STRONGHOLD SCOTLAND

The Pre-historic and Roman Fortifications Revealed

STRONGHOLD SCOTLAND

The Pre-historic and
Roman Fortifications Revealed

GEOFFREY WILLIAMS

Illustrations and Plans
by

DR. C.E. SIENIAWSKA

Riverside Publishing Solutions

The images in this book are almost entirely the authors own collection.
Every attempt has been made to gain permission for the use of Images
not from the authors collection in this book.
Any omissions will be rectified in future editions.

ISBN (Hardback): 978-1-913012-50-2
ISBN (Paperback): 978-1-913012-51-9
ISBN (ePub): 978-1-913012-52-6

The moral right of the author has been asserted.

A full CIP record for this book is available from the British Library.

Published in association with Riverside Publishing Solutions, Salisbury, UK

www.riversidepublishingsolutions.com

Designed, typeset and printed by Riverside Publishing Solutions, Salisbury, UK

www.riversidepublishingsolutions.com

Printed and bound in the UK.

CONTENTS

(Strongholds marked * in the book, such as Mousa*,
are featured in the gazetteer.)

Part 1

INTRODUCTION

Well, you must have a sense for adventure. For this book reaches parts of Scotland that others do not seek, or even know exist. A Scotland of 2,000 or more years ago that was populated by numerous tribes, large and small, whom the Romans called 'barbarians'. But the real barbarians were the so-called, civilised Roman invaders.

Pre-historic Scotland may have been a land of milk and honey, but conflict and confrontation between tribes existed long before the Latin invaders arrived. These tribes were the builders of the magnificent, spectacularly sited and unique pre-historic strongholds. Many of these are located in some of the most attractive and remote countryside, and are rarely seen by native Scot or visitor alike. From the southern-most point of Galloway to the northern tip of the Shetland Islands, there are far more than 1,000 strongholds and this book will take you to 120 of the finest. Welcome to Scotland's Iron Age.

One of life's peculiarities is that, at school, we learn about the pyramids of ancient Egypt, the temples of Asia, the classical architecture of the ancient Greeks and Romans, and so on, but little or nothing of our own pre-historic forebears. Then, when adults, we visit may these world-renowned sites on every continent, but still ignore the jewels on our own doorstep.

This is not unique to Scotland, but the variety and quantity of Scotland's pre-historic and (not to be biased) Roman strongholds cannot be matched anywhere else. And still, with few exceptions, most are unknown and rarely visited. Just what have you been missing?

By exploring the strongholds featured here, it will enhance and give a purpose when you visit areas on and off the main tourist trails, bringing the past actively into the present. It will take you to a Scotland that is often lauded, but seldom seen, and is a passport to a world beyond the glossy brochures and away from the crowds. Within these pages, you will find internationally renowned pre-historic strongholds, such as Mousa Broch*. Once there, you may meet people from any part of the world. But you will enjoy most by yourself or with companions.

Then again, you may find your own favourite stronghold. One that only you visit regularly, where you can retreat to find peace, space, inspiration or simply to feel more at one with our distant ancestors. How about Dun Skeig*, two duns and a hillfort in Kintyre, for one of many? What you may not realise is that Scotland is virtually overflowing with such places.

Mousa Broch, in Shetland, is the only nigh-complete broch in existence.
Its cooling tower shape, encircling outer defences and dramatic location are all apparent here.

This finely carved stone at Aberlemno, one of three by the road,
shows that the Picts were anything but 'barbarians'.

There are far more glittering jewels in Scotland than those that require an entrance fee. You might, for instance, visit Dun Grugaig* on Skye and find it a bit of a disappointment: but what a location, what a journey. Alternatively, amid all the motorways and railways between Falkirk and Stirling, you will find the peace, tranquillity and tumbled beauty of Torwood Broch*. There are hundreds of other examples and this book introduces you to the best.

Have you ever read a book about the history of Scotland? How few even bother to mention the pre-historic past, or skate over it as though introducing an embarrassing relative? Who were the Picts, for example? Are modern Scots really directly descended from Celts and, if so, who inhabited the land before them? Such questions are often ignored. True, the answers might never be known with any degree of certainty – and some cannot even be guessed at, but to pass off more than 5,000 years of pre-history in a few timid pages is the height of ignorance.

Naturally, such books might mention the Neolithic and Bronze Age tombs and their sacred sites, while perhaps going a bit wild and daring, and slipping in the odd broch. It makes you wonder whether there really was a world before that of clans, kilts and malt whisky.

Why was it, in a land of probably far fewer than 500,000 people in the Iron Age, so many places were defended, ranging from a single home, to a tribal capital? More importantly, who built these places and why were they abandoned? Were these people related to us today? Answers to those questions are still pretty elusive, but by visiting our pre-historic strongholds, the questions can be pondered and not simply ignored.

Besides which, although mostly more than 2,000 years old, many strongholds are wonderfully attractive and often stand in the most spectacular locations. Others are situated where you would think it almost impossible to live, let alone build a stronghold. After all, tools were mostly bone, stone and antler – metal tools were a valuable rarity – so building was a massive, labour intensive task. Above everything, how on earth did our pre-historic ancestors survive in our climate living on top of a hill? And all that is just for starters.

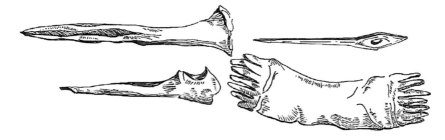

Drawings from a range of bone tools, including a comb, needle and gouge.

The greatest aid in visiting any pre-historic site, and not just a stronghold, is your imagination. Now, do not overdo it with a pre-historic version of the film *Braveheart*, but most strongholds are now isolated from the world in which they existed. With very few exceptions, their landscape has changed dramatically and emphatically.

Ignoring all the modern intrusions, such as roads, railways, power lines and even houses, this was a world of ancient tracks, field systems, outlying huts and farms. These now abandoned, ancient strongholds – even the un-finished hillfort of Durn Hill* – were once alive with the everyday sights, sounds and smells of human activity. Mousa Broch* might stand imperious and majestic today, and even appear hauntingly beautiful, but it was once a defended residence of a chief who dominated the little island. Life revolved round the broch and the broch was full of life. That is how to think of these strongholds, not as the cold and empty ruins seen today, no matter how romantic or beautiful the location.

Now, I know you cannot wait to get started, but let me introduce a very special lady who will help bring Scotland's pre-historic strongholds to life. Katia A.D. is the intrepid, time-travelling, roving reporter for the Roman Broadcasting Corporation (R.B.C). Katia A.D. goes where nobody else can, opening the door on the world of our pre-historic strongholds and meeting the people who lived there. By visiting our pre-historic world, she puts life into the pre-historic ruins. With her (fictitious) help, a new, yet very old, world is at your fingertips. Katia A.D. will give you more insight into the real pre-historic Scotland and its people than any digging, aerial imaging, geo-physical survey or metal detecting ever could.

Katia A.D. (left) approaching a large hillfort in the Borders.

So, enough chatter. Get out there and see for yourself that the land that is now Scotland has been a great country for more than the last few centuries. Before the English, before the French, before even the Romans came to our shores, our forebears were building strongholds that are unique. Their society, far from being barbaric or primitive, was clearly sophisticated and well organised to undertake such major works. We really are fortunate to be able to go and find these for ourselves today.

USE OF IMPERIAL MEASUREMENTS

As this book is about Scottish strongholds, and not those of a mere region of a federal Europe, the appropriate imperial measurements and weights have been used. Unlike the alien and artificial metric system, body measurements, such as a foot or a yard, are more relevant to pre-historic strongholds, and our imperial system developed from the long and protracted use of units that could be easily identified by all.

Should you need to convert to a metric equivalent, the following will help:

12 inches = 1 foot
3 feet = 1 yard = a pace
1 yard, plus a middle finger (approx.) = 1 metre
10 ft. = 3 metres

CHAPTER ONE

Scotland and its Pre-history:
Its Place in Time and Space

Without looking over the page, can you put the following historical eras into chronological order: Mesolithic, Dark Ages, Bronze Age, Palaeolithic, Iron Age, Medieval and Neolithic? Yes? Right, now put approximate dates against each of these eras, as they relate to Scotland. Finally, for those who are really on the ball, which of these eras are pre-historic and which are not?

Pre-history refers to the time before a society used writing, or was recorded in written form. So, pre-historic can easily mean completely different timescales from one society, or region, to another. For example, right into the 20th century there were African hunter-gatherer tribes whose lifestyle was little different from Scotland's inhabitants more than 5,000 years ago. These were effectively pre-historic tribes most definitely living in the world of mass communication, yet, were more or less untouched by the modern industrial world.

The coming of the Romans to the Third World island off the north coast of Europe – the one we now call Britain – led first by Julius Caesar in 55 B.C. and, rather more permanently, with the Claudian invasion of 43 A.D., is popularly regarded as being the catalyst for Britain's emergence from pre-history. Even so, that was some 3,000 years after the first recorded accounts were made in the advanced city-states of Sumeria. In any case, the accepted date of Britain leaving the murk of pre-history and entering the enlightened ages – with the ending of the Iron Age in c. 60 A.D., is all very well when applied to England, and is not too far out for Wales either, but it hardly applies to Scotland.

The first recorded accounts of England date back to the 4th century B.C. and are concerned with the Phoenician tin trading voyages to Cornwall. Scotland first really enters known records in c. 80 A.D. when Agricola attempted to conquer northern Britannia. And herein lies another problem. Despite Agricola's brilliant campaign against Scotland's Iron Age tribes, his rout of the Caledonii at the Battle of Mons Graupius in 83 A.D., his building of miles of roads and numerous forts, and the circumnavigation of Scotland by his fleet, well, just like Julius Caesar before him, he came, he saw and he conquered...but not for long.

By c. 100 A.D., the Romans had been forcibly and unceremoniously ejected to the south of the Cheviots. They spent much of the 2nd century grimly holding a tenuous grip on the Borders and Galloway and, like a punch-drunk boxer, came back for more early in the 3rd century. Lastly, they could not resist a final flourish a century later. Each time, their not-quite-so courtly advances were stoutly resisted by the increasingly unified tribes of Scotland.

Unlike the rest of Britain, Scotland rejected the so-called light of the Roman empire and opted to remain in the pitch-black of the pre-historic Iron Age and, later, the almost equally gloomy Dark Ages. It was early on in that time of great turmoil, with the arrival of Columba from Ireland, that Scotland finally boarded the train due to depart pre-history at 563 A.D. precisely; as with today's railways, a punctual time of arrival was envisaged, but far from guaranteed.

Well, here is the list to check your historical knowledge. The dates are very broad approximations and do not apply to the whole of Scotland at any one time, particularly as the eras changed.

Palaeolithic (Old Stone Age)	: Down to c. 7000 B.C.
Mesolithic (Middle Stone Age)	: 7000 to 4500 B.C.
Neolithic (New Stone Age)	: 4500 to 2000 B.C.
Bronze Age	: 2000 to 600 B.C.
Iron Age	: 600 B.C. to 500 A.D.
Dark Ages	: 500 to 1100 A.D.
Middle Ages	: 1100 to 1500 A.D.

Any serious disagreements? These eras have been imposed relatively recently and would certainly not have been recognised at their respective times. I mean, can you imagine two tribesmen wandering down a highland glen and having the following conversation on 7th January 599 B.C.?

"I say, did you hear the Iron Age started last week? I've only just traded a new bronze sword. You wait until I see Cerdic, the old scoundrel. I'll teach him to give me out-of-date goods."

Somehow, I think not. So, what was Scotland like in those pre-historic eras? Just how barbaric were our so-called Barbarian ancestors? And has history done our pre-historic forebears justice, or just done them?

STONE AGE SCOTLAND

As far as can be ascertained, the fabulous Flintstone age society passed by Scotland. Had Fred Flintstone and Barney Rubble visited Scotland in Palaeolithic times, overcrowding would not have been a problem they encountered: there was certainly no equivalent to the infamous town of 'Bedrock'. One might surmise that the climate would hardly be that of a south seas' island paradise either, though it was possibly warmer than it is today.

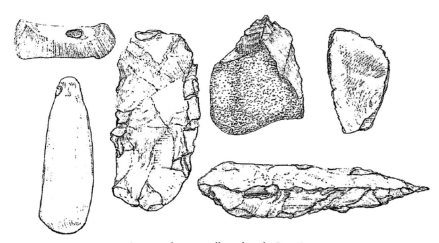

Stone tools were still used in the Iron Age.

It has been claimed, though one wonders just how on earth anyone could come up with such a figure – without wearing a big smile, that about 50 people occupied Scotland, c. 6000 B.C. Fanciful though such a notion might be, it gives some idea that the famed 'tartan army' would have been little more than a pithy Palaeolithic platoon.

The Mesolithic Age saw a steady improvement in the climate, which encouraged groups of hunter-gatherers to occupy some coastal regions. Occasional human traces from those times have been found, but Scotland was heavily forested and was home to the kind of wild animals you would not want to meet in a dark, lonely glade, such as bears and wolves. All in all, though, the land could not have been too inhospitable or those first hunter-gatherers would have turned smartly on their heels and departed back south.

The next era, the Neolithic Age, is the first where sweeping generalisations, such as 'they were all nomads', do not apply to Scotland as an entity. In some areas, say the Borders, traces of permanent Neolithic settlement are rare; yes, there is the large, possibly defended site at Meldon Bridge (Peebles) and other field-systems and settlements, but not many.

That does not mean all the Neolithic people in the Borders were nomads, nor that the area was un-inhabited, but further evidence either awaits discovery or has, more likely, been destroyed over the passing centuries. On the other hand, as peat has been cut in parts of the Shetland Isles and the Isle of Lewis, the remains of long established, late-Neolithic communities have been uncovered. This may apply elsewhere.

Nevertheless, the Neolithic Age was an era of great changes. A wider range of stone tools and weapons was developed, vast areas of forest were cleared, permanent settlements were established and, most obviously, many great – possibly semi-communal – passage and gallery tombs were built. The land was occasionally divided into farms and field-systems, and all this begs an obvious question: were these changes caused by an influx of outsiders and, if so, from where did they come?

These houses at the Knap of Howar, on Papa Westray, Orkney,
were thought to be Iron Age, but are now dated from c. 3500 B.C.

It is no use sending in your answers, for the truth will never be known to any degree of certainty. However, it is not beyond the bounds of probability that immigrants did arrive to ultimately usurp – or change – the Mesolithic hunter-gatherers and, in all likelihood, they came from what is now England.

You may have heard about the small settlement on the Orcadian island of Papa Westray, called the Knap of Howar. This well-preserved site was occupied for about half the 4th millennium B.C.; the still more comprehensive settlement at Skara Brae, on Orkney's Mainland, is almost as old. Recent research has established tenuous links between the inhabitants of Skara Brae and the builders of the massive Maes Howe tomb. Was this the equivalent of the village burial ground? It might have been, but one must be wary of drawing parallel conclusions and stating, for example, that each burial chamber must have been associated with a village or settlement. Many are those who have fallen into that particular trap. Nevertheless, it seems likely that many parts of Scotland were home to, at least, semi-permanent settlements of Neolithic man.

Some way into the Neolithic Age, man began to develop the first permanent ritual sites: the great henges are some of the most visual today. In Wessex, there is a long tradition of building henges without stones: Stonehenge and Avebury are exceptions, with the stones being added later.

Scotland's earliest henges date to the 4th millennium B.C., a little after, say, Avebury. However, Scotland's Neolithic inhabitants were quicker to the draw than their English counterparts when it came to erecting stones at henges. Take the henge of Stenness

The interior of a house at Skara Brae, the most complete Neolithic settlement in Britain, dating back nearly 5,000 years, truly remarkable.

(Orkney) as an example. Excavating archaeologists considered that the stones were probably erected before the henge ditch was dug. If that is the case, the stone circle – of which little now remains, was begun c. 3000 B.C., or up to 500 years before the first large stones were erected at Stonehenge.

Perhaps more important than these great ceremonial and burial sites, is that they demonstrate the ability of Neolithic man to produce an agricultural surplus, which enabled their building. Not only that, but Neolithic society clearly had the structure to organise and plan such long-term projects. None of the henges, circles, cairns and tombs is on anything like the scale of, say, the Seven Wonders of the Ancient World, to say nothing of the organisation in Fred Flintstone's Bedrock, but the larger sites, such as Maes Howe, are not trailing that far behind.

THE INTRODUCTION OF METALS

Scotland's Neolithic society became increasingly sophisticated, but, about 4,000 years ago, there was another, nigh-revolutionary sea-change. The earliest metals were introduced: first copper, but soon the amalgam with tin to make bronze. This was no

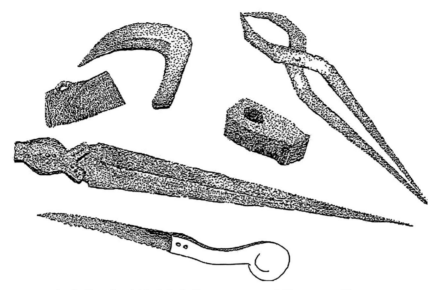

A selection of metal tools including an axe, saw, sickle, tongs and hammer.

straight-forward transition. For a start, copper ores are not found widely in Scotland, and there are no extensive copper mines such as that at the Gt. Orme, near Llandudno, while tin came from Cornwall. Now, what does that tell you about the extent of trade and awareness in those times? You do not need newspapers, the internet and endless radio and television news bulletins to keep abreast of the most useful things in life.

Simultaneously with the arrival of the Bronze Age came signs of a new race of people, the Beakers. So named not because they had different shaped heads – nor due to the size of their noses, but because of the distinctively shaped beaker-style pots found at their burial sites, these people may have introduced metal-working to the indigenous populace. There was a similar situation in England during the centuries before 2000 B.C. So, who were these people and from where did they come?

It is unlikely that they were military invaders; more likely, a steady stream of immigrants arrived from Europe. Perhaps these were the first Celts to reach our shores, for stone decoration – such as cup-and-ring marked stones, quite apart from the new vogue of standing stone monument building, is associated with them. Alternatively, beaker-style pottery and other influences might have arrived in Scotland through trade and then been copied, without there ever being a human influx of any size.

PRE-HISTORIC CLIMATE CHANGE

Oh yes, there is nothing new here, except that in pre-historic times it was not man-made. As society slowly, yet remorselessly developed, metal tools, implements, jewellery and weapons, though hardly common-place, were used more widely within communities. But change was in the air – quite literally, as it happens.

Just as higher ground was being farmed from early in the 2nd millennium B.C., probably due to a rising population, so the last centuries of that millennium witnessed a retreat from the uplands. Beneath the present blankets of peat, signs of Bronze/Iron Age landscapes on the Isle of Lewis, or Neolithic – but 2nd millennium B.C. – settlements on the Shetland Isles, are occasionally uncovered. Given the vast tracts of Scotland still engulfed by peat, the possibilities for future excavations could be almost limit-less.

So, what caused this climatic change, the opposite of the dreaded global warming? Not unlike the concern over the tropical rain forests, the drive to cultivate and farm the higher ground led to the destruction of woodland and forest. Much of southern and western Scotland had been, effectively, de-forested by c. 1500 B.C. The consequences of this could have been, at the very least, detrimental to soil regeneration.

The light, infertile soils of the uplands, rocky islands and some coastal areas, could never sustain an intensive agricultural economy – they still cannot. In any case, if yields were low on the rich soils of the valleys, one might assume they could be, at best, marginal on the higher ground, even in good years. Primitive farming methods and low yields required more land to produce enough food, and contributed to soil degeneration. From about c. 1500 B.C. in the north, and certainly by 1200 B.C., the peat blanket was forming. Why?

Well, the climate became steadily cooler and wetter, just the right conditions for peat. This was no mini-Ice Age either: all it takes is a small drop in average temperature and a few more inches of rain a year – each and every year, and crops will not grow or ripen at above, say, the 1,000 ft. contour. So, in time, the barren land was, not un-naturally, abandoned; peat soon takes over. Even today, peat is a relentless opponent. On the Shetland island of Yell, the crofters achieve the odd victory and reclaim a piece of land here and there. In no time at all, though, they are quickly on the back foot, fighting yet another fruitless, rear-guard action; all this despite tractors and fertilisers. Three thousand years ago, it was a hopeless task.

So, did the mass clearance of the upland woods cause the deteriorating climate? It hardly helped, but, in 1159 B.C., the Icelandic volcano Hekla erupted. This did rather more than prevent flying for a few days – as happened in 2010, it caused something akin to a nuclear winter. There was some fall-out and a dust cloud partially blocked the sun: this was nature's equivalent to acid rain or the Chernobyl disaster.

That, though, does not account for deteriorating weather before Hekla blew its top. Perhaps it was the combination of a small climatic change, not helped by the clearance of trees, primitive farming methods and finally Hekla, the straw – or more likely plank – that broke the camel's back and pushed matters over the edge, and farming off the hills.

THE FIRST PERMANENT STRONGHOLDS

The result of all this was that people migrated to the valleys and lower, more fertile ground. This would, over time, have created social conditions associated with a considerable growth in population, with all the attendant troubles and tensions. Was this the catalyst for the first permanently defended settlements that become the fore-runners of the multitudinous Iron Age strongholds?

Ptolomy's tribal map of Scotland

These first defended settlements, even if defying the description stronghold, certainly came about before the use of iron. In our list of historical eras, the Iron Age began c. 600 B.C., but some hillforts, crannogs and defended farmsteads – the fore-runner of brochs and duns – were in existence long before that time. The edges of the pre-historic eras become very blurred, especially when one considers Scotland and all the outlying islands as a whole.

Despite that, most of Scotland's known pre-historic strongholds date from the Iron Age. Over its first six hundred years, defended residences and settlements were built throughout Scotland: a scale of building not equalled until the Middle Ages. Hillforts spread like a rash in the Borders, but were found in lesser numbers in all over the mainland. Most are pretty small, fewer than 3 acres and often much less, but some expanded to become the equivalent of towns and even cities. Unlike the rest of Britain, the inhabitants of the western and northern coastal areas and the islands usually opted for smaller defended settlements such as duns, brochs and crannogs.

Hand in glove with this drive towards defended, more permanent settlements went an increasing concentration into tribal groups. A Roman named Ptolemy produced a map of the tribes of Britain in the 1st century A.D. This might be anything but accurate – even fantasy – with regards the north and west, areas the Romans never penetrated, but it demonstrates a general trend towards a more uniform, organised way of life.

This was certainly true in the Borders when Agricola invaded. There, the powerful Votadini tribe was seemingly treated with a degree of leniency not afforded its neighbours. And while the 30,000 Caledonii, who supposedly confronted Agricola at the Battle of Mons Graupius, belonged a temporary confederation of loosely associated small tribes – solely to see-off the Latin invaders, just two centuries later, they formed the basis of the Pictish kingdom that dominated north and east Scotland beyond the Clyde/Forth isthmus.

WHO WERE THE PICTS?

Ah! Well, there is no point in putting off the inevitable. You just cannot avoid becoming embroiled with these people of mystery and controversy. So, what about the Picts? Although the Pict kingdom formally existed until 843 A.D., and no doubt, effectively, lasted a good deal longer, what little has been written about them comes mostly from external sources.

The name was bestowed upon them by the Romans in 297 A.D.: Picti being the painted ones. It is not known if the Picts referred to themselves as such, but possibly not as it was unlikely to have been a complimentary term, just as our troops referred to the Germans as the b.....d Huns in the Great War.

The Picts emanate from the Caledonii of the central Highlands, who eventually amalgamated with other tribes and Pictland became a kingdom. A list of Pict kings is about the only written record and was compiled in the 9th century. King Bruide was the first to be noted and he was supposedly visited by St. Columba, in the 6th century (see Craig Phadrig* hillfort in the gazetteer). So, you can see that the blur between the ending of the pre-historic Iron Age, c. 500 A.D., and the start of the Dark Ages, and enlightenment – or should we say enwritenment – is more of a dirty great smudge. Such a cavalier attitude to our historic eras justifies the inclusion of several Dark Ages' strongholds in the gazetteer as well.

The Picts might have spoken, or understood, two languages: P-Celtic, not dissimilar to modern Welsh; and a non-European language, from which the Ogham inscriptions are derived. The latter may have been a pre-Celtic language that survived alongside the later Celtic tongue; in the manner of the Tsar-era Russian nobility speaking French, while the peasants and serfs spoke Russian. Eventually, those languages were superseded by Q-Celtic, or Gaelic, spoken by the Scotti tribe who migrated to Argyll from Ulster, from about the 5th century A.D., although some people contend, with some justification, this happened possibly a thousand or more years before. Such a confusion of Celtic languages gives added meaning to the phrase 'mind your Ps and Qs'!

All of which brings us to our arbitrary date to mark the end of the Iron Age, c. 500 A.D. This is some 450 years after the rest of mainland Britain – and a century after the more widely recognised date, yet still might have been before writing was introduced to Scotland's shores. As with most events in Scottish pre-history, one can easily argue 100 years either way, so 500 A.D. is a safety first mid-point. By that time, as the Scotti gained its toe-holds in Argyll, the Pict kingdom was firmly established; Britons occupied Galloway and Strathclyde, and the Angles first penetrated the Borders. Illiterate pre-history was thus being attacked on all fronts and, although it continued to survive for several hundred years – in parts, the writing-on-the-wall could be clearly seen, even if not read.

PRE-HISTORY BEYOND SCOTLAND'S SHORES

Meanwhile, although a few colours have been applied in an impressionistic fashion to the painting by numbers canvas that comprises Scotland's pre-historic past, to give a bit of depth and perspective it is essential to consider what was going on in the great wide world beyond our shores.

By about 4000 B.C., the differences between the people of England and Scotland, and not forgetting Wales, are mostly environmental. In south and east England, wood and earth were used to build great tombs, though stone was used elsewhere. Henges and causeway camps were built, while the Beaker culture reached the south coast before Scotland. The differences were mostly of the hair-splitting kind, although nothing south of the Cheviots can readily compare with the magnificence of the stonework at some Scotland's great northern tombs.

Then again, elsewhere in the world events were moving even faster, particularly at either end of the Fertile Crescent in Sumeria and Egypt. The Bronze Age of those civilisations began well over a thousand years before metal-working reached Scottish shores, c. 3200 to 1200 B.C. Indeed, the area to the north of the Persian Gulf, the scene of so much strife in recent decades, is a possible cradle of civilisation, and some of the first city-states were established in Sumeria, or Mesopotamia, long before 3000 B.C. The oldest known written records date from that time, and although there are no continuous or comprehensive records extant, Sumerian pre-history ended over three thousand years before Scotland's.

Simultaneously, and quite possibly unknown to the Sumerians, the Egyptians were building their first pyramids, c. 3300 B.C. Once again, although at a later date, they also began to leave written records – and their pre-historic past behind. It is quite a salutary thought that, while our ancestors were building Maes Howe, the Egyptians were not only creating the pyramids, but the various sculptures in stone and precious metals that are still so mightily impressive today.

About 2000 B.C., just as parts of Scotland first entered the Bronze Age, the Babylonian Empire, a successor to Sumeria, was flourishing, while the civilisations at Troy,

*Maes Howe magnificence. Would you believe this tomb was
built 5,000 years ago in the remote Orkney Islands?*

Mycenae and the Minoan Empire had been founded. As for the Egyptians, they were
yet to rise to their greatest heights over the ensuing millennium, with Tutankhamen
being Pharaoh in 1250 B.C. The sea-faring civilisation of Phoenicia emerged during
the second millennium B.C., as did the first flowering of the Greek city-states, but not
before sliding back into illiteracy, with the fall of Mycenae, c. 1200 B.C.

Thus, by 1000 B.C., while our inhabitants grappled with problems caused by a
worsening climate and were being over-run by peat, much of the Middle East and the
Mediterranean world was comfortably into its Iron Age. The independent city-state
empires were well and truly established.

Thereabouts also occurred one of the most one-sided contests ever staged by man,
on papyrus at least. The flyweight champ, David, challenged the invincible heavyweight
Goliath, over 15 rounds; a contest that the Marquess of Queensberry would surely
not have sanctioned. The biggest shock of all was that the mighty man was felled
by the minnow, the knockout-blow being a direct hit from a dastardly sling-stone.
Now that was a weapon that did not reach Scotland for another 500 years, but it had
a not inconsiderable impact with stronghold building.

Some 200 years later, in 814 B.C., Carthage was founded, while the written word
gradually came into vogue throughout the ancient world. Europe saw the rise of
the Celts out of the Aryans from the Asian steppes, Homer composed the *Iliad* and
Odyssey, c. 700 B.C., and Confucius wrote his *Analects* a little later. It is, in fact, these
ancient civilisations that provide the first written accounts of the Celts. In 390 B.C., the
Celtic 'barbarians' crossed the Alps and sacked Rome: an action that would be neither
forgotten, nor forgiven. This may have been the catalyst for the eventual establishment

of the mighty empire. The Greeks were also having to come to grips with the war-like people from the north, and just managed to beat them back when the Celts attacked Delphi in 279 B.C.

Europe was not the only continent having a bit of bother with the Celts either. The Aryans had been driven west by the Mongols, who also caused the Chinese a problem or two. Their solution was to begin the mighty and incredible Great Wall of China, from c. 220 B.C., as a much-needed barrier. For a while at least, this was rather more successful at withstanding an influx of Celts, than was the sea round Britain's shores, but not for long.

THE ARRIVAL OF THE CELTS

Nobody really knows when the Celts arrived in Britain, let alone Scotland. One thing is certain, that for all the gullible tripe mentioned about Celtic revivals these days, they are not Britain's indigenous population, but interlopers who were themselves pushed to the very margins by successive invaders.

If Celtic blood exists to any real extent in Britain's inhabitants these days, it is most likely to be in Scotland's west coast and islands, where an amalgam of the Celtic Picts and Irish-Celtic Scots formed the late-Dark Ages' kingdom. It might be a very big 'if' as well.

In any case, there were the Aryan Celts and the Belgic Celts. The latter were the particularly violent and nomadic people who gave the Romans such

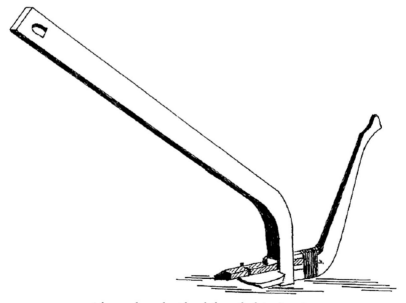

A bow ard wooden plough from the later Iron Age.

grief – and the occasional hiding, especially in the 1st century A.D. They arrived in southern England and caused great upheavals in society, but they also introduced the first coins in the 2nd century B.C., long before Scotland saw such a means of exchange.

One theory regarding the building of the northern coastal brochs, is that they were ranged against invaders. If this were the case, could these so-called invaders have been the Picts who were, perhaps, Belgic Celts? You may remember, the Romans latterly called the Scottish tribes Picts because of their painted bodies; Julius Caesar also described the Belgic Celts of south-east England as having woad-painted bodies, more than 300 years earlier. It is possible that these were one and the same people, although there is no evidence to suggest that the Belgic Celts occupied the rather large chunk of land in between England's south coast and Scotland, so why should they have sailed north?

It is also likely that the Belgic Celts introduced the potter's-wheel and the heavier ard-plough to Britain, as well. Evidence of these is quite apparent in southern England, with their distinctive wheel-thrown pottery and the ploughing of heavier soils, but much less so elsewhere and not at all in Scotland. So, the, relatively scant, evidence is inconclusive. Belgic or not, the Celts certainly played a dominant role in Scotland's Iron Age society. If only the strongholds could talk.

IRON AGE EVOLUTION

The beginning of Scotland's Iron Age is still a mystery. Iron, and its manufacturing techniques, probably reached central and northern Europe through trade with the Mediterranean region. The Phoenicians certainly sailed to Cornwall for tin and might have done so for many centuries. Could iron have been introduced to Scotland via the Atlantic trading routes to the west coast and islands, rather than overland from England?

The introduction of iron does not necessarily herald the dawn of a new age, though. Iron objects are noted more for their scarcity at Scottish excavations than the opposite. Of course, you would not expect homogeneity of society through such a large and disparate land, but the introduction of iron was, seemingly, a catalyst for change.

The existence of metal jewellery, decorated weapons and domestic utensils suggests that some sections of Scottish pre-historic society had reached material standards not dissimilar to those of the medieval period, more than 1,000 years later. For example, permanent towns – or oppida – existed where trade and manufacturing took place, while warrior-chiefs occupied strongholds as the focal-point of farms and field systems; a scenario perhaps equating to that of the medieval laird, with a castle at the centre of his lands. The Iron Age people probably had religious leaders, maybe even the dreaded Druids: again, that situation has parallels with the church in later times. One wonders whether the common-man of the late-Iron Age was a serf, tied to the land, as was his medieval counterpart. Although pure speculation, that could have been the case in certain times and places.

On the other hand, the farther north one looks, the less organised the tribal system may have been. The Caledonii, for example, was more a loose confederation of small tribes than a cohesive tribe on the scale of, say, the Votadini. They had probably changed little from the late-Bronze Age, especially in their use of metals, pottery, a lack of a common medium of exchange and from what little can be determined of their social organisation.

These differences in the deportment of the various tribes showed in their reaction to the first Roman invasion. Some were not wholly opposed – such as the Votadini;

Christianity reaches the Picts. This stone cross at Aberlemno's church may appear to be Christian, but the symbols and images on the rear suggest a Pict heritage.

others were totally hostile – such as the Caledonii; and still others were divided – like the Selgovae. At least the response to change was no different in the Iron Age from that of today – rarely unanimous.

What, then, caused the demise of the Iron Age and when did this occur? Obviously, the arrival of the first Christians was a catalyst, but there was no immediate change; hence the approximation of the dates. By 400 A.D., the area north of the Clyde/Forth isthmus was looking ever more ripe for the establishment of the Pictish kingdom. To the south, the Britons were seemingly in control, though to what extent there was any form of central organisation is open to very hot debate. Within 50 years, the Scotti was inhabiting parts of Argyll and before a century was out Dalriada was established. St. Columba and his fellow Christians followed and with the rise of the Christian movement in the Galloway and Northumbria, pre-history – and with it the Iron Age – flickered and died.

Did life for the archetypal common-man alter much, though? Probably not. He more than likely still lived in his round or rectangular house, perhaps even in an un-defended settlement. He probably worked the fields, either by himself or in common with others, and paid his dues or homage to a local chief, and the same probably applied to the women. Oh yes, our pre-historic common-man might easily recognise the lot of the medieval serf without too much difficulty, and even the daily grind of the crofter until the early 20th century.

*This reconstruction of a large Iron Age house shows both art
and architecture were of a high standard.*

For all the great changes in climate, strongholds, tribal formations, invasions and so forth, the lot of the poor old common-man might have remained pretty constant during the 1,100 years of Scotland's Iron Age. That, more than anything, needs to be borne in mind when considering the different pre-historic eras and, especially, when visiting pre-historic strongholds.

Nevertheless, the impact of the Iron Age was enormous. Quite apart from the gradual integration of small tribes into the hierarchical structure of larger tribes – especially the Picts, trading patterns were established along the Atlantic seaboard that ultimately brought the Scotti to Scotland. Although a long and turbulent voyage lay ahead, Scotland first became recognised as a distinct land – if not country – in the Iron Age. The Borders would continue to change hands again and again over the ensuing centuries, but at least the inhabitants knew their heritage. There was no doubting which way they would jump when Scotland, as we know it, came of age.

Rear of Aberlemno stone.

CHAPTER TWO

The People and Society
of Pre-historic Scotland

"I'm here at a Votadini hillfort in the hills to the north of our Britannia province. This area is known as Tweedale and we've been under siege all day long. The barrage from the occupants of a neighbouring Selgovae hillfort has intensified in the last half-hour, with sling-stones inflicting many casualties: men, women and children alike, and even one of my R.B.C. crew. Several of the inhabitants' circular, thatched houses have been set ablaze by lighted javelins thrown over the ramparts, but the fires have now been contained.

"Amidst all the confusion, the marauding Selgovae have captured many cattle and sheep. This is a devastating loss, as my hosts had just re-stocked following a similar raid last year. Considerable damage has been caused, although it now looks as though the defences will hold firm. Even so, it is almost certain that aid supplies from the Votadinian oppidum at Traprain Law will be needed over the coming winter.

"The northern border-country of our great empire has become an increasingly violent place, with constant raiding by, and among, the various uncivilised tribes of barbarians. It is a seemingly pointless fracas in a forgotten part of the world, overshadowed by the recent emphatic victories of Agricola in the land called Wales. The rumour is, that Agricola's attention will soon be turned to this corner of Barbaria, bringing yet further glory and wealth to our great empire, and ordered civility to the savages beyond.

"This is Katia A.D., for the Roman Broadcasting Corporation Six o'clock News, in Tweedale, northern Britannia, 78 A.D."

Perhaps this might a bit over-dramatic, but there was considerable unrest in the Borders during the last decades of the 1st century A.D. The Votadini tribal lands stretched from the Firth of Forth to the south of the Cheviot's, possibly down to the Tyne valley. There had been internecine warfare in the Brigantes tribe of northern England in the 70s A.D., and this probably affected the Votadini, Selgovae and Novantae tribes of the Borders and Galloway. They, in turn, may have taken full advantage of Roman discomfort in the Pennines.

Today, Scotland is often perceived as being divided on a north/south basis, but in the Iron Age it had a rather different divide: one based on an east/west axis. Cultural

After the attack. Katia A.D. talks to a local chief after a small raid on his hillfort.

influences and traditions were carried along the Atlantic trading routes, from Galloway to the coastal areas and islands of Argyll, the west and the north. So, an inhabitant of Dun Kildonan*, on Kintyre, might have more in common with a Shetland islander or a Cornishman than, say, a member of the Selgovae tribe in the Borders.

The trading routes of the Atlantic seaboard stretched from the Mediterranean via Iberia, Brittany and Cornwall to the west coast of Britain and Ireland. This does not mean that the inhabitants of Scotland's Atlantic zone were inveterate traders, just that their horizons were shaped by influences carried along the western seas. In the same way, the Votadini tribe possibly had more dealings with the Brigantes to the south, than the Novantae in Galloway.

CELTIC ANCESTRY

Despite Scotland being divided into numerous tribal areas, by the late-1st millennium B.C., if not well before, many inhabitants were probably Celts. Today, such a notion is often accepted without a second thought, but just who were the Celts and from where did they come?

In Chapter 1, it was suggested that the Beaker people might have been Celts, but this is not a favoured option. Traditionally, the Celts are thought to have arrived in Europe from the Asian steppes towards the end of the 2nd millennium B.C., following the breakdown of the Greek city states. Out of this cauldron of human confusion developed the Urnfield culture, with its possible Celtic origins. Well, that is a popular theory, but if this traditional scenario holds water, then the first Celts cannot have reached Scotland before the beginning of the 1st millennium B.C.

In any case, the Celtic movement was probably more of a cultural migration, rather than a physical invasion of northern and central Europe by marauding bands of apparent wild madmen. There is no doubt, though, that these central Asian emigrants invaded both the Greek and Italian peninsulas, and caused considerable mayhem. In Britain, the old, so-called invasion-thesis of 'wave after wave' of tribes invading our shores has, alas, fallen from archaeological fashion and favour in recent decades. Still, it was entirely in keeping with the Celtic traditions of heroic and adventurous deeds.

On the other hand, while pottery, tin, ores and other goods can be traded along the Atlantic seaboard, it is not so easy to import the traditional mores of Celtic culture, such as heroism, art, jewellery, ostentatious dress and seemingly wanton violence being treated as a virtual sport. (One wonders if this latter notion is behind the founding and eager playing of such potentially violent games as rugby, hockey and hurley by the Britons, Irish, Bretons and Iberians: after all, each has long Celtic traditions.)

So, there was little chance of an organised Celtic invasion of Britain in the manner of the Normans. But for most of Scotland and Britain to be considered Celtic-populated by the mid-1st millennium B.C., then, surely, some Celts must have long been settled to establish their ways and, most importantly, their language.

Metal Iron Age jewellery could be very fine work, as with the mirror, brooch and gold torcs.

The pre-Roman Celts of Britain left no written records: even coins from southern England bore Latin inscriptions. As a result, it is even beyond the miracles of modern archaeology to unearth evidence of languages spoken in pre-Roman Britain. As a result, opinion is, not un-surprisingly, divided on the matter of what language(s) our pre-historic ancestors spoke. Yet, it is not entirely implausible that a common language was understood throughout much of Britain, though with quite distinct regional variations – rather like today.

Another theory contends that the Celtic language first came to Britain during the Neolithic Age. Certainly, the notion that the Celts arrived before the Iron Age makes sense, at least in having a widely spoken Celtic language, for they were definitely established before Julius Caesar invaded southern England, in 55 and 54 B.C.

Had the Celts first arrived in the mid-1st millennium B.C., they would need to get a move on to impose themselves, their culture and language throughout Britain. All of which brings us back to the possibility that the Beaker people might have been Celts. However unlikely, especially as the Celts were supposedly driven from the central Asian steppes centuries after the first Beaker people arrived in Scotland, 2,000 years or so should have been long enough to establish a new universal language.

Today, two strands of Celtic language are spoken in Britain: Welsh and Gaelic. The older of the two is Gaelic, or Q-Celtic, but one plausible scenario suggests this had been ousted by the Brythonic, P-Celtic, language – similar to Welsh, by the 1st millennium B.C.: Q-Celtic was, by that time, possibly only spoken in the outlying islands. The Picts probably spoke P-Celtic, while Q-Celtic was re-introduced to mainland Scotland in the 5th century A.D. by the Scotti, who came from Ulster. The Scotti founded Dalriada, which, in the 9th century A.D., eventually overcame Pictland, and Q-Celtic once again became the dominant language, albeit briefly. This is still spoken, mostly, in the Hebrides.

Evidence about the Celts and other inhabitants of pre-historic Scotland is piecemeal and confused, if not downright contradictory. Glimpses of the people occur, from time to time, that favour one particular theory over another, but never offer anything like an all-encompassing answer as to who were the Celts. Tacitus, writing about the Agricolan campaign of the 80s A.D., describes the Caledonii as being physically different from other Britons – Britannia being considered as a whole – with their large limbs and reddish hair. Such a description suggests a central European, perhaps Germanic heritage, a curious link with substantial possibilities.

Quite a number of Scottish hillforts had timber-laced ramparts with horizontal supporting timbers through the drystone walls: these are some of the earliest to have been built. This building technique – known as *murus gallicus*, though rare elsewhere in Britain, was used by contemporary Celts in Germany. This incidence (or co-incidence?) suggests a potential direct contact with Germanic Celts, through either trade or migration. Do not, though, rule out the possibility that such techniques may have evolved in complete isolation in both Scotland and Germany, through simple trial and error. Nevertheless, one can see how scraps of archaeological evidence can be fused to become the catalyst for a theory about Scotland's Iron Age inhabitants being Celtic migrants from Germany.

This is not any old wall, but a reconstruction of a timber-laced, murus gallicus, *wall at Bibract's museum in France. A formidable sight to Iron Age eyes.*

Unfortunately, it is all too easy to end up chasing our tails over the business of who were the Celts, and how and when they arrived. It is probably safest to state that, by the mid-Iron Age, Scotland was a far from cohesive, yet mostly Celtic land. The Belgic Celts arriving in southern England from the 2nd century B.C. may never have reached Scotland, but that only raises the question as to why were all the coastal brochs built? Were, in fact, the Picts in any way connected with the woad-painted Belgic warriors who opposed Julius Caesar in 55 B.C. on the shores of the English Channel.

IRON AGE POPULATION

If the above raises far more questions than can possibly be answered, then it is no different regarding the size of Scotland's Iron Age population. Reasonably accurate population figures have only existed for the last 200 years or so and anything before that becomes increasingly less fact, more fiction. The population of Great Britain today is about 68 million, with about 5 1/2 million in Scotland. As Britain possibly had about 5 million people in the Middle Ages and, as no more than a best guess, some 2 million in the Iron Age, one might assume that Scotland's proportion was similar to that of today, about 200,000.

You may recall that the climate deteriorated during the Bronze Age, latterly causing a retreat from the marginal higher ground and increasing the demand for lower-lying land. The mass-building of strongholds also began at that time. Now, as night follows day, once people have established territorial rights, they invariably attempt to improve their domestic situation: improve the land, build a better house, that sort of thing. Such a settled, domestic outlook invariably encourages breeding; a scenario demonstrated the world over. So, the population pressures in Scotland at the beginning of the Iron Age were coming from two sources: migration and an increased birth rate. Friction was inevitable.

Excluding migration, for a population to increase either the birth rate must rise, and/or the death rate fall. As recently as the 18th century, the average life-span in Britain was no more than 40 years – compared with today's 80-plus years – so, one might assume, the average Iron Age life would be similarly short. A secure domestic existence, often in a defended settlement, would provide the impetus and wherewithal for the birth rate to rise.

Food production would need to keep pace with a growing population, while there were undoubtedly occasional famines or plagues – not irregular features of European life even two centuries ago, or even a fore-runner of our coronavirus 'scamdemic'. A fall in the death rate would have been less likely given the additional pressure on the land. The massive growth in defended settlements, throughout the first half of the Iron Age, was probably a response to an increase in raiding.

It is likely that with the growth of permanent settlements the population rose modestly, but unevenly, throughout the Iron Age. Perhaps this was as much as a two-fold increase during the 1st millennium B.C. These figures might not seem much today, a rise from, say, 100,000 to 200,000, but that would equate to a doubling of today's population to 11 million: makes you think, doesn't it?

SOCIAL STRUCTURE

Once a tribal system becomes established – at first on a small scale, but eventually to the extent mapped by Ptolemy, so new social structures would evolve. Even today, there are still tribes in the world that are ruled by elders, or other favoured groups.

Among the Celts, it seems that a warrior class – that is the strongest – assumed power. This would have been perfectly natural at that time, and even today, in sport, how often is the best player appointed the team captain? Once a hierarchy is accepted, a pecking-order is established, with off-shoots for those of higher intelligence (learned/religious class) and those with an aptitude for making things (craft/art class). It is not a particularly great step, then, to perpetuate this social hierarchy through offspring and, before you know it, a lineage tradition maintains the status quo.

If all this sounds too theoretically fanciful and convenient, especially as any evidence of Iron Age social structures is decidedly flimsy, neither is it pure kibosh. Examples fitting this hypothesis can be found in many societies and tribes, but Irish literature is more specific about the social hierarchy of Dark Ages' Celtic society. In this, a king ruled over a rigid, hierarchical structure of nobles, free-commoners and the un-free. Each class was sub-divided: the nobles – warriors, men of learning, priests, specialists and master craftsmen; the free-commoners – peasant farmers and basic craftsmen; and the un-free – the vast majority.

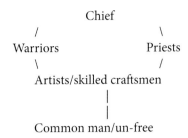

This Irish-Celtic social structure bears more than a passing resemblance to that of the Celtic tribes in Gaul, as described by Julius Caesar, and, possibly, the Belgic tribes of southern England. It is unwise to try to transpose a social hierarchy from one region to another, even if both societies were Celtic (just imagine how often we would be mistaken today), but this broad social structure may have had some similarities in Scotland. In particular, at about the time of Agricola's invasion, the tribes of southern Scotland might have had a social hierarchy not dissimilar from that of the later Irish-Celts, while the tribes of the north may have done likewise when Pictland was established, towards the end of the Iron Age.

In any case, the power of the warriors probably increased during the Iron Age. The un-free would have found themselves in a position not unlike that of the medieval serf: tied to the land and supposedly dependent on the lord, or warrior, for protection, but usually subjugated by him. Certainly, the growth of the defended settlement and the primitive land management that was exercised, points towards a greater organisation and control of society than before and, very likely, the existence of a ruling class. This possibly resulted in the establishment of the tribal areas mapped by Ptolemy, although these may have been quite fluid.

Central to Iron Age society was the family unit; more the extended family (grandparents/parents/children), than the nuclear family of modern times. That would enforce a rigidly hierarchical caste system and, especially in the mid-Iron Age, restricted social mobility.

The economy of Iron Age Scotland would have centred on the family as a fairly self-sufficient production unit. Above this, the population of a settlement would also be virtually self-contained, at least during the early Iron Age. The growth of the domineering tribal centre, such as Traprain Law*, is only really obvious in the south and, in any case, dates to the centuries immediately before the Romans arrived. Even then, what authority the leaders at, say, Traprain Law exercised over a small hillfort in Tweedale – perhaps that visited by Katia A.D. at the beginning of this chapter – is unknown.

Many pre-historians consider brochs to be defended residences of local chiefs, while the same has been said of small hillforts and duns. No doubt, this was often the case with the Broch of Gurness*, for example, where houses for 20 to 30 families surrounded the tower. But, what about Keiss*, where three brochs stand within a quarter mile of each other? Scotland's pre-historic strongholds were by no means all contemporary with each other, but there are surely still too many for them to be solely residences of chieftains.

*This view of the Broch of Gurness shows the outer defences, broch and additional dwellings.
A century ago, this was a large mound of earth. Copyright North Link Ferries.*

No doubt, a defended residence was a symbol of a chief's stature, and a degree of extravagant monumental display would probably be too much for an ostentatious Celt to resist. In Dark Ages' Ireland, the size of one's residence was determined by rank, and strict measurements were laid down. As ever, this was not necessarily the case in Iron Age Scotland, just because both were Celtic societies, but something similar may have applied.

Another measurement of social stature may be the old favourite of the number of cattle and sheep one possessed. Land might have been another, but be absolutely sure of one thing, stature and status – both among society in general and especially the nobility – certainly developed as the Iron Age progressed. Perhaps that was one reason for the Celtic tradition of combat, a means of establishing or raising one's superiority.

One rank of society not usually given a fanfare is that of slaves. Archaeological evidence of slavery in pre-historic Britain is rare. Manacles have occasionally been found, but these could have been for prisoners. Yet, the Romans' insatiable demand for slaves is well known, and slaves from Britain were certainly exported to the Roman Empire.

On the other hand, what happened to prisoners from local raids, as witnessed by our roving R.B.C. reporter Katia A.D.? Were they slaughtered, set free, held in captivity, bartered or used as slave labour? In all truth, we have no idea. Then again, just how free were the 'un-free' in Dark Ages' Ireland? Such details will remain obscure, but Celtic society in Iron Age Scotland, diverse though it undoubtedly was, almost certainly had social divisions that were wider, more discriminating and difficult to transcend than the assumed more egalitarian Bronze Age society.

WHAT ABOUT THE WOMEN?

Amid all this, I have omitted to mention, and avoided becoming embroiled in, the arguments about the position of women in pre-historic society. As with many things, until recent decades archaeology was male dominated. So, it has been assumed that the men did all the raiding, drinking, singing, hunting and farming, leaving the women to get on with their sewing, cooking, looking after the home, other domestic duties and child rearing.

For some, that is the natural order of things; while others ask where is the evidence to support such a thesis. As with much else about pre-historic Scotland, evidence is random and inconclusive. The above-mentioned roles for the male and females could easily be accurate, reversed or shared; who can tell? Like it or not, though, in physical matters it is the male that usually dominates. And there is no doubt about it, Iron Age society was most definitely physical.

Still, there is a tradition that matriarchy existed in Pict society. Not that a woman could become the new chief – don't be daft, but the line would pass through to her nearest related male, perhaps her husband.

Then again, who has not heard of Queen Boadicea who led the Iceni tribe of East Anglia in a violent revolt against the Romans, in 60 A.D.? There was also Queen

Was looking after an Iron Age home the limit of a woman's role in pre-historic society?

Cartimandua of the Brigantes tribe who, after a split with her husband, had Roman backing in the internecine troubles of the 60s/70s A.D. These led to the Romans taking a keener interest in the north of England and the Borders and, ultimately, to Agricola's invasion of Scotland. These are exceptions, but might there not have been other women who held similar positions before the Romans recorded such events?

It is clearly wrong to assume that because society has been male dominated for centuries, so it was in the Iron Age, despite the average male being stronger than the average female and more suited to heavy work. However, as the average life-span was possibly about 40 years, then the proportion of a woman's life spent child-bearing would be far greater than it is today. As a result, many tasks might have been evenly divided between males and females – and I am sure it was all hands-to-the-pumps at busy times of the agricultural year. But surely, the bearing of children, if not their entire rearing, would place more of the domestic duties on the female?

One would not suggest that Iron Age society reached the point of the upper classes in Victorian Britain, where women were there to look pretty and very little else. Realistically, males probably undertook most of the physically arduous work, such as building and heavy agriculture, and women did whatever tasks for which they were physically capable at any given time.

ECONOMIC ACTIVITY

Be that as it may, as the Iron Age ran its course, the general trend was towards a more unified tribal society under an established ruling elite, especially in the south and increasingly so in the north. As with many Third World countries today, the economy of Iron Age Scotland was based on agriculture, often at little more than subsistence level. That a surplus was extracted is demonstrated not only by the labour required to build strongholds, but the existence of both the ruling class and religious leaders with their attendant luxury possessions – such as jewellery, all appropriated from the common-man.

The one glaring omission in Scotland's Iron Age economy is the seeming lack of a means of exchange, either in non-Roman coins, or tokens, such as iron currency bars. Did barter predominate, perhaps with payment-in-kind to a chief, or a tithe to the priests? This is in direct contrast to southern England where coins appeared in the 2nd century B.C. That was not a market economy either, but the use of coins and tokens would have enhanced the growth of trade in southern Britain, much of which exists in the archaeological record.

It is the lack of such evidence that suggests Scotland's pre-historic economy operated at a primitive subsistence level. Yes, decorated pins, brooches, armlets, dice and other items of jewellery have been found, but only in relatively small quantities. The great silver hoard of Traprain Law* may have been either booty, or even payment by the Romans for services rendered, but such metalwork is a rarity, anywhere north of Hadrian's Wall.

Production also seems to have been aimed more towards personal use than for trade, whether in agriculture or other economic activities. There are occasional examples of larger-scale manufacture, such as an iron founder's hearth at Mid-Howe*,

A Celtic chariot as probably used in Iron Age Scotland.

but this is an apparent exception rather than the rule. Yet, surely communities the size of Jarlshof*, Gurness* and especially the larger hillforts would have supported specialists who produced for tribal distribution. Perhaps much more waits to be found.

Yet, the sheer number of strongholds, whether for an extended family of the Atlantic zone or the great oppida of the Borders, shows that there was an agricultural surplus, as there had been in the Neolithic and Bronze Ages. No doubt, there were peaks and troughs, but the agricultural year allows periods of slack and this was probably when the building, extension or repair of strongholds and houses took place.

Trade, without a means of common exchange, would not have been extensive either, even along the Atlantic coast. Occasional Roman objects have been found, mostly in the Borders, but also in the north, west and northern islands. Again, though, it is their rarity that makes these conspicuous.

Still, the Caledonii had chariots, and the Romans utilised native tracks, so there was long-distance mobility: were these primitive trading routes? It is only industrial society that has enabled the widespread transportation of the most basic products. Before that, even in Early Modern times, it was usually only luxury items that were traded afar. So it might have been in the Iron Age, but pottery, metal tools and weapons, and even woollen clothing, as well as the more obvious items such as jewellery, could have been regarded as luxuries.

AGRICULTURE

The main economic activity throughout pre-history was, to no great surprise, agriculture. The scale undertaken would depend entirely upon the region and its population. If one

A man and two oxen using an ard plough.

considers an Atlantic zone broch, even a large one such as Gurness*, the inhabitants probably indulged in a mixture of fishing, arable and pastoral farming, and hunting.

Farther south, at say Dreva Craig* hillfort, field systems can still be seen, suggesting not only an ordered society, but one with a fair degree of organisation. Even so, crop yields would not have been particularly high, although un-ripened corn could have been dried and used as winter cattle fodder.

Crop yields can be measured as a ratio to the seed corn. Today, yields are very high – it was not always so. In the mid-18th century, wheat yields were about 7:1 or far less. Two hundred years before, the ratios were about half that, and lower still for barley, oats and rye. One might assume that yields were similar (at best) in the Iron Age and, as they varied, little more than the seed-corn was produced in some years, even in extensive, organised field systems.

A major restriction on arable farming was the light ard plough. These merely cut the surface and did not turn the sod, so it was usual to plough a field up and down, and then from side to side – very time consuming. The light ard plough – occasionally used in the early 20th century – was unable to cut into the heavier clay soils of the valleys and so farming was often restricted to the less productive land, at least until the last centuries of the Iron Age. Pre-historic life was most surely a struggle.

Crops had been developed from grasses over the millennia, and those of the Iron Age are easy to recognise today. Wheat, oats, barley and rye formed the basis of the staple diet. Spelt wheat was introduced during the Iron Age, which produced better flour and allowed for sowing in both autumn and spring. Spelt was suited to the heavier, more productive clay soil of the lowlands that was farmed as heavier ploughs developed. Root crops, such as turnips, swedes and so on, were not grown, but beans, lentils and peas were an essential part of the diet and provided winter cattle fodder.

Livestock was the other major farming activity. Although there is considerable evidence of pre-historic weaving, animal skins provided clothing and bones were used for tools. Meat was an important part of the diet, but possibly less so in the south, where the economy might have been more organised. It is unlikely that whole herds were slaughtered each winter and, in any case, the dairy produce would have been invaluable. It might also be that the cow was something of a status symbol and, also, served as a draught animal.

Cattle and sheep were probably allowed to roam the hills each spring, and linear dykes and banks can still be seen that probably acted as boundaries. These animals would also fertilise the land. Several hillforts, especially in the south and north-east, may have combined defended areas for both animals and people: Arbory Hill* and Barmekin of Echt*, for example.

CULTURE, RITUAL AND RELIGION

As with the economy, most cultural activities would be based within the family or tribal-group. Celtic society is often perceived as having an heroic ethos. Raiding, combat, hunting, feasting and raucous games all contribute to this picture, but one would assume that everyday life for Iron Age man was considerably more mundane or less varied than it is today. There seems to have been a distinct raiding season, with a raid probably being preceded or celebrated by a feast. Perhaps the large number of vitrified hillforts is evidence of successful raids, though few strongholds without timber-laced walls have produced archaeological evidence of destruction.

The problem with other assumed cultural activities, such as singing, ostentatious dress and so forth, is that they rarely show in the archaeological record. It is certain that Irish Celtic society of the 1st millennium A.D. indulged in these activities, but the folly of such transpositions is very evident. Nevertheless, what appear to be gaming dice and marked stones have been found at several Scottish pre-historic strongholds: life cannot have been all work and no play, especially during the long winter nights.

Hard though life was, there was still time for leisure and play.

Religion is another aspect of pre-historic society of which little is known. In parts of England, Wales and Gaul, Druids were the religious leaders, at least in the 1st centuries B.C. and A.D. The Romans, although they seemingly tolerated other religions – as with the Jews, did not take too kindly to the Druids and wantonly massacred them and destroyed their sacred sites. In any case, there is no real evidence that Druids were in Scotland, but given the number of Neolithic and Bronze Age sacred sites, such as henges and stone circles, one might assume that religious leaders existed.

While most of those sacred sites do not originally date from the main era of pre-historic strongholds, the Iron Age, that does not mean that they were not used at that time. Many cathedrals, abbeys and churches were founded centuries ago and, even if comprehensively rebuilt, most have continued in use, often despite a change in religious denomination. This could have been so in pre-history.

Sites of possible religious sanctity have been found at hillforts in England and this is likely to be the case for Scotland. As one might appreciate, a large house in a hillfort with a well-used track leading to it may appear to be a shrine, especially if apparent sacrificial animal bones are found in great quantities thereabouts. Then again, it could be a pre-historic butcher's shop or slaughter-house.

Without knowing for certain, some Celts, at least, seem to have worshipped Mother Earth. In many parts of England, swords and shields have been dredged from rivers: the assumption is that they were thrown in as an offering to the gods, probably on the owner's death. Such a trend is not so obvious in Scotland. That begs the question, did Scotland's pre-historic inhabitants have a similar religion as those in England and, if not, why? Because most were not Celts? Or because each tribe had its own religious ceremonies and beliefs? But St. Ninian certainly introduced Christianity to Galloway and the south long before the Romans withdrew from Britain, c. 410 A.D.

Cairnpapple Hill, with its henge and cairn, dating from c. 3000 B.C.,
overlooks much of central Scotland.

Whatever the religions of pre-historic Scotland, ritual probably played an important part in both the tribal calendar and family life. No doubt, seasonal changes were celebrated and there may have been a plethora of gods: worship of these possibly brought extended family groups together in tribal gatherings. Religious leaders would, no doubt, have been consulted by, if not formed a part of, the ruling class, especially with regards agricultural seasons and possibly stronghold building and dedication, and even a raid. Well, might as well have the gods' blessing before you go to burn and plunder your neighbour's stronghold.

The Iron Age witnessed many important changes in society, as one would expect. On the eve of this new era, c. 600 B.C., defended settlements were far from being common-place, as were large settlements in general. Small groups, either an extended family or a community, formed the majority of settlements round the country, but that was to change. Whether there really was a large-scale migration of Celts from England, the North Sea coasts of Europe, or via the Atlantic zone may never be known with certainty. However, not only were considerable numbers of defended residences and settlements built throughout Scotland in the ensuing centuries, there was also a movement towards larger tribal groups.

That scenario is most visible in the Borders, Galloway and possibly the north-east, but occurred even in the outer island groups: hence, the tribal areas recorded by Ptolemy in the 1st century A.D. Still later, the formerly loose confederation of tribes that formed the Caledonii, and fought Agricola, became the nucleus of Pictland. Even in the 1st century A.D., the Romans may have agreed a treaty with the Orcadian tribes prior to their invasion, suggesting a degree of homogeneity in those islands. After all, the Romans did not usually conduct deals with disorganised hordes.

During the last two centuries of the Iron Age, to c. 500 A.D., much of the area to the north of the Forth/Clyde isthmus was considered to be Pictland, while Celtic Britons occupied the Borders and Galloway. Still later, the Britons were forced solely into Galloway and Strathclyde, and what had been Votadini and Selgovae territories became the land of the invading Angles.

Then, in the 5th century, the Scotti began to arrive in Argyll and the western islands, probably to areas where the Pict presence, if at all, was not over-riding: these lands, you might remember, might still have been populated by Q-Celtic speaking people. By the end of the Iron Age, the embryonic Dalriada had been established, possibly with its tribal centre at Dunadd*, and the seeds of the downfall of the Picts were sown, if not to be reaped for another 350 years.

All in all, Iron Age Scotland witnessed the ending of a semi-settled or nomadic pre-history, to be replaced first by smaller tribes, and then the formation of large supra-tribal areas. In some parts, notably southern Scotland, this was completed by the new millennium: these tribes were probably closer to those of England in organisation, than those of, say, Caithness. But then, in 80 A.D., the Romans arrived...

CHAPTER THREE

The Romans Came and Saw, But Failed to Conquer

Why did the various tribes and natives of Scotland build all the defensive strongholds, from the simplest palisade enclosures to the sophisticated brochs and their settlements? One presumes it was for protection, from neighbouring tribes or possible overseas raiders. But, the surprising thing among all these strongholds is limited evidence of destruction in action.

That could be due to the passage of time, plus the difficulty in determining whether the, for example, vitrified wall at a hillfort was caused by accident or deadly design. Or it could be that sling-stones and bronze or early iron weapons were no match for stone-built strongholds. Either – or any other – way, any battle or siege experience our pre-historic forebears had gained was on a minute scale compared with what they were about to face in 79 A.D.

In that fateful year, the Romans decided it was time to complete the conquest of all the island of Britannia. Their arrival in the Borders was on a scale no native would ever have hitherto imagined. The sheer numbers of highly trained and organised soldiers, with gleaming armour, weapons and artillery must have seemed astounding. It has been claimed that as the leading soldiers entered a fort after a day's march, the baggage trains and other support units at the rear would be leaving the previous fort. Such a sight must have been mesmerising for the natives.

For the various tribes, facing the Romans would have been the equivalent of a few partisans coming up against a Nazi SS-led blitzkrieg in the Second World War. For a start, the Romans seldom took prisoners; those who died in combat were the lucky ones. The survivors could be butchered there and then, marched off – often thousands of miles – into slavery, or end up as entertainment in one of the many amphitheatres where they would come to a grisly end. As for those left behind, the Romans were far from queasy about committing genocide on a scale of which the Nazis would approve. That was how the civilised Romans fought! And yet…

While the tribes of Scotland did not welcome the Romans with wide-open arms, not all were wholly opposed either. It is likely that the Votadini tribe (based in the Borders) enjoyed a somewhat privileged relationship with the Latin invaders – a sort of client-tribe. Although some hillforts were abandoned or rendered defenceless, their great oppidum

A Roman Legionary soldier.

at Traprain Law* fairly flourished. The same could not be said of the neighbouring Selgovae tribe, whose oppidum – at Eildon Hill* – was not only cleared, but the Romans built a signal station at its summit; their important Newstead fort was down below.

THE AGRICOLAN INVASION

Gnaeus Julius Agricola, the new Roman governor, arrived in Britain during 78 A.D. and had no intention of messing about with truculent tribes. Almost immediately, he sorted out the less than co-operative Welsh tribes, with devastating effect, and then comprehensively put down any unrest in northern England.

Let us, again, make one thing clear; the Romans regarded Scotland's inhabitants as uncivilised barbarians – wild and uncultured, only one up from savages. There were no altruistic reasons behind their invasion, aiming to civilise them and that sort of thing. Oh no, it was purely to extend and safeguard their empire, for good old profit: if they gained a few slaves for their trouble, all well and good. There was no choice and, as the people of Scotland were about to find out, not much hope of resistance – initially, at any rate.

The invasion began in 79 A.D. with a two-pronged attack. The IX legion pushed north from Corbridge and crossed the Cheviots and Tweedale to set up a fort at Inveresk, on the south bank of the Firth of Forth. They were joined by the XX legion, from Carlisle, which pushed up Clydesdale and then ventured through the central area. It seems that these legions might have made forays up to Tayside, but spent the next year consolidating their gains in the Forth/Clyde isthmus, and building forts and roads.

In 81 A.D., Agricola turned his attention westwards. Off he pushed into Galloway, joined by a sea-borne landing from across the Solway Firth – just to ensure all the odds were in his favour – and made his way to the west coast. From there, Agricola could see Ireland and perhaps thinking that an island free from Roman rule might put ideas into native minds, considered suppressing the Emerald Isle with one legion and a few auxiliaries. Perhaps it was just as well for his reputation that he did not try; the Irish Question might have damned him just as it has damned so many others since.

Roman roads with the surface dressing are rare. There are some doubts about Blackstone Edge, in Lancashire, but it gives a good impression of the real thing.

In all this time, with Galloway, the Borders and parts of Strathclyde subdued, the barbarians proved no match for Agricola. Then, in 82 A.D., he decided to complete the conquest of the mainland and set off for the north-east. Agricola split his forces to cause the maximum disruption and also to locate the main body of the hitherto elusive enemy.

The Caledonii seemed to have little interest in being engaged in battle, they simply preferred cowardly guerrilla warfare. Agricola's fleet sailed along the east coast, to both harry the natives and to provide supplies, but the Romans could not afford to let their guard fall. One night, Agricola's divided forces almost came a cropper when the IX legion was attacked in its camp. It was only saved from annihilation by a timely intervention by Agricola himself; a harsh lesson was sorely learned.

THE BATTLE OF THE MONS GRAUPIUS

After a winter by the Tay, Agricola decided to finally sort out the Caledonii, in 83 A.D. Spring passed into summer, but still he failed to coax them into battle. Then, towards autumn, the big moment arrived and the Caledonii succumbed to temptation. The site of the great Battle of Mons Graupius remains a mystery – for great it most surely was, but it may have been on the slopes beneath the distinctive Mither Tap o' Bennachie*, with its hillfort. The Caledonii chose the higher ground, presumably to wring-out

Could this be the site of the Battle of Mons Graupius, beneath the Mither Tap o' Bennachie?

every ounce of home advantage, and fully 30,000 of them lined up to throw the Latin invaders back from whence they came.

Thanks to a Roman called Tacitus, a relative of Agricola, there is a (unbiased?) description of the invasion and fanciful account about this great battle – the first recorded in Scotland, no less. As is usually the case in such literature, the opposition was trumped-up: after all, there is not much glory in saying that your army has comprehensively thrashed a hopelessly out-numbered, ill-disciplined bunch of barbaric cowards, is there? The Caledonii were far from that, though, but were no match for the well-drilled Roman legionaries and auxiliaries, both in tactics and, especially, close combat.

The Roman forces supposedly comprised about 8,000 Auxiliaries in the centre, flanked by some 5,000 cavalry, with the two legions drawn up behind. Assuming these were at full strength, the Romans would have exceeded 20,000, although Tacitus claimed there were only 11,000. Initially, the Caledonian charioteers paraded in front of their lines and taunted the Romans, who replied more effectively with volleys of javelins. The natives hardly batted an eye-lid, which clearly impressed the Romans. Then they got down to serious business and Agricola led the Auxiliaries into the mass of the natives in close combat, while his cavalry routed the chariots.

The rear ranks of Caledonians then surged down the hill, but Agricola sent forth four cavalry squadrons held back for such an eventuality. They swept through the Caledonians, attacked from behind and, in the ensuing chaos, about 10,000 natives were left dead on the battlefield: reputedly, only 360 Roman soldiers bit the dust (really?). Interestingly, neither legion took an active part in the fighting; they simply let the Auxiliaries get on with it.

This was a comprehensive victory and so, surely, the rest of Scotland was at Agricola's mercy? Not quite. About 20,000 Caledonians vanished into the highland mists,

The rampart and ditch of Fendoch Roman watch-tower, under the heather in the foreground, commanded the entrance into the Sma' Glen for the nearby Roman fort.

able and ready to fight again. No amount of scouting could locate them, so, as far as the Romans were concerned, a serious threat remained, ready to attack whenever they dropped their guard; how right they were.

It is perfectly true to say that the Caledonii lost the battle; but, though bloodied and perhaps bowed a little, they never quite lost the war. Agricola had a string of forts and watch-towers built at the southern entrances to the glens, but he was recalled to Rome that very winter, and a long drawn-out withdrawal was soon under way.

By 90 A.D., the Romans had retreated south of the Forth/Clyde isthmus – rebuilding many forts, yet by the new century they were back in England. Forts such as Newstead and Corbridge, and several others, had been burned and, although some might have been deliberately slighted, others were most certainly not. This seems to have been the work of the chariot-borne chief Argiragus, who was only too pleased to assist the Romans on their way south.

ANTONINE, SEVERUS AND BEYOND

Not for the last time in history, the Borders was a land of disputed territory. Emperor Hadrian had begun his wall by 120 A.D. to demonstrate Roman authority, but by 140 A.D. Roman eyes were cast northwards again.

Nothing bolstered an emperor's standing in Rome more than a conquest, with a good thrashing of the subdued natives for good measure. Much of the known world

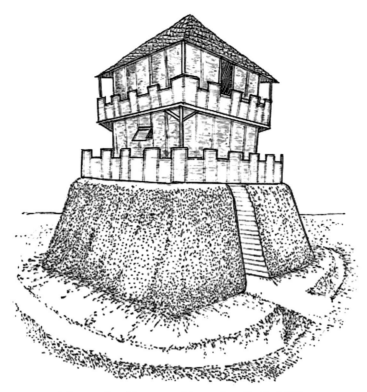

A Roman signal tower, possibly one from the Gask Ridge.

was in the Roman Empire, but there was always those insolent natives of Barbaria, north of Hadrian's Wall, who still needed to be taught a thing or two.

Rome's new emperor, Antoninus Pius, needed a military victory to cement his reputation and where better than against some barbarians in a far-flung corner of the world? Barbarians, furthermore, who had been comprehensively thrashed before and, even in the event of a defeat, well, it was so far away it could easily be hushed up.

So, by 140, Britannia's new Roman governor, Quintus Lollius Urbicus, had pushed into the Borders, and by 142 Antoninus Pius was accepting his one and only salutation for a great victory: the location and details of any battles are not recorded. The Antonine Wall was begun at that time, forts were built both to the north and south of the wall, and all looked rosy: if one were Roman that is.

Unfortunately, there was no Tacitus about at that time, so what happened next, as with most of our pre-historic past, is open to – heated – debate. At some stage in mid-century, the Antonine Wall was first abandoned and then re-occupied again, possibly in the 160s or even 180s. It was certainly abandoned by 196, when troops were withdrawn to Gaul. The few written accounts that exist only confuse matters, as references to 'the wall' could be either Hadrian's or Antonine's.

This section of the Antonine Wall at Rough Castle shows how formidable could be a turf wall.

Then, as the Borders' tribes had been taking full advantage – revolting barbarians – of the absence of Roman soldiers during the campaigns that eventually saw Septimus Severus become emperor, he exacted a terrible revenge with a series of devastating campaigns in Scotland, from 208 to 211. These started with an invasion that included the largest known marching camp in the empire, at St. Leonard's (173 acres) near Lauder. Although nothing can now be seen, this could house up to 35,000 men.

Once again, the Romans made their way to the north-east, building at least 15 temporary forts north from the Forth, through Strathmore right into Aberdeenshire. Severus failed to bring the Caledonii to battle, but died in York in 211 and withdrawal swiftly followed, leaving just the odd base, perhaps Cramond or Carpow.

Thereafter, for almost a century, Hadrian's Wall and the Borders seem to be virtually free from northern raids. Why was this? One theory contends that Severus' army destroyed all crops and so devastated the land that much of central and north-east Scotland was uninhabitable: in other words, genocide on a grand scale.

There were further punitive Roman raids in the mid-4th century, followed by two Pict wars: one c. 390; another c. 398. Yes, the Romans won a temporary respite in those campaigns, but by then the empire was under pressure from all sides. By the first decade of the 5th century, Scotland had seen the last of them.

The impact of Scotland's Latin invaders was obviously not so great as in England. On the other hand, they were less than welcome neighbours and invaders to the tribes of the Borders and Galloway for almost 150 years, the Votadini excepted. It is quite possible that the Romans' occasional incursions had much to do with the drawing-together of the smaller tribal groups that formed the Caledonii: the embryonic

The Volubilous triumphal arch in Morocco commemorates the success of Septimus Severus's campaign in Scotland.

Pictland. The two wars the Romans fought in the 390s were against the Picts, by that time a constant nuisance to the soldiers on Hadrian's Wall. The ever-present threat of Roman action in the Borders would undoubtedly be resented, and by the 3rd and 4th centuries even the wealth of Roman artefacts at Traprain Law* had virtually dried up; booty, or payment for mercenary troops, aside.

However, to really get a flavour of how Scotland's native barbarians felt about the Romans, we need to get beyond mundane written accounts and enlist the aid of our R.B.C. roving reporter Katia A.D. As ever, she is only too keen to get right to the heart of the matter.

"I've come to a small dun in the Caledonian hills, to interview a former chief of the Caledonii tribe on the 30th anniversary of the Battle of Mons Graupius.

"Calgacus 'the swordsman', were you chief of the whole Caledonii tribe?"

"Oh no, Katia. You see the Caledonii, as you Romans called us, was not a tribe in the sense that the Votadinian traitors were. We were a confederacy of many tribal groups: some large, others – like my own – reasonably small."

"Then how did you come to be the leader at Mons Graupius?"

"That was the will of the gods. All the tribal chiefs from the lands of our lordly mountains and beyond, assembled to decide how we should meet the threat posed not only by your army, but also by our brother compliant tribes. Our religious leaders consulted the gods, and it was they who appointed me the great chief, purely for the duration, of course."

"Calgacus, what tactics did you use to fight Agricola and his army?"

"Well, Katia, it seemed to me that, with an irregular force, we should simply use our advantage of local knowledge to its best effect."

"You mean guerrilla warfare?"

"Quite so. Why join in mass combat with a well-drilled, supremely armed fighting machine when we could inflict much damage by a series of short, sharp raids with everything in our favour?"

"That I understand, so why did you eventually face Agricola and his army?"

"We had kept up our campaign for two raiding seasons, but still Agricola could not be stopped. There was pressure from within our forces to cease this, if you will pardon the expression, effeminate form of combat, and to have it out with the Romans, once and for all. Eventually, I had to accede to the will of the gods, so we chose our ground well giving us the advantage in the battle, and an escape route should it be needed."

"According to our great writer, Tacitus, you heavily outnumbered Agricola's forces. Yet still you lost."

"Don't believe that. I had about 30,000 men, with many chariot-borne chiefs. Agricola lined up behind his Auxiliary infantry that included, I'm ashamed to say, Britons from the south, with cavalry and the main legion detachments in support. I'd say we were pretty evenly matched."

"So, what went wrong?"

"Essentially, Katia, your army fought to a disciplined plan, whereas we fought as if it were a local raid, only on a larger scale. Many of our chiefs paraded up and down on their chariots, but Agricola would not be drawn. We then exchanged volleys of missiles and javelins, of which we probably had the better. Then, just as many of our chiefs felt that Agricola was not a worthy opponent, he dismounted and led his infantry into battle."

"How did you meet this?"

"Head-on, in our time-honoured way, but it was the cavalry charge, which routed our charioteers, that was the defining action. Our long swords were more difficult to wield in the confined battleground, whereas your infantry and, I might add, Agricola himself, were at a distinct advantage with their short, stabbing sword."

"Did you retreat at that point?"

"No, far from it. I extricated myself to assess the situation, but saw the mass charge of our warriors running down the hill to engage the rear of your army – the famed legions. That was our big mistake. The Roman reserve cavalry charged through and attacked us from our rear. We were trapped fore and aft, and many paid the ultimate price, but died honourably with sword in hand, in battle."

"What did you do from there?"

"I had no control. We had to get as many out alive as possible, rather than gain eternal life through a glorious death. Well, you know the rest, but well over half our men got away. It was a bad defeat, and we have since heard that our lands were there for the taking. Maybe, but though the battle was lost, the war was eventually won."

"You mean, that the Romans withdrew?"

"Aye, that they did, but we – along with fellow tribes from the south – kicked them out, destroyed their forts and put them to the sword. As Newstead burned, we remembered our fallen heroes at Mons Graupius, and our gods had shown us the way to avenge the accursed ones."

"Well Calgacus, your land has remained free; is this your greatest achievement?"

Katia A.D. interviews Calgacus in his retirement hut.

"It was not solely my doing, fair lady. I eventually returned to my tribe and left the fighting to the younger ones. Mons Graupius was not the end, it was not even the beginning of the end, but it marked the end of the beginning. Rome was in retreat from then on, never mind the circumnavigation of our land by their fleet. Yes, I suppose that if I should live for a thousand years, I will still say, this was my finest hour."

"Calgacus, thank you very much for allowing me safe passage to your land on this special occasion. This is Katia A.D. for the R.B.C. 'Pan-Romorama', Caledonia, in 113 A.D."

This overview of Iron Age Scotland probably conceals more than it reveals, but one thing is crystal clear, it was constantly changing, if not quite at today's pace. To an Iron Age man from the north in c. 600 B.C., a large Votadinian hillfort on the eve of the Roman invasion of 80 A.D. would have seemed almost as unrelated to him as life today would be for someone time-transported from 1800.

Far from being un-civilised, Iron Age society in the 5th century A.D. had many traits we would recognise today. True, it was not as advanced as Rome, but it was increasingly poised to make that leap from the dark into the light. This situation might not have been universal throughout Scotland, but, even in the farthest-flung corners of offshore islands, society had developed far beyond that encountered as the Bronze Age drew to its close. Illiterate our forebears might have been, un-civilised barbarians they most certainly were not.

CHAPTER FOUR

──────── ✺ ────────

Individual Types of Strongholds

This chapter has been sub-divided into sections on the individual types of stronghold.

BLOCKHOUSES

Not unlike the Liberal Democrats political party, blockhouses are neither one thing, nor the other: neither hillfort, nor dun. But, unlike the political party, they are not just distinctive; they are unique and distinctly rare. There are only five known blockhouses and, unlike so many clone-like politicians, no two blockhouses are exactly alike in design. Furthermore, the only place you will see a blockhouse is on the Shetland Islands.

Not too long ago, only four blockhouses were known, but the remains of another was discovered at Scatness north, little more than a sling-shot away from the almost complete Ness of Burgi* blockhouse at the south of Shetland's Mainland. Not only might others be awaiting discovery on the Shetland Islands, but some archaeologists have started seeing blockhouses, if not in their sleep, then on the Orkney Islands and even mainland Scotland. None of those has yet been shown to be a blockhouse, without many shadows of doubt.

Of the five known blockhouses, four of them feature in the gazetteer and, should you ever visit the Shetland Islands – and if you are interested enough in pre-history, then you really must – you ought to see them all. Not only are no two alike, but, unlike brochs, there is no broad set of definitions to convey exactly what is a blockhouse.

Three are free-standing, apparent gateways: two at a promontory fort and one within a walled fort. Two are on islands in lochs, only one of which forms part of the main enclosing wall; and one stands within, but just about adjoining, a walled enclosure. Three have central entrances with cells either side – Scatness north probably had a very wide entrance, and one does not have an entrance, but has an enlarged cell, or open area, behind.

Despite these apparent conflicting variations, you should recognise a blockhouse when you see one. The best preserved is at Clickhimin*, where it stands between the later broch and the entrance to the walled fort. It rises to first floor level and there is a scarcement where once stood lean-to buildings. The odd thing here, and at all blockhouses – except the one at Loch of Huxter, is that it can seemingly be out-flanked with ease by anyone gaining entry to the fort.

Shetland's blockhouses are unique and all different. This one, at Clickhimin, is free-standing.
The blue shirt marks the central entrance, and the red bag the scarcement.

So, it may be that blockhouses were the chief's residence, a sort of personal citadel within the main fort, although one would think that, if attacked, burning lean-to buildings would soon smoke out the chief. More recently, though, an alternative, if less than popular, thesis contends that blockhouses might have been entrances to ceremonial centres, or even nothing more than a means of displaying one's status. Who can say what is right or wrong?

In many respects, these drystone strongholds betray their ancestry not only with their fine stonework, but also in the similarity of their entrance passages to those of brochs and duns. The arrangement of door-jambs and bar holes at three blockhouses is very similar to those in many brochs and duns. In the case of Clickhimin*, the blockhouse was pre-broch (although by how much?), but that does not mean that all blockhouses were. It could be that they were a local development in the broch era: whereas people elsewhere built a dun instead of a broch, so some Shetland Islanders might have built a blockhouse and its associated fort.

The location of blockhouses is another source of mystery. Two are on coastal peninsulas at the south of Mainland; two are on islands in inland lochs – Clickhimin* on Mainland and Loch of Huxter on Whalsay – and Burgi Geos* is miles from anywhere on the north-west coast of Yell. This dispersion makes one wonder how blockhouses evolved, and also whether they were built by people independent of each other or not. Or perhaps they really were merely a local variation to a broch or dun?

While there is no evidence that any blockhouse was slighted in battle, this applies to most other pre-historic strongholds. Still, it seems that the defining feature of a blockhouse was that they all form part of a greater stronghold. A dun is a dun, a broch often stands alone, and the majority of coastal promontory forts are just that. A blockhouse is not a self-contained stronghold. In that sense, it is sub-species, and a local one at that. Blockhouses cannot be fitted into any grand, all-encompassing chronological building scheme so favoured by archaeologists of yore; they are often treated as merely an adjunct to the main theme.

As with our smaller political parties, blockhouses may never predominate among pre-historic strongholds, but neither can they be ignored entirely.

BROCHS

'At least history never changes'. How often have you heard that remark? In a sense, it is not entirely without foundation. After all, every Scot knows that the Battle of Bannockburn was fought in 1314. That date is inviolable, but fresh research can unearth new facts about the battle that may lead to a radical re-interpretation: were the English really so emphatically defeated, for instance?

Six decades ago, debate about Scotland's unique Iron Age strongholds, the brochs, was mostly based on theories originating in the 19th century. A broch was defined as a circular, defensive drystone tower, rising anywhere up to 50 feet high. Furthermore, it was commonly stated that there were about 500 examples, despite most being little more than an overgrown pile of rubble. Any real disagreement seemed to centre on whether brochs were built first in either the northern or the western isles. In many respects, this popular image has changed little since then. Crucially, though, not in all respects.

Despite few brochs having been excavated, interpretations have been revised… revised again…and probably will continue to be revised far into the future. No longer is it accepted that there was a convenient ladder of stronghold development from hillfort, to dun, to semi-broch and, finally, to the brochs themselves. Neither is the grandiose scheme whereby brochs were developed in the western isles and refined in the northern isles, with each region thereafter trading architectural improvements, still discussed in revered tones. Broch architecture and design often differs from island to island, let alone between regions, while in some areas, notably Argyll, duns were used long before, and after, brochs had come and gone.

What is more, the identity of brochs as a separate class of stronghold has been questioned. You might think that historians debating such matters have gone completely mad and ought to get a proper job; after all, what is Mousa* if it is not a broch? Then again, Mousa* is a unique survivor and, out of 500 and more known brochs, barely a handful rise above 15 feet in height today. So, this is going to be anything but a cosy bedtime read to help you doze off.

All brochs that have been excavated, or dug into – as the less pompous 19th century antiquarians described their activities, possess several common, defining defensive features. The main ones are the assumed height of the tower, the lack of external

The majesty Mousa broch. The only survivor and possibly the tallest and finest broch of all.

apertures and a long, narrow and often low entrance passage closed by one or, occasionally, two doors – long since vanished. Yet, despite this seemingly insurmountable evidence, it is not universally agreed that brochs were defended homesteads, let alone strongholds.

Many are situated near the coast and some might have been lookout towers, or even beacons to guide in-coming boats: Scotland's own Pharos, perhaps? Such a notion might not apply to Mousa*, the one broch in nigh-original condition, but who is to say that it did not apply elsewhere? As you will see, there appears to be more academic venom spit over brochs than ever there was blood spilt fighting over them during the Iron Age.

Occasionally, a name can offer a clue as to the origins of a site. The term broch is derived from the Old Norse word 'borg', which means a fortified place: so far, so good. However, when visiting brochs you will find that many are called 'Dun', for example Dun Telve* and Dun Troddan*. 'Dun' is widely used to describe many places, defended or not, so this only confuses, rather than clarifies, the matter. Oh yes, there are so many almost contradictory possibilities over the question 'what is a broch'.

Nevertheless, it is fair to say that a broch is a tapered, circular drystone tower with defensive properties that dates from the Iron Age. It could withstand a typical, short Iron Age siege and, perhaps of more importance, would have appeared capable of so doing to contemporary eyes. That, at least, gets this show on the road and now we can get on with the more interesting business of finding out about brochs, the people who built and lived in them, and the world in which they existed.

A typical broch will have an overall diameter of 35 to 70 ft., a courtyard of 15 to 45 ft. diameter, a wall 10 to 20 ft. thick at the base, and would rise from 20 to 50 ft. in height. Those dimensions, clearly, leave considerable scope for variation, but that is only a part of it. Most brochs had a solid stone wall to first floor level and, effectively, two walls tied together with cross-slabs thereafter. This is a galleried-wall and it was essential for building higher levels. In the western isles, though, many brochs had galleried-walls down to the ground.

Inside a few brochs, a scarcement ledge can be seen running round the inner wall at about first floor level and also, in a handful, still higher. This, coupled with some evidence of post-holes in the floor, suggests that a wooden mezzanine floor or floors,

The entrance passage and two scarcements at Dun Telve broch are seen from the courtyard.

possibly with a hole in the middle, formed the main living quarters. The top may have remained either fully or partially open, but there may have been an overall thatched, or hide, roof at some distance below the wall-head. There were probably a great many variations.

The theory of a thatched roof has been making a comeback, but, quite apart from the strain such a roof could put on the galleried-wall, it could undermine a broch's defensive capacity. A single lighted spear thrown onto a fully enclosed roof would turn this most secure of Iron Age strongholds into a blazing inferno, and a death-trap for the inhabitants.

While these features cannot be seen today, there are others of considerable interest. Many brochs have intra-mural rooms, or cells, at ground level, and some have an

The interior of Mid-Howe, with various hearths, divisions, rooms and stairs may be rather elaborate, but it is unlikely any broch courtyard would have been empty.

intra-mural staircase, or evidence of one. The galleries within the wall above first floor level were probably unsuitable for use as anything other than a passageway, or possibly a store.

Perhaps of most interest is the guard-chamber(s) that usually leads off the entrance passage. A few still have a corbelled roof and a low doorway, which would surely hinder a fast exit in an emergency. Some entrance passages still retain their bar-holes and door-jambs to secure the door or, very occasionally, doors. These features are rarely seen outside Scotland at a British pre-historic stronghold. Regrettably, at most brochs the courtyard is usually either grassed over or, more often, filled with tumbled stones from the collapsed wall. This often hides hearths, storage tanks and other domestic refinements.

As with medieval castles, each broch, though quite individual, conforms to certain basic standards. These will become apparent the more brochs you visit. Accepting the oft-quoted figure of there being about 500 brochs, it might seem that one does not have to travel far to find one. That depends on where you are. The vast majority are on the Orkney and Shetland groups of islands (more than 150), Caithness (another 100 or so), and along the eastern and northern coasts, and glens, of Sutherland. In places, the sheer density of brochs, assuming most were contemporary, suggests that they were not simply the prerogative of a local chief.

Outside the far north and the aforementioned islands, the western isles house the next largest number, especially Skye with more than 20 examples. Quite interestingly, as with the northern isles, many of these overlook the coast, as do some in Ross and Cromarty, west Sutherland and Lewis. Were these the pre-historic equivalent of England's Martello Towers built to defend against a French Napoleonic invasion, or were they situated to guard safe anchorages for trade and fishing? Either could easily be correct, along with many other suggestions, as archaeology rarely produces un-contentious answers.

The sheer weight of numbers suggests that brochs were a phenomenon of the Atlantic and northern coasts, but there are clusters that turn up in the most unlikely places. Several exist in Tayside and in Fife. There are some in the central Lowlands, near Stirling, and three more coastal brochs in Wigtownshire. Perhaps the most surprising of all are the handful widely distributed in the Borders, all miles inland. It seems likely that these were built after the majority of northern brochs.

The dating of anything pre-historic is, as you can imagine, fraught with problems and often depends on artefacts from a site, or the site itself, fitting into the recognised chronological order. This is fine, as each succeeding generation considers its chronological scheme to be the correct one, but later excavations and new dating methods can lead to a revised sequence. In short, what is today's accepted wisdom may be disregarded by 2040.

Brochs provide a practical example of such revisions. Until the 1970s, many pre-historians thought that brochs were built in the 1st centuries B.C. and A.D., with some built a little before, and others – especially those in southern Scotland – a little after. It was assumed that most brochs were abandoned by the 3rd century A.D. The few brochs that had been excavated and produced artefacts that could be C-14 dated, hardly contradicted such a time-span.

*This small cell within the wall of Dun Mor broch would have a corbel roof,
but look at the low entrance.*

Then, in 1976, an excavation of Bu Broch, on Orkney's Mainland, threw up some alternative notions. The archaeological report, published in 1987, gave C-14 dating of artefacts that suggested Phase II at the site – that of the broch – may have begun before 600 B.C. This date, as you can see, is considerably earlier than that hitherto bandied about as the era of the brochs. It does not mean that all previous dating is wrong, as the dates at Bu Broch pertain only to itself, but it certainly opened up options.

Unfortunately, it became something of a fad to dig into brochs in the 19th century – many being the better examples, to boot. Any modern excavation of such a broch would be unlikely to produce artefacts that could be reliably dated in a correct chronological sequence. They would have been disturbed and be little more than a rough guide, but that was not the case at Bu Broch.

It is not wise to become embroiled in the niceties of academic debate here, for when theories and reputations are at stake, the going can get spiteful. Some authorities have questioned whether Bu was a broch, and its wall was substantially thickened later to enable it to be built higher, but C-14 dating is gradually showing that the era of the brochs began well before 100 B.C. So, it is safe to say that the era of the brochs stretched from c. 100 B.C. to 100 A.D. and beyond, while earlier, Possibly, less refined brochs were built several centuries before.

While it is difficult to ascertain the history of a pre-historic site from the archaeological record, that is as nothing when it comes to trying to understand the people who built and lived in them. There is often little tangible evidence. The Romans initially thought of Britain's inhabitants as uncivilised, and the farther north one went the more backward they became. Then, you had the barbarians of Caledonia! Well, the Romans came and saw, but they failed to conquer Scotland's pre-historic ancestors. Yet, more than anything, the brochs show that the people of Scotland were far from being primitive barbarians. Nowhere else in pre-Roman Britain are there such complicated drystone buildings, so there must have been a complex social organisation and structure capable of organising and undertaking such building.

To find out about the people who built and lived in brochs, then, all there is to go on is the artefacts found within or nearby. Differing interpretations of these can lead to some surprising and opposing theories as to who built the brochs and why. So, what are these artefacts? As you would expect, anything made from wood, fabric or

The galleried-wall and stairs at Dun Telve. A galleried-wall, with horizontal ties, would lighten the upper storeys. Unlike Dun Telve, some brochs had a solid floor to first floor level.

animal skins has usually long-since perished, so mainly we are referring to pottery, bone, stone and metal tools or implements, and other in-organic refuse. Thus, there is a one-sided picture of a workaday society with few cultural embellishments. The odd glass bead, polished stone and piece of decorated pottery or metal have been found in brochs, but the archaeological evidence suggests a very uninspiring, spartan life, but how does one recover evidence of entertainment, for example?

What about all the Celtic traditions of myths and legendary story telling, singing, music and decorative clothing? Unfortunately, even the most punctilious of archaeologists will find it difficult to dig up an Iron Age song. No, when it comes to considering the broch people, a large helping of common sense needs to be added to the archaeological evidence.

As with most things, people rarely wake-up and launch an aspect of society off into a completely new direction: steady, measurable progress is the norm. So it probably was with the broch builders, who certainly had the stonework tradition and experience. Scotland's renowned chambered cairns, some pre-dating the Romans by more than 3,000 years, show that the builders had considerable planning, organisation and masonry skills. Likewise with the inhabitants of Skara Brae and Jarlshof*, among others, while hillfort ramparts display a further development of these skills into the Iron Age. The brochs certainly required and utilised skills that had been developed over thousands of years.

Despite that, not all academics agree that the native population developed and built the brochs. There is a theory that brochs were built by immigrants to the various islands and north Scotland, possibly for protection or, rather as the Normans used motte and bailey castles, as a means of exercising control and subduing the natives. One might assume that such incursions would have to be on a large, organised scale, and one might then question from where people capable of such feats might come.

Dun Mor*, on 'sunny' Tiree, may offer a possible answer. When excavated in the 1960s, pottery was found similar to that from the Glastonbury Lake Villages, dating to c. 1st century B.C. Similar shards have been unearthed at other nearby sites, which might indicate that brochs were built by, for want of a better word, invaders. This theory is given further credence in that the guard-chamber at Dun Mor* has similarities with those at some hillforts in southern England.

Furthermore, Belgic-Celts settled in southern England at about that time and gradually spread west and north. Did the displaced natives migrate to the western isles? Perhaps, but such pottery could have reached the western isles via the Atlantic-zone trading routes. As for Dun Mor's* guard chamber, it looks similar to those at other brochs and duns. This shows how interpretations of archaeological evidence can differ widely, or even wildly, and just how contrary and insubstantial many theories can be.

All of which suggests that the question of who built the brochs is unlikely to be answered. If brochs were not built by immigrants, then, one assumes, it must have been the natives, who further developed stone-work techniques handed down the generations.

Although there are dense concentrations of brochs, especially in the far north, surely not every family or extended family would have one. Given the work involved in

A cutaway interior of how a broch might have looked.

planning and building, brochs were probably owned by people of some social stature: perhaps a local chief. This was likely to be the case in the western Highlands and islands, but in Caithness and the northern islands there must have been either a large population or an awful lot of chiefs. It might be that many farmers in the north had a broch as a defended homestead, as they feared coastal raids on a scale not dissimilar to those by the later Vikings.

Another possibility is that some brochs were communal defensive refuges. Several have been built over an older settlement and, particularly in the north, have additional dwellings nearby, or even form a central defensive citadel amidst a village. It was once considered that settlements round a broch were later additions, but recent research and re-interpretations of earlier excavation reports show this was not exclusively the case.

Ownership aside, brochs are so specialised that many may have been planned and built by a skilled, roving group of broch designers and builders. This was the case with the railways, some churches and tower-houses during the medieval era, so perhaps brochs established an historical precedent. Now, that certainly implies a degree of organisation beyond mere barbarians.

Quite why brochs were built and developed is another conundrum. Despite their obvious defensive qualities, only a few have shown signs of being destroyed in a conflict. Was that a

This aerial view of Nybster Broch shows the outer defences of the promontory and the broch surrounded by various buildings. The broch's courtyard is relatively small.

sign of their ultimate success? The great number of defended settlements suggests that the Iron Age was at least an uncertain and violent time: why else go to all the trouble to build them? On the other hand, given the variety of Scottish Iron Age strongholds, it may have been a time when a monumental pile was used to display one's social standing. The broch-owning family was certainly one of some importance in its vicinity and such a domineering structure would have left absolutely no doubt in other people's minds.

While it is tempting to view the development of brochs as a natural progression from hillforts, duns and so on, this is a trap that has snared many theories. Carbon-14 dating has shown that there is considerable overlap between these strongholds, even within a locality. I suspect, for example, that many duns were built simply because they suited local needs better than brochs. It also seems reasonable to surmise that smaller brochs generally pre-dated tall ones and, quite probably, that a broch with a solid wall at ground level, post-dated a neighbouring one with a galleried-wall from the ground upwards. It would be quite wrong, though, to use this scheme as anything other than a very general rule of thumb.

As at other types of stronghold, it is the lack of metal tools and weapons that is most surprising, although iron slag has occasionally been found at brochs. This may indicate that, apart from a metal weapon being of great value, Iron Age society was not so violent as might be assumed from the proliferation of strongholds. In any case, a broch was built to withstand a short Celtic-type siege, and not a massed, concentrated Roman attack.

Evidence is somewhat patchy, but it seems that the two centuries following the Battle of Mons Graupius saw the abandonment of many brochs as defended dwellings. Towers were sometimes dismantled and the stone re-used, while others were used as manufacturing premises, the main living quarters being moved outside; a sort of pre-historic industrial estate. These changes occurred after an external threat receded. Maybe the Roman invasion really did act as a catalyst for the fusing of society into larger tribes.

It was not just brochs that were abandoned from the 2nd century A.D. either. Perhaps, as society developed and tribes melded together, life became more settled and stabilised and such monumental piles became unnecessary. After all, it would have taken a fair amount of maintenance to keep a broch fully defensible. Excavations have shown broch collapses were not uncommon, so some, quite literally, fell out of use. Thus, brochs and their owners may have followed the same path as those of the fledgling nobility in the Middle Ages, who abandoned their tower-houses or made them more comfortable, as their status was secured and society became more established

Brochs hold an esteemed position in the distinguished ranks of Scottish strongholds. The drystone walls are highly complex compared with others elsewhere in Britain, but clearly utilised skills that were first seen in the Neolithic chambered cairns built

At Mousa, the stairs lead within the galleried-wall all the way to the top.
The wall ties are clearly visible.

3,000 years before. Despite doubts about an Iron Age stronghold chronology running from hillforts to brochs, drystone building reached its zenith with the broch-towers.

Thereafter, monumental building fell into decline until the Middle Ages. Then, pele-towers, tower-houses, castles and bastles, though not of drystone build, have sprung up to seemingly resurrect and develop a lost art. These later strongholds are as distinctive of their own eras as are brochs to the Iron Age. All these contribute to Scotland's unique blend of stone-built strongholds. Within these ranks, brochs stand right at the forefront.

The biggest misfortune is that only a handful of brochs survive to any height. The gazetteer, nevertheless, gives details of many brochs worth visiting. As with most pre-historic strongholds, brochs are 2,000-year-old ruins and one needs to carry a mental picture of what one probably looked like and, most important, an impression of the people who lived there. These were not the cold empty ruins of today, but were alive with the sights, sounds and smells of extended families, with everyone going about their daily tasks. Even in their present ruinous state, it is easy to appreciate the skills used in the planning and building of the brochs. Their impact on contemporary eyes would exceed that which sky-scrapers have on us today; and many are situated in attractive locations.

For far too long our pre-history has been overlooked: how many general history books barely mention the Iron Age? Yet, this was a time when some of the most magnificent, spectacularly sited and impressive strongholds ever were built. Arguably, brochs were the finest of all and demand the attention of everyone with an interest in our great heritage.

Our understanding of brochs, their development, demise and the society that built them might be patchy, but archaeological research is continuously adding to the wealth

Today, all brochs bar Mousa are but a ruin. But a great many, as seen here of Dun Bhoraraig on Isla, are in marvellous locations and, usually, far from the madding crowds.

of knowledge. It might sometimes seem to be a cauldron of controversy and petty back-biting, but whatever the historical disputes, we can try to understand the arguments while, more than anything, fully appreciating the splendour of the brochs themselves.

CRANNOGS

This is a type of pre-historic dwelling of which no examples have been listed in the gazetteer. Neither can any be visited in conjunction with any of the other sites, but the O/S maps show that there are, or were, crannogs in many lochs. That is not surprising, for there are more than 600 known examples in Scotland, plus un unknown number just below the water surface. As such, it is easy to choose a route to a pre-historic stronghold in the gazetteer that will take you past a crannog.

It is, perhaps, stretching limits to describe a crannog as a stronghold – a 'defended dwelling' might be more appropriate or a (fairly) 'secure settlement'. A crannog is, usually, an artificial island formed by boulders placed a suitable distance off-shore; often, but not always, in a loch. Stakes and piles were then driven in and a base built above the water line, on which, it is assumed, a timber-framed thatched house was built. Many crannogs, presumably, had a causeway to the shore – some, perhaps, just beneath the water level – and probably had a landing stage as well. Water, and a precarious passage along the causeway, with the odd trap for the unwary, was the main defence, although some crannogs might have had a wooden fence, or even a stone wall round the perimeter.

As one would expect, no crannogs retain anything of their superstructure today, and most need a boat to reach them. Nevertheless, they are worth making a detour for en route to another stronghold just to see. For archaeologists, though, crannogs, with their preserved underwater timbers and middens, can provide a metaphoric, gold-mine of sources rarely found on land.

As with wheelhouses, just a few decades ago crannogs were thought to date from the late-Iron Age. They are found in all five countries of Great Britain and Ireland and, in fact, it was considered that those of Ireland were the first built. Since then, crannog studies have begun to take-off rather in the manner of broch studies in the late-19th century, although on a more scientific scale.

Carbon-14 dating of crannog timbers in Galloway has shown that they were probably built from c. 8th century B.C. to c. 13th century A.D. As further studies are undertaken, these will probably not be the ultimate dated limits of crannog use. A crannog at Loch Olabhat in North Uist has produced much pottery and waterlogged timbers that suggest it might date from Neolithic times. In Ireland, on the other hand, a sample of crannogs that have been C-14 dated shows that they were built after the 5th century A.D. Thus, it could be that after members of the Scotti tribe migrated from Ulster to Argyll, so some returned with the knowledge of the crannog dwelling for their families. It is far too presumptuous to say that this is what happened, but is a more likely scenario than the other way round.

Undoubtedly, more evidence is coming from crannogs that not only enhances knowledge of crannogs, but adds considerably to the understanding of our past: pre- and post-historic. The potential for finding organic matter at a crannog, such as

*This shows Loch Tay's re-created crannog before it sadly burned down in the summer of 2021.
As seen here represents how hundreds now submerged might have looked.*

timber, leather and food waste, is far greater than on land. Underwater archaeology has developed considerably and the opportunities of finding and understanding such artefacts and evidence have never been greater.

Visible crannogs usually appear as little more than pretty islands these days, yet are potentially archaeological Aladdin's caves. We might not only expect more than the odd revision of a pet thesis in the years to come, but some hard facts about diet, clothing and other everyday aspects of life have already come forth.

On the other hand, too much is known – and too many reputations are at stake – to expect any earth-shattering revelations about our pre-historic strongholds. Crannogs may offer a unique opportunity, at least, to discover more about the daily lives of our pre-historic forebears. Such matters might not rock the world, but will give substance to what are, on the whole, generalisations of yard-brush dimensions.

Although the Loch Tay crannog has been destroyed, buildings on the shore survived, housing domestic re-creations. Do contact the phone number below before making a visit.

Scottish Crannog Centre,
Kenmore,
Loch Tay,
Perthshire.
Tel 01887-830583
www.crannog.co.uk

West of Aberfeldy on south bank of Loch Tay
Re-creation by Scottish Trust for Underwater Archaeology

DUNS

When is a dun not a dun? When it is a broch, a hillfort or simply a hill. Dun is the Gaelic word for a fortified hill or dwelling, yet some hills that are not, and never were, fortified are called Dun something or another. Naturally, most genuine duns are called Dun Fighting, or something similar, though not all. This anomaly is not dissimilar to a country house being called a castle, but not being in the least bit defensive, such as Inveraray Castle. So, be aware.

Then again, what exactly constitutes a dun in archaeological terms is also a matter of debate. Several sites in the gazetteer have been defined as brochs, but have been referred to elsewhere as duns, such as Dun Cuir*, Tirefour Castle* and Dun Lagaidh*. Alternatively, Dun Torcuill* is considered a dun here, but has been described as a broch elsewhere.

The boundaries are similarly blurred when one comes to define what is a large dun and what is a small hillfort, especially as examples of both have vitrified, timber-laced stone walls. It is no different with regards promontory duns and promontory hillforts. Again, the differences can be either great, or hair-splitting. Just for good measure, there are also strongholds that have been described as semi-brochs, but these are called duns in this book.

All this demonstrates that Iron Age man did not build a particular type of stronghold as we would, say, a semi-detached house, but probably built to suit a particular location, set of needs and to a standard of which he was capable ('I was not sure whether to build a dun or a broch, so I've built a semi-broch'. Somehow, I doubt it.).

There are two basic types of duns: those with galleried-walls; and those with solid walls. Duns with galleried-walls have been considered as the more advanced and, by implication, closely related to brochs. That ignores the fact that many Hebridean duns have solid walls, some of which were built in the Middle Ages. As ever, you can take nothing for granted with pre-historic strongholds, and still less with regards duns.

Both galleried and solid-wall duns are built to a variety of different styles and shapes. They range from round to almost rectangular. Naturally, this is probably determined by the location, such as a rocky knoll or an island in a loch, to which the builders were attracted. As many duns were built during or after the main broch-building era, so this is a more likely scenario than slavishly following the latest style of designer-dun.

And then there are the promontory duns. These are mostly built on the coast and can be split into several types. Sgarbach's* defences comprise little more than a single wall cutting across the neck of the narrow promontory; sheer cliffs take care of the other sides. The difference between such a promontory dun and a promontory fort, such as St. John's Point*, is mostly one of size and the fact that the latter has a rampart rather than a drystone wall. On the other hand, the Brough of Stoal* is a smaller promontory fort than Sgarbach*. Its, admittedly three, ramparts were probably stone-faced and, in the Iron Age, may have appeared little different from that at Sgarbach*; of course, a stone-faced glacis rampart is unlikely to have an intra-mural gallery.

Another type of promontory dun encloses most of its promontory, rather in the manner of a dun on a rocky knoll. Dun Ringill* is one example, whereas nearby

The entrance is all that remains at Dun Grugaig (Skye), but traces of a perimeter wall have been found. It is another in a spectacular location.

Dun Grugaig* (Skye) is similar, but its wall near the cliff edge must have been far less substantial than the entrance wall.

Finally, the most unusual – and controversial – type of dun is the so-called semi-broch. They are usually C- or D-shaped strongholds that display broch features, such as a galleried-wall, entrance design and intra-mural cells, yet were never circular towers. Although they form something of a half-way house between brochs and duns, the notion of a chronological ladder, whereby hillforts preceded duns, which preceded brochs, is unlikely.

Dun Ardtrek* is the premier example of the semi-broch, standing on a large rocky knoll with its galleried wall forming a C-shape round and back to the cliff edge. However, as Dun Ardtrek* was built during the main broch-building era, it certainly does not fit into a cosy chronological ladder.

Dun Grugaig* (Inverness-shire) is another member of the elusive semi-broch club, high above a river. A more interesting example is Rhiroy Broch*, which has been described as both a broch and a semi-broch: it could also be a dun, for good measure. That just about sums up the whole argument regarding semi-brochs. Surely, there is little to be gained by adding yet another category of pre-historic stronghold. Of all the so-called semi-brochs that I have seen, they give the impression that they are simply duns with some architectural features also found in brochs. No big deal and as simple as that.

By far the majority of duns are in Argyll and the Hebridean islands, with a few in Galloway, the hills around Perth, and some dotted about the Highlands. Occasional

Dun Ardtrek is one of the so-called semi-brochs: half dun, half broch. It features architectural aspects of both, but what a place to live.

ones can be found along the Atlantic seaboard, such as Sgarbach*, and possibly even the pre-broch settlement at Nybster*, both in Caithness. As with brochs, some were small, defended settlements, while others possibly served an extended family. Once again, some may have been the residence of a local chief, perhaps serving as a communal refuge for the people who lived in open settlements nearby in times of danger. It is impossible to prove, but it would not be beyond the realms of fantasy to assume that the wide variety of sizes and styles reflected an equal number of uses.

With regards building details, many dun walls have a rubble core with inner and outer stone facings, not unlike hillfort ramparts; others had timber-laced walls. Neither of these could have supported a broch-like tower. Other duns had solid stone, or galleried-walls that were probably a development of rubble-core walls. This suggests that duns with a rubble-core wall pre-dated most brochs, at least in the western Highlands and islands. Remember, though, take nothing for granted.

Walls were often stabilised with timber-lacing, as at Dun Skeig*, by having a broch-like tapered wall-face, as at An Sean*, or with an inner revetting, as can be seen at Dun Kildonan*. Some duns have many features that show an affinity with brochs, such as galleried-walls, intra-mural cells and stairs, guard chambers and entrance design, a scarcement and even first floor galleries.

Inside, timber lean-to buildings against the wall often featured, as at some hillforts, while it is assumed that intra-mural stairs often led to a wall-head walk. As such, duns can certainly appear to be a mid-point between hillforts and brochs, but that ignores

Rhiroy, or Dun an Ruigh Ruadh, is another potential semi-broch. It is not on the coast, but still lost part of the wall over an edge.

all dating evidence that shows that some brochs can pre-date either of these. All of which demonstrates how various architectural details can find themselves in different types of building or stronghold.

Whether duns ever preceded brochs or not may be open to debate, but there is little doubt that they continued in use far longer than brochs. This may be purely due to regional differences. Duns were inhabited in Argyll and the Hebrides into the Middle Ages, though not continuously, and there are considerably more duns than brochs in those areas. Even so, several brochs have also produced evidence of use beyond the Iron Age.

Another reason duns endured a longer period of use than brochs is that they would not deteriorate so markedly, or quickly, if abandoned. The same applies to hillforts. Some, possibly most, brochs undoubtedly collapsed, while a dun, even if in a poor state of repair, would not take too long to make habitable and defensively secure again. As Argyll and the Hebrides were often embroiled in violent encounters and invasion in the Dark Ages and Middle Ages, so duns were used to take refuge in a Norse raid, while some were even used in later clan feuds. So, despite isolated exceptions, duns may have outlasted brochs by about a thousand years.

Clearly, duns are a diverse type of stronghold. It would be interesting to join Katia A.D. on her time-travelling and return to various Iron Age sites to hear how the inhabitants referred to them; a few archaeological disagreements might then be resolved. Until such times as a Tardis goes into mass-production, we must satisfy ourselves as to what classification any particular site falls into: it is a purely personal and subjective matter.

The classifications used here will not have archaeological unanimity, but part of the fun in visiting strongholds – and especially duns – is to decide for yourself. Pre-historic strongholds are not always spectacular, but neither is pre-history straight forward and mundane either.

HILLFORTS

Just about every book with a section on pre-historic Britain attempts to define what is a hillfort and to explain them. Many divide the word with a hyphen, hill-fort: a fort being a defensive military establishment, while a hill is...well, a hill. Add the two together and you have a defended military establishment on a hill; only you do not. I suppose out of the 1,000 or so hillforts in Scotland, some might fit that description, but few, if any, would have been built purely for use by a militia or warriors.

So, hillforts are not forts in the usual sense, but defended settlements, ranging from half an acre or less – when some can be confused with a dun, to more than 40 acres, as at Eildon Hill*. There is no upper limit: Stanwick hillfort, in Yorkshire, enclosed about 850 acres – and neither is it on a hill, for good measure.

Which introduces the second matter. Not all hillforts are on hills, while many stand on hillside plateaux and can be easily overlooked, such as Edinshall* for example. So, 'hillfort' is not an entirely satisfactory descriptive word, but that is the term that has stuck and is universally accepted.

No doubt, many Neolithic settlements had a fence to keep out wild animals and strangers, and to protect their animals. These palisade enclosures are not hillforts and few traces of them can be seen today, though many early hillforts developed from them, such as Hownam Rings*. The defining feature of a hillfort is its defences:

Hillforts are best photographed from above and none better than Edinshall. The layout of the defences, open settlement to the left and broch are all clearly visible.

at least a wall or rampart, usually in conjunction with a ditch. Such defences are rather more permanent and, in many cases, the ruins are still visible. About 50 hillforts are featured in the gazetteer and, although there are many different types and styles, it is the permanence of the defences that distinguishes them from the palisade enclosure.

As with other types of pre-historic stronghold, hillforts are often concentrated in specific areas. In the main, these are the Borders – where there are hundreds, Galloway, the central Lowlands and the north-east; there are surprisingly few in the Highlands and the north. Promontory forts are a feature of the northern islands and, although they are a rarity in Argyll and the Hebrides, Islay's Dun Nosebridge* is a wonderful, inland specimen. In short, you are never too far from a hillfort, at least if you have a car and a good pair of legs.

There was a time, not so long ago, when all hillforts were claimed to herald from the Iron Age. Well, the majority seem to, but, thanks to carbon-14 dating, several are known to have existed in the 8th century B.C., at least: about 200 years before iron reached our shores. So, now there are some Bronze Age hillforts that were inhabited through most of the Iron Age. Eildon Hill*, for example, was occupied for about 1,000 years. True, the extent of its Bronze Age defences, if any, are not known, but other hillforts have some visible remains.

Hillforts continued to be built throughout the Iron Age. Some were abandoned and re-fortified, or re-used as open settlements – as with Edinshall*, while others were not only inhabited into the Dark Ages, but were built then: especially the nuclear forts, such as Dundurn*. Hillforts, like duns, have a long heritage of build, use and re-use. They are as much a feature of the Borders and north-east, as are duns to Argyll and the Hebrides, and brochs to the Orkney and Shetland Islands. However, unlike elsewhere in Britain, a good number of Scottish hillforts possibly continued to in use for more than 1,500 years, from hamlet to city, to chieftain's stronghold, with periods of abandonment in between. Such a varied and lengthy heritage makes, for example, tower-houses seem relatively recent interlopers in the great canvas of Scottish history.

There are two broad types of hillfort, both of which can be further sub-divided: the univallate hillfort, with a single defensive wall or rampart; and the multivallate, with two or more ramparts. For two seemingly straight-forward types, the permutations of build and development can be mind-boggling. Some univallate hillforts remained just so throughout their existence. Some had additional lines of defences built at a later date, while others expanded in size and also gained additional defences. A few contracted in size, while others expanded and then contracted. In reality, the possibilities were endless, to suit the requirements of the inhabitants at any particular time.

The same applies to multivallate hillforts. Some were maintained as built with multiple lines of defences, while others had further defences added. Perhaps the strangest of the lot were those multivallate hillforts that expanded, and finally contracted to a small univallate type. As with life, it takes all sorts and that is certainly the case with hillforts.

Some early palisade enclosures had a pre-historic equivalent of our 'upgrading' with their fence being replaced by a rampart or wall to become a true hillfort. These were often the initial phases from which developed the contour hillfort, one of the more common types found in Scotland. As the name implies, the defences of this type of hillfort followed the contours of a hill, perhaps enclosing the whole summit area, as at Ben Freiceadain*. With these, as with duns built on a rocky knoll, the site would have conformed to the needs of the builders, and the defences were built round the contours.

Another variation is the plateau hillfort. With these, the area enclosed by the defences is not dictated by the contours of the hill. Many plateau hillforts are located at hill summits, only part of which is enclosed as it was far too big: the rest could be used for cattle enclosures. Other hillforts stand on a plateau part-way down a hill and, surprisingly – given that the interior can often be overlooked, these are not exactly rare.

Promontory hillforts are a common feature of the rugged coastlines of Cornwall and Pembrokeshire, but are comparatively rare in Scotland. Many duns and brochs are built in such places instead, but the large St. John's Point* is a magnificent exception to the general trend. Once again, the dividing line between a small promontory fort and a promontory dun can be quite fine, as near as would have made no difference to the builders, no doubt.

Not all promontory hillforts are at the coast, though. The hillfort at Inchtuthil* occupies a promontory above a former bend in the River Tay, while others enclose a promontory or a spur of a hill. The major feature of promontory hillforts is the, usually, extensive defences that cut across the easy approach, such as the five – yes five – ramparts at Inchtuthil*, and the modest, or even absence of, defences on the other sides. Hillforts on a ridge are often similar, but usually have fully encircling defences.

One final type is the un-finished hillfort. Durn Hill* is the sole example included in the gazetteer. It is worth visiting if only to see how a hillfort was planned, and to inspect the incomplete works. More than anything, un-finished hillforts have been invaluable for enabling archaeologists to study exactly how our pre-historic ancestors went about planning and building the great defences.

All of which brings us to the details of the defences. The wooden fence, even when accompanied by a ditch, belongs to the palisade enclosure rather than the hillfort. There are three main types of hillfort rampart. The simple glacis rampart, comprising spoil from a ditch is the most simple. The box rampart comprised an inner core (rubble and spoil) enclosed by a wooden rampart or, sometimes with just an outer wall of timber revetting. Most interesting (and not visible) is the timber-laced or *murus gallicus* rampart. This was a rubble core, revetted by stone and tied with internal horizontal timber-lacing. Some hillforts also had a solid stone wall.

Somewhat surprisingly, the simple glacis rampart was possibly the most recent development in Scotland. They are often associated with additional outer ramparts that, for example, converted a univallate into a multivallate hillfort, possibly to combat the introduction of the sling as a weapon (or was it the other way round?). They can be seen at many Borders' hillforts, such as Arbory Hill*, or those in the north-east, such as Barmekin of Echt*, but hillforts defended only with glacis ramparts are relatively rare in Scotland, no matter how common elsewhere.

Today, glacis ramparts are eroded by 2,000 years of wind and rain, and are often covered by nature's finest efforts, from grass to dense undergrowth and trees.

 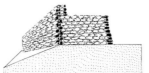 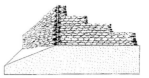

Three stone-faced ramparts.

Yet, many were more than 15 ft. high – double that if you were unfortunate enough to find yourself at the bottom of the adjoining ditch – and their original appearance, and visual impact, is completely lost. Oh yes, glacis ramparts can seem quite harmless now, but when fully maintained they were formidable defences: and remember, they were often only the outer ones.

Timber box ramparts were mostly found in the south and probably originated in the Bronze Age. These could be anything up to 20 ft. high, and the same in width, and could prove to be a very effective defence. However, fire was always a hazard, while the timbers would need maintaining. The stoutest timber could last about 25 years, perhaps a pre-historic lifetime, but others might need replacing, if not annually, certainly with an annoying regularity. Just try leaving your window frames un-painted and you will soon find out.

The solid stone wall was widely used in duns and brochs, and it is a stone wall with a rubble core that is often associated with the hillfort. Many walls were supported with an internal timber frame, known as timber-lacing or *murus gallicus*. This was more common than is readily apparent as the timber has rotted and, as a result, the wall has collapsed. Today, it is virtually impossible to tell whether the piles of rubble were a timber-laced or a solid drystone wall.

Only a handful of hillforts have revealed the horizontal holes for the timber-laced ramparts, but, fortunately for us – though not the inhabitants, some were burnt and the stones melded together, or vitrified: hence, Scotland's vitrified hillforts. Back in

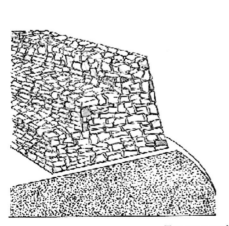 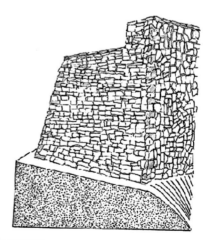

Two stone wall ramparts.

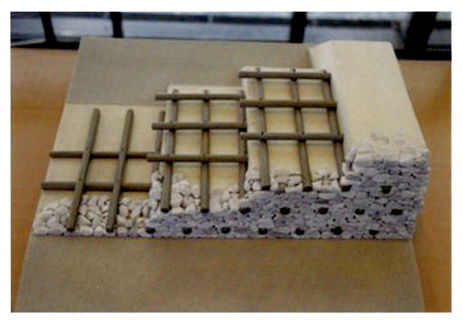

This model of a timber-laced rampart, or murus gallicus, *shows the method of construction.*

the earlier days of archaeology, it was thought that such ramparts were deliberately set on fire to increase the defensive capability of such walls; it is likely to have had the opposite effect.

Neither was vitrification necessarily, or even likely, to have been the result of battle or siege. No, experiments in more recent times have shown that to achieve the constant and high temperatures needed to melt and meld the stones, a fire would need to be deliberately made and maintained. Not a likely scenario during a raid – no matter how successful, or the cause of a domestic accident in lean-to houses.

It seems that vitrification was an act of deliberate destruction, perhaps after a hillfort was taken in battle, or after one was no longer used – possibly to make it fairly useless for any foe. Were the Romans involved in this? However, charcoal from vitrified hillforts has been C-14 dated to the late-Bronze Age (very early for such sophisticated defences and contemporary with similar rampart styles found in Germany). So, was timber-lacing brought to Scotland by traders, immigrants or invaders from Germany, or did it evolve independently? These are answers that may never be known, but dates for these have been pushed ever-further back in time.

Ditches are an, almost, essential part of hillfort defences: one done on the cheap when digging the core for ramparts. In the case of a glacis rampart, the ditch is usually about the same size as its rampart and equally effective. Ditches would often be 10 ft. or more deep, sometimes of a 'V' profile, and sometimes with a flat bottom. At up to 40 ft. across and, in conjunction with wooden stakes in the bottom – a *chevaux de frise* – or other obstacles, ditches could be a formidable barrier.

Mid-Howe broch has a rare example of a stronghold ditch in original condition.
The man is 5 ft. 6 in. tall (or small), showing the ditch as a major obstacle.

Unfortunately, ditches today are usually heavily silted and much of their defensive capability is lost. Naturally, given our climate, they would need to be maintained – probably being cleared out annually – and this spoil was often thrown to the outer edge, eventually forming a counterscarp bank. In the, past antiquarians sometimes thought that these were ramparts, but they are usually easy to distinguish and were an additional benefit from an otherwise arduous task. Incidentally, the ditch at Mid-Howe* broch is still near to its original depth and shows how an attacker, stuck at the bottom, could be in a perilous position.

As with all strongholds, the entrance was the main potential weak spot. Several hillforts with timber-laced ramparts have produced vitrified material from entrances that were probably attacked and burnt. Earlier entrances, as at palisade enclosures,

The stones of a chevaux de frise *would not necessarily stop a mass-charge, but would undoubtedly be a hindrance. This one is at Cademuir hillfort.*

tended to be simple gateways that would not take much to breach. So, as at brochs and duns, hillfort gateways became deeper: inturned rampart ends formed an elongated passageway where an enemy could be attacked from the side walls.

Even these entrances had their limitations, though, and as the Iron Age progressed, so various elaborations were introduced. Multivallate hillforts could have staggered entrances, forcing attackers to turn and expose their flanks. Out-workings were developed, while innovations such as two sets of gates, bridges, guard-chambers and even *chevaux de frise* provided additional protection. Although there are very few examples of *chevaux de frise* to be seen, rows of wooden stakes arranged to prevent a mass-charge would have been highly effective, easy to maintain and no longer exist. They were possibly more common than it appears today.

As you visit the hillforts in the gazetteer, you will find several with a stone wall and no apparent entrance, such as the White Caterthun*. Now, entrances in some of these might come to light if excavated, but by no means all. In those cases, a wooden structure was possibly used that could be dismantled in the event of a raid, or simply ladders. Although these might seem an impractical method of entry – reminiscent of late nights when scaling college walls to get in, at least it negated the most vulnerable point in the defences. (Such an impractical means of entry, for daily use, raises the question of such hillforts only being used in times of danger.)

Gates at hillforts would have been wooden, as was probably the case with many duns and brochs. Entrances would be heavily used, probably having a metalled track and, in larger hillforts, there may have been a pair of gates divided by a central pillar, the gates being supported on pivot stones. One might assume that the gates were left open in the day, but closed at the first sign of trouble. That was when they would be put to the test, an examination, judging by the number of hillforts with vitrified entrances, some seem to have failed quite miserably.

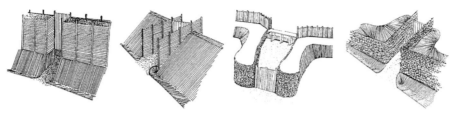

1 Timber fence and palisade gap; 2 A palisade gap with extensions; 3 An inturned entrance with bridge; 4 A simple inturned entrance.

It is all very well having massive and complex defences, but people needed to live in the hillforts as well. House circles and platforms on which round houses were built can be seen at several hillforts, and some seem to be covered in them; mind you, not all were necessarily occupied simultaneously. The same applies to the assumption that each family occupied one house. Some families may have had one for living in and another for work, while some might have been for living and others for sleeping. We cannot tell, but some seem too small to serve all the needs of a family, unless they were a pre-historic bachelor-pad.

Then again, evidence from vitrified hillforts has suggested that terraces of lean-to houses lined the ramparts. This was certainly the case at some German hillforts. A good proportion of known, Scottish timber-laced hillforts have produced vitrified material at points other than the entrance. Unless the entrance was particularly heavily fortified – and few hillforts had really elaborate entrances, then one might assume that nobody would attack a blank wall. In these cases, vitrified destruction may have been caused by a domestic incident. Once timber-lacing caught fire it could soon spread and wooden lean-to buildings would be particularly vulnerable. If one went up in flames, those nearby could soon be consumed.

Food storage was another important consideration. In southern England, many hillforts had large storage pits – sometimes hundreds. These are rare in Scotland, although many souterrains have been found. Several English hillforts had rows of buildings on stilts or piles, which were probably granaries. Perhaps some of our pre-historic forebears stored food this way, as did the Romans, although archaeological evidence is sparse. But what about a log cabin resting on the ground? These leave virtually no marks, and certainly none for discovery 2,000 years later, so who knows? An absence of evidence is not evidence of absence.

As for water, occasionally what are assumed to be storage tanks have been found, though nobody knows whether they were used for water. Wells are similarly rare and

Food storage must have been a problem in the Iron Age. Underground souterrains were one solution, and this one at Castle Law (Mid-Lothian) hillfort has been restored.

while hollows might have served as dew ponds, there are very few hillforts having evidence of springs rising within, or running through their confines.

Duns and brochs are often sited near streams, although many are a fair walk away, but there are probably hundreds of hillforts that are a long way from any obvious source of water. How did the inhabitants manage? Were, in fact, such hillforts ever permanently occupied, or were they merely refuges? As evidence points to most hillforts being permanently occupied, so the question of water supply, and sewage disposal, is something that is not going to yield up any easy answers. Dew ponds might have been in universal use, but how are we to find out, either way?

As you can see, hillfort – like dun and broch – is a simple word that opens up a whole gamut of possibilities. There are other sub-types that I have omitted, for this book is all about getting out and visiting our pre-historic strongholds. If you really want to become an 'expert' or 'nerd', there are plenty of archaeological reports that make for, shall we say, compulsive reading.

One should not be so vain, but allow me to quote from my book, *The Iron Age Hillforts of England*, '... (hillforts) are some of the most magnificent, spectacularly sited and greatest of man's work...' So, get out there to visit some of the finest strongholds in Scotland. Strongholds, moreover, that are well off the main tourist routes and enable you to see parts of Scotland the glossiest guide books fail to reach. You will be anything but disappointed.

ROMAN STRONGHOLDS

If there is such a thing as reincarnation, a native of Scotland from, say, 150 A.D. who bought this book today might be more than a little miffed to find a section devoted to the strongholds of these less-than-welcome invaders. These belonged to the people who, after all, caused enormous and, at times, devastating, disruption for the natives, brought no benefit to the country and who were – finally and emphatically – given the order of the boot. To include what our re-born Scotsman would probably have seen symbols of oppression, perhaps as significant as the Nazi jack-boot during the Second World War, might be considered an act of treachery.

It is easy to agree with such sentiments and Roman sites would not be included in a book about English pre-historic strongholds. Scotland, though, proved to be a far tougher nut to crack and, ultimately, the Romans, for all their bluster and mayhem, failed to conquer the land and extend the empire. For better or for worse, Scotland's pre-history carried on for a further 400 years after the Agricolan invasion, and so the Roman strongholds, whether wanted or not, fall within Scottish pre-history. From a visiting point of view, the Roman strongholds featured in the gazetteer, occasionally in conjunction with those of the natives, offer a welcome addition to the not inconsiderable variety already found in Scotland.

Chapter 3 covered the three main phases of Roman activity in Scotland, none of which really involved civilian settlement to any great extent: the Agricolan

The largest of the Pennymuir Roman camps (see Woden Law*)
could house two legions in its 42 acres.

*The defences of Ardoch fort are the most extensive still to be seen in Scotland.
There were several temporary camps nearby.*

campaign, from c. 79 to 90 A.D.; the Antonine period, from c. 140 to 180 A.D.; and the destructive Severan campaign, from c. 208 to 212 A.D. The latter two invasions had a tendency to re-use forts at or nearby those of Agricola's time. Even after the abandonment of Scotland following the death of Septimus Severus, the Romans maintained forts at High Rochester, Bewcastle, Netherby and Risingham from which patrols may have reached as far north as the River Tay, until the 4th century. The Borders, especially the lands of the Votadini, was possibly akin to Vichy France in the Second World War.

Perhaps surprisingly, there is quite a variety of Roman strongholds, from the most temporary, overnight marching camps to a great legionary fortress. In between, there were forts, fortlets, watch-towers, signal stations, semi-permanent marching camps, practice siege-works and the Antonine Wall. Examples of each have not been included in the gazetteer as most of the temporary camps are barely visible, and this book aims to feature the best sites worth seeing.

The Agricolan forts usually resembled a playing card and have a 'V' shaped ditch surrounding a turf or spoil rampart. Even overnight camps had wooden stakes on top of the rampart, and permanent forts often had the rampart built on wooden foundations, with a wooden revetment to prevent it sliding into the ditch. Later, many of these – as with the Antonine Wall* – were rebuilt on stone foundations.

Outside the rampart, some forts, such as Ardoch*, had a series of ditches, and there were many other defensive refinements, but the general plan remained. Sometimes, ditches had straight sides to prevent an attacker getting out, thus becoming a target in a lethal coconut-shy. The area in front of the rampart could be a veritable killing ground and artillery would probably have been needed to mount a successful assault:

This re-creation of a Roman gateway is at South Shields. It may be a bit grand for anything actually built in Scotland, but illustrates what might have been built had the Romans been victorious.

the Scottish tribes did not possess such things. These Roman forts seldom look as impressive as many hillforts today, but the Roman defensive planning was certainly proved in battle – many times over.

This general layout, with each side usually having an entrance, was the same for virtually all Roman strongholds, from an overnight camp to the great, intended legionary fortress at Inchtuthil*. But, surely, an entrance is the weak-spot of any stronghold? That is usually the case, but the Romans did not intend cowering behind their defences if under attack. No, they wanted to get out and at the attackers as quickly as possible, hence the numerous entrances. An enemy could virtually seal one entrance, but, if at all possible, the Romans would emerge from the opposite side to meet them out in the open, and the attackers had better be prepared.

The Romans certainly were. They cleared two native hillforts possibly to use for siege practice, Woden Law* and Burnswark*, and both of these have artillery mounds. Surprisingly, perhaps, sieges of occupied hillforts are noted more by their absence. Few have produced archaeological evidence of their destruction by the Romans; even the great oppidum and probable tribal centre at Eildon Hill* was seemingly given up without a fight. Such a scenario rests uneasily with a mental picture of a brave and heroic Celtic populace, but it seems that the sheer sight, and perhaps a little demonstration of firepower, of an indomitable Roman army could be enough to encourage capitulation.

The three artillery mounds, known as the 'Three Brethren'
at the fort near Burnswark hillfort.

You do not have to visit many hillforts to realise that most are built on high ground overlooking what was probably the inhabitants' territory. The Romans seem almost to have gone out of their way to build their strongholds on low-lying ground, sometimes even being overlooked by, presumably, cleared hillforts, as at Woden Law* and Eildon Hill*. Were they confident, or arrogant, enough to know that their defences could withstand an attack, especially with their highly trained troops and tactics? Mind you, Newstead fort was one of several that perished in a native raid.

The internal arrangements at Roman strongholds were as stereotyped as were the defences. Consider a marching camp, for instance. Tents for the soldiers were set up in rows, with each centurion's troops housed together. In the centre would be the senior officers' tents. The same layout was used at a fortress, with the barrack-rooms being laid out round the periphery, and the *Principia* – commandant's and officers' quarters and shrine – being in the centre. A small fortlet usually had the same arrangement, with perhaps no central buildings.

As can be clearly seen at Rough Castle* on the Antonine Wall, forts often had an annexe. This might contain the baths – possibly, as they were a fire risk, extra storage, workshops and perhaps even a training ground. Larger forts often had other ancillary buildings such as a hospital and granaries. Agricola ensured his main forts, at least, had provisions to last a winter, just in case one was cut-off for any length of time.

This demonstrates the high degree of planning and organisation of the Romans, and though their strongholds seem to be quite inflexible, many brochs also conform to a general standard design. In any case, the Romans had developed their fortresses through long, battle-hardened experience.

One thing absent from virtually all Roman forts in Scotland, but quite common south of Hadrian's Wall, is an adjacent civilian settlement. This demonstrates the nature of the Roman presence in Scotland: military invaders, not civilian settlers. Even in Nazi-occupied countries during the Second World War, natives worked for, or collaborated with, those regarded as the occupiers. Not apparently so in Scotland, and that includes the Votadini tribe as well, who enjoyed a favoured position with the Romans, with considerable quantities of Roman artefacts and coins having been found at some of their settlements. The Romans certainly did not endear themselves to the Scots.

Whatever the rights and wrongs of including Roman strongholds with those of the native population, Roman intervention in Scotland did not bring about the end of pre-history, and so their sites sit – somewhat uneasily – alongside our own 1,900 years later. It is to Scotland's credit that the Romans were seen-off; how many others resisted their onslaughts successfully?

In any case, the Roman strongholds are a welcome addition today, and offer a still greater variety as we set out to investigate the greatest defended strongholds of our pre-historic forebears.

WHEELHOUSES

You might consider wheelhouses to be a strange inclusion in this book on two counts: firstly, wheelhouses – so far as is known – were not strongholds; secondly, there are no specific examples featured in the gazetteer, as they are not the most visual of sites to visit.

Before you think I am about to include wattle-and-daub huts, just for good measure, the remains of a few wheelhouses can be seen at some brochs, while they are also a sub-group of the Atlantic roundhouse type of dwelling to which brochs also belong. So, are those good enough reasons?

Wheelhouses are only found on the Hebridean and Shetland islands, except that the secondary inner wall-face at some brochs, such as Borwick Broch* (Orkney) might have been a wheelhouse-type conversion. Until fairly recently, wheelhouses were assumed to have been built when brochs fell into dis-use, at some time after the 2nd century A.D. As several brochs were converted into wheelhouse-type dwellings, it was considered possible that wheelhouses, as separate dwellings, were developed from these broch conversions. That notion has now begun to change.

Recent C-14 dating of wheelhouses has confirmed their use into the Dark Ages, and also, more interestingly, that the first ones date back to, at least, the 4th century B.C. No doubt, as more wheelhouses are excavated and produce material that can be C-14 dated, such an early date may appear more often. This will have a profound effect on many theories of the development of the Atlantic roundhouses. The former nice and

*Wheelhouses were probably not strongholds, but some brochs were so converted
or had wheelhouses built nearby, as at Jarlshof.*

neat ladder of duns, semi-brochs, brochs and finally wheelhouses seems to have just a
few rungs that are, shall we say, loose.

As the name infers, wheelhouses are circular houses, sunk into the ground, with
radiating stone piers as spokes and a hearth as a hub. The piers divide the interior and,
probably, acted as the rafter supports for the turf or thatch roof. In some wheelhouses,
the piers were not joined to the outer wall, or rim, except by a lintel; these are called
aisled roundhouses. We need not become too drawn into the niceties of these
structures, for obvious reasons (were there such things as quick-release wheelhouses,
for example?), but a few general observations might be of interest.

There are three broad types of wheelhouse: the free-standing, as at Clettraval on
North Uist; those revetted against, often, sand dunes, such as Kilpheder on South Uist;
and those converted from brochs. The wheelhouse at Clettraval seems to have been a
farmhouse, while Kilpheder is more typical of the accepted wheelhouse. There, it is
quite probable that only the upper wall, or just the roof would have risen above the sand
dunes, not unlike the Neolithic houses at Skara Brae. The top of the roof might have
risen fully 20 ft. above the ground floor, though, and such a wheelhouse could never be
considered as a stronghold. In any case, evidence from some wheelhouses suggests that
they might have been used more for ritual or religious activity than a residence.

Needless to say, it is the wheelhouse conversions of brochs that are most likely to have
been capable of being defended. Clickhimin*, Mousa* and, possibly Borwick* brochs
were all so transformed. None of these have their stone piers in position – although the

former two did into the 19th century, but the additional inner-wall facings are clearly visible. By far the best example of a wheelhouse conversion of a broch, plus additional wheelhouses themselves, is at Jarlshof*. This great archaeological site features at some length in the gazetteer, and the wheelhouse phase, clearly post-broch in this case, is one of many on view.

One suspects that there is a great deal more to be discovered about wheelhouses. Yes, they will never be dramatic, like a broch, spectacular, like many hillforts, or mighty, as are many duns. Most are quite anonymous, but some are a unique development of our great drystone building heritage. Some may provide a rich source of investigation for archaeologists for years to come, in a way that many brochs no longer can.

CHAPTER FIVE

Scottish Pre-history Revisited:
A Blast from the Past

For some, it is a sad fact of life; for others, this is precisely how it should be. No, I am not considering the dominance of Scottish football by the 'Old Firm', but merely commenting on the rapidly changing world in which we live. Conditions on even the remotest croft in the Shetland Islands or the Hebrides have changed more in the last half-century or so than at any other time in the past.

Take, for example, the typical village. In 1851 a village was a community that was, more often than not, a hive of activity. Many were probably tied to a particular industry, landowner or employer, but a range of essential services would usually have been available within a village's boundary. A century later, in 1951, there had certainly been many changes, but the same basic principles would have applied, although often to a lesser extent.

Nowadays, despite the coronavirus effect, many villages are little more than a virtually deserted commuter estate during weekdays, especially those near the larger towns and cities. Specialist shops, such as a butcher, are forever closing and as for other services…there is about as much chance of Stranraer winning the Scottish F.A. Cup, as there is of finding exactly what you are looking for.

No, like it or not, life is constantly evolving, but the scale of change has been phenomenal in recent decades. Even our hypothetical village of 1951 would have obvious similarities with a small pre-historic community; commuting to our Iron Age ancestors probably meant a walk to the fishing boat or the fields. Far too many of us understand just what that word means today.

Nevertheless, the cumulative knowledge from numerous published reports on pre-historic defended sites gives a good basic impression of daily life in, say, the Iron Age. However, to get right to the heart of the matter and to see what life was really like, we need to resort to the efforts of our intrepid, Roman Broadcasting Corporation (R.B.C.) roving reporter, Katia A.D. As luck would have it, she was due to make a special documentary about north Scotland in the decade after Agricola's campaign wound down. So, let us go over to her in 95 A.D., shortly after she had arrived on the east coast of Caithness.

Dun Ringill's splendid location above Loch Slapin must have been as magnificent in the Iron Age as it appears today.

"After a boat journey of several days, we landed beneath the cliffs of northern Britannia. We were greeted not as adversaries – and neither as friends, but with a tolerance made all the more welcoming by our gifts. Our boat's crew was well known in these parts, and recalled the time when Agricola's fleet passed by on its way round Britannia, perilously close to the edge of the world.

"The sound crew and I climbed to the cliff-top, where we were met by two guides. They led us through several small fields and our progress was watched keenly by the men, women and children busy tilling and sowing in the time-honoured fashion. After about a (Roman) mile, we reached a group of undefended round huts where a light meal had been laid out for us. Here we were to rest for the afternoon.

"Our hut was similar to those in the northern lands of Britannia province: the circular stone wall having a large thatched roof. The guides acted as interpreters, and I was told that these huts are only used by those who work directly for the chief. The fields seemed particularly productive and the chief controlled not only the distribution of the corn, but the rota for working the land.

"That evening, we were ushered to stay at the chief's former residence, called a promontory dun. Last autumn saw the completion of his new fortified residence and the promontory dun is now used by the guards of the land nearby.

"The dun was defended by a stone wall built across the neck of land that jutted out from the cliffs. It was wild and exposed, and all but a few small huts were positioned in the lee of the wall. The R.B.C. crew and I, six of us, were quartered in the chief's former residence, adjoining the back of the defensive wall, with further accommodation within the wall.

A group of round huts possibly like those visited by Katia A.D. and her sound crew.

"Dinner that evening was taken with our guides and the six families who occupied the dun: they clearly regarded it as an opportunity to display their renowned hospitality. The meal comprised bread, soup and meat, the latter in copious quantities – well above the norm so I gathered. It was quite apparent that they intended to impress us, their honoured guests. Milk and water were provided as liquid refreshment while later, a drink peculiar to these islanders – made from grain, and called 'beer' – was brought forth. The climate of northern Britannia is far too severe for grapes to grow, and wine is not found in this tribal area.

"Our hosts were neither slaves, nor the equivalent of our citizens. They worked the land and looked after the chief's cattle, in exchange for which he, and others of similar exalted stature, purported to protect them. Despite the presence of our guides, this latter point was treated with a good deal of sarcasm, as, in most cases, it was the men who did the bulk of the protecting themselves. Only three weeks ago, they were summoned to prepare to fight off a tribe from the northern islands. This proved to be a false alarm, but rumour was rife that they might be called to arms once again, at short notice.

"These people, having returned from their daily duties, transformed their appearance by donning gaily woven tunics fastened by pins and clasps of some beauty, despite their lowly stature. The men were quite rowdy and, as the evening wore on, so their tales of heroism grew as long as the hours.

"Animals were kept as objects of pleasure and pride, rather than a source of food, and our hosts had a variety of dogs, fowl and even hares for the children. Having seen the children to bed, the women gave an impression of being subservient to the men. This image was somewhat dispelled by the time the, by then, boisterous men were summarily ordered to their beds, in view of the tasks awaiting their attention the following day.

"A meal prepared from grain, called 'porridge', was provided to help us on our way the next day. Most people were already hard at their appointed tasks by the time we were ready to leave and, being spring, there was a backlog of work to be done after the particularly severe winter.

"Our guide took us inland along tracks between the fields where, again, people were busy tending the land. We followed a small river, gradually making our way to the higher ground where crops gave way to grazing pasture: sheep and cattle were much in evidence. The rumours of a possible raid from the northern islands seemed to be the main topic of conversation among any passing natives."

A couple of hours later, Katia A.D. and her crew came to the new stronghold. This was built to the latest style and was a source of great pride, as it was the first 'broch' in the vicinity. So, let us go over and join Katia A.D. for live coverage as she makes her approach on this unique occasion.

Reaping what you sow. Especially arduous work in the Iron Age.

"Welcome to this most historic moment as the R.B.C. brings you live to northern Britannia, an island off the north coast of Europe – partially beyond the limits of our great empire, and close to the edge of the world. We are arriving at a native 'broch' stronghold and, although our presence is expected, we have to undergo the visitors' entrance procedure.

"As we approach the outer defensive wall, we are being watched – with an apparent degree of suspicion, I might add – by natives who have temporarily ceased their work. There is a great deal of noise from cattle that were brought into the vicinity of the new broch, just in case the barbarians from across the water decide to pay an unwanted visit.

"We are now approaching the outer gates and, from the encircling wall, a number of men – each armed with a spear, a long sword and a small circular shield – are taking a keen interest in our party. A guard is advancing towards us. He is asking our guides who we are, what is our business and on whose authority has our presence been granted. The replies seem to have been satisfactory, as we have been beckoned through.

"This, then, is the moment for which we have travelled a long and hazardous journey. We are passing through the narrow gateway and entering a stronghold that belongs to the natives defeated by Agricola, but who have, so far, still maintained their independence. The outer wall is skilfully built of stone and stands to the height of more than two men. The wooden gates are a little crude in their operation, but are made from heavy timbers and appear to be very stout. One must admit, the wall would not look entirely out of place at a small town near our glorious Rome. However, as is the case with all native building in Britannia, cement is not used to bind the stones together, simply the weight of the stones: the natives call this drystone walling.

"Several guards are looking down from the parapet as we stand within the outer courtyard. Ahead is the great broch tower, the first we have seen from close quarters, although we passed several along the coast on our voyage north. This stronghold is mightily impressive, and two guards have emerged to meet us from its low and narrow entrance.

"Our guide has spoken to them and we are gestured to pass through to the broch's inner courtyard. The new guards will be our guides during our stay. As we bid farewell, our original guides confirm that the number of guards on duty is due to the heightened state of readiness, just in case...

"The long entrance into the broch is both cramped and claustrophobic, and it is not possible to stand upright. There are two doors: the wider outer one is wooden; and the still narrower inner one is an unwieldy stone slab. In between these, two dimly lit and smoky guard chambers lead off the passage.

"I have now entered the inner courtyard, which is surprisingly small, awfully gloomy – despite being open to the elements – and has two circular, mezzanine-type upper levels that protrude from the wall, not unlike balconies. These are supported by a circle of stout wooden posts and are partially covered with thatch. The broch is some 25 paces in diameter, but the courtyard is barely a dozen paces across; such is the depth of the solid defensive wall.

"We have been gestured to our quarters on the first floor mezzanine balcony, beside those of the chief, who is out hunting with his warriors. The stairs are within the massive wall that, from first floor level, is cleverly divided by a gallery. It is dark as we make our way upward and Agrippa, one of the R.B.C. crew, has just fallen on the very narrow steps.

"Our balcony rooms have wooden partitions and basic facilities. Basic, that is, by our standards, for the Caledonii do not bathe as we do and, although they can bear an attractive appearance, their personal hygiene is as expected of barbarians. I have just been told that light refreshments will be provided shortly and then we will be able to inspect this stronghold at close quarters before this evening's feast. So, until then, this is Katia A.D. in far-northern Britannia handing you back to the R.B.C. studio."

There is no doubt about it, despite the miracles of modern archaeology, we could never hope to find out exactly how such a stronghold's defences were manned and operated, without the work

A Celtic warrior ready to fight the Romans.

of the intrepid Katia A.D. So, after a meal and good rest, Katia was invited to tour the stronghold – one of the most advanced of its kind – and to meet the people who lived there. She is accompanied by her guides – as Katia does not speak Celtic – and they will act as her interpreters.

"I am standing in the outer courtyard, which is a hive of activity. The perimeter wall is lined with lean-to houses, and there are several free-standing huts as well. One large hut – really a hall – is, our guide has explained, to be the venue for tonight's feast. This is in honour both of our visit, and to gird the warriors for the deeds of bravery they will be expected to perform if the northern barbarians carry out their threat and attack. Although the broch is solely for the chief and his family, with senior warriors and advisers residing in the outer courtyard, the population density, though not on a level with our great cities, is high.

"I have just asked a guide about the two rectangular buildings on wooden stilts to our right. He told me they are granaries and we are going to inspect them. An ox is currently being loaded with baskets of grain. I am now inside one of the granaries,

A timber granary raised off the ground to keep out pests.

where baskets of grain are piled up to the rafters. The guide explained that grain stored here is for general consumption, a similar arrangement to many native settlements within Britannia province."

Although Katia A.D. has seen some of the basic features of a native stronghold, she has not yet had a chance to meet the ordinary residents. Let us now join her as she goes among the people and their quarters, accompanied by her guides. Remember, though, that Katia A.D. does not speak the language and requires her guides to act as interpreters.

"I am at a group of huts where activity is almost at fever-pitch. Iron ores from the south are being smelted and the metal-workers are busy forging and finishing long swords, spear-heads and shield bosses. Each item takes a long time to be worked up and there is no time to talk to me: the more items made, the greater the number of men who will be able to resist any raid. Normally used to making objects of high quality, the present manufactures are strictly of functional standard.

"A little further along, women, children and some men are undertaking a variety of tasks, such as grinding corn, patching huts and baking bread. Unlike the metal-workers, there is little sense of urgency and people are willing to chat. One lady, for example, appears to be suggesting that all this is a fuss over nothing, especially now that they have the new broch. Her friend does not appear to be quite so sure.

"Others are busy selecting sling-stones. There is a surprising, neat orderliness about the way the inhabitants' work. Children, in-between their tasks, are running about challenging each other in mock duels. My guide has explained that the distinct air of purposefulness is due solely to an expected raid and that normally life is a little more relaxed.

"I can only say that these people appear to live a world apart from the barbarians slaughtered by Agricola. They seem almost civilised and their seemingly egalitarian society means that people work in a variety of communal tasks. Of course, I have not yet met the chief and his entourage and so I shall return to my quarters to await tonight's great feast, laid on in honour of our visit."

A feast might have been a not uncommon public display of both material possessions and personal abilities, and was very much a part of Iron Age life, at least for some. This particular feast had an additional importance, for not only were guests present – with Katia A.D. and her R.B.C. crew, but reputations needed to be enhanced and fighting spirits lifted by recalling great deeds of derring-do. So, let us return to see what Katia A.D. has to report of the evening's events.

"It's now long past midnight and the feast, attended by most of the warriors, is drawing to a raucous finale. The personal attire of those present was even finer than that of our hosts at the promontory dun. Everyone wore jewellery and functional items of considerable splendour and craft, and each, in turn, drank from the chief's ceremonial goblet. Food, in particular meat, was served in lavish quantities, washed down by that native drink called beer.

"Almost from the outset, glories of past generations were regaled, while each warrior tried to out-do the rest, both in the story they told and their embellished boasts of personal triumph. As the beer flowed, so the heroics flowered, but I received

Dun Carloway broch might have been not unlike the broch Katia A.D. was to be almost trapped inside. It was occupied during the inter-clan wars of recent centuries.

no answers to my questions regarding the tribe from whom a raid is now regarded as being almost certain, indeed invited.

"It was pointed out that, in this tribe at least, the chief-elect is the husband of the chief's eldest daughter. His son only becomes chief if there are no daughters: in other words, the female line predominates, though the chief is always a male. This eldest daughter's husband – the chief-in-waiting – is selected by the warriors, with spiritual guidance offered by the religious leaders. This guidance is, I gather, invariably followed.

"The chief himself brought the feast to its exultant climax with a tale about how he slew the leader of a northern isle's tribe last year, while on a raid. This so demoralised them that they fled to their strongholds leaving behind a great many cattle, some of which were brought back to the mainland. I fear that revenge will not be long in coming."

There was to be no encore as the chief's tale brought the evening to its close. It proved to be a memorable evening for Katia A.D. and her R.B.C. crew, but was a mere precursor for the events of the following day. We will now join Katia A.D. live on the broch wall-head in the early afternoon of the morrow.

"I was awoken this morning by frantic, almost frenzied activity within the broch. A large group – one would hardly call them an army by our own glorious standards – approached from the north, led by chariot-mounted warriors with support from armed men on foot. A desperate effort was made to get all cattle and people within the confines of the outer wall, while the warriors and others prepared to go out and meet the enemy. The sheer number of cattle and all the excitement caused mayhem, but eventually our warriors, supported by all the able-bodied men, emerged onto the plain outside the entrance to face the assembled ranks of the northern barbarians.

"The invaders created an almighty din with long trumpet-like instruments and war cries, while individual warriors sallied forth from their ranks to boast about their great deeds and to, apparently, taunt and belittle our warriors. From my vantage point, it all looked like a bit of good-natured fun, but eventually one of our warriors strode out to engage in single-combat. It was not a clever move. Seconds later he was slain by several savage sword blows. Cries of derision rose from the ranks of the barbarians, and tension rose still further when their victor severed our warrior's head and paraded up and down waving his gruesome trophy.

"Three more of our warriors went forth in single-combat, one losing his life – and his head, and another getting back to the ranks severely wounded. The boasts of the previous night were beginning to seem foolhardy. As the third warrior finally retreated – bloodied, but unbowed – so our spirits seemed to flag while those of the enemy reached fever-pitch. Then, our chief ventured out to join in single-combat with his opposite number: to do, or to die.

"Our chief was deposited in the field by his chariot and faced the barbarians' chief. They began to taunt each other and eventually, almost tentatively, engaged in combat roared on by both ranks of men. This proved to be an even, increasingly violent contest with both men fighting bravely, their personal and tribal honour at stake. At long last,

*Dun Lagaidh hillfort and dun would probably not be faced with a direct
frontal attack as Katia A.D's hosts experienced.*

our chief went the way of his fellow warriors, but before his head was severed, the field
was engulfed by an on-rushing mass of the barbaric hordes.

"As they charged towards our stronghold, many of our men, disheartened by the
demise of their leader, turned and fled towards the gates. Most got in, but the gates
were closed before the enemy arrived, leaving some to either fight to a very bitter end,
or to flee. The walls by the gateway were defended by men too old or infirm to fight,
and also some women, and those from the field reinforced these.

"Soon, men of both sides resorted to using slings as their main weapons: our
defenders fired down on the barbarians with lethal accuracy, while they attempted to
clear the wall near the entrance. It soon became obvious why; as chariots were driven
up to the gates and stooks of burning straw were piled against them. Eventually, the
gates began to burn and groups of the enemy ran forward, with shields over their
heads – *testudo* fashion – to try and force an entry. They took many, many casualties,
but the gates were forced about an hour ago.

"Since then, a battle raged round the outer courtyard wall. Some of our warriors
made it into the broch, but others, including women, were left outside: no prisoners
were taken. All the lean-to buildings and huts were soon ablaze, including the large
feasting hall. One could not help but recall how our warriors' boasts seemed rather
more substantial than their combat skills.

"A further attack was pressed forward to force an entry to the broch: if they got in
we would all have perished. Once again, the barbarians attempted to set fire to the
wooden outer door, this being a relatively new innovation. I gather this had some
success, but volleys of sling-stones and boulders dropped from the broch's wall-head

took a fearful toll on the barbarians. I have been unable to see, but am reliably told that there has been a wholesale slaughter as the barbarians tried to press home their attack. Certainly, their spirit has diminished and they resorted to aiming sling-stones from the outer wall, which had little effect.

"As I speak now, most barbarians are making their way from the scene of the battle, leaving many corpses behind. Once the initial attack on the broch had been repulsed, they seemed bereft of any alternative strategy, much to my R.B.C. crew's surprise and delight, and to the relief of all. A few barbarians have remained to taunt our defenders in between the odd volley of sling-stones. The rest have rounded up what few cattle were left and are driving them away. The spoils of victory are meagre; the cost, for both sides, is daunting.

"It has been a disastrous day for our hosts. The chief is dead as are many warriors, leaders and their families, and the physical destruction in the outer courtyard is beyond description: nothing, absolutely nothing, survives. On the other hand, the broch has not been breached, but whether it could withstand a sustained siege from our glorious legions, is doubtful.

"We had intended to depart tomorrow and, in one respect, the sooner we get away the better. We might be regarded as unlucky omens – even spies, so had better help clear the damage and be prepared to work our passage to freedom. This is Katia A.D. for the Roman Broadcasting Corporation, 'Pan-Romorama' in northern Britannia."

Dundurn was a probable Pict stronghold of the late-Iron Age
and Dark Ages, and was besieged in 683 A.D.

Ah, the miracles of technology and we thought radio was a 20th century invention. While Katia A.D. might have spiced-up the account of her visit a bit, raids were certainly not an everyday, or even annual, occurrence. However, she has tried to convey an impression of what an occupied broch was really like, while the course of the raid might not be too far-fetched. Whatever, Katia's account is the only contemporary report of how a Scottish pre-historic stronghold was able to cope in times of duress. We ought to be grateful that Rome was advanced enough to set up such a broadcasting network...

It is, though, to the decline of our pre-historic strongholds that we must now turn. In England, native strongholds were abandoned soon after the Roman invasion. With odd exceptions, that is how they remain to this day. It was quite different in Scotland.

As in England, those strongholds that featured either wooden revetted ramparts, or timber-laced walls, soon fell into decay. The vast majority of brochs also seem to have collapsed and had the stone pillaged, but several hillforts and duns, usually with solid stone walls, survived not only into the Dark Ages, but were intermittently occupied right into the Middle Ages.

Several sites in the gazetteer date solely to the Dark Ages, such as Dundurn*, while others straddle the divide between the Iron Age and the Dark Ages, such as Burghead* and Craig Phadrig*. Some were built in the Iron Age, were abandoned and then re-used in the Dark Ages and even the Middle Ages: Kildonan* dun, Clickhimin* and Mousa* all endured a similar history. At Tynron Doon* hillfort, not only were Dark Ages' artefacts found at the site, but a tower-house was built c. 1500 A.D., of which nothing now remains. Much further north, at Dun Lagaidh*, the broch and hillfort formed the basis of a 13th century castle and bailey.

These are some of the better known examples of the re-use of pre-historic strongholds, but many duns in Argyll and the Hebrides were occupied at different periods throughout the last 2,000 years. Some were built during that time, though the occupancy was probably quite short. Until the King of Norway was defeated at the Battle of Largs in 1263, Argyll, the Hebrides and the northern counties were seldom free from conflict and, one might suggest, did not remain so for several centuries hence. Thus, we find that Dun Carloway* broch was occupied during an inter-clan conflict only a few centuries ago.

Some pre-historic strongholds enjoyed a more genteel use, usually in recent times. Hoxa Broch* was rebuilt to form a sheltered wall-garden, while Nybster Broch* has what can best be described as a carbuncle of a monument built beside it. If nothing else, it can be easily seen from the road. More than these, the transformations from mounds of earth to the brochs we can see today, at Gurness* and Mid-Howe*, have immeasurably advanced our knowledge of these structures and the world from which they herald.

Other sites have not fared so well. The Antonine Wall* has suffered badly because it is located right across the industrial heartland of Scotland: a good thing, too, a time-travelling, Iron Age Scot might add. Whoever permitted the quarrying of the great Traprain Law*, even though it has now stopped, needs dressing up as a Roman

Does the monument to Sir Francis Tress Barry grace or desecrate the adjacent Nybster Broch? It makes it easy to find, though.

soldier and transporting back 2,000 years to the great oppidum, all by himself. I know stone is needed for roads, but to destroy one of Scotland's foremost pre-historic sites? What next, Edinburgh Castle, or perhaps the Stone of Scone? Such establishment-authorised vandalism must never happen again. And yet, given the chance, or 'need'?

The emphasis on confrontation in this chapter, no doubt over-states its incidence in the distant past. Pre-historic strongholds had defence as a priority and as Celtic society is often considered to be heroic – both in the Iron Age and later, such emphasis has not been misplaced entirely. Epic encounters, both of single-combat and tribal raids, abound in Celtic legends and mythology. These usually referred to the warrior-leaders and not the common-man, in the same way that the champion sportsman, top actor or famous musical performer is regaled in modern society, while most people go about their daily lives in relative anonymity.

The common-man might have led a mundane existence in the Iron Age, but surely, life was not all work and no play. Routine tasks were undertaken on behalf of a senior ranking class who supposedly ruled and protected in return. Yet the common-man must have had time to indulge in individual or group pleasures, and to tend to his personal tasks; not a great deal of difference from today, if you strip away the fripperies. Mind you, widespread social mobility has only really been possible in the last century, so there would not have been much of an opportunity for the Iron Age common-man to raise his status. I cannot see an Iron Age chief willingly handing over his position and privileges.

Whatever your opinion of the monument at Nybster Broch, there is no doubt the quarrying at Traprain Law has not been beneficial. Is Arthur's Seat next?

Anthropological studies have demonstrated numerous differences between social hierarchies and relationships in industrial and non-industrial societies. Yet, there are many similarities between societies separated by thousands of miles and hundreds of years in civilised development, so is it not beyond the bounds of possibility that Iron Age society had much in common with ours, on a day to day basis? Naturally, that cannot be stated with certainty, but the dominance of industrial, commercial or administrative work in our lives would have been matched by the inevitable predominance of agricultural tasks for Iron Age man.

True, there are many more leisure alternatives today, but many of these are more passive than active, such as watching a play or television, let alone playing computer games, or even going to a pub. It is, perhaps, the latter activity that would fit easiest into the life of the Iron Age common-man, although participating in sport, music and other performing arts might also have figured highly.

Whatever the daily routine of Iron Age life in Scotland, it is the defensive nature of the strongholds that reminds us of the – possibly exaggerated – violence of that time. Perhaps such defended settlements distort our mental image of those days, for hard evidence of attacks is limited. Unlike many castles and tower-houses, few pre-historic strongholds readily show the scars of a siege or a battle, except for vitrified gateways or the slighting of ramparts. As when visiting a castle, though, an insight into Iron Age life will enhance your visit and enable you to go back in time and to find an empathy with the people.

Yet, there is so much to see and this book is aimed at helping and guiding you to visit and appreciate some of the finest sites and sights in the land. So, enough of historical fact, theory and innuendo, take to the road, track and path and search out the past that most history books about Scotland ignore. It is in the remote hillforts, duns and brochs and, above all else, the people who lived in them, that we find the proud heritage of our clans and country.

Now it is time to get out and see Scotland's varied pre-historic strongholds for yourself. But remember, while they are now mostly 2,000-year-old cold and empty ruins, they were once hives of activity where people lived, worked and played. The key to getting the most from visiting Scotland's pre-historic strongholds is to re-create them as being full of life in the mind's eye and, if in doubt, enlist the words of Katia A.D. to help you out.

Part 2

The Gazetteer

INFORMATION FOR VISITING
THE STRONGHOLDS

The strongholds in this book stand on public, private or common-owned land. All have public access and, in many cases, the directions given are but one of several options. Most strongholds can be reached by public footpath or track, but not all. If in the slightest doubt, ask permission from the nearest house or farm. Out of thousands of archaeological sites visited in Britain and Ireland, I have never been refused entry to any.

I have arbitrarily divided Scotland into five areas, based on either groups of counties or islands, and the strongholds are listed alphabetically within these areas. Directions are given from the nearest town, so a road atlas will be useful: do not entirely trust a sat-nav.

It might seem obvious, but under no circumstances must you damage, dig into or remove any material whatsoever (unless it is litter) at any pre-historic or archaeological site. There are no treasures to be found, so digging will do nothing but cause irreparable damage; even tidying up a bit – clearing stones and so forth – will do nothing but harm for any future excavations. If you were at a picture gallery and did not like a painting, you would not get out your paints and alter it, would you? (Don't answer, I know it can be tempting with some modern works.) These strongholds are even more valuable: they are our past, present and future. Treat them with the utmost respect. While some archaeologists do not like people walking over our archaeological sites, hard-cheese, but do not walk on stone walls, even if they are tumbled. Drystone walls may collapse.

Also, treat our countryside as you would your most prized possession: it is, after all, irreplaceable. Close and secure all gates, do not trample crops and certainly do not disturb animals, while keeping your own under control – especially the species known as children. These are all straight-forward, common-sense matters, but, as any farmer and landowner will tell you, there is always one idiot about. Make sure that it is not you.

USE OF MAPS

All maps referred to are from the Ordnance Survey Landranger 1:50,000 series, of 1¼ in. to the mile, which I used to visit all the sites featured, plus a great many more.

You should not have any serious problems in locating a stronghold without a map, but one will enable you to appreciate it within its environment. These maps are widely available, or can be loaned from a library.

For those unfamiliar with the six-figure map reference number, say 012345, the first two figures (0 and 1) refer to the vertical grid reference 01 found at the top and bottom of the O/S map. By dividing the distance between the vertical lines 01 and 02 into an imaginary ten, our no. 2 is approximately one-fifth of the way across. Numbers 3 and 4 refer to the horizontal grid line 34 that can be found at the map sides. No. 5 is, once again, an imaginary line – the mid-point – between the horizontal grid lines of 34 and 35. By drawing these two points together, you will find the location of the stronghold. Have a couple of goes and it soon becomes second nature.

When the famed Highland mists roll in, a compass might be useful, too – even better if you know how to use one.

Map of Scotland's Counties

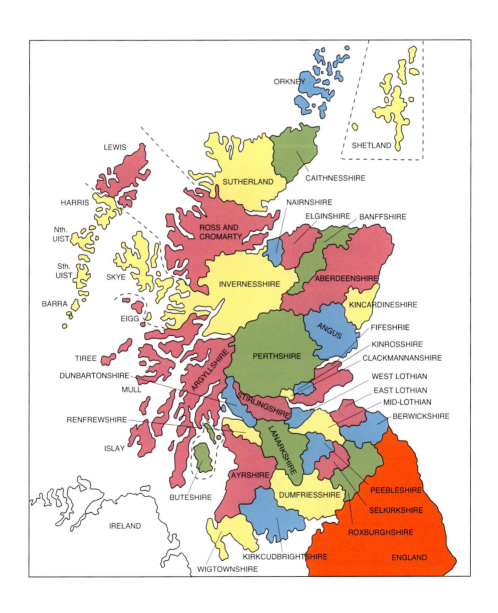

ALPHABETICAL LIST OF PRE-HISTORIC AND ROMAN STRONGHOLDS

SITE	COUNTY	O/S MAP	MAP ref.	OTHER
Addinston	Berwick	73	523536	Hillfort
Am Baghan Burblach	Inverness	33	832199	Hillfort
An Sean	Mull	47	431563	Dun
An Sgurr	Eigg	39	460648	Hillfort
Antonine Wall	Stirling	65	843799	Rough Castle fort
Antonine Wall)	Stirling	65	814793	Seabegs Wood fort
Antonine Wall)	Stirling	65	865798	Watling Lodge
Antonine Wall)	Stirling	65	855798	Tentfield Plantation
Arbory Hill	Lanark	72	944238	Hillfort
Ardifuir Dun)_	Argyll	55	789969	Dun
Duntroon)	"	55	803960	Hillfort
Ardoch	Perth	57/58	839099	Roman fort
Ardwell Broch	Wigtown	82	066466	+ promon. H/F
Ashie Moor	Inverness	26	600316	Hillfort
Auchteraur	Inverness	34	349070	Vitrified dun
Bar Hill	Dunbarton (det.)	64	707759	Roman fort
Barmekin of Echt	Aberdeen	38	725070	Hillfort
Barry Hill	Perth	53	262504	Hillfort
Barsalloch Point	Wigtown	82	347412	Promontory H/F
Ben Freiceadain	Caithness	12	059558	Hillfort
Birrens	Dumfries	85	218753	Roman fort
Bochastle	Perth	57	601075	Hillfort
Boreraig Broch	Skye	23	195532	Broch
Borwick Broch	Orkney	6	225168	
Bragor Broch	Lewis	8	286474	Broch
Broch of Burland	Shetland	4	446360	Broch
Broch of Gurness	Orkney	6	383268	Broch
Brough of Stoal	Shetland	1	547873	Promontory H/F
Burghead	Moray	28	109691	Damaged H/F
Burgi Geos	Shetland	1	478034	H/F + Blockhouse

(continued)

SITE	COUNTY	O/S MAP	MAP ref.	OTHER
Burnswark Hillfort	Dumfries	78	185785 &	Roman siege-practice camps
Burra Ness Broch	Shetland	1	556957	Broch
Burrian Broch	Orkney	5	762513	
Cademuir Hillfort)	Peebles	73	230375	
" Hillfort)	"	73	225371	
" Settlement)	"	73	235379	
Cairn Liath	Sutherland	17	871013	Broch
Caisteal Grugaig	Ross & Crom	33	866251	Broch
Carrol Broch	Sutherland	17	846065	
Castle Greg	West Lothian	65	050592	Roman camp
Castle Haven Dun	Kirkcudbright	83	594483	Galleried dun
Castlehill Wood Dun	Stirling	57	750909	Dun
Castle Law	Mid-Lothian	66	229638	H/F + souterrain
Castle Law	Perth	58	100155	Hillfort
Caterthun (Brown)	Angus	44	555668	Hillfort
Caterthun (White)	Angus	44	548660	Hillfort
Cinn Trolla Broch	Sutherland	17	929081	
Clickhimin	Shetland	4	465408	Broch, Fort & Blockhouse
Coldoch Broch	Perth	57	697982	
Cow Castle	Lanark	72	042331	Several phases
Craig Phadrig	Inverness	26	640453	Vitrified H/F & Dark Ages
Culswick Broch	Shetland	4	254448	
Dreva Craig	Peebles	72	126353	Hillfort
Duchary Rock	Sutherland	17	850050	Hillfort
Dun Aisgain	Mull	47	377452	Dun
Dun an Ruigh Ruaidh	Ross & Crom	20	149901	Broch
Dun an Sticir	North Uist	18	897777	Broch
Dun Ardtrek	Skye	32	885595	Dun
Dun Baravat	Lewis	13	156356	Dun
Dun Beag	Skye	32	339387	Broch
Dun Bhoraraig	Islay	60	417658	Broch
Dun Carloway	Lewis	8	190412	Broch
Dun Cuier	Barra	31	664034	Broch
Dun Dornadilla	Sutherland	9	460449	Broch
Dun Fiadhairt	Skye	32	231504	Broch
Dun Grugaig	Inverness	33	851159	Dun
Dun Grugaig	Skye	32	535124	Dun
Dun Hallin	Skye	23	257593	Broch
Dun Lagaidh	Ross & Crom	20	142915	H/F + Broch
Dun Mhuirich	Argyll	55	722845	Dun
Dun Mor	Tiree	44	046493	Broch

(continued)

SITE	COUNTY	O/S MAP	MAP ref.	OTHER
Dun Nan Gall	Mull	47	433431	Broch
Dun Nosebridge	Islay	60	371601	Hillfort
Dun Ringill	Skye	32	561170	Broch
Dun Skeig	Argyll	62	757571	H/F + Duns
Dun Telve	Inverness	33	829173	Broch
Dun Trodden	Inverness	33	834173	Broch
Dun Torcuill	Nth. Uist	18	888737	Galleried Dun
Dunadd	Argyll	55	837936	H/F + Dark Ages settlement
Dundurn Hillfort	Perth	51	707233	
Dunsinane Hillfort	Perth	53	214316	+ Souterrain
Durn Hill	Banff	29	571638	un-finished H/F
Durisdeer	Dumfries	78	903048	Roman Fortlet
Edinshall	Berwick	67	772603	H/F + broch
Eildon Hill North	Roxburgh	73	555328	H/F + Roman Signal Station
Finavon	Angus	54	506556	Vitrified H/F
Gask Ridge	Perth	58	various	Roman watch-towers
Haerfaulds Hillfort	Berwick	73	544501	+ Roman settlement
Hownam Rings)_	Roxburgh	67	790194	Hillfort
Hownam Law)	Roxburgh	74	796220	Hillfort
Hoxa Broch	Orkney	7	425940	
Inchtuthill	Perth	53	125397	Roman legionary fort
Jarlshof	Shetland	4	397096	Broch & Wheelhouses
Keiss Brochs x 3	Caithness	12	348615	
Kildonan	Argyll	68	780277	Dun
Kilphedir Broch	Sutherland	17	995187	
Knockfarril	Inverness	26	505585	Vitrified H/F
Loch of Houlland	Shetland	3	213792	Broch
Loch of Huxter	Shetland	2	558620	Fort & Blockhouse
Mid-Howe Broch	Orkney	6	371308	& Chambered barrow
Mither Tap o'Bennachie	Aberdeen	38	683224	Hillfort
Mote of Mark	Kirkcudbright	84	845540	Vitrified Dark Ages Fort
Mousa Broch	Shetland	4	457237	Broch
Mullach	Dumfries	78	929870	Vitrified H/F
Ness of Burgi	Shetland	4	388084	Fort & Blockhouse
Norman's Law	Fife	59	305202	Hillfort
Nybster Broch	Caithness	12	370632	& Promontory Dun
Ousdale Broch	Caithness	17	072188	
Rispain Camp	Wigtown	83	429399	Hillfort
Rubh'an Dunain	Skye	32	396160	Galleried dun
Sgarbach	Caithness	12	373637	Promontory dun

(continued)

SITE	COUNTY	O/S MAP	MAP ref.	OTHER
Sheep Hill Hillfort	Dunbarton	64	435746	+ cup & ring carvings
St. John's Point	Caithness	12	310751	Promontory H/F
Stoer Broch	Sutherland	15	036278	
Tap o' Noth	Aberdeen	37	485293	Hillfort
Tirefour Castle	Lismore	49	867429	Broch
Torwood Broch	Stirling	65	833849	Broch
Traprain Law	E. Lothian	67	851746	Hillfort
Tynron Doon	Dumfries	78	820939	Hillfort
White Castle	E. Lothian	67	613686	Hillfort
Whiteside	Peebles	72	768461	Hillfort
Woden Law	Roxburgh	80	768125	& Roman Practice Camps

BORDERS AND GALLOWAY
STRONGHOLDS AND MAP

SITE	COUNTY	O/S MAP	MAP ref.	OTHER
1 Addinston	Berwick	73	523536	Hillfort
2 Arbory Hill	Lanark	72	944238	Hillfort
3 Ardwell Broch	Wigtown	82	066466	& Promontory H/F
4 Barsalloch Point	Wigtown	82	347412	Promontory H/F
5 The Birrens	Dumfries	85	218753	Roman fort
6 Burnswark Hillfort	Dumfries	78	185785	& Roman practice camps
7 Cademuir Hillfort	Peebles	73	230375	
" Hillfort	"	73	225371	
" Settlement	"	73	235379	
8 Castle Haven Dun	Kirkcudbright	83	594483	Galleried dun
9 Cow Castle	Lanark	72	042331	Several phases
10 Dreva Craig	Peebles	72	126353	Hillfort
11 Durisdeer	Dumfries	78	903048	Roman Fortlet
12 Edinshall	Berwick	67	772603	H/F & broch
13 Eildon Hill North	Roxburgh	73	555328	H/F & Roman sig. sta.
14 Haerfaulds Hillfort	Berwick	73	544501	& Roman settlement
15 Hownham Rings	Roxburgh	67	790194	Hillfort
16 Hownham Law	Roxburgh	74	796220	Hillfort
17 Mote of Mark	Kirkcudbright	84	845540	Vitrified H/F
18 Mullach	Dumfries	78	929870	Vitrified H/F
19 Rispain Camp	Wigtown	83	429399	Fort. settlement
20 Traprain Law	E. Lothian	67	851746	Hillfort
21 Tynron Doon	Dumfries	78	820939	Hillfort
22 White Castle	E. Lothian	67	613686	Hillfort
23 Whiteside	Peebles	72	768461	Hillfort
24 Woden Law	Roxburgh	80	768125	& Roman Camp

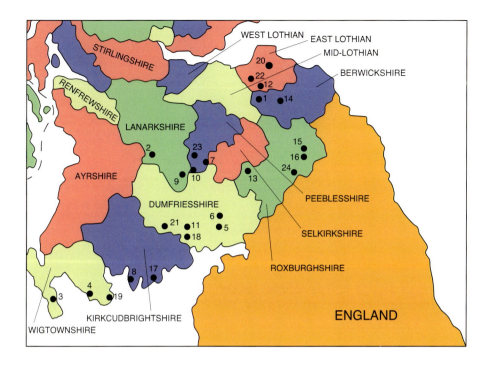

ADDINSTON HILLFORT

Berwickshire O/S Landranger map no. 73 ref. 523536

Directions: Take the A68 south from Edinburgh to Carfraemill and turn left on the A697. The ramparts can be seen in the hills to the south of the junction. Turn left along the road to Addinston Farm, where it becomes a track. Two wooden signs point the way up the hill and the hillfort is at the south-east end of a spur on the right.

The A68 through the Borders passes through some attractive scenery, particularly in Lauderdale. More pertinent, there are several historic sites within a few miles either side of the road, of which Addinston is but one, albeit rather good, example.

Lying equidistant between the two, assumed, great tribal strongholds of the Selgovae, at Eildon Hills, and the Votadini, at Traprain Law*, Addinston could have been in either tribal area. At 990 feet above sea level, it overlooks Cleekhimmin Burn to the south-east and is an ideal place to command the upper reaches of Lauderdale. Such strategic matters were probably important to our Iron Age ancestors, as demonstrated by the similar hillfort of Longcroft just to the north-east, across Soonhope Burn. So, Addinston may have been an outpost of the Selgovae tribe, while Longcroft belonged to the Votadini, each casting a wary eye over the other. Perhaps, but as with all such matters concerning our pre-historic forebears, that is mere conjecture.

Addinston is a well-preserved, almost triangular-shaped hillfort measuring about 280 ft. x 160 ft. It is protected by two powerfully built ramparts, each with an external ditch, the outer-most having a counterscarp bank. At the highest point, in the north-west, the ramparts rise 16 feet above the bottom of the ditch, which, despite the fact that they are 2,000 year old ruins, gives a good impression of the power that they would have exuded. The entrance is in the south, where the ramparts widen.

Defences on this scale suggest a date of 1st century B.C., or 1st century A.D. Perhaps Addinston was built when word of Roman activity spread ahead of the Agricolan invasion, but, unlike Longcroft, which was fortified on two occasions, Addinston has only one set of defences.

Within these, there are several grass-covered, circular hut foundations. These probably belonged to the original inhabitants, but the largest, and most obviously visible with a 42 feet diameter, may be of a later date – it is anything but a hut. There are many examples of Iron Age strongholds being re-used either in the late-Iron Age, or during the Dark Ages, as semi-open settlements, and this may be one of them.

While little of Addinston's past is known, that should not detract from your enjoyment of a fine, typical Borders' hillfort. The walk up the hill, the good all-round views and the fine quality of the pre-historic remains make Addinston a most enjoyable and interesting hillfort to visit. Its proximity to Longcroft hillfort will also give you plenty to ponder.

Other Pre-historic Sites
Blackchester Hillfort Map 66 Ref. 508504.
Longcroft Hillfort Map 66 Ref. 532543.

ARBORY HILL (Hillfort)

Lanarkshire O/S Landranger map 72 ref. 944238

Directions: Leave the M74 at Junction 13 and turn into Abington. Turn left into Station Rd., cross the railway and turn left at the junction. Continue north – Arbory Hill is on the right – until you come to the railway bridge. Park beside the railway, just before the bridge. Go down to the burn, pass through the gate and head for the gate near the woods on the left. Cross the next field diagonally to the far gate and then walk straight to the summit.

A glance at the O/S map, and the sites at the end of this site entry, shows that the route through Clydesdale was as important to our pre-historic ancestors and Roman invaders as it today. The Romans linked up native track ways in driving their road north, which descends to Raggengill Burn to the south-west of Arbory Hill. The Caledonian Railway pushed its main line through the valley to all points north, and the M74 is one of the least pleasant roads in Scotland today.

Whether the inhabitants of the nearby hillforts belonged the Selgovae tribe, centred at Eildon Hill*, is unknown, but all have a similar, oval, stone inner rampart. As none has been properly excavated, little else can be determined with any certainty, including whether or not any were occupied simultaneously.

If this does not sound particularly enticing, then it is misleading for Arbory Hill is one of the most rewarding hillforts to visit. Built in two or even three stages, it towers 600 ft. over the winding valley below and occupies the western promontory of Tewsgill Hill. Yet, at 1,406 ft., is more than 400 ft. below the summit.

Somewhat oddly, the first phase(s) of building was probably of the middle and outer ramparts. Each still rises up to 10 ft. above its ditch and is of glacis construction, possibly having been stone-revetted. The middle rampart has entrances in the east, south and north-west and encloses about an acre. The outer rampart is concentric to it and encloses about 2 1/4 acres. The main entrance is in the east, where the rampart is opened out to give an off-set approach. The area between these two ramparts might have been used to herd cattle, and the widened entrance would allow for quicker and easier movement of hefty beasts in times of danger. But cattle at 1,400 ft.? Surely not. As for the other entrance gaps, two of them approximate to those in the middle rampart in the south and north-west, and that in the west seems to be superfluous.

The spread of stones that once constituted the inner rampart is not unimpressive, but is a mere shadow of its pre-historic self, rising only about 5 ft. high. This was 10 ft. thick and enclosed about half an acre. Again, it is concentric with the other ramparts and has two entrances. That on the east roughly aligns with those in the other ramparts, but the one in the south-west only gives entry to the area between the inner and middle ramparts. If Arbory Hill were intended for both man and beast, and was built as outlined, then perhaps with more cattle, and/or fewer inhabitants, the living area was decreased with the building of the inner rampart, hence the need for a gap to the cattle area in the west.

Of course, if an excavation could show that the inner rampart was timber-laced, then the building phases could be reversed. Stone ramparts are quite common in this part of Scotland, although several others elsewhere have no sign of an entrance. Although there are few large hillforts in Scotland many were reduced in size, or, in the north, were often replaced by smaller duns and even brochs. Whether this was due to a falling population, or simply changes in stronghold building is unknown. However, Arbory Hill is one of the best hillforts where stages of development (or contraction) can be readily seen.

Within the inner rampart there are traces of hut circles, while there may be some between the inner and middle ramparts. If that is the case, the inner rampart could be the most recent, but the surface traces are too indeterminate.

Pre-historic strongholds should not be considered in isolation, as they often appear today, but as part of a whole pre-historic landscape. About 80 yards to the east of Arbory Hill, a linear earthwork once cut off the hillfort's promontory from the rest of the hill. Could this have been a boundary to keep the cattle off the cultivated land between it and the hillfort? It was unlikely to have any defensive properties.

These days, it is not easy to envisage an Iron Age stronghold within its wider environment, as it is usually only the stronghold that has survived. A visit to Arbory Hill offers a tantalising glimpse into what a hillfort's immediate environment might have been like, with cattle being allowed to roam on Tewsgill Hill and, perhaps, corn being grown. Thus divided, the land would just about enable the inhabitants to feed themselves, always assuming crops would grow at 1,400 ft. in the pre-Roman Iron Age.

Although much of Arbory Hill's past is open to speculation that should not spoil your visit. Its magnificent location above Clydesdale, an area that positively oozes pre-history, makes this a wonderful place to visit. An even better view of the hillfort can be gained from the summit to the east. Allow plenty of time to enjoy this hillfort and its environs, and perhaps visit one of the others nearby as well. Clydesdale will never quite seem the same again.

Other Pre-historic Sites
Black Hill (hillfort) Map 72 ref. 908239
Crawford (hillfort) Map 72 ref. 952219
Crawford (settlement) Map 72 ref. 944215
Bodsberry Hill (hillfort) Map 72 ref. 963169
Devonshaw Hill (hillfort) Map 72 ref. 953284
Normangill (henge) Map 72 ref. 972221

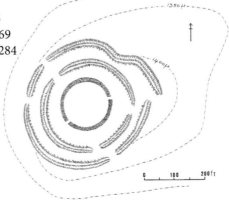

ARDWELL BROCH

Wigtownshire O/S Landranger map 82 ref. 066466

Directions: Leave Stranraer, heading south, on the A77. Turn left on the A716 and turn right on the minor road after Sandhead. Follow this when it becomes a track and stop at the second car park. Walk south round the headland and the broch is on a promontory south of Ardwell Point.

One usually associates brochs with the north and west of Scotland. Galloway seems to be somewhat less in need of pre-historic strongholds, but it features hillforts, duns and, out of the blue, the most southerly examples of the brochs. Ardwell is by far the best preserved of them and is often referred to as Doon Castle.

Do not expect Ardwell to equal the best of the northern brochs, but it has one most distinctive feature. Like several northern brochs, Ardwell sits on a rocky spit that projects into the sea. The spit is cut off by a wall and ditch, with a distinct causeway through it. The basic layout is thus typical of many coastal brochs.

Unlike the other possible brochs in Galloway, many of Ardwell's features are visible. The wall is 13 ft. thick and encloses a courtyard of 30 ft. diameter. Although the interior is full of tumbled stones, the inner wall-face is visible. Two intra-mural cells can also be seen, so Ardwell broadly follows the classic broch plan. Mind you, given the ratio

The late evening sun makes the remote Ardwell Broch a special attraction.

of wall:courtyard diameter, it is most unlikely that Ardwell would have reached the height of Mousa*.

The entrance faces the sea, quite common among coastal brochs, but what makes Ardwell most unusual – and almost unique, is a second entrance opposite. This may be secondary, perhaps added after the tower was demolished, but there is no evidence either way and it looks like an original feature. Of course, a second entrance would weaken the broch's defensive properties, and it may have been added when the broch was still a tower, if there was little likelihood of attack. Certainly, it would have made life easier.

As with much else about Ardwell Broch, that is pure speculation, but there is no doubt that it is a marvellously located broch. Quite why four brochs should appear in apparent splendid isolation on, or near, The Rhins of Galloway is not known. Did the builders come from Ulster, perhaps having gone there first from the Western Isles, or did they simply come straight from, say, Kintyre? Although there are several hillforts on the Rhins, the inhabitants must have had contact with broch builders and seen the advantages of such a structure. All such conjecture aside Ardwell, though not of the very latest design, may have been built before the Romans arrived in the 1st century A.D.

As usual, there are few answers and many questions concerning the activities of our pre-historic forebears. Ardwell has even fewer answers than most yet, for all that, is a rewarding broch to visit, at an outstanding location. Likewise Galloway, as under-rated a region as any in Scotland.

Other Pre-historic Sites
Kemp's Walk (hillfort) map 82 ref. 974598
Kirklauchlane (hillfort) map 82 ref. 035506
Dunman (hillfort) map 82 ref. 096335
Jamieson's Point (dun) map 82 ref. 033710
Teroy (broch) map 82 ref. 099641
Crammag Head (broch?) map 82 ref. 088340, small section west of lighthouse.

BARSALLOCH POINT (Hillfort)

Wigtownshire O/S Landranger map 82 ref. 347412

Directions: On the bend just north of Moncrieff on the A747. Sign post. Short, steep climb.

Had Barsalloch Point been situated across the Solway Firth in England, at barely 1/2 an acre in size, it would have been considered more a defended homestead than a hillfort. As it is, the Iron Age inhabitants of Scotland were either less populous, or preferred the smaller defended residence – perhaps of the extended family, to the larger town/village-type of hillfort. Even so, as Scottish hillforts go, Barsalloch Point is small.

Let not size deter you from visiting this hillfort, though, for its location is inspiring. It is situated in an area of much pre-historic interest and its defences have much to commend them. For a start, the geography of the immediate area has, not surprisingly, changed since the Iron Age. The A747 is built on what was the old beach and the hillfort used the cliff as a defence. If you take the direct route to the hillfort from the road, up the steep cliff, you will soon understand why the inhabitants did not see the need to provide additional defences on this side.

Once in the 'D' shaped hillfort, the defences curve round from cliff-edge to cliff-edge, to enclose a small, featureless area. Nevertheless, the defences are impressive and comprise two ramparts separated by a ditch. This is about 30 ft. wide and the ramparts rise up to 10 ft. above, the whole defensive system being up to 70 ft. in overall width; these, remember, are 2,000+ years old ruins. In more recent times, these defences formed part of a field boundary, and the north-east entrance is still partly obscured by this.

In a sense, the two ramparts with a central ditch give the lie to attempts at placing pre-historic strongholds into a chronological format, such as single rampart hillforts, multiple-rampart hillforts, duns, brochs and so on. Here is a hillfort, in an area of brochs and duns, which might well post-date some of the latter, yet has a rampart both with and without a ditch in one system. It is almost as if Barsalloch Point were a hillfort-ised dun, or vice versa. What the defences suggest is that the inhabitants did not build to any current fad or fancy, but were capable of creating defences applicable to a specific site. This was probably the case with the majority of pre-historic strongholds.

Although little above sea level, and still less in the Iron Age, Barsalloch Point has extensive coastal views along the Whithorn peninsula and across Luce Bay to The Rhins of Galloway. No doubt, inhabitants of the promontory forts on The Rhins looked over to Barsalloch Point as well. All this makes for a distinctly attractive hillfort to visit, despite lacking details of its past. These cliffs above the former coast were obviously attractive to our pre-historic ancestors, for various Mesolithic sites have been discovered. A hearth at Barsalloch, which included a number of geometric microliths, has given a C-14 dating of c. 4050 B.C. to show that the area has a long history of human habitation.

Within a few miles of Barsalloch Point hillfort there is a diverse range of pre-historic sites that give the area a distinct appeal, from the Mesolithic, through the Bronze and Iron Ages to the early Christian period. Like Barsalloch Point hillfort, it is worth spending time to savour the atmosphere.

Other Pre-historic Sites
Fell of Barhullion, hillfort Map 83 ref. 375419
Burrow Head, hillfort Map 83 ref. 454341
North Balfern, cup and ring marked stones Map 83 ref. 433510
Drumtroddan, cup and ring marked stones Map 83 ref. 362444
Torhousekie, stone circle Map 82 ref. 383565
St. Ninian's Cave, early Christian site Map 83 ref. 422360

THE BIRRENS (Roman Fort)

Dumfries-shire O/S Landranger map 85 ref. 218753

Directions: Leave the M74 at Junction 19. Go east of Ecclefechan to join the B725 to Middlebie. Turn right up the lane and the fort is on the right by a signpost, after about 3/4 mile, before crossing Mein Water.

The border country has been a source of conflict for many centuries. It was no different for the Romans when they decided to invade what is now Scotland. The Birrens, or Blatobulgium to give its Latin name, was built beside the main Roman route to south-west Scotland. As with many Roman forts, what is seen today is but the most recent of several periods of occupation.

Unfortunately, Birrens is very much a '...what might've been...' for, although built on the scale of, say, Ardoch* fort, the visible remains are much less impressive. Still, Birrens is one of the most important forts in south-west Scotland and, as far as archaeology is concerned, has proved a valuable resource. It was excavated in the 19th century, in the 1930s and, most importantly and extensively, in the 1960s. The results of these excavations have been important not only for understanding Birrens – for example it is the only fort in south-west Scotland where the original name is known, but has helped to clarify dates and routes taken during various Roman campaigns. Some geophysical surveys have been undertaken recently, including noted an annexe.

There are three, no longer visible, temporary camps and an annexe to the west. The first probably dates to the Agricolan invasion of c. 80 A.D., while a permanent 4 acre fort was established shortly after, no doubt to guard the route north. This fort was abandoned late in the 1st century, but a second fort was built in the early decades of the 2nd century. This was later destroyed, possibly during an uprising that caused the abandonment of the Antonine Wall*, in about 158 A.D. It was rebuilt again, possibly by the 2nd Cohort of Tungrians, and occupied as an outpost of Hadrian's Wall after the abandonment of the Antonine Wall*. The plan shows the likely layout of The Birrens at that time. It was finally abandoned towards the end of the century.

The plan also shows that, despite having six closely set ditches similar to those at Ardoch fort, the remains are poorly preserved. For a start, the road on which you arrived runs right through the eastern defences, while the western defences have long since been ploughed. Although most of the fort's interior is intact, under which the stone foundations of the barracks and the principia were discovered and subsequently covered again, the southern defences have been eroded by the river. All that remains of the six concentric ditches, is the section across the north side and its entrance, plus slight traces of the outer three ditches for a few yards on the east side of the road.

Even these have not survived particularly well and are merely hollows in the ground. They are not, then, on the scale to make you gaze in wonder, or to admire the planning and building skills of the Roman invaders – not without a good deal of imaginative artistic licence, at any rate. Then again, it is not as though Scotland is over-flowing with decently preserved Roman forts, and that is why The Birrens is both historically important and worth visiting.

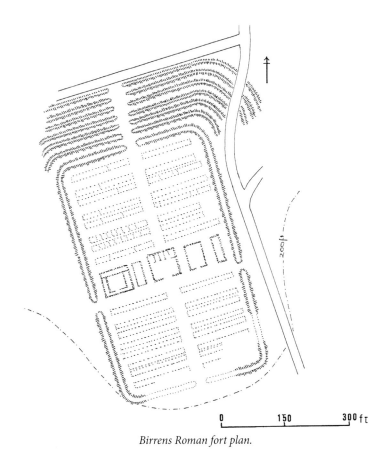

Birrens Roman fort plan.

Whenever you visit a pre-historic site, one must view it both as it stands today, and with a reasonably accurate re-creation of how it may have once appeared. The Birrens, more than most sites, is better appreciated if you can take the latter view. For what you can see is only a small part of the story; what the Birrens meant and stood for to the native people in the 1st and 2nd centuries, was something very different. There was no doubting its status and less than endearing role then. As with the Berlin Wall, the natives were, no doubt, pretty glad to see its demise.

BURNSWARK (Hillfort and Roman Forts)

Dumfries-shire O/S Landranger map 85 ref. 185785

Directions: Leave the M74 at Junction 19 as for The Birrens*. Go east of Ecclefechan to join the B725 towards Middlebie. Turn left after crossing the railway and follow the narrow road up the hill until it becomes a track. Park by the bins and walk through the pine trees, emerging to walk up the steep hill to the right hand summit.

Many years ago, while a post-graduate student, a university porter asked what I was studying. When I said history, he replied, '...at least that doesn't change...' Oh no? Sixty or so years ago, it was thought that Burnswark hillfort, high on its hill, was surrounded by two Roman camps, possibly joined by a small bank, and captured after a mighty demonstration of artillery fire-power.

This was backed by considerable evidence unearthed at excavations undertaken in 1898, when 67 ballista-bolts were found embedded in the hillfort ramparts. Furthermore, the three artillery mounds – known as the Three Brethren and from which the ballistae were fired – were prominent landmarks. Here, so it seemed, was a cut-and-dried example of how clinically the Romans dealt with any native resistance. The only possible queries concerned the small Roman fortlet in a corner of the southern fort, and the time it would have taken for the Romans to build their defences.

Then, excavations in the 1960s/70s seemed to comprehensively blow away those ideas just as surely as that decade's pop culture swept aside many traditional inhibitions. Not only that, but a few tasty morsels were thrown into the new historical soup, showing that Burnswark hillfort, as it appears today, was not the first settlement on the hill either.

From all this, a new sequence of events was suggested, which included the Iron Age hillfort being cleared of natives and being used for siege and artillery practice by the Romans. Well, it makes sense, doesn't it? That was that, until, following recent work, the theory of the Roman siege has come back in favour. Who knows what light future excavations might shed on the once oh-so-simple and straight-forward interpretation of Burnswark's dim and distant past. History never changes...

The 1960s excavations showed that a single palisade fence enclosed the east end of the hillfort on the western knoll of the hill. A double palisade separated, possibly,

The Three Brethren artillery mounds, the south Roman fort and the small fort in the corner are all seen in this picture at Burnswark.

by a fighting platform was discovered elsewhere. This measured 300 yds. x 220 yds. And the defences may have been the result of two phases of building. Carbon-14 suggested this dated to about the 6th or 7th centuries B.C.

Somewhat later, these defences were replaced by two glacis ramparts, the inner one having an external stone facing. The entrance was in the south, but when the hillfort was extended round the eastern knoll to enclose 17 acres, three more south-east facing entrances were added. These are opposite the northern entrances to the south Roman fort, so the Romans may have built them. The rampart that divides the east and west halves of the hillfort is now very slight.

There is no question that Burnswark was of considerable importance, quite likely a major stronghold of the Novantae tribe. There are few Scottish hillforts of comparable size and it controlled a route into south-west Scotland. Certainly, the Romans recognised the strategic value of Burnswark for they built The Birrens* fort – Blatobulgium – only a few miles to the south-east.

The sequence of events following the arrival of the Latin invaders is far from certain, but the fortlet in the north-east corner of the south Roman fort pre-dates both larger forts. This fortlet might date from c. 140 A.D., although it could be an Agricolan fort. The hillfort was probably rendered defenceless, although an undefended settlement survived as the south entrance was re-paved after the destruction of the ramparts.

The Roman forts are, in many ways, even more interesting. The northern one is not the usual rectangular shape, being 330 yards long and had six entrances, only four of which can still be seen. This fort is quite distant from the hillfort, and beyond throwing range, but the southern one is much closer. That has the more usual playing card shape, with an entrance in the centre of each side; that in the north is flanked by two more. The Three Brethren artillery platforms, from which missiles were directed against the defences, stand outside. Only, according to theories from the 1960s/70s, there were no defenders. So, these Roman camps were used for siege practice and not the real thing.

This seems plausible as, being so close to The Birrens* fort, it is likely that Roman troops were billeted at Burnswark for siege and fighting practice. Quite how long this lasted is unclear, for the Roman presence in the area became irregular in the last decades of the 2nd century. It seems as though the 1960s excavations, like so much else from that decade, demolished older attitudes while failing to effectively replace them.

So, the original nice, clear-cut and exciting theory of Burnswark hillfort being under siege by the Romans, developed – or degenerated – into the much more mundane likelihood that it was merely a military training ground. Still a unique site, but without the drama. Until…

Work in the last decade, using geo-physics, aerial imaging, metal detecting and excavation has picked up Burnswark's balls and tossed them into the air again, coming down in favour of the siege theory. The concentration of ballista bolts and balls, arrows and lead sling-shot on a quarter-mile section of the hillfort's southern rampart has been interpreted as being from a major assault.

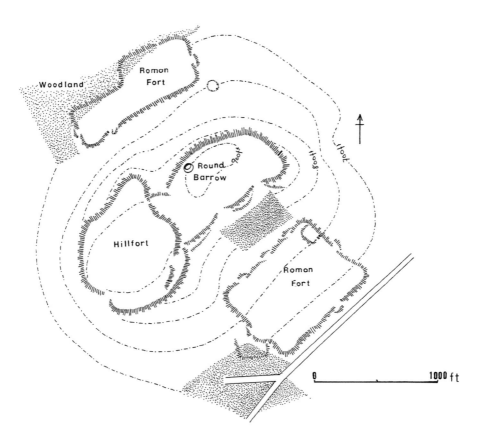

But why was there an attack of a scale, unknown at any other native stronghold in Britain? Was this the Romans under Quintus Lollius Urbicus making their presence felt at the start of the 140 A.D. (Antonine Wall) invasion? Or was it in revenge for the possible sacking of The Birrens fort in the 150s? Or was it simply concentrated target practice? For now, the siege theory is back in favour. Ironically, history has given us a taste of the future, but it remains as indistinct as ever.

There is a bit more to Burnswark, though. The burial mound at the highest point within the hillfort dates from the Bronze Age and the hillfort also had its uses in more recent times. There is a 17th century artillery redoubt just inside the south entrance, while it was also used as a mapping station in the 19th century. More than anything, though, here is a site where the native defences can be seen alongside those of the invaders who caused their abandonment, forming one of Scotland's most fascinating pre-historic sites.

It might appear that the land hereabouts is unchanging, though the roar from the M74, when carried on the wind, reminds you otherwise. History ultimately never really changes, only our interpretation. Burnswark's muddled past will certainly benefit from a further comprehensive investigation. Truth will out – eventually.

CADEMUIR (Hillforts and Settlement)

Peebles-shire O/S Landranger map 73 refs. (west H/F) 225371, (east H/F) 230375 (settlement) 235379

Directions: Head west from Peebles on the A72. Turn left after 1 1/2 miles. Park at the picnic place, after crossing Manor Water and the cattle grid, and walk up to the middle of the three summits on the left. That is Cademuir II.

Cademuir Hill, though not the highest in the area, overlooks a stretch of upper Tweedale, plus several lesser valleys. The hillforts on the south-western spur are ideally perched above Manor Water and command useful pre-historic routes both from east to west, and north to south. It is not known what relationship the two hillforts or the undefended settlement had with each other, or whether they were contemporary.

The west hillfort, Cademuir II, is the smaller one, built on a minor summit of the south-west ridge, rising to 1,087 ft. above sea level. A tumbled drystone wall encloses an area of 230 ft. x 150 ft., with slopes to the north, south and west being utilised to save on the building required. The substantial eastern rampart is about 20 ft. thick and has both facings still visible in places. There are entrances in the south-west and the north.

Outside the central citadel are five secondary enclosures adjoining the rampart on all sides except the south. These vary considerably in size, ranging from the large one in the north-west, to a small triangular affair just beyond the eastern wall, adding further to its strength. And it is the eastern approach that required the stoutest defences as it faces the higher mass of Cademuir Hill, and is approached over a number of ridges.

In the ridge immediately before the hillfort is a *chevaux de frise*, comprising about 140 stones blocking the approach. Many of these have now fallen, but it is clear and its effectiveness can easily be imagined. This would have prevented a mass charge either on horse or foot, and is one of only two *chevaux de frise's* on mainland Scotland; the other being at Dreva Craig* hillfort nearby. It has been cleverly sited so as to be almost invisible until one is near the top of the ridge.

Little else is known about the west hillfort on Cademuir Hill; it was once thought to have been post-Iron Age, while the lack of any stone huts has been interpreted as dating it to the early Iron Age. It is certainly an unusual and yet impressive structure and, with its *chevaux de frise*, bears an almost unique distinction.

Almost half-a-mile up the hill to the north-east, at 1,314 ft., is the larger of the Cademuir hillforts. This is diamond-shaped and sits on a summit of the south-western ridge with commanding views over Tweedale and Manor Water. A single stone rampart about 10 ft. thick encloses 8 acres within maximum extremities of 230 x 130 yds., so this is considerably bigger than Cademuir II. As such, it has been considered to be a minor oppidum – possibly a regional centre - of the Selgovae tribe. That is,

*The massive, tumbled, stone rampart at Cademuir II hillfort overlooks Tweedale,
but the larger Cademuir I hillfort overlooks this one.*

of course, nothing more than a speculative guess, but this was hardly your run-of-the-mill Borders hillfort.

There are reasonably steep approaches to all sides except the south-west, where lies the simple main entrance through the tumbled wall. There is another entrance in the east, while much of the south-east wall has fallen down the hill. Most of the wall is protected by an unfinished outer rampart about 10 yds. away. This is an earth and rubble glacis affair that may have been hastily thrown up to repel an approaching enemy; either that or the threat vanished and there was no need to finish it. Something, perhaps, such as the Roman invasion of c. 80 A.D.? The Romans probably only engaged the major native strongholds, and defences, such as those at Cademuir, even when strengthened, would have been useless against the highly organised and vastly experienced Latin forces.

This hillfort seems to date from the mid-first millennium B.C., while it appears to have been abandoned abruptly. Inside are the remains of about 40 well-spaced, timber-framed houses ranging from 15 to 35 ft. in diameter; most measuring about 25 ft. Even if these were all occupied simultaneously, the population cannot have been particularly high, despite this being quite a large hillfort for the Borders. It is the lack of any stone house circles, or any other secondary structures, that suggests Cademuir was not used in the later Iron Age, perhaps after the Romans first arrived on the scene.

If this hillfort were a victim of the first Roman invasion, its abandonment aligns with that of most native strongholds, with exceptions in the Votadini tribal area, in the Borders. Once the Romans departed, few hillforts were re-used and many became open settlements. Once abandoned for several decades, a hillfort would need considerable work to become a defensible stronghold again.

Should there have been no need for a stronghold, it would remain abandoned unless it was close to good agricultural land. In that case, walls were often robbed for their stones, but both hillforts on Cademuir Hill are too high to have succumbed. Maybe one superseded the other, but we can only speculate.

Fortunately, though, these two hillforts have survived, while the open settlement is a further half-mile to the east, still nearer the summit of Cademuir Hill.

Other Pre-historic Sites
Harehope Palisade Settlement Map 73 ref. 203448
Harehope Rings Hillfort Map 72 ref. 196445
White Meldon Hillfort Map 72 ref. 219427
Kerr's Knowe Hillfort Map 72 ref. 182384

CASTLE HAVEN DUN

Kirkcudbright O/S Landranger map 83 ref. 594483

Directions: Leave Kirkcudbright heading west on the A755. Turn left on the B727 to Borgue and take the minor coast road through Kirkandrews. About 220 yards east of Corseyard Tower, the dun can be seen from the road above the shore. You need to walk from that point.

Whatever grandiose theory archaeologists put forward for a chronological order and location of pre-historic strongholds, there are always exceptions that have to be either explained away – or simply ignored. All the various theories about the founding and development of brochs, for instance, whether in the northern or the western isles, come a cropper when having to explain how they are found in Galloway and, especially, the Borders.

The same can be said about duns, in particular those with galleried-walls. True to form, these are mostly found in the Hebrides, Western Highlands and Argyll. Then, up pops Castle Haven 50 miles to the south. Being on the coast, Castle Haven could have been built by migrants from Argyll, been influenced through trading links along the Atlantic seaboard, or it could simply have been a one-off. Whatever its origins, though, Castle Haven is an honest-to-goodness typical example of the D-shaped galleried-dun.

It is both attractively and, no doubt, strategically sited above the shore overlooking Wigtown Bay and this makes a visit all the more pleasing and rewarding. Castle Haven was cleared and partially restored in 1905. This is a great disappointment to modern

Castle Haven Dun lies attractively on the Galloway coast.
No wonder it was occupied on several occasions.

archaeologists, as the disturbance will play havoc with evidence from any future excavation, but makes the site more visually interesting for visitors. Unfortunately, it can be a bit overgrown in the summer months, while the ivy is doing its best to obscure the drystone wall. Let not this put you off, though, for all the main features are readily apparent.

The drystone wall encloses a courtyard of about 60 ft. x 35 ft. and has two entrances. The main one is in the north-east, while a narrower one in the south leads down to a natural landing stage; access to the sea would have been important for transport, trade and fishing. The walls, even though restored, are not unduly high, but within these are three narrow galleries with six entrances opening onto the interior of the dun. There might have been a stairway built against the perimeter wall. The dun was confirmed to date from the Iron Age by various artefacts found in 1905.

All of this is surrounded by a similarly shaped enclosure about twice the size. At the north and west sides, the outer wall is close to the dun, but much further away elsewhere. There are entrances in the north and south that align with those in the dun, but this outer wall may date from the Dark Ages. A few of the artefacts confirm its continued use in the Dark Ages/early Medieval periods, and the outer wall has been considered to form a Dark Ages' stock enclosure. Mind you, these were hardly unknown in the Iron Age either so, until that wall is excavated using modern techniques, there is no evidence one way or another.

The sheer attractiveness of the location apart, Castle Haven Dun is one of Galloway's many important pre-historic sites. It was certainly occupied, if not continuously, for several centuries and may have even played a part in more recent Scottish history, as a refuge for Edward Balliol in the 14th century.

Here, then, is a fine example from the extraordinary range of pre-historic sites along the coast of Galloway. It is almost as if this diverse range were intended to confound and compromise all the various archaeological theories. For the visitor, that can range is only of benefit.

Other Pre-historic Sites
Barnheugh Hillfort Map 83 ref. 599475
Borness Batteries hillfort Map 83 ref. 619446
Trusty's Hill hillfort Map 83 ref. 588561
Cardoness House cup and ring marked stones Map 83 ref. 565535
Lower Laggan House cup and ring marked stones Map 83 ref. 545526
Cairnholy I and II chambered cairns Map 83 ref. 517538

COW CASTLE

Lanarkshire O/S Landranger map 72 ref. 042331

Directions: Leave Biggar on the A702 to Coulter. Turn left in Coulter to Culteralles and turn left up the track to Nisbet Farm. Walk east along the track from the farmyard to the knoll, on which the hillfort lies.

Not surprisingly, there are many building styles on display at the hundreds of Borders' hillforts. Naturally, these reflect the environment, materials, the tribe or people who lived in the hillfort, and the reasons for its building. Cow Castle is a good example of a hillfort that has been reduced in size. Many hillforts were altered during their life-time and most were expanded, but that was not always the case in the Borders. Here is a site where a later hillfort was built right on top of an earlier one.

Standing almost 1,050 ft. above sea level, 300 ft. above tributaries of Culter Water to the north and west – and overlooking Culter Water itself, Cow Castle commands a prominent location; it is not alone in this, though. It lies at the west end of a long spur, to the north of Culter Fell, with White Hill and Mitchelhill Rings hillforts farther to the north-east. Assuming they were occupied during an over-lapping period, the inhabitants of these three hillforts can hardly have lived in splendid isolation. Both of the latter hillforts were probably developed over more than one stage, White Hill's second phase being clearly un-finished. Mitchelhill Rings, like Cow Castle, may have been reduced in size during its lifetime.

But of the three, it is Cow Castle that is the most impressive hillfort to visit. It is D-shaped and the original single rampart and ditch – where room permitted – enclosed an area of about 230 ft. x 150 ft. The entrance was in the north-west and was retained for the later hillfort. Though most of these defences have been subsequently superseded by the second hillfort, they are still visible in the south-west. Unfortunately, no dating is known at the present.

A second, D-shaped hillfort was built mostly within the lines of the earlier one, enclosing an area 140 ft. x 100 ft. This gives the appearance of a hillfort with two ramparts and ditches on all sides, but an additional rampart and ditch were only required in the south-west. A new entrance was made through the earlier defences to align with that of the later hillfort. Finally, an annexe was built outside the first hillfort's defences in the north-east, possibly as a cattle enclosure.

It is quite easy to work out the building sequence once you are at Cow Castle. Traces of 4 huts can be seen, three within the second hillfort, while the fourth is in the north-eastern annexe. (I wonder if this hut was a pre-historic equivalent of a granny-annexe?) These huts could all date from the same period and are quite typical of the timber-framed type visible at many Borders' hillforts.

Despite the miracles of modern archaeological excavation techniques, it is unlikely that anyone will find out if Cow Castle was inhabited by members of the Selgovae tribe in whose area, in Roman times, it lay. Given the proximity of the two aforementioned hillforts, it is likely that it was built by an extended family; possibly the Borders' equivalent of, say, the Mid-Howe* broch and settlement on the Orkney Islands.

One can only guess as to why Cow Castle was reduced in size – famine, or victims of a raid, if you want to be morbid – but this was probably not unconnected with the fate of its neighbours.

Other Pre-historic Sites
White Hill hillfort Map 72 ref. 055338
Mitchelhill Rings hillfort Map 72 ref. 062341

DREVA CRAIG (Hillfort)

Peebles-shire O/S Landranger map 72 ref. 126353

Directions: Take the B7016 east from the A72 at Biggar, to Broughton. Cross the A701 and take the minor road south-east. After descending, the road rises again about a mile from Broughton and the hillfort can be seen to the south, on a knoll overlooking the valley.

Almost every river, stream and hill is covered from every possible angle by a multitude of hillforts in this part of the Borders. Most are relatively small, many enclosing less than an acre, but display wide variations in construction. Dreva Craig is not untypical, but has two highly distinctive features: its spectacular and strategically dominating location; and a *chevaux de frise* protecting the gentle approach to its south-western flank. The former makes Dreva Craig a particularly enjoyable hillfort to visit.

Approaching from the north-east, where traces of an early open settlement lie in the field above, Dreva Craig stands on top of a knoll 898 ft. above sea level and almost 300 ft. above the various rivers nearby. Thus, it gives spectacular views along Biggar Water and overlooks the confluences with both Holms Water and the River Tweed. While this makes an attractive location, it was surely the strategic benefits of observing, if not controlling, what passed in the valley below that was of considerable importance to the Iron Age inhabitants.

At the foot of the knoll is an open settlement with several house circles. These are probably late-Iron Age and post-date the hillfort, while there is a number of large stones of no apparent use standing among them. Was this settlement built on another *chevaux de frise*? The north-east approach to Dreva Craig is easy and a *chevaux de frise* was intended to prevent a mass attack, either on horse or foot. So, there may have originally been one at this location. In any case, this serves as a precursor of the real thing.

Beyond the open settlement, the base of the knoll, on which the hillfort stands, is defended by a fairly ruinous stone wall, best seen at the south and west. The north and east sides of this defensive line mostly comprise the rocky outcrops of the knoll. The wall, as far as can be determined, was about 12 ft. thick and had a rubble core, much in evidence now, with a stone facing. In the main, it is pretty standard fare.

The inner wall is of much the same build – perhaps a little wider, but is in a better state of preservation. This encloses about 1/2 acre at the summit of the knoll, measuring almost 200 ft. x 150 ft. Once again, the builders utilised a rocky outcrop in the north-west to save on the building work with the entrance in the east; a simple gap approached through a gully in the rock. The combination of sound defences and a good natural position must have given Dreva Craig an air of invincibility in the Iron Age.

Historically, the most significant aspect of the hillfort is the *chevaux de frise* that blocks the south-western approach – there is certainly no idle speculation about this one. Approximately 200 stones cover an area of 100 ft. x 70 ft. directly outside the outer rampart. About half still stand to their original height, about 3 ft., with the rest having fallen or been broken, but the site is otherwise mostly complete. In the summer, the effect is somewhat spoiled by the bracken, so it is best seen earlier in the year. Nevertheless, this is a rare survivor of what was a seemingly little-used defensive measure, in Britain at any rate. It may be a co-incidence, but the only other particularly good example in mainland Scotland is at nearby Cademuir* hillfort.

Within the hillfort are four hut circles, with another near the outer wall at the south-west. As these appear to be built within the debris of the wall, they were probably built after Dreva Craig ceased to be defended.

Down the hill to the north-west, though, a large open settlement can be seen, with an extensive field system beyond. Traces of several boundary dykes give an insight into how the land was divided in the Iron Age. Whether for cultivation or animals, the rich land of the river valleys was as valuable in the Iron Age as it is today. Another open settlement has been traced down the south-west slope near Biggar Water; this, as with those to the north-east and north-west of the hillfort, is thought to post-date the hillfort, but still date to the Iron Age.

With traces of four open settlements in its immediate vicinity, an extensive field system, a magnificently attractive location and its *chevaux de frise*, to say nothing of the hillfort itself, Dreva Craig is a pre-historic explorer's paradise. This rich combination is compelling; add the large number of hillforts in the close environs and a visit to the area is compulsive. Whether you are particularly interested in Scotland's pre-history or not, Dreva Craig will certainly impress you, while it is an ideal place from which to appreciate the Borders.

Other Pre-historic Sites
Tinnis Castle Hillfort and Medieval castle Map 72 ref. 141344
Henry's Brae Hillfort Map 72 ref. 139339
Helm End Hillfort Map 72 ref. 110335
Langlaw Hill Hillfort Map 72 ref. 100382
Chester Rig Hillfort Map 72 ref. 0993204

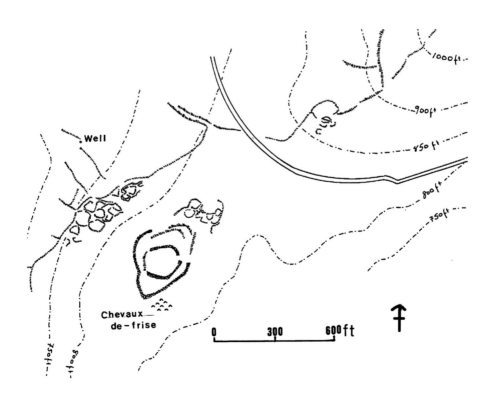

DURISDEER (Roman Fortlet)

Dumfries-shire O/S Map 78 ref. 903048

Directions: Take the A76 north from Dumfries and continue on the A702. Turn right into Durisdeer and park beside the attractive church. Follow the track beside the church and look out for the signpost on the left to the fort, and two more pointing across the burn to the fort up on a hillock. About 1 mile walk.

This is something of a very pleasant surprise. Many of Scotland's Roman forts require a fair helping of imagination to get the best out of a visit, yet this minor fortlet compares favourably with many hillforts.

The Roman road dates from the Agricolan period and ran between the fort at Dalswinton, in Nithsdale, and the fort at Crawford in upper Clydesdale: for the Romans, this was bandit territory. Durisdeer fortlet dates from the Antonine period when, as a means of exerting control over the unruly natives, fortlets were built at about 12 mile intervals.

The fort sits on a ridge above the burn and road. Its defences comprise a deep encircling ditch with a counterscarp on its outer lip, and a large earth rampart,

Surely Roman soldiers appreciated a (peaceful?) posting at the remote Durisdeer fortlet?

about 27 ft. wide: the interior measures 105 ft. x 60 ft. The entrance causeway faces north-east with a second, now shallow, ditch beyond. In short, it is a compact, well-fortified base for a small detachment. Remains of timber buildings, probably barracks, have been found but, of course, cannot now be seen.

Both the fortlet and its dominating and picturesque location are best appreciated from the hill to the north-east. Once there, all doubts about such a remote site are banished. The Romans were no fools. Durisdeer, though overlooked, could hardly be attacked from the hills and yet commands the pass. There is no finer stronghold of its type in Scotland today.

The nearby Church of Scotland church is also very interesting.

EDINSHALL HILLFORT and BROCH

Berwickshire O/S Landranger map 67 ref. 772604

Directions: Leave Duns along the A6112 towards Preston. Turn left on the B6365 and left again on the B6355. Turn first right towards St. Bathan's and park after 1 1/2 miles at a right angle, left-hand bend. A sign indicates the route. Walk down the path and cross Ellerburn brook. Follow the path, parallel with Whiteadder Water, which climbs the hill and passes through two gates. The hillfort is on top of a promontory overlooking the river valley. About 3/4 mile.

Edinshall is unusual in several important respects. Most obviously, unlike most hillforts, it does not command the locality. Anything but, for, at about 660 feet above sea level, Edinshall is still more than 300 feet lower than the small hillfort at the summit of Cockburn Law, 1/2 mile to the south. There is also considerable visual evidence of at least three periods of settlement. But the really important factor, and probably of most interest, is the second phase, the broch: something of a rarity in the Borders.

As with most defended pre-historic sites, Edinshall has not been thoroughly excavated, but its past can be pieced together from a combination of the visual remains and other known events. It is one of numerous small hillforts within the Votadini tribal area, whose centre was on the massive rock of Traprain Law*. Two stone-faced ramparts with outer ditches enclose 2 acres with entrances at the south-west and east. The ramparts are still quite impressive and must have been strong for a small hillfort. Their tumbled stone-work is exposed at the east, but is grass-covered at the west. It is possible that the outer rampart was a later, pre-broch addition.

The oval hillfort was probably built long before c. 100 B.C. and commands a good stretch of Whiteadder Water, possibly a strategic factor for its location. The hillfort at the summit of Cockburn Law – with slight defences – may have been connected with Edinshall as, between them, they command the land for several miles about.

There is nothing to see of the original interior layout, due to subsequent settlements, but the hillfort was probably abandoned – or at least rendered defenceless – with the arrival of Agricola and the Romans in c. 80 A.D. Many Votadini hillforts continued to be occupied during those troubled times, so perhaps the tribe entered into a pact with the invaders, who pushed-on farther north.

Nevertheless, this is hardly exceptional and it is the broch that gives Edinshall its distinction. This stands in the western half of the hillfort and utilises the north ramparts, along with an additional rampart and ditch to create a bailey. The broch is both unusually large and has well preserved, restored walls. With a solid wall about 16 feet thick enclosing a courtyard 45 feet across, it has just about the biggest area of any broch and is considerably larger than many renowned northern brochs.

Unfortunately, the walls are less than 6 feet high, but are complete in their circuit: you do not need much imagination to re-create scenes of about 1,900 years ago. The narrow entrance passage faces east, with guard-chambers either side. These, like the rest of the broch, are clear of rubble and particularly interesting. There are intra-mural cells at the north and west, while the stairs to the upper levels are at the south.

The broch may have been built following the Roman withdrawal c. 100 A.D., quite likely utilising stones from the hillfort ramparts. What happened thereafter is unknown, but within the eastern half of the hillfort, and even over the ramparts, lays a settlement of circular huts. Some have additional enclosures and the largest, measuring 45 feet across with walls 8 feet thick, is almost in the centre of the hillfort. This open settlement has obliterated the hillfort's east entrance, which hints that life had become more peaceful in the later Iron Age.

The Romans returned in c. 140 A.D. and may have remained until c. 200 A.D. Thus, the broch may have been built before the Romans returned and abandoned later. The open settlement was probably built following the final withdrawal of the Romans, near the end of the 2nd century A.D. Such a chronology cannot be determined without a thorough excavation, but the different phases of building coincide with the comings and goings of the Latin invaders. At least it gives plenty to see when you visit. The location over Whiteadder Water is pretty enough, but served a strategic purpose in the Iron Age.

The broch has always been referred to as a broch, yet its wall width:courtyard diameter ratio suggests it this never reached anything like the height of Mousa. In that respect, it has more in common with a dun, though it seems to be an advanced, later broch design. Yet, if a broch is taken to be a drystone, circular tower upwards of, say, 30 feet upwards in height, then, for Edinshall, it might have been a fairly close-run thing.

What of the name, though? It may be derived from 'Wooden's Hall', or Woden's Hall, the Saxon god of war. Another alternative is that of the giant Etin, who supposedly lived in the broch – the broch is certainly giant-sized. And the link with Scotland's capital city's name is obvious.

There is plenty to be pondered at this most impressive site in state care. So peaceful is its location that you can look to the south and easily imagine Roman soldiers marching down the hill towards you. They stop at nothing and you are in their path.

The broch within the hillfort may have been a 'semi-broch' to an extent, as its large courtyard suggests the walls cannot have reached the height of many northern brochs.

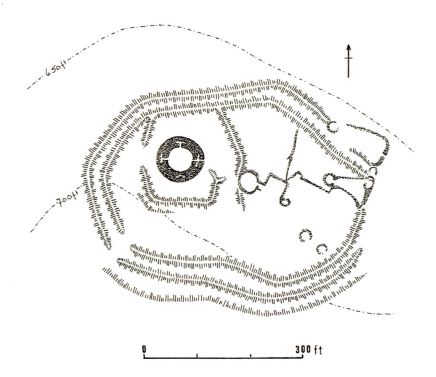

EILDON HILL (Hillfort)

Roxburghshire O/S Landranger map 73 ref. 555328

Directions: From the Market Place in Melrose, walk south along the B6359. Pass under the by-pass, and a footpath marked 'Eildon Walk' leads off left. Follow this over the stiles, turn right and keep to the path that leads to the summit of the north hill. The hillfort ramparts enclose this hill.

For all its size – and at 40 acres this is, if not the largest, the greatest of Scottish hillforts along with Traprain Law* – Eildon Hill is a bit like Frank Bruno the former heavyweight boxer: massive, impressive, but flatters to deceive. Eildon Hill is so much larger than all other hillforts in the assumed Selgovae tribal area, that it can have been little other than the capital or main centre.

To be sure, Eildon Hill is a multi-phase, multi-rampart hillfort. However, the defences today are fairly modest and fail to dominate the former volcano in the manner of some gems of Borders' hillforts. Despite these negative comparisons, there is a great deal from the Iron Age to see at Eildon Hill, while there are also some truly magnificent views. One can fully understand just why Eildon Hill played such a major part in Iron Age society in the Borders.

As with so many hillforts, though, it started on a much more modest scale. A single rampart defended a running-track shaped enclosure of about 600 ft. x 175 ft. on the summit: about 1 3/4 acres. This would have dated far back into the first millennium B.C. and, to all intents and purposes, is invisible today, although slight traces may be seen.

At a later date, the best part of the summit area was enclosed with a single rampart, including the whole of the original fort. This covered fully 9 acres, to make it one of the leading Borders' hillforts and, from that time, Eildon Hill was probably a tribal centre. This rampart is visible in places as a low bank or a terrace. At 1,327 feet above sea level, and 1,000 feet above the River Tweed, this large hillfort clearly dominates all but its fellow Eildon Hills for miles about, especially eastwards along Tweedale. It is clearly much bigger than any of the nearby hillforts.

Yet, there was more to come. At a later date, a further massive expansion was undertaken. A single stone rampart – almost a mile in length – encircled the whole of the hill and the two older hillforts. This was further strengthened by one or two additional lengths of rampart in the west, where the approach is easiest. There were four entrances: two in the west; and two in the east. The whole complex combined defences on a scale un-rivalled in the Borders, with a commanding strategic location that could not fail to be seen from afar.

What is so interesting is that the interiors of the two earlier hillforts are covered by about 300 hut circles, while hut platforms indent the western flanks of the hill. Another 100 or so might have been destroyed by the plantation at the south. Such figures suggest a population of about 2,000, but whatever the figure, it would have been exceptionally large for those times. Surely, Eildon Hill was nothing less than a tribal capital of considerable clout, in the decades before the Roman invasion? However, reasonably recent excavations have shown that the huts date from the late-Bronze Age right up to the 1st century A.D. Clearly they were not all contemporary.

Unfortunately, such a rich promise of pre-historic defences does not materialise. In most areas, the ramparts have slipped down the hill and only the terraces on which they once stood remain. There are good sections in the south-west, especially one where the turf has been cleared to reveal a section of the wall-face. Otherwise, it is a bit of a let-down. As for the hut platforms, heather has covered the majority of these and what promises so much, as with Frank Bruno, fails to deliver when it comes to the crunch.

This, once great, tribal capital that developed over many centuries, seems to have met a quick end. Despite there being no obvious sign of violence, Eildon Hill was probably cleared by the Romans, c. 80 A.D. Towards the west end of the summit, a shallow section of ditch marks the site of a Roman signal station, almost certainly connected with Newstead fort, Trimontium – of which nothing remains, a mile away to the north-east. That, more than anything, hints at the marvellous views one can expect from the summit of Eildon Hill.

There is quite a bit to see at Eildon Hill, although one might have hoped for more from one of Scotland's premier hillforts. Nevertheless, so long as you visit on a reasonably clear day, you will be rewarded by the combination of pre-historic remains and good views. That, and the knowledge that here was a truly major centre of population less than 2,000 years ago, and today there is nothing. What price Edinburgh going the same way by 4000 A.D.?

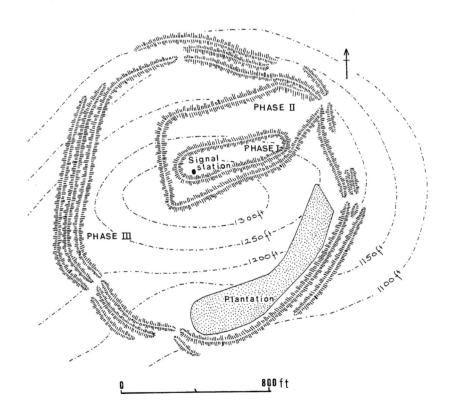

Other Pre-historic Sites
Little Twopenny (Hillfort) Map 74 ref. 631256
Castle Hill, Ancrum (Hillfort) Map 74 ref. 624249
Peniel Heugh (Hillfort) Map 74 ref. 654263
Ringleyhall (Hillfort) Map 74 ref. 667312

HAERFAULDS (Hillfort)

Berwickshire O/S Landranger map 73 ref. 574501

Directions: Head north from Kelso on the A6089 and turn left on the A697. At the tiny hamlet of Cambridge, turn right along the lane running north-east and 1/2 mile farther on take the track on the left, north-west, to 1/4 mile past Blythe Farm. Then head west across the moor for 1/4 mile to the hillfort.

Lying on the southern slopes of the Lammermuir Hills, and also on the eastern flanks of Lauderdale, Haerfaulds is deep in the heart of Borders' hillfort country. It is ideally placed on good stock-raising ground on the edge of the southern spur of Scoured Rig, 200 feet above Blythe Water to the south.

Haerfaulds is overlooked by the hills to the north, so a good-sized stone wall encloses an oval area about 375 ft. x 250 ft. The wall is now tumbled and spread to about 15 feet, although it was probably originally 10 feet thick. Nothing is known about its build, for it has been robbed of stone for huts, but it could have been of timber-laced construction. Nevertheless, the sheer quantity of stone is impressive.

Within the hillfort are several hut circles and other foundations. Most of these are close to the wall, and some utilised some scavenged material. The inference is that these buildings formed a Romano-British open settlement, but others could date from when the hillfort era, or perhaps much more recently.

As with many Borders' hillforts, dating remains elusive, but one would expect it to have been inhabited far back into the first millennium B.C. Haerfaulds is another of the strongly fortified small Borders' hillforts, probably of a cattle raising people under the suzerainty of a chief at Eildon Hill*, or perhaps even an out-post of the Votadini tribe. In either case, it was built to last and may have done so until the arrival of the Romans.

While little is known with even minimal certainty about this hillfort, it is still a fascinating place to visit out in the open spaces of the Borders' hills.

HOWNAM LAW (Hillfort)

Roxburghshire O/S Landranger map 74 ref. 796220

Directions: Head south from Kelso on the B6436 to Morebattle. Turn left southwards towards Hownam, following Kale Water. After 3 miles, turn left to Howgate, cross the river and turn left. Follow the track and path in a north-east direction for 1 mile. The hillfort is on top of the hill.

Hownam Law, at 22 acres, is one of the biggest hillforts in Scotland, in reality being more of an oppidum. It is situated on a hill fully 1,472 feet above sea level on the north-western slopes of the Cheviot Hills. From Hownam Law, there are magnificent views north over the Tweed and Teviot valleys to the Lammermuir Hills beyond, while in the north-west lie the Eildon Hills, with the even larger oppidum on the northern mass.

Considering its credentials, one might expect that Hownam Law would be one of the better known Scottish pre-historic strongholds. Certainly, one would not expect it to be completely overshadowed, in archaeological terms, by its relatively miniature neighbour, Hownam Rings*. But that is the case, even if the occupants of the oppidum could look down almost dismissively on the little upstart to the south. This situation is due entirely to Hownam Rings* having been excavated to a high standard, while Hownam Law has been comparatively ignored. In the Iron Age, there is no doubt as to which was the most important hillfort.

As Hownam Law rests between the oppida of Eildon Hills and Yeavering Bell, in Northumberland, one might suspect that these three rather dominated affairs in this part of the Borders. Eildon Hill* was probably a tribal capital of the Selgovae, but it would seem likely that Hownam Law belonged to another tribe. As Yeavering Bell is only about 8 miles away to the north-east, these two could be oppida of the same tribal group.

Enough of such hypotheses, though. Never mind the ifs-and-buts, what is there to see? Well, like Eildon Hill*, Hownam Law is a little disappointing. A stone rampart, fully 3/4 mile in circumference – and now quite tumbled and robbed, encloses the summit and a large area of gently sloping ground to the north-west. The wall was about 10 feet thick and would have required an immense amount of stone, although it cannot be clearly traced round its whole circuit today. On the summit rests a cairn, while below this are two ponds on a fairly level stretch of ground.

More obviously, inside lie the remains of at least 150 hut platforms or circles. Heather covers much of the oppidum and so even more may be awaiting discovery – it is certainly not overcrowded. Yeavering Bell has about the same number, yet is only 13 acres, while twice that number is visible at Eildon Hill*, with another 100 or so being destroyed. In any case, Hownam Law's population would have been considerable.

There appears to have been only one entrance, in the south-west, which would have been pretty busy at times. Presumably, the land towards Kale Water was farmed, but such an oppidum would probably have been a trading, manufacturing and ruling centre, so it may not have been necessary to till the vast acreage required to feed such a large populace. In the north-east corner, there is a much smaller enclosure of a later date. This uses the oppidum wall round its eastern flank and has an entrance in the north-west. It may not date from pre-historic times.

Given its defensive and likely historic details, one would expect Hownam Law to be almost breathtaking. Unfortunately, all of Scotland's biggest hillforts are somewhat visually disappointing, but the combination of the magnificent views and all those house sites ensure a visit to Hownam Law is rewarding. All it needs is a decent excavation and Hownam Law could once again put the little upstart, Hownam Rings*, back in its place.

HOWNAM RINGS (Hillfort)

Roxburghshire O/S Landranger map 80 ref. 790194

Directions: From Hownam Law*, return to Howgate and go back to the minor road. Turn left, heading south to Hownam. Turn left in the village and follow the track and path east for 3/4 mile. The hillfort is about 1/4 mile due north across the moors.
Hownam Rings gained its pre-eminent position among Scottish pre-historic strongholds neither for what is visible, nor for its association with any historic event. No, it was something much more recent.

Hownam Rings was excavated in 1948 and the results were more significant to archaeology in general, than to the hillfort itself. The excavation showed a long period of occupation and a considerable sequence of development, from a palisade camp, through an increasingly fortified hillfort, to, finally, an open settlement. Such results were a major archaeological breakthrough at the time, and remain an important step in the history and development of British archaeology.

Now, cynics might feel that money spent investigating the past is wasted and is of little relevance today: such people might need to consider those opinions carefully in the light of what has happened since. The excavators' thought the earliest settlement dated from the 2nd century B.C., at the earliest. As an indication of how archaeological developments are improving the knowledge and understanding of the past, and Scotland's development into a nation, it is now known that the first phase at Hownam Rings dates back to the 7th century B.C., or the end of the Bronze Age. Not that such nomenclature would have meant anything to the people at the time, but this allows a greater accuracy of understanding today.

The hillfort lies at the raised north end of a plateau 1,117 feet above sea level, on the north-west slopes of the Cheviot Hills. As with Hownam Law*, it enjoys good views to the north-west across the Teviot and Tweed valleys, but The Cheviot Hills restrict those views to the south and east. Hownam Law lies just over a mile to the north, while about 5 miles to the south is Woden Law*. With various oppida, hillforts and settlements, you do not have to go far hereabouts to find a place of pre-historic interest.

Back to Hownam Rings, though. The 1948 excavation showed that the simple, Phase 1 palisade camp enclosed about 1 1/2 acres, measuring 300 ft. x 250 ft. Nothing of this is now visible, nor of its successor, the Phase 2 palisade camp. This was a rebuilding of the original palisade on a slightly different line from the original camp, presumably as the timbers were replaced.

Then, just inside the line of the palisade camps, the first true hillfort was built in the 5th century B.C., Phase 3. This comprised a stone wall about 10 feet thick, the lowest courses of which can still be seen on the west and south sides. This is typical of contemporary Borders' hillforts, but, as it was dismantled in antiquity, it is not known if it was timber-laced or not.

The final stage in Hownam Rings' defended development, Phase 4, may have occurred in response to the imminent arrival of the Romans, c. 80 A.D. Alternatively,

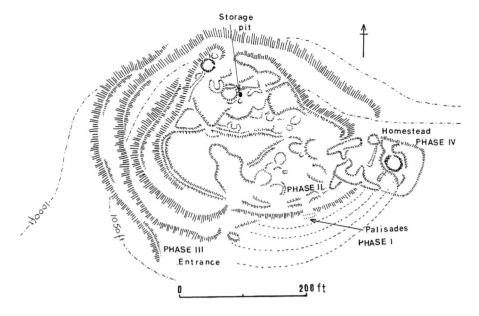

it may have been in response to weaponry developments, such as the introduction of the sling or javelin in the last centuries B.C.

The stone wall was dismantled and a rampart and ditch built outside, or on top of this. Two further ramparts, each about 15 feet thick, and ditches were built outside, while a fourth exists in the west. The whole combination of defences measured up to 150 feet across, a considerable size given the relatively small area enclosed. There was a simple entrance through these defences in the south, not aligned with the previous strongholds' entrances in the same vicinity.

The two outer ramparts are only visible on the west side, but the other two rise to about 4 feet in height. The inner rampart is built of stone from the Phase 3 wall, while the second rampart utilises material from its ditch. The excavators discovered that the Phase 4 hillfort, as designated here, fell into ruin soon after completion. Hence, the possibility that it was comprehensively rebuilt just before the Romans arrived.

Still Hownam Rings was not finished, though. At a later time, possibly soon after the Romans invaded the Borders, an open settlement of circular huts was established. These can still be seen within the hillfort, though some may date to the hillfort's time, and quite a large one lies over the eastern ramparts. Such a development could have been the work of the hillfort's inhabitants, after the defences were dismantled in the wake of the Romans: a scenario with parallels elsewhere in the Borders.

The final stages, Phase 5, include the rectangular homestead built round the large hut over the ramparts in the east. This is much larger, covering an area of about 100 ft. x 80 ft., and would probably have belonged to a farmer and family, probably of the late-Roman, or even post-Roman period. This can still be clearly seen today.

So, the complex development of Hownam Rings may have evolved over a thousand years. Were it not for the ground-breaking excavation of 1948, nothing of Phases 1 and 2 – and possibly even Phase 3 – would have been known, let alone a sequence of dating. Here, then, a seemingly typical Borders' hillfort with a succeeding open settlement has been found to have a much longer lineage.

All that seems fairly straight-forward and, let's face it, logical and easy to believe. Unfortunately, for the visitor, that is no longer thought to be the case and Phases 1 to 3 are considered, at least, not so certain and, at worst, unreliable and probably wrong. Fortunately – now you have made all the effort to visit Hownam Rings, the most visible phases of all, that of the multi-vallate hillfort (Phase 4) and the homestead (Phase 5), have passed muster – so far – and these are what you will see high on the hill.

Despite the great strides made in the 70-odd years since Hownam Rings was excavated, little is known about the vast majority of pre-historic strongholds, and the chain of events in the Bronze and Iron Ages remains a mystery. Many fundamental questions remain unanswered. Yet, Hownam Rings has demonstrated how a good, thorough excavation can bring unexpected dividends – and fuel future revisions. Many more are needed. Just what secrets the hundreds of other Borders' hillforts hide is anybody's guess.

Other Pre-historic Site
Eleven Shearers (Stone rows) Map 80 ref. 792193

MOTE OF MARK (Dark Ages' Fort)

Kirkudbrightshire O/S Landranger map 84 ref. 845540

Directions: Leave Dumfries heading south on the A710 and follow the Solway Firth coast to Colvend. Turn left along the road to the coast at Rockcliffe, and a path from opposite the entrance to the Baron's Craig Hotel leads to the fort.

One might be justified in wondering just what a Dark Ages' stronghold is doing in a book devoted to pre-history. This is especially so when the fort in question has associations with the Arthurian legends: in particular King Mark of Dumnonia, or Cornwall; and the tragic romance of Tristan and Isolda. In addition, the Mote of Mark was thought to be the residence of a chieftain of the Dark Ages' kingdom of Rheged. So, where is the pre-historic connection?

Back in 1913, the Mote of Mark was excavated. The report showed that a badly tumbled and overgrown, timber-laced stone wall enclosed some 270 ft. x 100 to 50 ft. of this triangular-shaped rocky eminence, 100 feet above Rough Firth. There seemed to be two entrances in the west, and though the wall was in a poor condition, it was presumed to be about 10 feet thick and of similar height. In addition, along with many walls at Scottish hillforts, it was found to be vitrified. Although this wall was badly robbed of its stone, traces of an inner rampart were also seen. It was considered that the outer wall was deliberately set on fire by the inhabitants, who possibly built the inner wall, as recently as the 9th century A.D.

The excavators noted the large quantity of animal bones and considerable evidence of metal-working, while a rotary quern, fragments of Roman pottery and many clay moulds – dating to the 8th to 9th centuries A.D. – were also found. It was commented that the lack of native Iron Age relics was odd. Nevertheless, here it seemed was an Iron Age hillfort that was occupied into the Roman period, was then abandoned, and was finally re-occupied in the 9th century A.D.

That was the accepted chronology of Mote of Mark for 60 years as worked out, not by a simple surface survey, but an excavation: it had archaeological authority behind it. Then, in 1973, a second excavation was begun and this suggested a quite different story. Once again, there was a good haul of fragmentary artefacts. These included fine glassware, possibly from Germany, much evidence of metal working – including gold and silver – and jewellery manufacture, more clay moulds and confirmation that the vitrified outer wall was shored up with rubble before being finally abandoned. Dark Ages' pottery was also found.

The real difference between the two excavations – fortified by a third in 1979 – was that the timber-laced wall was found to have been built no earlier than the 5th century A.D., and was destroyed about 200 years later. The Mote of Mark was not an Iron Age stronghold after all, but dated from a later period and was probably a settlement of considerable importance in Dark Ages' Galloway. It may even have been destroyed by Northumbrian Angles, so it was unlikely to be a mere village of no significance.

The later settlement and clay moulds of the 8th to 9th centuries, relate to a re-use of the site, probably after a period of abandonment. So, it is just possible that the Mote of Mark was occupied, if not fortified, in the Iron Age. Not only has history changed tack in the light of the new evidence, but this serves as a salutary warning not to make sweeping statements about Scotland's many unexcavated hillforts. Most are presumed to date from the Iron Age, based on their similarity at a handful of excavated sites, but, as with the Mote of Mark, there might be other exceptions.

The Mote of Mark towers over the cottage down by the Rough Firth.

Although the visible remains are somewhat scant, there are fine views over the Solway Firth to the mountains of the Lake District, and along the nearby coastline. Such sights give a real clue as to why this site was occupied in the first place, and continued to be so for several centuries, whether pre-historic or not.

MULLACH (Hillfort)

Dumfries-shire O/S Landranger map 78 ref. 929870

Directions: Take the A76 north from Dumfries and, after about 6 miles, take the farm road north-east at the junction with the road from Dalswinton, on the right. Just before High Auldgirth, walk 1/2 mile south-west to the summit of the hill.

Commanding long views over Nithsdale, to the hills of Kirkcudbright in the west, Mullach is a well-located hillfort, but, unlike many in Clydesdale and, to a lesser extent, Annandale, it is almost isolated. In its own way, that makes it more attractive to visit and probably enhanced Mullach's importance in the Iron Age. The Roman fort near Dalswinton was a mile to the south, but there is nothing left to see.

That is certainly not the case with Mullach, though. The summit is almost 800 feet above sea level and is surrounded by the considerable ruins of two, timber-laced stone ramparts, with much grass covering. The outer rampart is an oval, enclosing about 300 ft. x 250 ft., while the inner rampart is about 100 feet inside and concentric with it. Among the remains of these ramparts can be seen several lumps of vitrified material, denoting not only the ramparts' type of build, but also the likely cause of Mullach's ultimate demise. There have been satellite images of a possible third rampart in the north-west.

Mullach has not been excavated and so nothing of its past can be determined to any extent. It is assumed to date from the 8th to 4th centuries B.C., because of its timber-laced ramparts, but such guessing is not exactly certain of accuracy. In the case of Mullach, though, it appears similar to other early/middle-Iron Age hillforts, especially with regards its location. That is quite spectacular, despite not being of any particular height, and would have controlled an important route in the Iron Age. One later followed by the Romans, the railway and the main A76 road.

Other Pre-historic Site
Barrs Hill (Hillfort) Map 78 ref. 015834

RISPAIN CAMP (Defended Farmstead)

Wigtownshire O/S Landranger map 83 ref. 429399

Directions: Leave Whithorn heading south on the A746. After 1/2 mile, turn right along the track to Rispain Farm and park where indicated. The hillfort is 200 yds. beyond.

Following an excavation in 1901, the small, compact and well-preserved Rispain Camp was thought to be a medieval site, but the possibility of it being a Roman fortlet was not completely ruled out. It just shows how wrong one can be. Further excavations from 1978 to 1981 produced material that was C-14 dated to the mid-1st century B.C. Thus, it qualifies as being an Iron Age hillfort, but, in reality, was more of a defended farmstead.

About 3/4 acre was enclosed by two ramparts and a central ditch. This latter is in fine condition, was formerly of 'V' shape and was almost 20 ft. deep. It is nothing like that now, but still gives a good idea of its defensive capability. The two ramparts are now low mounds, but the whole is a good example of the defended homesteads that abounded in southern Scotland.

A causeway in the north-east leads to a probable timber-framed entrance; a metalled track led to the interior. A large circular house, 44 ft. across, stood in the north-west, adding to the impression that this belonged to a farmer of substance. The possible translation of the name, rhurospen – in Welsh, means 'the chief of the cultivated country', adding to this impression.

An enamelled bronze plate, dating to the 1st or 2nd centuries A.D., was found, and the likelihood is that Rispain Camp was occupied for about 300 years from about 100 B.C. This is a particularly attractive homestead situated in gentle countryside. While there were many defended homesteads, few have survived, and still fewer approach the condition of Rispain Camp.

TRAPRAIN LAW (Hillfort)

East Lothian O/S Landranger map 67 ref. 581746

Directions: Leave Haddington heading east on the A119 to East Linton. Turn right along the road through Traprain and turn right along the minor road that runs to the north of the rock. There is a car park and an information board just beyond the old quarry. It is a steep walk to the summit.

Traprain Law is a conundrum, especially for 21st century visitors. This great massif that towers majestically over East Lothian is one of Scotland's outstanding, magnificent sites of immense historical importance. Yet, it is a disappointment for its visible pre-historic remains. Fortunately, the outstanding views from the summit compensate, but it is a bit like going to watch your favourite footballer when he has an off day, yet his team plays well. The visit will still be worthwhile, but one feels just a little let down.

For a start, as will be obvious when you arrive, a large chunk of Traprain Law has been quarried away for road stone, although this desecration has ceased. It was akin to demolishing a wing of Edinburgh Castle to use the material for modern housing. Some people just do not appreciate our wonderful world.

It likely that no other Scottish pre-historic stronghold has been the focus for so many excavations, surveys and field visits as Traprain Law. A decade of excavations from 1914 unearthed the famous hoard of cut up Roman silver, weighing about 75 lbs., followed by others in 1939, 1947 and almost every decade to the end of the century. Then, after

a severe fire on the summit in 2003 – one of several, another series of excavations and surveys took place, on and off, through to 2018. After all these, you might imagine that there is nothing left to discover about Traprain Law. Much information and artefacts were, indeed, revealed, but also much debate and doubt – bordering on confusion – as to the chronology, and even layout, of the various defences has been created.

The plan of Traprain Law shows a simplified version of its possible development, in the most general of generalised ways. Artefacts from the Neolithic and Bronze Ages have been found, but the first defences formed a 10-acre enclosure at the summit, C-14 dated from the late-2nd millennium to c. 8th century B.C. Excavations showed this to have begun as palisade trenches, replaced by a bank and ditch, and finally an earth rampart with an outer stone face. This is only visible in parts – and barely, at that. The summit may have been occupied before this, but was probably not fortified.

The next defences are the 20-acre hillfort, possibly dating from a century or so before the Romans arrived. These curve round the west to the south and some banks may have been turned into terraces when Traprain Law was extended later. The intervening period between these two strongholds seems to have been one of reduced activity, but this enlargement suggests that the number of people living here was increasing by the end of the 1st millennium B.C. This possibly cemented the importance of Traprain Law to the nascent Votadini tribal area. Another extension of the defences to the south-west followed, enclosing 30 acres. Yet, there was more.

A further rampart was built to the south and west, enclosing 40 acres. These are the most substantial seen today, more than half-a-mile long and up to 15 ft. wide and 10 ft. high. There are entrances in the north, south and south-west, the latter two possibly from the 30 acre hillfort, while it overlays older defences in places. Artefacts found near this rampart, dated to the 1st and 2nd centuries A.D. so these defences were probably pre-Roman. Evidence from recent excavations suggests that, at the time the Romans arrived, in the 80s A.D., there was considerable activity on Traprain Law and possibly an increasingly dense population.

Thereafter, there may, or may not, have been several attempts at rebuilding, re-aligning or reducing the defences – even a period of abandonment – all before the end of the Iron Age. Despite many attempts at giving a chronology for both pre-historic and post-Roman settlements on Traprain Law, with six or more phases, there is no defining version.

One of the very late- or even post-Iron Age phases included streets and a square, while rectangular houses with rounded corners – perhaps not unlike the Black Cottages of the north and west Scotland – were also found. Another theory suggests that Traprain might have been a flourishing town called Dunpheldur in the 6th century A.D.

The range of artefacts found at Traprain Law, more than anything, shows just how long it has been occupied. Neolithic polished stone axes, Bronze Age metalwork, numerous objects from the Iron Age and more Roman artefacts than from any other site in Scotland, including the famous Traprain hoard of Roman silver. The list does not stop there, for coins, beads, jewellery, an impressive Dark Ages' silver chain – possibly connected with the aforementioned Dunpheldur, early Christian and medieval pottery, and even a stylus from the late Iron Age – inferring that somebody, at least, could write – have all been found.

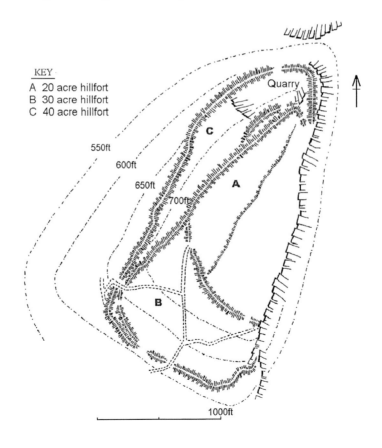

KEY
A 20 acre hillfort
B 30 acre hillfort
C 40 acre hillfort

Quarry

550ft
600ft
650ft
700ft

C

A

B

1000ft

By the 5th or 6th centuries A.D. events at Traprain are no longer relevant to pre-historic strongholds, although occupation has been confirmed in the Middle Ages and beyond – possibly more off than on. So much of Traprain's history seems to be known, compared with most pre-historic strongholds, yet it is merely a tantalising, confusing glimpse that shows there is still much to discover.

Considering all this, anyone who regularly visits pre-historic strongholds will find their expectations somewhat unfulfilled. After all, this was a major pre-historic town, nothing less. Its only real equivalents were Eildon Hill*, cleared by the Romans in c. 80 A.D., and possibly Tap o' Noth*, at a much later date. Traprain Law not only survived, but flourished and grew during those centuries when the Romans came and went like confetti blowing in the wind.

Yes, you can see Bass Rock off the coast and appreciate the commanding view over the north-east route to the south. But, bearing in mind Traprain Law's importance, the scale and length of occupation, and the number of artefacts found – plus the effort to reach the summit – the defences are underwhelming. Yet, despite all that, Traprain Law really is worth visiting and is not easily forgotten.

Other Pre-historic Sites
Pencraig Hill (Standing stone) Map 67 ref. 581768
Kirklandhill (Standing stone) Map 67 ref. 616776
The Chesters (Hillfort) Map 66 ref. 507782

TYNRON DOON (Hillfort)

Dumfries-shire O/S Landranger map 78 ref. 820939

Directions: Take the A76 north from Dumfries and turn left along the A702 at Thornhill. Take the second minor road on the right after Penpont towards Tynron, and Clonrae Farm is 3/4 mile farther along on the right. Follow a track from there up the hill, to the east of the hillfort, which is on a south-eastern spur of the hill.

It is not often one can write about a pre-historic site where one knows the farmer of the land on which the hillfort stands. Well, that still eludes me, but the son of the farmer was a loyal and devoted member of my hockey club – to say nothing about being a good player, before moving away to manufacture disposable nappies. Unfortunately, as is so often the case, he knew next to nothing about Tynron Doon, except that is was a lovely hillfort to visit.

Of that, there is no doubt. It is spectacularly sited, while there is a probable Dark Ages' courtyard in the north-east that was converted to become a motte castle. Even more recently, an L-shaped tower-house was built in the north-west corner, towards the end of the 16th century. Disappointingly, nothing of that now remains, but it must have looked particularly grand in such a location.

Lying on the south-eastern spur of Auchengibbert Hill, at almost 950 feet above sea level, Tynron Doon towers over Scar Water to the east, with Nithsdale and the Lowther Hills beyond, and Shinnel Water to the west along with the distant Galloway hills. Although the Keir Hills rise to the south, there are reasonably long vistas in that direction, too. One might easily assume that such a dominating location was a reason for the initial and continued use of Tynron Doon.

A central citadel of 150 ft. x 130 ft. is protected by an overgrown stone wall with an entrance in the south-west. This is nothing special, but outside, to the west and south-west, three massive earth and rock ramparts and ditches provide further defences. These may be later additions, but still rise to 20 feet above the bottom of the ditches: remember, not only are the ramparts ruined, but the ditches are heavily silted and may be less than half their original depth. Such defences would have sent very clear messages to all who had nefarious intentions. Anyone who wanted to lay waste to Tynron Doon was in for a fight.

The chronology of Tynron Doon is confused somewhat by the discovery of a midden, or rubbish tip, on the south side. This produced many Dark Ages' artefacts, such as bone implements and a blue glass bead. Of much more interest was a gold panel that was found in 1927. This dates from the 6th to 8th centuries A.D. and is of Anglian origin. As several other pre-historic strongholds in Galloway were also re-used in the Dark Ages, and some were found not to be pre-historic at all, the lack of Iron Age artefacts from Tynron Doon should not come as a surprise.

This attractive hillfort, with its considerable defences from several building phases, is a fascinating site to visit. If the central citadel dates from the Iron Age, then the site could have been defended, on and off, for about 1,500 years until relatively recently. That is quite rare for a pre-historic site, and especially a hillfort, but one can understand why the owner of the tower-house abandoned his exposed pile, especially if marauding bands were no longer likely to threaten his wellbeing.

One wonders just how much of the original Iron Age stonework was used to build the tower-house, and how much has been subsequently re-used in my friend's family home?

WHITE CASTLE (Hillfort)

East Lothian O/S Landranger map 67 ref. 613686

Directions: From Edinshall hillfort, return to the B6355, turn right and continue until the Whiteadder Reservoir is crossed. Turn right along the minor road at the end of the reservoir and the hillfort is on the right after about 3 miles.

Lying on the northern slopes of the Lammermuir Hills, White Castle is overlooked by hills to the south, east and west, while to the north looms the daunting, distant mass of the one-time oppidum of Traprain Law*. This is the heart of the Votadini tribal territory in which there are many small hillforts. White Castle is not only a good example of these, but it is next to the road and has an informative notice board.

There could not be an easier hillfort to visit, though. One practically falls out of the car into it. Three ramparts and ditches enclose an area of 230 ft. x 180 ft. These can best be seen in the southern half, for the steeper northern side probably did not warrant such defences and there has been some slippage down the hill.

White Castle, foreground, has views of Traprain Law (centre) and North Berwick Law (back, right) hillforts and across the Firth of Forth to Fife (back, left).

The aforementioned notice board once suggested that the hillfort dated to c. 600 B.C., but from 2010 to 2013, inclusive, a series of excavations gave a modified insight into the hillfort's past. It now seems that the inner rampart was built c. 400 B.C., at the site of a possible earlier enclosure. This comprised soil and spoil between stone kerbs and was about 10 ft. wide, it is now barely a foot high, with an 8 ft. wide ditch.

The other two ramparts, the more prominent ones facing the road, were built a bit later in much the same way, with the middle one built in two phases and being 15 ft. wide, and the outer one about 12 ft. wide. Despite their size at the south, the excavations found these two ramparts were terraces facing the downward slopes to the north: evidence of a palisade fence was also found on that side. There are entrances in the south-east, south-west and north-west.

Inside, a few, feint hut circles/platforms could be made out, but the excavations discovered 18. These were probably occupied until the 2nd century B.C., aligning with a C-14 date from the outer rampart. It was found that the outer rampart and ditch had collapsed in places several times – probably not an entirely unusual occurrence, giving the impression that White Castle was slowly deteriorating towards abandonment.

So, White Castle was probably a small settlement of farming people, one of hundreds in the Borders. A defended settlement rather than a true stronghold, as were probably the vast majority of similar pre-historic sites. Was it ever occupied when the Votadini was a recognised tribe and when Romans came, I wonder?

This is the best of the three colour-named hillforts near each other, but was unlikely to be a site of any greater, or lesser, importance in the Iron Age. It is certainly worth visiting en route from Edinshall* to Traprain Law* and is, quite rarely, a hillfort that can be viewed from above, or from the comfort of your car.

Other Pre-historic Sites
Friar's Nose (Hillfort) Map 67 ref. 664632
Black Castle (Hillfort) Map 67 ref. 580662
Green Castle (Hillfort) Map 67 ref. 582657

WHITESIDE HILL (Hillfort)

Peebles-shire O/S Landranger map 72 ref. 168461

Directions: Leave Peebles on the A72 heading west. Turn right on the B7059 towards Romannobridge and, after nearly 2 miles, a track leads to Whiteside Farm on the right. Follow this and a path leads up to the hillfort.

More so than almost anywhere else in Scotland, the numerous Borders' hillforts come in all shapes and sizes. Whiteside is a circular hillfort with multiple lines of ramparts that encompass at least four distinct phases of occupation. At first, it expanded, but latterly contracted to barely half its greatest size. For this, Whiteside is not unique, though it is a very attractive hillfort that can be seen from the A72.

Situated on a spur of Whiteside Hill, the hillfort overlooks the confluence of Flemington Burn and Lyne Water. Although 1,200 feet above sea level, that means nothing in the Borders and the only views of any real distance are to the south and west. It also stands above cultivation terraces that might date to Roman times – the invading Latins having a considerable interest in this part of Scotland for an unwanted length of time.

Whiteside's earliest defences are the single rampart and ditch that enclose about 250 feet of the spur. These were joined in pre-Roman times by two outer ramparts and ditches. Together, these formed a series of defences that gave considerable advantages of depth and height to the inhabitants. Within the interior are hut platforms that probably date from these earlier phases. In addition, cutting-off the easiest approaches, from the north-east and south-west, are outer enclosures formed by a bank and ditch – these might have been used for herding cattle and sheep.

It is likely that these pre-historic phases of occupation may have been followed by a period of abandonment, for in Roman times a stone wall was erected within the earliest defences. Although quite ruinous, this wall is visible throughout its circuit and encloses an area with a diameter of about 200 feet.

Following another period of abandonment, Whiteside's final occupation is defined by a badly ruined wall enclosing only some 140 ft. x 80 ft. of the interior. The reduction of Whiteside hillfort can be put in context if viewed as the original hillfort expanding as the Iron Age prospered, before the arrival of the Romans. This was followed by a period of dis-use and then re-occupation – possibly between the Roman invasions of the 1st and 2nd centuries A.D. Finally, once the Romans had mostly left for good, a final re-occupation took place in advance of more settled times. Such a chronology is, of course, no more than conjecture.

The combination of four phases of occupation, a pleasant location and the condition of the various ruined defences, make Whiteside one of the more fascinating Borders' hillforts to visit. It is situated in an area thickly populated with hillforts, Roman forts and other pre-historic defences, to say nothing of medieval and later fortifications. The Borders has almost always been an area of turmoil, and the sheer number of defended settlements suggests that pre-historic times were as violent as any.

Other Pre-historic Sites
Henderland Hill (Hillfort) Map 72 ref. 149459
Harehope Rings (Hillfort) Map 72 ref. 196445
Hallyne Roman Fort Map 72 ref. 185405

WODEN LAW (Hillfort and Roman Practice Camp)

Roxburgh-shire O/S Landranger map 80 ref. 768125
Pennymuir Roman camps ref. 755138
Chew Green Roman Forts (Northumberland) ref. 787085

Directions to Woden Law: Take the minor road from Jedburgh through Oxnam and turn left along the road that follows Oxnam Water, past Swinside Hall. At the junction, turn left for a mile, and then turn right: the best of the Pennymuir Roman camps are on the right. Continue along the road to Kale Water. Park on the right. Cross Kale Water at the ford and the track ahead follows Dere Street. Once at the top, Woden Law is on the right.

It is easy to visit the Pennymuir camps and Woden Law together, but if your interest is restricted to native fortresses, then Woden Law is equally fascinating by itself. Although, on initial acquaintance, it has the impression of being a multi-vallate hillfort, it is a product of three distinct phases.

The most obvious aspect of the hillfort is its dominating location. To the north, one can see towards Hownham Law* hillfort, while The Cheviot broods away in the north-east. Yet, despite this outstandingly strategic site, fully 1,390 feet above sea level, the land to the east was convenient to farm.

A single stone-faced rampart enclosed 450 ft. x 180 ft. for the first hillfort; the second bank from the interior. This had entrances in the north, east and south-west, and probably dates from the later centuries in the first millennium B.C. As such, this would have been similar to hundreds of other Borders' hillforts.

At a later date, possibly in response to an external threat, such as the arrival of Agricola and the Romans in c. 80 A.D., a pair of ramparts and median ditch were built outside the original wall on all bar the effectively inaccessible west side. The inner of these ramparts was built of spoil from the original rampart and was faced by its stone; the outer rampart was of glacis construction revetted with timber. These Phase

2 defences offered increased protection in depth, although the interior was still within range of a javelin or sling-stone. There was also an additional enclosure, possibly for cattle and sheep, to the immediate south.

No matter how substantial were these defences, they were no match for the Romans who demolished them and cleared the hillfort. Whether this was with or without resistance is not known, but would Woden's – or any strongholds – residents have simply abandoned their hillfort, and effectively their entire world, without a fight? Either way, whatever pact the Latin invaders had with the Votadini tribe, and Woden Law may have been within the Selgovae tribal area in any case, they were not going to allow the natives to occupy a hillfort in such a strategic position. Woden Law most certainly commands both the Pennymuir camps and Dere St. for miles into the distance, and cleared it was.

At this stage, leave the hillfort, but not before observing the two banks and three ditches that encircle it on all except the west side. These were the first Roman practice siege-works at the site, probably used by soldiers from the Pennymuir camps. In reality, these are within throwing distance of the hillfort, far too close to be the real thing, as you can find out for yourself. Roman soldiers might have a fearless reputation, but trying to build such works under a hail of missiles would surely have been beyond even them.

Further outside these are two sets of incomplete ditches with a median rampart. These are joined by a similar east-west traverse to the south, and are probably a later work, possibly following the Roman re-occupation of the Borders in the mid-2nd century A.D. Near the traverse bank there is also a suspected ballista mound, just for good measure. All these make for a pretty impressive set of siege-works, although a bit overkill for what would have been a relatively easy hillfort to capture. Limited excavation, in 1950, confirmed that these siege-works were merely for practice.

Returning to the hillfort, after the Romans had finally departed, Woden Law was re-fortified once again. The inner-most wall, another grass-covered mound about 9 feet thick, enclosed about 400 ft. x 160 ft. within the original wall. You can have a bit of fun in spotting the sites of many round houses in the north, although they might belong to any of the hillfort's three phases of occupation.

Woden Law is a wondrous site as a hillfort, both for its strategic location and for the outstanding Roman siege works. It is compact and is easy to reach, while still being secluded, just the sort of place where one's imagination can run wild. Looking down on Dere St., are you sure that isn't a squadron of Roman soldiers marching from Chew Green to the Pennymuir camps? A sight far from welcome to the original occupants.

Pennymuir Roman Camps

The largest camp is to the south-west of the junction and encloses 42 acres within a bank and ditch. The bank is up to 4 feet high in places, the ditch about 3 feet deep. There were six entrances, only five of which survive, and the whole could accommodate two legions in tents, about 10,000 men.

Within the south-east corner of this camp is a second, later camp. This is considerably smaller, not quite so obviously apparent, but is still visible, and also has several entrances. There are also the faint remains of two more camps: one to the east, between Dere St.

and Kale Water; the other astride the road running east from the road junction. These are the finest preserved marching camps, as opposed to permanent forts, in Scotland.

Chew Green Roman Camps

To visit the Chew Green camps, you can take an 8-mile circular walk. From your car parked for Woden Law, walk south along the track following Kale Water for 1 1/2 miles, to Nether Hindhope Farm. Follow the track on the left and take the path on the right up the hill. After 1 1/4 miles, turn left, east, along the Pennine Way for 3/4 mile – crossing into England – and where the Pennine Way turns sharp left, Chew Green sits in the angle. To return to Woden Law, follow the Pennine Way north for a further 1 1/4 miles and then take the Roman road, Dere St., on the left for 2 miles. Woden Law is on the left before the descent back to Kale Water. A most fascinating walk and quite beautiful scenery.

Four camps overlay each other at this complex site. The first dates to the Agricolan campaign, while a convoy protection post dates to the Antonine invasion. There were wagon parks onto Dere St., the Roman equivalent of lorry parks on, say, the A1. Dere St. was, after all, the major route from north-east England into Scotland and was, in all probability, an important pre-historic route long before the Romans annexed it. For the really energetic, there are further marching camps to the south, along Dere St., at grid ref. 815057, and also at High Rochester, ref. 833986, with its stone ruins.

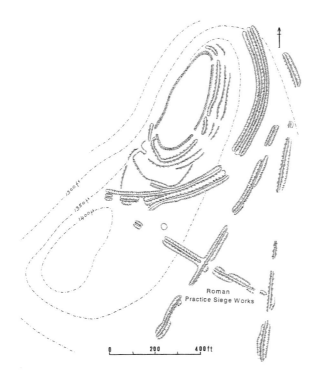

CENTRAL SCOTLAND AND ANGUS
STRONGHOLDS AND MAP

SITE	COUNTY	O/S MAP	MAP ref.	OTHER
1 Antonine Wall	Stirling	65	814793	Seabegs Wood
1 Antonine Wall	Stirling	65	865798	Watling Lodge
1 Antonine Wall	Stirling	65	855798	Tentfield Plantation
2 Ardoch	Perth	57/58	839099	Roman fort
3 Bar Hill	Dunbarton (det.)	64	707759	Roman fort
4 Barry Hill	Perth	53	262504	Hillfort
5 Bochastle	Perth	57	601075	Hillfort
6 Castle Greg	West Lothian	65	050592	Roman camp
7 Castlehill Wood Dun	Stirling	57	750909	Dun
8 Castle Law	Mid-Lothian	66	229638	H/F & souterrain
9 Castle Law	Perth	58	100155	Hillfort
10 Caterthun (Brown)	Angus	44	555668	Hillfort
11 Caterthun (White)	Angus	44	548660	Hillfort
12 Coldoch Broch	Perth	57	697982	
13 Dundurn Hillfort	Perth	51	707233	
14 Dunsinane Hillfort	Perth	53	214316	& Souterrain
15 Finavon	Angus	54`	506556	Vitrified H/F
16 Gask Ridge	Perth	58	various	Roman watch-towers
17 Inchtuthil	Perth	53	125397	Roman fort
18 Norman's Law	Fife	59	305202	Hillfort
19 Rough Castle	Stirling	65	843799	& Roman wall
20 Sheep Hill Hillfort	Dunbarton	64	435746	& Cup & ring carvings
21 Torwood Broch	Stirling	65	833849	Broch

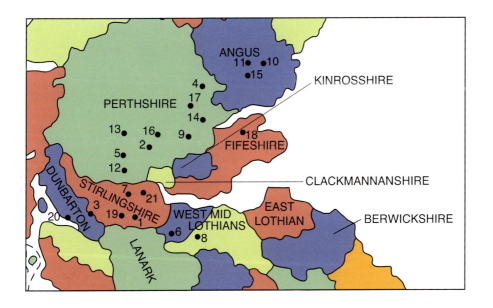

ANTONINE WALL (Roman Wall)

Stirlingshire O/S Landranger map 65 Seabegs Wood ref. 814793,
Tentfield Plantation ref. 855798, Watling Lodge ref. 865798

Directions:

Watling Lodge. Leave Falkirk on the A803. Turn left onto the B816 towards High Bonnybridge along Tamfourhill Rd., at Camelon. A sign-post indicates the site after 3/4 mile.

Tentfield Plantation. Continue farther west along the B816. Turn right at the cross-roads and a sign indicates the site on the left.

Seabegs Wood. Continue west along the B816 through High Bonnybridge. Pass under two railway bridges (the road to Rough Castle* is through the small industrial estate on the right) and turn left on the road to Castlecary. A sign indicates the site, nearly one mile along the road on the left.

The Antonine Wall was one of the great Roman structures. It runs for 37 miles from Bo'ness, on the Forth, to Old Kilpatrick on the Clyde and effectively cuts Scotland in half. So ideal was its course that, for the most part, the defensive wall and ditch, and most of its 16 known – and 19 supposed – forts, have been either destroyed, or subsequently built upon. Anyone thinking that they will see ruins on the scale of Hadrian's Wall will be disappointed, but there are several sections that give a fine impression of the scale of the original wall.

For a start, the Antonine Wall was not built of stone, but of turf on a stone base. There is nothing surprising about this – rather Hadrian's Wall is unusual, but it was obviously more susceptible to weathering over the 1,880 years since first begun. Despite there being a fair amount of archaeological and historical evidence of events at the time of the Antonine Wall, historians are still unsure and divided as to why the wall was built, and what was its ultimate fate.

Antoninus Pius succeeded Hadrian as Roman Emperor in 138 A.D. He appointed Quintus Lollius Urbicus as Governor of Britain and, shortly afterwards, incursions into southern Scotland began. These lands had been subdued by Agricola in the 80s A.D., but after his recall to Rome, all direct control was lost.

By 142 A.D., the Romans had built a fort at Cramond, on the Forth, and it seems that the Antonine Wall was begun at that time. Certainly, Antoninus accepted the salutation of Imperator for the invasion of Scotland, the only military accolade in his name, so this seems a reasonable date. The wall was built by men from the three legions then stationed in Britain: II Augusta (from Caerleon), VI Vitrix (York) and the XX Valeria Vitrix, (Chester). So, the campaign had the full weight of Roman military power behind it.

The wall was heavily garrisoned and forts were built and occupied to the north. This scenario did not last long, for by the mid-150s A.D. trouble was brewing, probably with the Brigantes tribe in northern England. Re-inforcements were brought in from Germany and the Antonine Wall and forts were evacuated and burnt, most likely by the departing Romans. Scotland's natives seem to have taken this opportunity to help the Romans on their way, for there is evidence of a slaughter at the large Roman base of Newstead, but whether similar results were achieved at any of the Antonine Wall forts is unknown.

Then, after the supposed Brigantian uprising was put down, the Antonine Wall was re-occupied c. 160 A.D., but was abandoned again in about 163 A.D., after the death of Antoninus Pius. That might have been that for the wall, although it might have been re-occupied again in the late-2nd century. As yet, hard supporting evidence is at a premium.

Quite why the Antonine invasion ever took place is another matter for much conjecture. None of the Scottish campaigns, from Agricola's onwards, ever gave the Romans any substantial economic or political gains, so why did Antoninus think he could do any better? One theory contends that, as he had no military reputation, here was an opportunity to gain one at little risk to his position. After all, a military reverse by the unco-ordinated tribes of Scotland would hardly threaten the empire itself, while that very fact increased the likelihood of an easy victory. If this were the case, then Antoninus seems to have been both successful and right. It was just unfortunate that the, supposed, Brigantian uprising caused problems when it did.

The three sites mentioned here can all be visited in one trip, along with Rough Castle.

Watling Lodge

Here stood an important northern gateway, though nothing can be seen as it lies under the house bearing the name. There is, however, the only stretch of the ditch to the original V shape, measuring 40 feet wide and 15 feet deep. Unfortunately, the wall is not seen to its best advantage and neither is the fortlet that guarded the entrance. This was revealed by excavation in 1972-4 and measured 50 ft. x 60 ft., but is now buried beneath some recent houses.

Tentfield Plantation

You can walk from here to Rough Castle*, but it is overgrown in the summer. The wall is still about 4 feet high and its line can be traced through the woods. Two of the 6 known beacon platforms are also visible, one about 170 yards beyond Lime Rd. and the second 45 yards east of the railway crossing.

Seabegs Wood

Nothing remains of the fort, but there is a good length of ditch visible with the wall up to 3 ft. 6 in. high behind it. There is also perhaps the best section of the Military Way road that ran parallel to the wall. This appears as a mound about 1 foot high and 24 ft. wide and can be seen to the south of the wall.

Other Antonine Wall Sites in Book
Rough Castle (fort), Bar Hill (fort)

ARDOCH (Roman fort)

Perthshire O/S Landranger map 57 ref. 839099

Directions: Take the A9 north from Stirling, through Dunblane. Turn left on the A822 and as you leave Braco at a sharp left-hand bend, there is a small parking area. The Roman fort is through a gate on the right of the road.

Though this book contains the best Roman sites, Scotland is not renown for any particularly spectacular strongholds built by our Latin invaders. Yet, some Roman historians regard Ardoch's earthworks as not only the finest in Britain, but the best within the former Roman Empire. They were very effective when built, remain very impressive and are quite rightly renown, both in general and for their complexity.

That says a great deal about the lack of public awareness of our native pre-historic strongholds, for if you visit all the sites in this book, Ardoch could easily fail to make it into your personal 'top ten'. Of course, any direct comparison needs to be tempered, as a great many Scottish Iron Age strongholds had drystone walls and not turf ramparts. This is not to decry the merits of Ardoch, for it deserves its fine reputation, but puts matters into perspective.

As seen today, Ardoch fort dates from the Antonine-era: the mid-2nd century A.D. It is but one of several forts or marching camps in the immediate vicinity. The larger, temporary camps lie to the north and north-east, and over-lap both each other and the main fort.

The six ramparts and ditches in the north-east corner at Ardoch.

Traces of these can be seen, but they pale in comparison with Ardoch itself: two apparently date from the time of Agricola, c. 80 A.D., while the others were used during the campaigns of Septimus Severus in 208/9 A.D. One may have been able to hold 30,000 men.

Originally, at the time of Agricola's campaigns, Ardoch covered about 8 ½ acres and the outer three ramparts at the north and east date from that time. The fort, with the rest of the Roman strongholds north of the Forth/Clyde isthmus, was abandoned in the late-80s and was re-occupied during the Antonine period. A smaller fort was required, of about 5 ½ acres, so inner ramparts were added, reducing the size and strengthening the defences.

The interior contained the usual array of buildings associated with Roman forts, of which nothing is visible today. The western defences were never as extensive, but the road has reduced them further. The inner rampart and ditch are visible and continue round the south where faint traces of several outer ditches can be seen.

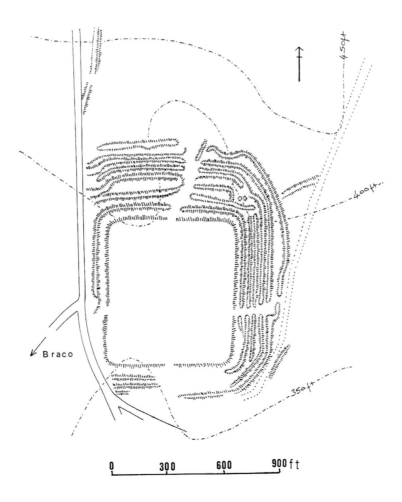

It is at the east side in particular, with an inner rampart and five external ditches all enclosed by a further rampart, that one can appreciate the sheer scale of Ardoch's defences. These are impressive and it would be unlikely that many potential attackers would have reached the inner rampart in one piece. There is a causeway across the ditches with an offset outer gateway; another can be seen in the north, and there would have been others through the west and south walls. Remember, the inner rampart would have had a tall, stout wooden palisade fence on top as well.

The eastern defences were not uniform round the whole fort; the north ditches are wider spaced and have an additional rampart. The outer rampart is continued round and, with marshy ground to the east and south, the fort would have been nigh-impregnable, except to the most determined attack.

During the Agricolan era campaigns, the Ardoch camps were intended as little more than temporary bases as the Romans pushed on north. The fort here was one of four along the Gask frontier system and was of considerable importance. In the Antonine period, the reduced size Ardoch fort was a lynch-pin of the advance defences for the Antonine Wall. Ardoch's ramparts are built of turf on a stone base, just like the wall itself.

Here, then, in the 150s A.D., Ardoch was the major Roman fort north of the Antonine Wall. Today, it offers a magnificent example of Roman defences and a rare opportunity to compare these with native strongholds. The latter may often appear to be more impressive but, with Roman soldiers, Ardoch would certainly be the more impregnable. Sections of the larger, temporary camps can be seen at map refs. 840107 and 839109.

BAR HILL (Roman Fort)

Dunbartonshire (det.) O/S Landranger map 64 ref. 707759

Directions: From Rough Castle*, also on the Antonine Wall, take the A803 west from Bonnybridge. Turn left at the junction at Queenzieburn, west of Kilsyth, turn right on the B8032 and immediately left. Cross the Forth and Clyde Canal in Twechar, park and follow the line of the Antonine Wall east for about a mile. The fort is to the south of the line of the wall.

The earthworks of Bar Hill fort do not compare with those of either Rough Castle*, or Ardoch* fort to the north. Nevertheless, it is interesting as the stone wall footings can be seen, unlike at either of the other aforementioned forts, while it is situated at the highest point of the wall.

Bar Hill is just to the south of the Antonine Wall. The former Military Way, also not visible, passed between the wall and the fort. Although not as well-preserved as at Rough Castle*, the line of the rampart can be seen, indicating the fort's size. At about 3 1/2 acres, Bar Hill is much bigger than Rough Castle* and lies between the forts of Croy Hill, to the east and Auchendavy. Here, then, was a fort of no little importance.

The foundations of the Principia at Bar Hill.

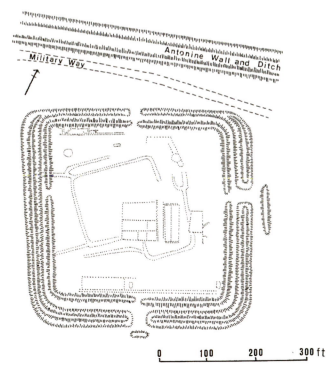

In the centre of the fort, the footings of the Principia can be seen, and sections of the bath-house and well have been consolidated and left open. At Rough Castle*, the bath-house, a potential fire hazard, was located in an annexe outside the fort. During excavations, from which the extensive report Bar Hill: A Roman Fort and Its Finds (Brit. Arch. Report no. 16, 1975) was compiled, several of the garrison's altars were found thrown down the well. This possibly occurred when the Romans abandoned Bar Hill, along with the rest of the Antonine Wall*, in the c. 160s A.D.

Bar Hill was an orthodox, rectangular fort with a single turf rampart, built on a stone base, and defended by two outer ditches on three sides and a single ditch to the north. There was a gateway in each of the four sides, with a causeway across the ditches, but the western gateway was not central and had no causeway either.

Of equal interest, though completely unseen today, was the discovery of a smaller, probably Agricolan, fort of about the size of Rough Castle*, within the main fort area. As at Ardoch, the Romans seem to have re-used several sites previously dating from the Agricolan campaigns of the late-1st century A.D. Perhaps the isthmus between the Forth and Clyde was selected as a site for a permanent boundary before Agricola was re-called to Rome and the campaign abandoned?

While the remains are something less than awe-inspiring, you still get a good idea of the strategic value of the Antonine Wall* at its highest point. The Campsie Fells are clearly visible, and a long section of the Forth-Clyde isthmus would have fallen under the immediate gaze of Romans patrolling the wall. Of that, nothing now remains, but there is a section of the ditch going east for about 1/2 mile, towards Croy Hill fort.

It is the location and the internal remains that make Bar Hill worth visiting. Many a native stronghold is visually superior, but the Roman incursions into Scotland were always somewhat transitory, and Bar Hill makes an interesting comparison with that of the better known Rough Castle*.

BARRY HILL (Hillfort)

Perthshire O/S Landranger map 53 ref. 262504

Directions: Take the A926 towards Aylth. Turn left on the B924 bypassing Aylth to the east. The hillfort is on the right about half-a-mile beyond the turning on the right to Shanzie, still on the B924.

The wide, fertile Strathmore, with its pleasant climate, has long held an attraction for both native and invader alike. The Romans, in the 80s A.D., briefly established control of the strath, and its importance in Iron Age times can be gauged by the number of hillforts with considerable defensive capability, along the flanking hills – several are featured in this book. Barry, or Barra, Hill overlooks Aylth Water and has extensive views in both directions along Strathmore.

From the above, one would be forgiven for assuming that Barry Hill was in a pretty dominant location but, once you arrive there, it is obvious that this is far from being the case. Yes, there are commanding views, but barely half-a-mile to the west, the Hill of Aylth overlooks the hillfort while, of course, the great mass of mountains to the north does likewise.

It is worth pondering why hillforts were built in such exposed locations, and by whom. Was Barry Hill a frontier post for a tribe based in the mountains, possibly like the Brown* and White Caterthuns*, while Finavon* and Kemp's Castle served the same purpose for a tribe from the south? Perhaps all these hillforts formed a deep frontier network of, say, the Vacomagi tribe to deter and keep out the wild hordes from the north? Nobody knows the answer, but one cannot ignore certain building similarities, whether coincidental, or otherwise.

Each of the above-mentioned hillforts has a single stone wall; all, bar Finavon*, have evidence of more than one period of building. Such facts may, or may not, be relevant, while the similarity of Barry Hill to the White Caterthun*, the Barmekin of Echt* and others, in having a stone rampart – seemingly without an entrance – built over an earlier, multi-rampart settlement, may also be co-incidental. I am afraid that you will have to try and decided for yourself, for archaeology has little excavated evidence to go on at the moment.

The single rampart, with stone visible on the south and on the inner edge of the north side, must have once been of quite grand proportions. It encloses an area about 250 feet long by 100 feet wide, about 1/2 acre. Its tumbled mass is now spread up to 30 feet wide in places, while it is still up to 8 feet above the interior. There is a ditch at the south that is partially scree-filled, and in this can be seen vitrified stone. This means that the main wall was very likely timber-laced, possibly being built on the early Iron Age and, given the great mass of stone, must surely have been pretty impressive.

To the south, running at an ever-increasing distance from the stone wall, until it is about 50 feet away on the east side, is an outer rampart. This finally becomes a huge club of a bank cutting-off the approach from the east, with a gap at the north for an entrance; there is no corresponding gap in the stone rampart. This, then, was a pretty

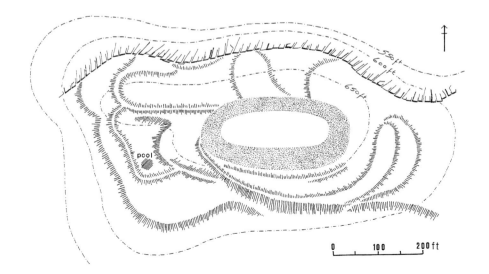

formidable hillfort that could undoubtedly withstand a typical Iron Age raid until, that is, fire was introduced into the equation. Here was the big weakness of the timber-laced stone rampart and Barry Hill, along with many others – including Finavon*, succumbed to the torch: either that, or one of the inhabitants was particularly careless.

Yet, for all that, there are confusing surface traces of an even earlier settlement. These include slight banks that run beneath the great wall and must clearly pre-date it. Whether Barry Hill was continuously occupied, or was abandoned between the two settlements, is unknown. Similarly with the pond to the west; it could have belonged to either period, or neither.

Overlooked or not, Barry Hill holds a commanding position. Making your way along the hillforts of Strathmore will give a better insight to their inter-dependence than any amount of book-work can currently deliver, and is far more fun, to boot.

BOCHASTLE (Hillfort)

Perthshire O/S Landranger map 57 ref. 601075

Directions: Leave Callander, heading west, on the A84 and turn left on the A821. After about 3/4 mile, there is a turning on the left. Park nearby and the hillfort is 1/4 mile up the hill to the north-west. It is best approached from the west.

Bochastle is known locally as Dunmore, the big fort, and, at barely 1/2 acre, one must assume that the 'big' refers to its defences. Quite rightly so. At 600 feet above the sea - yet over 2,200 feet below the summit of Ben Ledi to the north-west, it still takes a bit of an effort to visit it. The rocky knoll on which Bochastle stands, and the outline of its four ramparts, are clearly visible from the road 400 feet below. Bochastle seems to have been specifically built to overlook both Loch Venachar and the pass, as was the Roman fort 250 feet below the hillfort, to the south-west - now no longer visible.

The almost sheer drop to the east saved the Iron Age builders the trouble of erecting any defences there, but they made up for it with the mightily impressive defences elsewhere. Four stone, now mostly turf-covered, ramparts encircle the knoll, with the inner three ramparts each having an external ditch. In addition, a small plateau to the north is enclosed by a much slighter bank, through which there is an entrance where it adjoins the main defensive system. This bank ends just short of the cliff edge where, no doubt, entry was gained into the main fort.

The interior, which measures about 180 ft. x 150 ft., holds little of interest, other than a central depression that might have been a well. Yet, the scale of the defences indicates that Bochastle was more than, say, a simple defended village. As seen from without - in its Iron Age pomp, Bochastle's defences must have appeared awesome, sitting as they do right on the edge of the knoll, letting all and sundry know they were being watched.

At the south, there are original entrances through the outer and inner-most ramparts; the track through the middle two is modern. This indicates that the outer and inner ramparts were built first, or perhaps just one of them initially. However, the track

Bochastle is a compact, well-defended and strategically located hillfort.

through the other two might have destroyed an entrance, so such a chronology is not beyond question. Nevertheless, it seems likely that Bochastle, as with so many multi-rampart hillforts, was built in several phases. Whether occupation was continuous or not, is one of the many questions that, as usual, remains unanswered.

Bochastle's location is both spectacular and beautiful. Though east of Strath Gartney and The Trossachs, it commands a route through the glens important enough for the Romans to build a fort at its head in c. 85 A.D.; a so-called Glen Blocker fort. More than its location though, it is the scale of the defences that demand attention. Quite what was going on to determine the need for four ramparts and three ditches on what is, after all, a pretty inaccessible knoll is difficult to comprehend. It appears to be far more a stronghold than a defended settlement, and perhaps therein lies the key to its pre-historic past.

BROWN CATERTHUN (Hillfort)

Angus O/S Landranger map 44 ref. 555668

Directions: As for the White Caterthun, except it is along the path up the hill to the east on the right of the lay-by.

In most respects, as hillforts go, the White Caterthun* beats its neighbour hands-down. Quite apart from the massive stone rampart and the far better state of preservation of its defences, it is also situated 35 feet higher. Let that not put you off a visit to the Brown Caterthun, though, for with its five lines of roughly concentric defences, it, too, is an astonishing hillfort.

The defences are not particularly visual, especially on the western half that is covered in heather, but they combine to create one of Scotland's most fascinating hillforts. Yet, the inner-most defence, a circular stone wall that is covered by heather, is barely visible for much of its circuit. This encloses the summit area, measuring about 250 ft. x 200 ft., with an equally hard-to-distinguish well just beyond the fence. There is a single entrance in the north, so it is totally unlike the great central citadel of its neighbour.

Ranging from 60 to 175 feet outside this is a second line of defence that appears as a low bank, but which was probably a stone wall. In places, this is spread to about 25 ft. thick and has, wait for it, fully nine entrances, all a simple straight-through type: one had a timber-lined passage. If an entrance is a potential weakspot in a stronghold, then heaven-help the Brown Caterthun's inhabitants. These all appear to be original and, given their lack of sophistication, suggest the rampart may have been built early in the first millennium B.C. Or was it a stock enclosure or something similar?

It is tempting to say that no other Scottish pre-historic stronghold has so many entrances, but just outside this lies a third rampart with ditch and counterscarp bank, also with nine aligned entrances. One might well expect these two to be contemporary – and so they might be, but some archaeologists beg to differ.

Still farther outside is a fourth line of defence, roughly concentric, but with a distinct kink in the east. This was built from stone, earth and turf and was timber-laced, too, and is the most prominent of the defences, possibly dating to before 400 B.C. It has eight entrances, most of which roughly align with those of the inner ramparts, and beyond lies another rampart and ditch, with slight counterscarp bank. This fifth defensive line has an even more pronounced kink at the east, which opens out to form an enclosure between the two outer defensive lines: these defences are the easiest part of the hillfort to see. The fifth line of defence also has eight entrances, seven of which align with those of the fourth line, while six of those have additional low banks alongside the connecting causeway.

Some excavations were undertaken in 1995 and 1996, which revealed evidence of how the various ramparts were built and evolved. A cobbled entrance passage was found, along with evidence of a burned palisade fence. The largest rampart was dated to about 500 to 400 B.C., with other materials elsewhere dating from c. 800 to 150 B.C., so it appears to have had a long period of use.

As for a sequence of building, almost anything goes. About the only thing that can be stated with any certainty is that defensive lines four and five were probably contemporary. Some archaeologists feel that lines two, four and five may be of a similar age, while others think that lines two and three were. None of these, and any other combinations, has been comprehensively tested by excavation and, until that happens, guesswork rules the roost.

Perhaps of more interest is to consider just what role the Brown Caterthun played in Iron Age Strathmore. The sheer number of entrances almost precludes its use as an out-and-out stronghold, so the constant references to defensive lines may be inappropriate; it would probably have been indefensible in its current layout in any case. Some assistance might come from pondering its relationship with the White Caterthun*.

Now, it could be that the inhabitants of the Brown Caterthun moved and built the White Caterthun*, or vice versa. Of course, one or both hillforts could have been outposts, either for tribes based in the mountains to the north, or from Strathmore. On the other hand, the Brown Caterthun might be a cattle ranch with a central enclosure for the cattle hands, nominally under the auspices of the White Caterthun*. Something along those lines appears the most obvious choice, but, even so, it is unlikely that all the outer defensive lines were in use simultaneously.

A final possibility might be the use of the Brown Caterthun as a meeting venue or religious centre. It is not unlike an enlarged Neolithic causewayed camp, especially with its entrances, though such an analogy may only be a superficial impression. It is more than likely that the Brown Caterthun was a stock enclosure, at least for a part of its useful life.

While the Brown Caterthun's past remains firmly out of bounds, it is nothing that a decent, all-encompassing excavation could not put right, as with many pre-historic

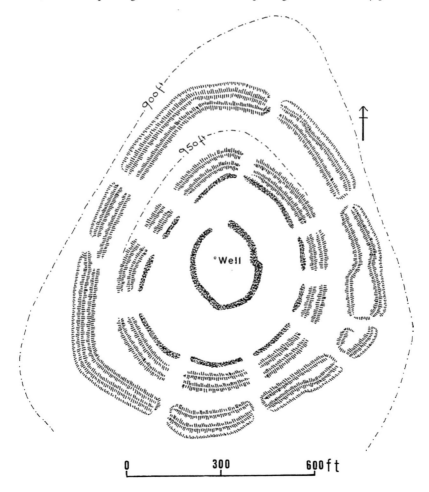

sites. Enough hillforts have had some form of investigation, so anything gained from the Brown Caterthun is only likely to be of value locally. In any case, with the increasing use of advanced archaeological techniques, hillforts might be considered to be old-hat.

Nevertheless, whereas a simple excavation might not have the same archaeological attraction as the discovery of an under-water midden at a crannog, it may be of more use to most people who might visit; people who, after all, create the wealth that allows specialists to indulge themselves. Still, with ever-scarce resources at hand, priorities have to be made, but he who pays the piper might occasionally be allowed some choice in a tune or two.

CASTLE GREG (Roman Fortlet)

West Lothian O/S Landranger map 65 ref. 050592

Directions: Leave Edinburgh heading south-west on the A70. Turn right on the B7008 towards West Calder for about 3/4 mile. The fortlet is a short walk from the road on the right, about 50 yards south of the summit of Camilty Hill, with surrounding woods.

Scotland might have a large number of Roman forts, fortlets and marching camps, but few of these are readily visible today. Rather too many are either invisible, or somewhat disappointing. Castle Greg cannot compare with, say, Ardoch* fort, but it is one of the best small fortlets and, as such, has much to commend a visit.

There is no obvious reason why Castle Greg was built. It lies on the lower northern slopes of the Pentland Hills, at about 900 ft. above sea level. As such, it is quite a way north of the great mass of Borders' hillforts, and does not appear to be near a Roman road either. That alone might suggest that Castle Greg dates from the very first Roman incursions into Scotland and was by-passed by the later roads.

Castle Greg lies on a small plateau just below the summit of Camilty Hill and is of the standard Roman design. A single rampart encloses an area measuring about 180 ft. x 150 ft. with an entrance facing east. This is further protected by a rampart and ditches on either side, giving the Romans their traditional killing fields in front of the main rampart. The causeway between the ditches and outer rampart is 22 ft. wide, but narrows to only 10 ft. at the inner rampart. It was just about big enough to squeeze 100 men within the defences.

The defences are best seen on the south and east sides, but are visible for the whole circuit. Naturally, nothing of the interior layout remains, but a hollow towards the centre indicates the position of a possible well; if so, Castle Greg might have been, at least, semi-permanently occupied.

It could be that Castle Greg was strategically placed just to let the locals know that the Romans were never far away. There are Roman military camps in all sorts of seemingly out-of-the-way places, but this is certainly more than a simple marching camp. Perhaps its relative isolation is one reason it has survived.

Excavations in the 19th century produced a large quantity of Roman coins from under a large stone. Surveys this century have revealed possible an annexe, but nothing visible to see.

Castle Greg will not take your breath away, either for its remains or location. It is a rare surviving example of a stronghold that was, if not common-place, seen throughout Britain in the early centuries A.D. The defences can also be readily compared with those of the numerous native hillforts of similar size not too far to the south.

CASTLE LAW (Hillfort)

Mid-Lothian O/S Landranger map 66 ref. 229638

Directions: Leave Edinburgh on the A702. About 3 miles south of the A720 outer ring road, the hillfort is signposted on the right, about 1/2 mile up a farm road to the car park. It is in the care of Historic Scotland.

Castle Law is a fine, typical small hillfort of the type so prevalent in the hills of southern Scotland. Standing on the lower slopes to the east of the Pentland Hills, it has good views in that direction, but is easily overlooked by hills on the other sides. This, at least, suggests that it was not of major strategic value, more a local stronghold.

It was excavated in 1931/2 and, as with so many small hillforts, the excavators thought that Castle Law developed over several centuries. Initially, in phase one, a palisade enclosure existed on the site, with a wooden fence and outer ditch enclosing an oval interior, measuring about 100 x 50 yds. Nothing of this can now be seen. The inner rampart of the second phase did not correspond exactly to the line of the palisade enclosure, at least in the vicinity of the main gateway.

This phase marked the building of the inner rampart, with outer ditch, both clearly visible today. The rampart was reinforced with timber beams on the inside and revetted with a rough stone wall on the outside. There was an entrance in the west and possibly another in the south. This seems to have sufficed until there was a need to strengthen the defences. Was this anything to do with the arrival of Agricola and the Romans in 80 A.D.? The additional outer ramparts and ditches that were then added would never have presented any sort of challenge to the Latin invaders, but their arrival did seem to have been the catalyst for numerous native hillforts to be strengthened in the southern Scotland hills.

What happened thereafter is open to speculation, but you can be sure that the Romans would not leave a fortified native hillfort in their midst. Still, the excavators found house foundations built along the ditches and, connected with these, a souterrain was built on the line of the middle ditch at the east end. Fortunately, this has been cleared and opened so you can now pass along this subterranean passage, complete with a once-corbelled cell 11 ft. across and 6 ft. high. This souterrain is the most impressive feature of Castle Law and dates to the 2nd or 3rd centuries A.D. A brooch, Roman pottery and glass from that period were found at the excavations.

Mind you, it is not absolutely certain that the chronological sequence of palisade enclosure, single rampart hillfort and finally multi-vallate hillfort added with the arrival of the Romans, is correct. Although perhaps not built at the time of the inner rampart and ditch, the outer ones might have been added soon after, rather than as a

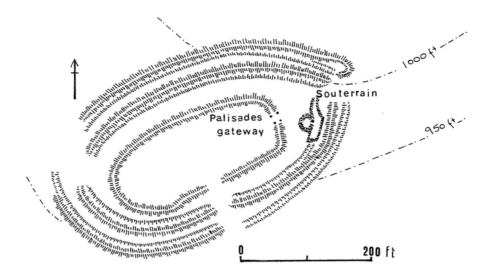

futile response to the arrival of the Romans. A modern excavation is needed to confirm the chronological sequence once and for all.

Castle Law is a decent, but not outstanding, example of what was a fairly common-place, native hillfort of south Scotland in the centuries prior to the Roman invasion. One advantage of it being in state care is the information boards, while it is one of Scotland's easiest hillforts to visit. More than anything, though, it is the enclosed souterrain that makes Castle Law such an interesting place; so far back in time, and so close to the modern capital city.

CASTLE LAW (Hillfort)

Perthshire O/S Landranger map 57 ref. 100155

Directions: Take the A912 south from Perth and turn right on the B935 towards Forgandenny. A mile after the junction, turn left along the minor road past Dummonie House and turn right at the T-junction to Glenearn. Walk south along the road and then south-west for 1/2 mile. Take the footpath on the left when you reach the electric cables, and follow this up the hill for 3/4 mile. The hillfort is on the right, to the north-east of the summit and triangulation point.

Lying 950 ft. above sea level and on top of a 700 ft. high slope, Castle Law offers fine views along Strathearn, towards the Firth of Tay and northwards to Perth. These views are worth the effort required to visit this hillfort, and walking boots are the order of the day.

The excavators of this hillfort in 1892 have teased archaeologists ever since by revealing that the sockets of the timber-laced stone walls were found intact, yet gave no further details. If found today, these could have provided invaluable evidence about timber-laced walls, but only a plan of the hillfort remains. (Excavations at Castle Law hillfort near Abernethy – see below – in 1896/8 also contained sockets for horizontal timbers running within the wall.)

Castle Law is quite unusual, but also has many similarities with other timber-laced hillforts. The main defences comprise two timber-laced stone walls on a hillock on the northern slopes of the Ochil Hills. The inner rampart encloses about 1/2 acre, measuring 180 ft. x 80 ft. with a wall about 18 ft. thick; this is the hillfort's most visible defensive feature and is likely to have been in excess of 10 ft. high. Outside this, about 25 to 50 ft. beyond, is a second, oval, timber-laced wall, barely visible in the north, up to 16 ft. thick. A much larger, less obvious enclosure surrounds this.

A survey in spring 2010, and geophysical survey and excavations in 2013 gave differing interpretations, but considered the large enclosure was possibly the earliest of all.

At the east end, there is yet another timber-laced wall that runs between and beyond the two walls. This somewhat unusual feature takes some explaining. There is an entrance to the outer enclosure at the north of this wall, but no entrance to the inner enclosure. This is not unique (see Barry Hill* or the White Caterthun*), but did not exactly make entry easy.

It may be that the outer enclosure was intended for cattle, with the inner enclosure for the inhabitants with entry being gained by a moveable structure. If this were the case, then perhaps the lateral wall was a means of gaining entry to the inner enclosure without the need to walk through the cattle enclosure. Although such an explanation might compromise the defensive attributes of the hillfort, it would be awkward for any attackers to cross this under fire from bows, spears and possibly sling-stones. Mind you, it seems an awkward way of doing things.

Castle Law is well sited strategically, but is overlooked from the south. To counter this, the depression to the south of the hillfort is traversed by a low bank and ditch, with a larger bank and ditch nearer the hillfort. This depression carries a stream in wet weather, and there are traces of two dams across at the south-western end.

To the north, the gentle sloping ground bears slight traces of a bank before the steeper slope downwards is resumed. Altogether, then, this is a well-planned and defended hillfort of a decent size. There is nothing of pre-historic note within the interior, but quite a number of families could have been housed in the inner enclosure. It certainly gives the impression of being quite a self-contained stronghold.

Quite what the tribal structure, if any, was in this part of central Scotland will remain forever unknown, but there are similarities between this hillfort and others near Tayside. This is also apparent with Castle Law hillfort at Abernethy, which suggests that, if nothing else, there was contact between the inhabitants of these defended settlements, and possibly a shared purpose.

Other Pre-historic Sites
Castle Law Hillfort, Abernethy Map 58 ref. 183153

CASTLEHILL WOOD DUN

Stirlingshire O/S Landranger map 57 ref. 750908

Directions: Leave Stirling heading south on the A9. Turn right on the A872 (Glasgow Road) and turn right into Borestone onto Barnsdale Road, which soon turns left. Turn right onto New Park Crescent, turn left into Bearside Road and turn right into Greystale Road. This crosses the motorway and continues for 3/4 mile. Park at the sign for the Absolutely Scotland Activity Centre and turn right up another track after 200 yards. Follow this beside the woods for 1/2 mile to the dun, marked by an 'Out of Bounds beyond this point' sign.

Somewhat surprisingly, there are several duns in Perthshire isolated from the majority on the western coast. Castlehill Wood, in Stirlingshire, is not only a good example close to a town, but was also excavated in 1955.

Standing on a rocky bluff on the north-east face of the Touch Hills, 650 feet above sea level, a mostly grass-covered, ruined stone wall up to 16 ft. thick encloses an egg-shaped area of 75 ft. x 50 ft. There is a good entrance in the east, complete with door-jambs and some paving stones, but the interior shows nothing, with natural rock breaking through in the centre.

The excavation revealed no permanent hearth or sign of other structures, but that does not mean the dun was not occupied. For example, wattle and daub built huts will not leave any traces after 2,000 years. Evidence was certainly uncovered that fires had been lit in various parts of the interior, so Castlehill Wood was certainly inhabited at times.

By far the most unusual facet of the dun was two intra-mural cells and passages. That in the north-west consists of a narrow passage about 6 ft. long leading to a circular chamber only 4 ft. in diameter. Just before the chamber, an even narrower passage, or perhaps a flue, left the main passage and ran for about 20 ft. within the wall, before emerging back at the dun interior. A similar passage was found in the south wall, but with an even smaller chamber. The excavator considered that these passages might have been used for grain-drying, even if this was not necessarily their original function. Quite what else these unusual features could have been used for is a matter of some conjecture.

A number of artefacts were found within the dun, including a saddle quern and some Roman glass. This rather suggests that Castlehill Wood was occupied into the 1st or 2nd centuries A.D. It is not an easy place to reach, but is a good example of a defended homestead: one in which the occupants might have had some connection with the Romans through trade rather than hostilities. It also has outstanding panoramic views, including towards Stirling Castle.

Castlehill Wood Dun lies close to several historic sites, of considerable relevance to modern Scotland, but is itself an important example of a pre-historic stronghold more readily associated with the Western Highlands and islands.

Other Pre-historic Sites
Sauchie Craig hillfort Map 57 ref. 763893
Braes hillfort Map 57 ref. 797847

COLDOCH BROCH

Perthshire O/S Landranger map 57 ref. 697982

Directions: Leave Stirling heading north-west on the A84. Turn left on the A873 and turn left again on the B8031. Go past two unmarked entrances to Coldoch House, on the left, past the wood and the first field to a track. Cross the field diagonally from the gate to the broch in the far corner. Permission to visit must be requested from Coldoch House.

This is the western-most of central Scotland's brochs. It occupies low-lying land on the north-western edge of Blairdrummond Moss. All the known brochs of central Scotland and the Borders appear to be advanced in basic design and, one might surmise, were built at about the time of the Roman incursions.

Today, trees grow from Coldoch's walls and the wall is covered in grass. It is not immediately impressive, but the inner wall and several interesting features can be seen amidst all the greenery.

Coldoch was cleared out in about 1870 and is one of the better preserved brochs away from the usual broch areas. Its courtyard is about 28 ft. across, protected by a solid wall almost 20 ft. thick. Such a ratio of wall:courtyard suggests that Coldoch was of a considerable height; more akin to Mousa* than, say, Edinshall*. Having no other natural defensive advantages further supports the likelihood that Coldoch was probably 30 ft. high, or more. The wall is built of small stones – as is Mousa* – and is now mostly only about 4 ft. high, but is a little more in the north-west.

The entrance is narrow, only about 2 ft. 6 in. inside the door-jambs, and has a bar hole. Leading off the interior are passages to three intra-mural cells, in the north, south and west. These are all small and rectangular, rather than the more usual oval shape. There are also stairs in the south-east, and two aumbries – or cupboards – low down in the wall; a feature seemingly restricted to the most recent brochs. So, although Coldoch might not immediately appear much to look at, it has many details worth inspecting.

One theory is that the brochs of central Scotland were built by specialists from the north for chiefs of the south, at the time of the Antonine invasion. Of course, this cannot be confirmed, but Coldoch has the appurtenances of the latest brochs and, as such, would not look out of place right up on the northern coast.

As for surviving a Roman attack though…

COW CASTLE

Lanarkshire O/S Landranger map 72 ref. 042331

Directions: Leave Biggar on the A702 to Coulter. Turn left in Coulter to Culteralles and turn left up the track to Nisbet Farm. Walk east along the track from the farmyard to the knoll, on which the hillfort lies.

Not surprisingly, there are many building styles on display at the hundreds of Borders' hillforts. Naturally, these reflect the environment, materials, the tribe or people who lived in the hillfort, and the reasons for its building. Cow Castle is a good example of a hillfort that has been reduced in size. Many hillforts were altered during their life-time and most were expanded, but that was not always the case in the Borders. Here is a site where a later hillfort was built right on top of an earlier one.

Standing almost 1,050 ft. above sea level, 300 ft. above tributaries of Culter Water to the north and west – and overlooking Culter Water itself, Cow Castle commands a prominent location; it is not alone in this, though. It lies at the west end of a long spur, to the north of Culter Fell, with White Hill and Mitchelhill Rings hillforts farther to the north-east. Assuming they were occupied during an over-lapping period, the inhabitants of these three hillforts can hardly have lived in splendid isolation. Both of the latter hillforts were probably developed over more than one stage, White Hill's second phase being clearly un-finished. Mitchelhill Rings, like Cow Castle, may have been reduced in size during its lifetime.

But of the three, it is Cow Castle that is the most impressive hillfort to visit. It is D-shaped and the original single rampart and ditch – where room permitted – enclosed an area of about 230 ft. x 150 ft. The entrance was in the north-west and was retained for the later hillfort. Though most of these defences have been subsequently superseded by the second hillfort, they are still visible in the south-west. Unfortunately, no dating is known at the present.

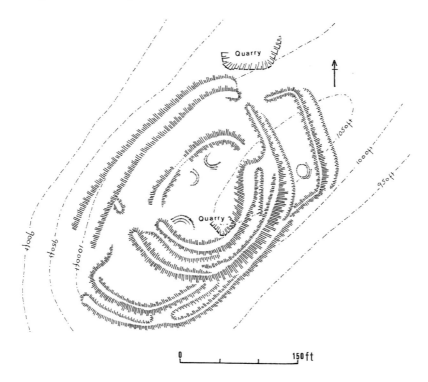

A second, D-shaped hillfort was built mostly within the lines of the earlier one, enclosing an area 140 ft. x 100 ft. This gives the appearance of a hillfort with two ramparts and ditches on all sides, but an additional rampart and ditch were only required in the south-west. A new entrance was made through the earlier defences to align with that of the later hillfort. Finally, an annexe was built outside the first hillfort's defences in the north-east, possibly as a cattle enclosure.

It is quite easy to work out the building sequence once you are at Cow Castle. Traces of 4 huts can be seen, three within the second hillfort, while the fourth is in the north-eastern annexe. (I wonder if this hut was a pre-historic equivalent of a granny-annexe?) These huts could all date from the same period and are quite typical of the timber-framed type visible at many Borders' hillforts.

Despite the miracles of modern archaeological excavation techniques, it is unlikely that anyone will find out if Cow Castle was inhabited by members of the Selgovae tribe in whose area, in Roman times, it lay. Given the proximity of the two aforementioned hillforts, it is likely that it was built by an extended family; possibly the Borders' equivalent of, say, the Mid-Howe* broch and settlement on the Orkney Islands.

One can only guess as to why Cow Castle was reduced in size – famine, or victims of a raid, if you want to be morbid – but this was probably not unconnected with the fate of its neighbours.

Other Pre-historic Sites
White Hill hillfort Map 72 ref. 055338
Mitchelhill Rings hillfort Map 72 ref. 062341

DUNDURN (Hillfort and Dark Ages)

Perthshire O/S Landranger map 51 ref. 707233

Directions: Take the A85 west from Crieff. Just before St. Fillan's, turn left along the road south of Loch Earn and park after crossing the bridge over the River Earn. Take the track east, signed to Western Dundurn, and follow this past the farm to St. Fillan's Chapel. Dundurn is up the north-west flank of the hill above.

Like Dunadd*, Dundurn is a Dark Ages' fortress built on several levels, with a central citadel thought to date from the Iron Age. Also like Dunadd*, it features in the 'Annals of Ulster', as being besieged in 683 A.D. – though Dundurn was probably a Pict stronghold. Whether Dundurn was besieged by the Dalriadans, or it was an internecine conflict, or even undertaken by, say, the Britons of Strathclyde is not clear, but it certainly commands the east-west pass of Strathearn. It was just the sort of place anyone attempting an invasion would have to overcome.

Dundurn dominated what may have been an important route between Dalriadan Argyll and the Highland Picts. It was excavated in the 1970s, from which a plausible chronological sequence emerged. Unfortunately, little was discovered of a pre-Dark Ages' settlement, although one could not be ruled out. Perhaps Dundurn is a little out of place here, but it will accompany Dunadd as another Dark Ages' stronghold with Iron Age antecedents.

The uppermost summit was fortified with a stout timber palisade. Fortunately, this has been C-14 dated to the 6th to 7th centuries A.D. What is immediately obvious is that such a stronghold would have been distinctly old-hat during anything but the early Iron Age, yet was considered good enough to last for more than 100 years in the Dark Ages. It could not be determined with any certainty whether any of the lower terraces were also fortified at that time, but that cannot be dismissed.

Phase two began with a repair of the earlier palisade and the creation of an upper citadel with a timber-laced stone wall. The timbers were secured into the wall, possibly by nails driven into the ends, as at Burghead* – another Pict stronghold. This rebuilding may have taken place before the siege of 683 A.D., or, as there was evidence of some burning, somewhat later.

A final phase involved a further rebuilding of the citadel's defences. The massive, tumbled stone wall that encloses the lower terraces was added at that time, and may have been about 15 ft. high, while additional stone walls and embankments were built lower down at the north and west. These might have been stock enclosures, but the enhanced main defences reflect a growing importance for Dundurn, whether as a

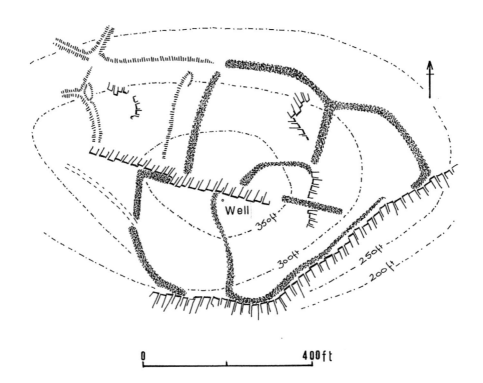

major stronghold similar to Dunadd*, or just an extremely important frontier post. There is little doubt that its command of Strathearn was for strategic purposes in those troubled times.

Among the varied artefacts found during the excavations were glass shards, some of which were imported and of fine quality, though the bone and antler artefacts were regarded as being quite poor. Most important of all was a fine leather shoe – a rare ancient recovery. This probably belonged to someone of standing (apologies for the pun) and, with the imported wares, the inference is that Dundurn was certainly a stronghold of considerable note for a lengthy period.

For the visitor, it is the massive tumbled stone walls that are the most impressive feature of this multi-phase stronghold – along with the views. Dundurn is a complex site that needs further work to determine whether there was an Iron Age hillfort or not. It may have been occupied well into, if not beyond, the 10th century A.D., but it is also the place where King Girig died, in 878 A.D. That, more than anything, shows that Dundurn has earned its place in Scottish history and deserves recognition as a rare major Dark Ages' stronghold.

DUNSINANE (Hillfort)

Perthshire O/S Landranger map 53 ref. 214316

Directions: Leave Perth, heading north-east, on the A94 and turn right along the B953. Take the second minor road on the left to Collace and at the sharp left-hand bend, just before Collace, a footpath leads south-east up to the hillfort.

Lying on a prominent hill of the north-western slopes of the Sidlaw Hills, and enjoying good views along and across Strathmore to the foothills of the Highlands, Dunsinane is a well-located hillfort. That it was one of the first hillforts to undergo a recorded digging – excavation is too grandiose a term for the damage caused – in 1854, also marks Dunsinane out as being special. However, it is Dunsinane's place in the Macbeth legend, thanks to Shakespeare, that has given it nigh-universal prominence.

That is somewhat ironic, for, quite apart from the tenuous Macbeth connection, Dunsinane is also supposedly the place where Kenneth, King of Alban, was murdered in 995 A.D. Whether true or not, Dunsinane seems to have the happy knack of featuring in the mists and myths of Scottish history at significant moments, and was surely a Dark Ages' fortress of some prominence.

Dunsinane is included here because it was an Iron Age stronghold. The conspicuous summit, measuring 180 ft. x 100 ft., is enclosed by an egg-shaped rampart. This is ruined and spreads about 30 feet across, but the early excavators thought it had been a timber-laced stone wall, having found vitrified stone among the rubble. They also found a souterrain in the interior, but this is not now visible. Unfortunately, much of the interior was damaged by the earlier diggings, particularly at the eastern end – no doubt in the hope of finding treasure connected with Macbeth. These diggings – what could be called wanton destruction nowadays – also unearthed some rectangular buildings in the interior, but the damage caused would severely compromise a modern excavation.

Two further ramparts and ditches, the latter now silted up and looking like terraces, surround the citadel at lower levels, on all bar the east side. They were built by casting the spoil downhill, so reducing the need to double-handle the material. A slighter rampart can be seen between the inner and middle ramparts from the north round to the east. The entrance cuts through all four ramparts in the north-east. So, Dunsinane was probably a heavily defended and nigh-impregnable Iron Age hillfort that almost certainly became a Dark Ages' stronghold, but forget images of grand palaces for Macbeth.

Outside, and quite a way down the hill, can be seen the traces of an additional rampart. This is best seen in the north-west, from where you approach, and also about 100 yards away to the south. The rampart can be traced for much of its triangular circuit to enclose about 5 acres, and could have been part of an earlier hillfort, or the outer defences of a hillfort now beneath the Dark Ages' ruins. This is not clear and another excavation is badly needed, but the entrance from the summit does curve round into the outer enclosure, which appears to have a gap in the west.

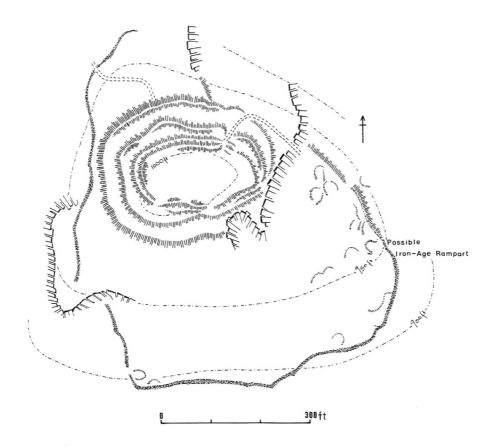

Possible
Iron-Age Rampart

0   300ft

A southwards view of Dunsinane hillfort and Strathmore. From Iron Age hillfort to Dark Ages stronghold and world-wide literary prominence, Dunsinane has few equals.

For followers of Shakespeare, Dunsinane may be a bit disappointing, though Birnam Wood is visible about 10 miles away to the north-west. But for readers interested in Scottish history – and especially the varied pre-historic strongholds, Dunsinane is an attractive, well-located site with views along Strathmore that may have had more significance in the Iron Age. Dunsinane is one of several hillforts facing each other across Strathmore, a sure sign of its importance in the Iron Age, and even earlier times.

Other Pre-historic Site
Little Dunsinane Hill (Broch) Map 53 ref. 222325
Evelick (Hillfort) Map 53 ref. 199257

FINAVON Hillfort

Angus O/S Landranger map 54 ref. 506556

Directions: Take the B9134 east from Forfar towards Brechin. Turn left after 4 miles along the twisting road that passes to the south of the summit. The hillfort is at the top of the hill. Go through the gate and follow the farm track.

Occupying the summit of the Hill of Finavon, 750 feet above sea level, but, more important, with long commanding views over Strathmore, Finavon is an early example of a timber-laced hillfort. Its single wall encloses about an acre in a running-track shape, measuring about 500 ft. x 120 ft., and still rises to over 6 feet in places. This, and the interior, is now clothed in grass, but that hides much more of considerable interest.

The general layout takes little account of the lie of the land: this is no contour hillfort, but was built to a definite size. As with many similar hillforts, there is no sign of an original entrance, the two gaps in the rampart being quite recent. At the east end, there is an external arc of wall connected to the main rampart, and a short length of horn-work to the south. It is possible that these may have been connected with moveable entrance ladders.

Finavon has benefited from two excavations, undertaken in 1933 to 35 and 1966. The former were more extensive and showed that the rampart was a timber-laced stone wall, about 20 feet wide, 12 feet high internally and about 16 feet externally. At a height of about 8 feet, the internal wall-face was set back by about 2 feet and, wherever tested, vitrified stone was found. This indicates that the wall timbers had caught fire and fused the stones together. Was this deliberate or accidental?

In addition, the excavators uncovered hearths, traces of wooden huts and quite rough, coarse pottery. The rock-cut well in the east may have proved to be dry, according to the excavators, and it is possible that the hillfort was extended to enclose the deep hollow inside the western arc, as a further source or receptacle of water. There is a suggestion of a curved rampart across the interior a little to the east of the farm track. A final conclusion of the 1930s excavation was that the wall may have been lined with lean-to huts and buildings, hence the 2 ft. indentation acting as a support. If so, and this is pure conjecture, Finavon may have been built by migrants from southern Germany who also built lean-to buildings at hillforts with timber-laced ramparts.

The 1966 excavation was more modest, but provided some quite startling material and information, for the time. A trench dug against the south rampart unearthed charcoal from what was thought to be a hut floor. C-14 dating of this suggested that Finavon was occupied from c. 700 to c. 400 B.C. Such a long occupation, and an early date of building, was quite unexpected and proved to be a bit of an archaeological eye-opener at that time.

From a visitor's point of view, all this adds to the general interest, but it is usually what is visible on the ground that is of more importance. Fortunately, Finavon is reasonably preserved with its rampart and well(s) all being clear and visible. Of most interest, though, are the large lumps of vitrified stone. There are not many clearly visible, but they are very impressive and it shows just how fierce the fire must have been to melt the stone in that way. Pity the poor inhabitants, yet Finavon is but one of many hillforts that display vitrified material, though few have such long sections clear of grass.

Here then, stands a most important hillfort, one surely sited with strategic considerations. Whether occupied by native or migrant, and whether it burned deliberately, fell in battle or by a domestic accident, Finavon has played an important role in determining Scottish pre-history and is a fine hillfort to visit. Yet, it is not alone, for Kemp's Castle is but half a mile to the south, and is almost 100 feet higher.

A chunk of vitrified stone, melded through fierce burning of a timber-laced rampart at Finavon hillfort.

Other Pre-historic, and historic, Sites
Aberlemno Pict Standing Stones
1) in Aberlemno churchyard
2) beside the road to the church
3) beside B9134 towards Brechin
Kemp's Castle or Turin Hill (Hillfort) Map 54 ref. 514535
Brechin Round Tower. In Brechin Cathedral grounds.

GASK RIDGE ROMAN WATCH-TOWERS

Perthshire O/S Landranger map no. 58 ref. see below

Directions: Take the A9 south from Perth and turn right 2 1/2 miles after the junction with the M90. After a mile, this road follows the line of the Roman road for nearly 3 miles, with the sites of the watch-towers either side.

While the advancing Romans usually established a temporary frontier before the winter set in, for example along the Forth-Clyde isthmus in 80 A.D., their first semi-permanent Scottish frontier was a system of observation or signalling watch-towers along the Gask Ridge, between the forts at Ardoch* and Bertha. As is usual with our pre-history, there is much uncertainty about this, despite more than a few excavations, but a frontier it most certainly was.

The frontier comprises Ardoch* fort, three watch-towers (of which nothing can be seen), Kaims Castle – a small fort, another watch-tower, Strageath fort, guarding the crossing of the River Earn, then 10 watch-towers – all with some visible remains – along the Gask Ridge, three more widely spaced watch-towers – of which nothing can be seen, and finally Bertha fort. As the towers are usually less than a mile apart and are close to the Roman road, they were presumably intended to control the frontier, signal, observe who passed through and impose conditions on any natives, and act as an early warning system. The towers were not expected to halt natives with warlike intentions, but acted as a warning system for the nearby forts, while letting all and sundry know that they were about to enter what we might now call a 'new normal': an area of Roman rule.

Recent theories have questioned the positioning of the watch-towers, suggesting if north/south visibility were the most important, several watch-towers could have been better sited. In view of this, it has been noted that the watch-towers offer good views over Strathearn into native territory beyond, offering advance warning of any potential conflict. In which case, the watch-towers could have fulfilled observation and signalling requirements farther afield, from a safer distance than at the potentially not entirely secure frontier.

The watch-towers seem to have followed a standard pattern, as one might expect of the Romans, except that those between Ardoch* and Strageath forts have two ditches. The square tower was about 12 ft. in diameter, with four corner posts, some 1 ft. 6 ins. across and sunk about 2 ft. into the ground. The tower was a 2 or 3-storey affair, probably with a wooden observation balcony. Accommodation was on the lower floor of the tower. This was protected by a rampart, probably surmounted with a fence, with an external ditch, 10 ft. wide and 4 ft. deep. Some watch-towers had a small counterscarp bank outside the ditch. Needless to say, there was only one entrance. The towers were manned by detachments from the nearby forts and, given the exposure out on the ridge, one might expect that such duties were not considered plum jobs.

The watch-tower system might have been extended south of Ardoch, although only one watch-tower has been discovered so far. There is also uncertainty as to when the Gask towers were built. Did they define the outer extent of the empire, while Agricola consolidated his gains to the south of the Forth/Clyde isthmus, c. 80 A.D., or were they built after Inchtuthil and the forts at the mouths of the glens, to the north and west, were abandoned, c. 85 A.D.? Either way, hard evidence is almost non-existent, but the latter scenario might be nearer the truth, for just such a system was developed in Germany at about the same time. That lasted rather longer, as there seems to be little doubt that the Gask Ridge watch-towers were abandoned, along with the rest of the Roman forts north of the Forth/Clyde isthmus, by 90 A.D. at the very latest.

Not all of the watch-towers are worth visiting, but those listed below have some remains to view.

WITCH KNOWE Map ref. 997196

Park opposite the lodge of Gask House and walk along the track north for 100 yds. Turn east for 100 yds. and the tower is in the woods. Despite the undergrowth, which makes finding the tower a bit of fun, the ditch, causeway and outer bank can still be seen.

MUIR O'FAULD Map ref. 982189
Continue west for a mile and park where the road turns sharp left, ref. 985191. Walk west along the track, that follows the Roman road, and the watch-tower is in a fenced enclosure to the south, after 1/4 mile. With its notice boards, and being clear of trees, this is the finest of the watch towers to visit. The rampart, ditch, causeway and outer bank are all clearly visible making the layout easy to understand.

ARDUNIE Map ref. 947187
Continue west along the minor road for 1 ½ mile and turn right. Park at the third sharp right-hand bend, after 1/2 mile, ref. 960188. Walk west along the Roman road for 3/4 mile and the watch-tower is in a fenced enclosure just south of the road. As for Muir o'Fauld, Ardunie is clear of trees and one can clearly see the ditch and causeway. Its overall diameter is only 40 ft., showing how small were the watch-towers.

PARKNEUK Map ref. 917185
Retrace your route to the main minor road, and head west. Turn right onto the B8062 for 1 1/2 miles. The road then turns left by Shearerston Farm, and park just round the corner at the Forestry Commission gate to Inverpeffray Woods. Follow the track north

Kaim's Castle (west of A822 at map ref. 85019) was a Roman fortlet north of Ardoch Fort leading towards the Gask Ridge.

for 50 yds., until the Roman road crosses at right angles. Turn east for 100 yds. and the watch-tower is just south of the road. Although mostly overgrown, the outer bank, ditch and rampart can be made out, enclosing an area of 22 ft. x 18 ft. So space around the tower would have been at a premium.

INCHTUTHIL (Hillfort and Roman Fort)

Perthshire O/S Landranger map 53 ref. (hillfort) 115393 (Roman fort) 125397

Directions: Leave Dunkeld heading east on the A984. Just after Spitalfield, at a sharp left hand bend, follow the track on the right through the woods for 3/4 mile, and a footpath leads to the Roman fort. The hillfort is to the south-west, reached by following the east-west edge of the plateau.

Though mostly covered by a golf course, if you lived hereabouts 1,900 years ago, there would be far more than a wayward white ball that you would need to keep a look out for. Here, on this plateau formed by the shifting course of the River Tay, was a legionary fortress from which the Romans intended to subdue the whole of Scotland. Political events and repercussions back in Rome brought the campaign to a swift end and a total, if temporary, withdrawal from Scotland of all invading forces. Within five years, the largest Roman fort in Scotland had come and gone with little left to see.

To put Inchtuthil in perspective, most permanent Roman forts in Scotland are smaller than 5 acres. One Pennymuir marching camp is 42 acres, yet Inchtuthil enclosed 50 acres in the classic Roman style. It was briefly the base for the XX Valeria Vitrix Legion – fully 6,000 men. Built in c. 83 A.D. over earlier camps, possibly used by the soldiers building it, Inchtuthil was defended by a stone and wood rampart and external ditch. Inside was the full complement of wooden buildings for every conceivable need, all laid out in the traditional Roman pattern. This was no temporary fort: the Romans came, and they intended to conquer and stay, but Agricola was re-called to Rome and soon after the invading force followed.

Rather than take everything back with them, the Romans destroyed all that they could not carry that would be of use to the natives. Thus, not only were pottery and glass smashed, but these were ground into the earth. The timber buildings were dismantled and carted away and about a million iron nails – fully 12 tons in weight – were buried beneath a workshop. Whether they were coming or going, the Romans never did things by halves.

All these details, and much more, were revealed by extensive excavations undertaken from 1952 to 1965. The layout of the fort, Pinnata Castra, is one result of those excavations, but much knowledge about the Romans, their invasion and how the army worked, is owed to those excavators. There is more, though. A redoubt was discovered down by the earlier course of the River Tay, to the south-east of the main fort, yet this little appendix was almost 5 acres, or twice the size of many Antonine Wall forts. A bath-house was also discovered: as usual, well away from the fort where it was not a fire risk. A long ditch farther to the west cut-off the approach to the fort from that direction, and there may have been others.

Despite the size of Inchtuthil, and all that was uncovered during the excavations, there is not a great deal to see today. The course of the ditch at the east is still visible and the rampart at the south remains impressive. Other than that, it is a case of using your imagination, but this is not too difficult given the lie of the land. This is an important site, one from which – had it not been for events in Rome – the history of Scotland might have taken a completely different course. Having already defeated the natives at the battle of Mons Graupius, the Highlands were seemingly at the mercy of the Latin army. Had the Romans gone on to conquer the rest of Scotland, Inchtuthil might have been impressed on every Scot today, rather in the manner of Stirling Castle.

Getting on for 1/2 mile to the south-west of the Roman fort, at the corner of the plateau, lies a post-Roman hillfort. This was dug into in 1901 and an earlier palisade camp was discovered inside. A palisade trench cut across the promontory enclosing an area of 200 ft. x 100 ft.: it was one of the first to be recognised in Scotland. While this cannot be seen today, the hillfort most certainly can. Five ramparts and ditches

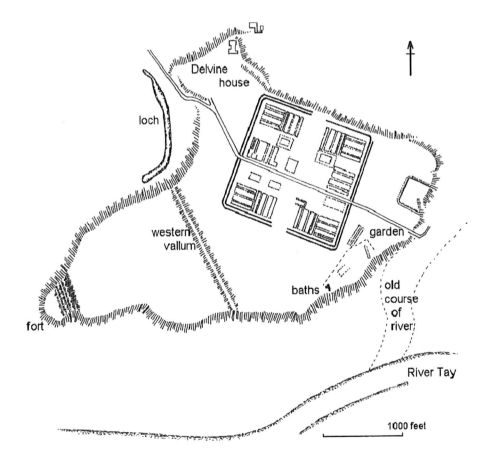

were later built farther out across the neck of the promontory, enclosing an area about 250 ft. x 150 ft. This would not have been able to withstand the Romans had they ever returned, but it was one of the most comprehensive sets of defences associated with our Iron Age ancestors.

These defences were 200 feet long and fully 300 feet wide, covering a much bigger area than the hillfort's interior, despite only protecting the east side – presumably the river surrounded the other sides. The inner rampart was faced using stone from the Roman fort, which confirms the post-Roman date, so the natives did gain something from Inchtuthil.

These two strongholds make strange bedfellows. One, a truly great structure, has all but disappeared, yet the least important, a mere appendage, remains – a bit of an archaeological David and Goliath. Some barrows overlay the Roman earthworks, as potentially rare examples of Iron Age burials.

Nothing is ever certain in pre-history and when the Romans began building Inchtuthil little did they realise how temporary it would be. Had it not been for the immense skill of the archaeologists, Inchtuthil would have kept its secrets to itself. Now, so much more is known. We might all be grateful that Inchtuthil never fulfilled the role intended for it, yet archaeology owes the site so much. Never were the Romans able to penetrate permanently so far north again.

NORMAN'S LAW (Hillfort)

Fife O/S Landranger map 59 ref. 305202

Directions: From Newburgh, take the A913 towards Cupar. After about 4 miles, turn left along the farm road to Denmuir and Denmuirhill Farms. Ask permission at the latter farm and the hillfort is 1/2 mile to the north-east on the summit of the hill.

As the Ochil Hills trail away east into Fife, their final outpost is at Norman's Law, 936 feet above sea level. The hillfort on top of this hill thus commands long views in all directions, especially north across and along the Firth of Tay, but also east and south over Fife. The mass of the Ochils rise increasingly in the west but, even so, this only adds to the diverse scenery from this vantage point.

No doubt, it was the strategic value of the location that resulted in there being at least three phases of fortified settlement, plus a probable open settlement, on Norman's Law. The whole, uneven summit is enclosed by a mostly tumbled stone wall, measuring about 700 ft. x 250 ft. This may be the first hillfort, dating from the early Iron Age. There are no obvious entrances and neither is the wall extended to the steeper slopes at the north side.

A wall divides this hillfort on a north/south axis, with a gap in the north-east. This may have been added later, but makes a compact enclosure to the west, complete with two short lengths of wall where the main and dividing walls are carried round at the north. Within this enclosure is the best preserved of the three strongholds on the hill, an oval hillfort of 170 ft. x 100 ft. defended by a wall about 12 feet thick. Sections of both wall facings are visible and this hillfort may be post-Roman but, in any case, seems to be the most recent. The western enclosure of the larger hillfort could have been created as an outer defence for this stronghold.

Outside the larger hillfort, the lower terraces at the south-west are enclosed by another wall. This runs from outside the western enclosure at the summit; right round to join the larger hillfort at its south-eastern angle. This enclosure, including the larger summit hillfort, measures 1,000 ft. x 550 ft. and may be the earliest on the hill, with an entrance at the south. On the other hand, it may also be an annexe of the larger hillfort, perhaps used for herding cattle. The wall follows the contours and is typical of the earlier Iron Age.

Within all three hillforts, and also partially built over the wall of the annexe in the south-east, can be seen a number of hut circles. These, and perhaps some of those on the terraces within, are obviously the latest on the site, and may represent a post-Roman, or even an early Dark Ages' open settlement. Any within the two summit hillforts may be contemporary with these hillforts.

There is plenty of interest to see on Norman's Law. The combination of the three hillforts – or two hillforts and an annexe, an open settlement, other hut circles and, not in the least, the long views make this a particularly interesting site. There are other Iron Age strongholds in Fife, but none to equal Norman's Law, either for their scale or their natural beauty.

Other Pre-historic Sites
Denork (Hillfort) Map 59 ref. 455137
Drumcarrow (Broch) Map 59 ref. 459133
East Lomond (Hillfort) Map 59 ref. 244062
Greencraig (Hillfort) Map 59 ref. 323215

ROUGH CASTLE (Roman Fort)

Stirlingshire O/S Landranger map 65 ref. 843799

Directions: This can be visited at the same time as Watling Lodge, Tentfield Plantation and Seabegs Wood (see Antonine Wall *). From the latter site, return back to and turn right along the B816, and turn left through the small industrial estate. Follow this road over the railway until the car park is reached. The fort is a furlong farther east.

Rough Castle and its attendant 1 1/2 mile stretch of Antonine Wall, from Bonnybridge House through to the Tentfield Plantation, are ideally situated in central Scotland. The odd smells and occasional bangs that emanate from the nearby factories give a different atmosphere from the more isolated sites and, with two busy main railway lines diverging nearby, one never has illusions of being back in Roman times.

An aerial picture of Rough Castle showing the layout of the fort, the annexe to the east, the adjoining Antonine Wall to the north, and the Rowan Tree burn to the west.

Images of a cohort of Roman soldiers marching along the Military Way rather lose their effect as a Glasgow to Edinburgh train races past in the background.

Although Rough Castle is the second smallest of the known Antonine Wall forts, there is no finer survivor. From the car park, follow the wall westwards where, 50 or so yards beyond the cattle grid and attached to the rear of the wall, is a probable signal station mound. There is a second closer to Bonnybridge House. This section of wall runs back east, across Rowan Tree burn to Rough Castle itself, making a pleasant place to walk and to view the relationship between the Roman wall, fort and road.

An indication of Rough Castle's archaeological importance can be gained with it having been partially excavated in 1903, 1932 to 1933 and 1957 to 1961, and consolidated in the 1970s. Such attention is not surprising, given that most of the Antonine Wall forts, and the wall, have been destroyed. Barely an acre is enclosed by a rampart and two external ditches on the east, west and south sides, and by the wall to the north; almost a square. The turf rampart was built on a stone foundation, as was the wall, and has been badly eroded over the years, but the whole defensive system remains intact. Apart from Ardoch fort, Rough Castle must rank as about the best preserved Roman stronghold in Scotland.

There are entrances through the centre of each side while, unseen today but revealed by excavation, a Principia, granary, the commandant's quarters and various barracks filled the interior. So, Rough Castle was an orthodox fort, one of which was sited approximately every two miles along the length of the wall. The Military Way runs through the fort on an east-west axis, but was later re-routed to the south. Several trees grace the fort and, far from detracting and obscuring it, they add to the scene, giving it the appearance of something other than a stark, simple defended field.

Immediately to the east, a slightly larger area is enclosed by a turf rampart, with a single ditch to the south opening into three, wide-spaced ditches to the east: these are now within the woods. This annexe contained the wooden bath houses, an important accoutrement of any permanent Roman fort. If possible, these were built away from the fort due to the risk of fire; this was serious if it consumed the bath houses, but quite another matter if the fort's timber buildings were also engulfed. Geophysical surveys this century showed further, indeterminate, timber buildings in the annexe.

Outside the fort's northern entrance lies Britain's only uncovered example of a *lilia* that comprised ten rows of holes, each about 7 ft. x 3 ft., and now only 2ft. 6in. deep. Each hole would have contained sharpened wooden stakes, which, presumably, would have been camouflaged. Like the *chevaux de frise*, seen at hillforts such as Dreva Craig* or Cademuir*, these would serve to break up a mass charge, either on horse or by foot. Any natives who decided to rush the wall would, if not impaled on the stakes, be trapped in the holes at the mercy of javelins thrown from the wall. The Romans were nothing if not ruthless.

A number of these lilia, minus the stakes, have been left open, although there were originally about four times as many. As with the *chevaux de frise*, *lilia* might have been used much more often than is readily apparent today.

The only example of lilia *still visible in Scotland. This is located in the gap in the trees to the right of the pylon in the last picture.*

The excavations of the late-1950s sectioned through part of the rampart and described the turf-work as being, '...brilliantly defined...', even after all these years. This excavation clearly demonstrated how a supposedly simple turf wall could be as defensively secure as one of stone. The rampart, of course, had a wooden fence on top.

The general history of Rough Castle is inextricably tied-in with that of the Antonine Wall. Built in the mid-2nd century A.D., it was abandoned after about 15 years, only to be re-occupied a few years later. Rough Castle may have been occupied by the Romans on three separate occasions in that century, although that is by no means certain. It was probably finally abandoned about 180 B.C.

There is so much to see in the vicinity of Bonnybridge that you need to commit some time to visit the four sites featured in this book. It is not a bad idea to visit the other three sites first, as by transposing your images of the Military Way and ditch – best seen at Seabegs Wood and Watling Lodge respectively – you will have a complete picture by the time you reach Rough Castle.

SHEEP HILL (Hillfort)

Dunbartonshire O/S Landranger map 64 ref. 435745

Directions: Leave Dumbarton on the A82 towards Glasgow. Turn left, northwards, up the winding minor road at the roundabout beyond Milton. The hillfort is to the west of the road at a sharp right hand bend, after about 1/2 mile.

Like the more famous Dumbarton Rock, Sheep Hill also stands on a knoll of volcanic basalt. Though very much on the lower south slopes of the Kilpatrick Hills, Sheep Hill commands extensive views along the great waterway of the River and Firth of Clyde. There is little doubt that these, and the route now followed by the main roads and railway, were of considerable importance in pre-historic times, giving the inhabitants of Sheep Hill a particularly powerful location. The hillfort was also unlikely to escape the attention of any rival tribal incursions along the river.

The remains of a timber-laced stone wall enclose a triangular area measuring 120 ft. x 70 ft. at the summit. This hillfort was excavated from 1966 to 1970 and was found to be the earliest stronghold on the site. There is now no obvious sign of an entrance, but, in the south-west, there are several examples of material that show how it met its end. Yes, Sheep Hill is yet another of Scotland's vitrified hillforts, and reddened, vitrified stone can be seen in several places.

The point must be made, yet again, that the fierce burning of the timber-lacing within the stone wall was not necessarily caused by aggressors: there were accidents then as now, or a deliberate burning, perhaps when abandoning it. Not too long after this, a second, larger hillfort was built that utilised not only the original north wall, but also considerable amounts of the burnt rubble. The second hillfort enclosed an area of 300 ft. x 150 ft., in an irregular shape that follows the contours, although what is left of the once massive stone wall, is a tumbled mess.

There were simple entrances in the north-west and south; the latter was additionally protected by a triangular enclosure with an outer entrance to the east. A short outer bank protected this entrance from a flanking attack from higher ground. Such a layout certainly brings to mind the motte and bailey castle layout of the early medieval period.

Evidence from the excavation, in particular debris buried beneath the second phase rampart, suggests that the builders might have been the inhabitants of the original hillfort. Although timber-laced stone walls were not exclusive to the early Iron Age, that is more usually the case – an assertion backed here by some pretty basic, gritty pottery that was found, which suggests an earlier rather than later date. Some clay mould fragments, several jet bracelets and a tiny glass bead were also found, possibly dating from the 1st centuries B.C. and A.D., and indicate trading connections.

As ever, we know nothing about the people who lived here, but they could have been from the Damnonii tribal group of north Galloway and Clydeside. What are of considerable interest are the two sets of rock carvings about 200 yards to the north of the hillfort. These include cup and ring marks, spirals and cups, and probably date to the Bronze Age, at map ref. 435746.

Unfortunately, at the time of writing, late-2020 the hillfort is under threat of destruction/desecration through an extension to the established quarry. This is doubly unbelievable at a time when Scotland is considering independence from Great Britain and yet may destroy important sites of its history, plus it shows that the lessons of the damage caused at Traprain Law* have been ignored. Who would trust such an administration? Is Arthur's Seat safe?

Other Pre-historic Site

Dumbarton Rock (Various phases of fortification) Map 64 ref. 400745

TORWOOD BROCH

Stirlingshire O/S Landranger map 65 ref. 833849

Directions: From Larbert, take the A9 heading north. Cross the motorway and turn left on reaching Torwood. Near the brow of the hill, a public right of way to Denovan, on the left, leads to a circular car park. Follow the path at the beginning of the car park, opposite the first telegraph pole, into the wood up the hill towards the summit. The broch is the heather-covered mound in a clearing on the right.

Torwood Broch is deceptive. Almost surrounded by trees, you need to imagine the commanding views it would have had in the Iron Age to appreciate the importance of its location. When you first see it, it might appear as a heather-covered mound, and, until 1864, that is just what it was.

Then it was dug away and mostly cleared-out, although the rubble still obscures the outer wall-face. But beyond that, and once you go up on the walls, you will see that Torwood is not only the best preserved broch in central Scotland, but is of advanced build and design.

In many ways, Torwood is similar to many northern brochs, thought to be the very latest thing in such strongholds. It sits on a rocky knoll above the cliff that faces north-west towards Bannockburn. Due to the woods, this is now the only direction with a view but the advantages of such a site can be appreciated. There is no need for additional defences at that point, but the north, east and south sides of the knoll are further protected by two ruinous walls: the outer being about 3 feet high; and the inner about 6 feet high. These were examined in 1949 and can best be appreciated from the path leading to the entrance. Whether these were built as outer defences for the broch, or the broch was built within existing – abandoned or otherwise – defences is unknown.

Another feature of Torwood is that the wall is fully 20 feet thick, while the courtyard is 35 feet across, although is not really circular. So, not only is this a large broch, but the wall:courtyard ratio suggests that it probably stood to a considerable height, while the massive scale of the wall confirms this as a broch of advanced design. This does nothing to diminish the oft-said inference that the few brochs in south Scotland were designed or built by specialists from the north.

The entrance passage contains a door-jamb and bar-hole, but no guard cell. This passage, and the courtyard, is filled with stones and hidden by bracken in the summer. There is a lintel over the passage and another over the entrance to the eight remaining steps.

A scarcement can be seen about 7 or 8 ft. above the original floor. While stones and bracken cover the courtyard floor and the external wall cannot be inspected, the internal wall-face shows high-quality, drystone building work. A dozen small cupboards, or aumbries, are sunk into the wall-face. These are seemingly found only at the more recent brochs, such as Mousa, and there are probably more at Torwood than at any other broch.

If you have visited some of the better surviving brochs, Torwood may seem nothing special, although it will be easy to appreciate its advanced design. There are no intra-mural cells, although the walls were probably galleried above first floor level. When first uncovered in 1864, the wall was still 11 feet high in the north, but it is now about 3 feet lower and nothing exists to show where the gallery began.

But why were brochs built so far south? Could they have been intended to repulse Roman raiding parties – unlikely? Or was Torwood, perhaps, built after the Antonine Wall* was finally abandoned and only occupied for a brief period? Incidentally, the Roman road from the Antonine Wall* towards Ardoch* fort passes to the west of the broch. A once-busy route that the Romans would surely never allow to be dominated by a native stronghold.

Torwood broch is a fascinating place to visit. It seems as though an excavation is only half-finished and that the archaeologists will return next year. Well, one has in 2014, but not specifically on the broch.

For those living in the central Lowlands, this is an easy and very interesting broch to reach. Rather than detract from one's enjoyment, its lack of any known history only adds to the eerie mysticism conveyed by its woodland setting. And some of the vegetation has been cleared.

WHITE CATERTHUN (Hillfort)

Angus O/S Landranger map 44 ref. 548660

Directions: Leave Brechin towards Little Brechin. After passing under the by-pass, turn first left and head north-west for about 5 miles, past the turn to Little Brechin. There is a lay-by at the top of the pass between the two Caterthun hillforts. The White Caterthun is on the left along the footpath.

Notwithstanding its comparatively diminutive size, when measured against, say, Eildon Hill* or Traprain Law*, the White Caterthun is one of Scotland's finest hillforts. Its massive, tumbled, inner stone wall is one of the most substantial not only in Scotland, but the whole of Britain. How did this vast quarry of building material escape being re-used for farms and crofts, when so many hillforts, duns and brochs have been decimated? After all, overlooking the wide expanses of fertile Strathmore, it is hardly off the beaten track.

The initial approach takes you through the eastern entrance in the outer defences. These comprise two glacis ramparts separated by a ditch. The outer rampart may be nothing more than a counterscarp bank, for it is only of any size on the south and west and almost invisible in the north. The elliptic circle of this outer defence measures about 425 yards x 275 yards; a hillfort of not inconsiderable size, but, as with most others, of no certain date. Another entrance lies in the west.

Immediately to the right of the east entrance, a simple bank forms a roughly rectangular enclosure on the east flank of the hill. There is no access to this from within the hillfort, so it may have been a stock enclosure and, as the outer defences can be traced within, is probably a later addition.

Passing through the east entrance, a low rampart with inner quarry ditch lies between the outer defences and the inner citadel, complete with aligned entrances. This may be contemporary and enclosed the inhabitants' living area, with the cattle in the outer enclosure, as at other similar hillforts. But there is more. Between these two defensive lines, another rampart has been noted running from the outer defences in the north, round the west to the south, possibly to join with the outer defences in the east. This is almost certainly of an earlier date.

For all these outer defences, what really makes the White Caterthun special is the stone wall that encloses the summit of the hill, 978 ft. above sea level. This is assumed to be the latest defensive structure. Strathmore opens out to the south, while the foothills of the Grampian Mountains are visible in the north. To the east, the complex ramparts of the Brown Caterthun* appear as small waves in a sea of heather a little below. All this gave the White Caterthun many strategic advantages.

It is the sheer scale of the stone rampart that, quite literally, tops the lot, though. Enclosing a modest 1 3/4 acres, and measuring barely 175 yds. x 70 yds., the wall is now spread up to about 100 feet across in places, often covering the encircling ditch. Even so, it still rises to a considerable height and was always very wide. Despite never having been excavated, many archaeologists have claimed that that it was two timber-laced walls, some being particularly brave and suggesting that the inner wall was 40 ft. thick and the outer 20 ft. thick. If so, that would be something of a unique application of two stone walls so close together.

Another theory is that it was one stone wall, but that the middle was lower to create a protected walkway. The outer section could have acted as a parapet and the inner being used for defenders in two ranks, with these having an un-impeded line of fire. This idea could be rather fanciful, or at least a case of imposing more recent tactics onto Iron Age defences, but it does appear to have been one wall.

Another suggestion has been that, to economise on materials, the inner section of the wall was built over a hollow timber frame. Despite this multitude of theories, the collapsed appearance is similar to those of other timber-laced stone walls. The big question is, though, against whom was such a massive, defensive wall built? Surely a threat much greater than that from a small, local, Iron Age tribe?

In common with many other hillforts with a central citadel, there is no sign of an entrance through this massive wall. If this were the case, then a wooden structure may have been used to gain entry. While such a method certainly eliminates the most obvious weak spot of any stronghold, it could have been a nuisance in daily life. Then again, that would be a small price to sleep in relative safety.

The interior reveals little of how or where the inhabitants lived. Traces of a rectangular enclosure in the north post-date the hillfort, but the deep hollow in the west was almost certainly a well. Nobody knows whether the White Caterthun

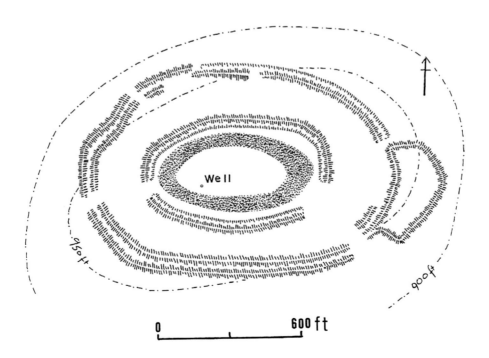

Well

950 ft

900 ft

0   600 ft

was occupied when the Romans entered Strathmore, but of all the native Iron Age strongholds, this was the one most likely to be able to withstand a Roman siege.

Some excavations of the annexe, outer ramparts and the stone covered ditch counterscarp bank outside the stone wall in 1997, but if ever there is a pre-historic stronghold deserving a comprehensive excavation, the White Caterthun is it – no half-measures will suffice. It might not advance archaeological techniques much, nor enhance pre-historical knowledge to any great degree, but how one of Britain's foremost pre-historic monuments – never mind stronghold – can remain a virtual stranger beggars belief.

This is one stronghold that will impress even the most experienced observer. The stone wall, despite its massive size, is a ruin and, with timber-laced support, would have been much higher. Never mind about recreating Shakespearean wooden theatres, or even reviving a scrapped steam locomotive, a full excavation followed by a restoration of a section of wall would really be something special. It would put even Hadrian's Wall firmly in its place.

The great, tumbled stone rampart of the White Caterthun, plus annexe, seen from the Brown Caterthun hillfort to the east.

HEBRIDES AND ARGYLL
STRONGHOLDS AND MAP

SITE	ISLAND	O/S MAP	MAP ref.	OTHER
1 An Sean	Mull	47	431563	Dun
2 An Sgurr	Eigg	39	460648	Hillfort
3 Boreraig Broch	Skye	23	195532	Broch
4 Bragar Broch	Lewis	8	286474	Broch
5 Dun Aisgain	Mull	47	377452	Dun
6 Dun an Sticir	North Uist/	18	897777	Broch
7 Dun Ardifuir	Argyll	55	789969	Dun
7 Duntroon	"	55	803960	Hillfort
8 Dun Ardtrek	Skye	32	885595	Dun
9 Dun Baravat	Lewis	13	156356	Dun
10 Dun Beag	Skye	32	339387	Broch
11 Dun Bhoraraig	Islay	60	417658	Broch
12 Dun Carloway	Lewis	8	190412	Broch
13 Dun Cuier	Barra	31	664034	Broch
14 Dun Fiadhairt	Skye	32	231504	Broch
15 Dun Grugaig	Skye	32	535124	Dun
16 Dun Hallin	Skye	23	257593	Broch
17 Dun Kildonan	Argyll	68	780277	Dun
18 Dun Mhuirich	Argyll	55	722845	Dun
19 Dun Mor	Tiree	44	046493	Broch
20 Dun Nan Gall	Mull	47	433431	Broch
21 Dun Nosebridge	Islay	60	371601	Hillfort
22 Dun Ringill	Skye	32	561170	Broch
23 Dun Skeig	Argyll	62	757571	H/F & Duns
24 Dun Torcuill	Nth. Uist	18	888737	Galleried dun
25 Dunadd	Argyll	55	837936	H/F & settlement
26 Rubh'an Dunain	Skye	32	396160	Galleried dun
27 Tirefour Castle	Lismore	49	867429	Broch

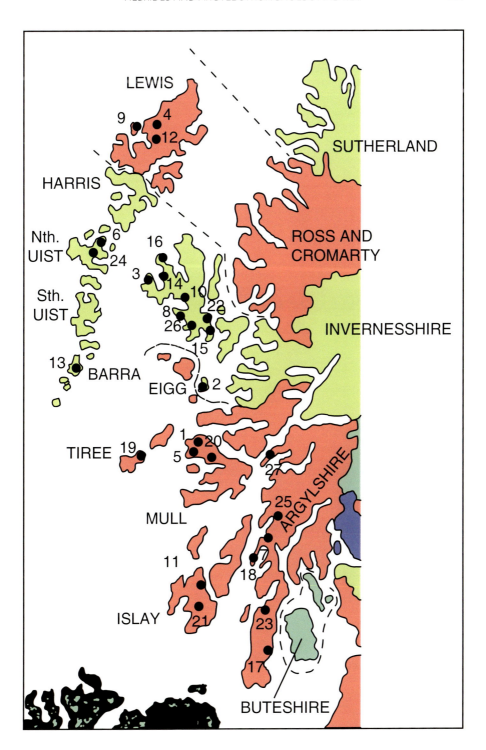

AN SEAN (Dun)

Isle of Mull O/S Landranger map 47 ref. 431563

Directions: Leave Tobermorey north-west on the B8073. After about a 1/2 mile, at a steep left hand bend, follow the minor road towards Glengorm Castle for about 4 miles. About a third of a mile before the castle (private), park and follow the track forking left through the woods. Go round the northern edge of the woods and then cross to the woods in the west. Follow the edge to the south, not the track through them, until you reach the southern-most tip. Then head in a west south-westerly direction until you come to the dun. About 1 1/2 mile walk.

Occupying the north-west end of a ridge between Loch Mingary and Glengorm, An Sean is ideally situated. An almost circular wall, about 10 feet thick, encloses a courtyard 32 feet across. Though there is a thick layer of debris inside, the wall still rises almost 4 feet above this, and part of a scarcement can be seen. The original floor level could be several feet below that visible today.

The wall is faced with large blocks and is complete internally, and almost so externally. This follows a style quite common in the western isles: that might indicate an early date of building, but could simply reflect local materials and the preferred style. The entrance passage is in the south-east and it may have had a guard cell, although it is difficult to tell with all the tumble about. Neither is it clear if there was a door-jamb or not, but there is evidence of a protective outwork having existed at some time.

There are rubble-filled, intra-mural galleries at the east and west sides, and a gap at the west probably led to stairs, although these cannot be seen either. Also in the south-west, a later, inferior structure has been built against the wall, indicating that the dun was re-used at some stage. None of An Sean's past has, as yet, been revealed and, given its internal condition, it is holding its cards pretty close to its chest.

Mind you, while there are duns in better condition, An Sean is located in a pretty remote corner of one of the less busy Hebridean islands. The views to Loch Mingary and over the coast, as well as its commanding land position, make a visit very worthwhile. The Isle of Mull was probably as sparsely populated in the Iron Age as it is today, considering its lack of strongholds compared with, say, the Isle of Skye; either that, or it was a particularly peaceful island.

But is An Sean a dun? Well, it certainly appears to be so, albeit one of no great size, but there is an alternative. Writing in the *Proceedings of the Society of Antiquaries of Scotland*, in 1942, V. Gordon-Childe said of An Sean, '...there can be scarcely any doubt that this is a broch...' Oh dear! So, ensure that you have visited other duns and brochs before you visit An Sean and then you will be able to make up your own mind.

Given the lack of funds available for archaeological excavation, you are unlikely to be proved wrong (or right) for some considerable time in the future.

AN SGURR (Hillfort)

Isle of Eigg O/S Landranger map 39 ref. 460648

Directions: From the ferry pier, walk west through Galmisdale. At a junction with the road from Sandavore, continue round the south of the hill, An Sgurr, that dominates the island. There is no easy approach, but by walking up the steep rocky slope from the west the main rampart is reached.

Unlike some pre-historic strongholds that can be difficult to locate, the summit of the pitchstone massif of An Sgurr can be seen long before you reach the island of Eigg. At 1,292 ft., it dominates the island and must have been nigh-impregnable in the Iron Age, although one might wonder who on earth would live in such an exposed place, and why.

With sheer drops of almost 400 feet at the north, east and south sides, the only possible approach to the summit is from the west. This is barred by a massive stone wall, about 10 feet thick and some 250 feet long, that links the north and south cliff edges. With such natural defensive advantages, there was no need for further defences.

Altogether, an area of 9 acres is enclosed, measuring 430 yards by 100 yards, making An Sgurr one of the largest hillforts in west Scotland. The wall looks to have lived a full life through each one of its 2,000+ years, but enough remains to demonstrate its defensive properties. There is little to see of any permanent habitation on the summit, so perhaps the islanders only used An Sgurr as a defensive retreat in the event of a crisis.

What really makes the effort all worthwhile, though, is the magnificent view in all directions. Whoever held An Sgurr controlled Eigg. The defensive wall would have taken a considerable effort to build, so there must have been a good reason to do so. Just what events brought about the need for this wall and hillfort remains unknown to us, but few people would surely choose to live in this exposed location if such drastic measures were unnecessary.

BORERAIG BROCH

Skye O/S Landranger map 23 ref. 195532

Directions: Head south from Dunvegan on the A863. Turn right on the B884 and after passing the turning to Colbost, take the minor road north, through Totaig. Follow this for 2 1/2 miles. A road joins from the left after 2 miles and the broch is 1/4 mile east across the moorland near the coast. Park near house no. 10, on the right before Boreraig, and walk up the drive. Cut across the fields to the south-east to the prominent broch.

Occupying a fine site overlooking Loch Dunvegan, Boreraig Broch is quite tumbled. Despite this, its remote location allows you to imagine it as it was 2,000 years ago, with the tower standing against the backdrop of the loch early in the morning.

Boreraig was no Mousa* though. Its wall was about 13 feet thick and enclosed a courtyard about 35 feet across. These bare figures alone suggest that it did not reach too great a height, perhaps about 30 feet or so. As with all brochs, except Mousa*, that is anything but the case today. Whether deliberately pulled down, or just collapsing, Boreraig now rises up to about 9 feet externally, with a scarcement being visible at about 7 feet in the south-west of the interior. There is an intra-mural gallery most of the way round and a cell near the entrance, in the west. This might have been a guard-cell, but the damage near the entrance is too widespread to tell.

The broch stands within a rectangular enclosure, so it could have been quite self-contained: this wall is about 4 feet thick, but might not have been contemporary with the broch. One matter of interest concerning brochs is the different methods of drystone construction. Enough of the facing remains to make Boreraig worth close inspection, and to draw your own comparisons and contrasts with others you have seen.

One such is Dun Osdale broch (ref. 240464), which you passed on the left of the B884 going to Boreraig. This, too, is reasonably well preserved and should be visited, if time allows.

BRAGAR BROCH

Lewis O/S Landranger map 8 ref. 286474

Directions: Leave Stornoway, heading north-west, on the A857. Turn left on the A858 and, as this by-passes Bragar village, the broch is in the loch south of the road.

The Isle of Lewis, as with all the Outer Hebridean islands, is not the easiest of places to visit, but, as if in compensation, its pre-historic sites require little effort to see them. A visit to Bragar broch, or Dun Loch an Duna, is as simple as stopping at a roadside shop; one only has to walk a few yards across the short causeway to the island on which it stands.

From the road, Bragar appears as a tumble of rocks and from close up the outer-face of the wall is difficult to see. Do not be put off. Its island lies in shallow water just off the edge of the small loch. In the dark and distant past, a second causeway led from the island to a crannog, barely 50 yards away. Now, Bragar broch cannot compare with Dun Carloway* broch – few can, but it has its own merits as seen from close quarters.

The wall is about 12 feet thick and encloses a courtyard of about 30 feet across. Despite its un-prepossessing appearance, the interior wall-face rises above the interior of tumbled stones covering the original floor, while a wide scarcement can be clearly seen. From within, one can begin to get an impression of just what an island broch would have been like. All embellishments are, of course, missing now, but enough exists – coupled with your own knowledge – to re-create Bragar Broch as it looked 2,000 years ago in the mind's eye.

With at least two levels of accommodation, Bragar would have been an ideal stronghold on its little island. It may well have stood about 30 feet high, which would

Travelling to/from Dun Carloway broch from Stornoway on the A858, you will pass right beside Bragar Broch in its loch. A pile of rubble it is not, as you will soon see.

have given it just the right air of impregnability in the Iron Age. Dun Carloway* might be more grand, but Bragor has its own distinctions, despite lacking any accurate knowledge of its past. Its remote setting in the loch only adds to the pleasure of a visit.

As with other duns and brochs in the remote islands, this may have been occupied – on and off – long after the Iron Age.

Other Pre-historic Sites
Rudha na Berie (Hillfort) Map 8 ref. 235474
Lower Bayable (Island dun) Map 8 ref. 516305

DUN AISGAIN (Dun)

Isle of Mull O/S Landranger map 47 ref. 377452

Directions: From Dun Nan Gall*, continue west along the B8073 for about 5 miles to Borg. The dun is about half-a-mile to the south and can be seen from the road. It is an undulating walk across country and, on occasions, the dun is lost from sight. There is a final steep climb to the dun.

This impregnable little stronghold overlooking the saline Loch Tuath and isle of Ulva to the south, is the best preserved example of a dun on Mull, and one of the better examples of a galleried-dun to be found. Standing on its rocky knoll, there is no easy approach for friend or foe, and an outer stone wall was built along the south-west approach just to put off any unwanted guests.

Despite dominating a considerable stretch of coastline, Dun Aisgain is overlooked from the north and west, possibly being within sling-shot range. Perhaps that is why it is a galleried-dun, the gallery originally allowing the wall to be quite high. So high, in fact, that it has been considered to be a broch – albeit not a typical broch – this century, due to the fallen lintel at the entrance, its mural gallery as first floor level and the scarcement. Never mind any archaeological debate, you can make up your own minds when you visit.

In places, the wall still stands up to 10 feet high, being a little less in thickness and is built of good sized stones, many now being strewn along the lower slopes of the knoll. Externally, the wall is reasonably well preserved and the facing can be observed in several places. Enough remains to gain a good impression of how it would have looked 2,000 years ago.

The interior is about 35 ft. diameter, quite small really, and filled with fallen stones. The intra-mural gallery is also mostly stone-filled, but can be seen for part of the circuit. Likewise the west-facing entrance. A door-jamb, three lintels and possibly a bar hole are still in place, but are difficult to see due to the tumbled rocks. This is the disappointing aspect of Dun Aisgain, but there is no doubt that it is impressively located.

There are not many Iron Age strongholds on Mull, at least in comparison with Skye, and, even then. Dun Aisgain is of no great size. Given the strategic benefits of its location and the equally difficult means of access, these suggest that Dun Aisgain perhaps had more of a strategic purpose than being a simple fortified homestead. If this were the case, then Dun Aisgain would not be taken easily. Its dramatic, and attractive, defensive location would ensure that.

DUN AN STICIR (Broch)

North Uist O/S Landranger map 18 ref. 897777

Directions: Head north from Lochmaddy on the A865. Turn right along the B893 towards Newtonferry. The broch is visible from the road in Loch an Sticir, just before the village. Walk along one of two causeways to an island in the loch, and another causeway leads to the island with the broch.

What appears as a great tumble of rocks from afar begins to take on a more meaningful shape as you make your way across the intricate approaches. The loch is saline and would have been very useful to the Iron Age inhabitants. Apart from a means of getting food, it would have enhanced the broch's defensive nature.

The entrance faces the causeway and includes a massive fallen lintel among the debris. There is a guard chamber, while sections of the main wall facings and those of the intra-mural passages can also be seen. The wall is about 8 ft. high and 12 ft. thick, and the upper gallery is visible, but the interior is filled with fallen stones. This is not an easy broch in which to spot the usual fittings.

A survey in 2012 noted footings of several buildings outside, all post-broch, but also a rectangular building inside, which adds to the difficulties of understanding the site. This may have been the stronghold of Hugh Macdonald, younger son of the MacDonald clan chief in the 16th century. In 1581, he reputedly invited three sons of Donald MacVicar – owner of much of North Uist – to a banquet at Dun an Sticir and slaughtered them. Later, in a failed family coup, Hugh was captured here – supposedly dressed as a woman – and died in the dungeons of Duntulm Castle, on Skye, in 1601.

Such later use of pre-historic strongholds in the mid-second millennium A.D. is not unknown in the Outer Hebrides – see Dun Carloway*, for example. Hugh starved to death chained to a wall and Dun an Sticir, similarly, seems to have died through neglect, even though it was reputedly the last pre-historic stronghold to be occupied on North Uist.

There is no doubt that it is the island location that gives Dun an Sticir its attraction today. That and the causeway approach, for these were quite common in the Outer Hebrides in the Iron Age, and the advantages can be easily appreciated, then and now.

Other Pre-historic Sites
Clettraval ch. cairn and wheelhouse Map 18 ref. 749714
Unival ch. cairn and I.A. house Map 18 ref. 800668

A broch in a loch gave additional protection and crossing a narrow, uneven causeway would not be ideal for enemies either.

DUN ARDIFUIR (Dun) and DUNTROON (hillfort)

Argyll O/S Landranger map 55 ref. 789969 (Dun), 803960 (hillfort)

Directions: Take the B8025 north from Crinan. Turn left at the crossroads. After 2 1/2 miles, Duntroon hillfort is above the road on the right. A track leads round it, followed by a short walk. For Ardifuir dun, follow the road past Duntrane Castle and continue to the farm at the end. Ask permission at the farm.

Duntroon

Overlooking Loch Crinan, the hillfort comprises a partially vitrified, timber-laced stone wall enclosing an oval area about 140 ft. x 90 ft. The wall was 10 ft. thick and would have been pretty much the standard fare for an early Iron Age hillfort in western Scotland.

Nothing dating to the Iron Age can be seen within the hillfort's wall, but outside, and generally concentric to the main wall, lies a similar, though thinner wall enclosing about 300 ft. x 180 ft. In addition, two further walls protect the south-west side, making Duntroon an impressively defended stronghold dating to c. 2,500 years ago.

Duntroon was excavated in 1904 and several saddle-querns were found, but none of the later rotary querns. These artefacts, along with the timber-laced inner rampart, suggest that Duntroon was built in the early Iron Age, perhaps as long ago as 800 B.C. As with other concentric hillforts, the outer rampart might have been built at a different time from the inner rampart, with the outer enclosure being used for herding cattle, and the inner one for the inhabitants. That is just one possibility.

One might also wish to consider the relationship, if any, between the inhabitants of the hillfort and those of the later Ardifuir dun. Could the hillfort inhabitants have built the dun, or were the dun builders immigrants or simply neighbours? We can never hope to know the answers to such questions, but pondering them can only add to the enjoyment of visiting such sites.

Ardifuir

If Duntroon is an orthodox concentric hillfort, Ardifuir is another matter. It is circular with a scarcement about 5 ft. above ground, has intra-mural stairs and passage, and an entrance with door-jambs and a guard cell. One could easily be describing a broch, but Ardifuir is something of a hybrid. Despite its many broch-like features, it is obvious that Ardifuir was a dun, albeit one that is virtually unique.

For a start, the wall is only 10 ft. thick and the courtyard's diameter is 65 ft. at the original floor level, and 68 ft. above the scarcement; there is a secondary inner-wall round part of the circumference. So, it is unlikely that the wall was more than 20 ft. high, as opposed to the 8 ft. of today. The paved entrance has a similar layout to those at many brochs, yet is nearly 9 ft. wide inside the door-jambs – wider than at any broch. Another feature is the entrance to the guard-chamber which is now only 2 ft. 6 ins. high, more suited to a dog than a man needing to get out in a hurry. This is not unique and seemingly inordinately flexible guards would have been needed at several brochs! One wonders whether the wide entrance was to enable cattle to be brought inside, into the living quarters.

Ardifuir is an impressive dun. The wall is complete in its circuit, and both the inner and outer wall facings can be seen. To all intents and purposes, it is an advance on the timber-laced hillforts, such as Duntroon, and appears to be a thoroughly well planned stronghold of the last centuries B.C. Except for one matter of not inconsiderable importance.

Ardifuir is overlooked by a hill to the west, plus two other sides. Bad news! Even I managed to throw a stone into the dun from up there. Give me a sling or a javelin and I might be deadly. To a well-practised Iron Age man, I dare say this would be easy. So, were not such weapons in use in Argyll at that time, or was this a peaceful area? If so, why build a stronghold at all? Suddenly, we are asking the same, un-answerable, questions as for Duntroon. You seem to go round in circles with pre-history, but it is never dull.

DUN ARDTREK (Dun)

Skye O/S Landranger map 32 ref. 335358

Directions: From Sligachan, take the A863 towards Dunvegan. After 6 miles, turn left along the B8009 and follow this for 5 miles. Turn left towards Fiskavaig and turn right along the minor road within a mile of the junction. Follow this road until it forks with a track, parking just before. Go through the farm yard and cross the fields, aiming at gates in the fences. Keep heading in a north north-easterly direction for the 1/4 mile walk to the coast.

Dun Ardtrek is another infamous, so-called semi-broch; part broch, part dun. As is sometimes (jokingly) said of the Liberal Democrat Party, it is neither one thing, nor the other. Giving pre-historic strongholds a specific type-name might be ingratiating them a touch too much. In the case of Dun Ardtrek, it is a dun with one or two broch-type features, and is more akin to a galleried-dun than any broch I know.

Dun Ardtrek sits on a rocky knoll facing the sea Lochs Bracadale and Harport, and the wall runs almost to the cliff edge, about 60 feet above the sea. There is no obvious sign of any wall along the top of the cliff and so, with its semi-circular wall to the land side, Dun Ardtrek is now a 'C'-shaped stronghold.

Along the top of the terrace of the rocky knoll are traces of an outer wall with a gateway and steps between the rocks; this was about 8 ft. thick. The dun wall itself is built on a rubble base and is faced with good quality rectangular stones. This is in fine condition, standing a little over 7 feet in height, and is particularly well built. The wall is just under 10 feet thick and encloses an area measuring some 43 ft. x 35 ft., and it is unlikely that the wall ever reached 20 feet high. The paved entrance is in the centre

Dun Ardtrek might have lost its defences on the seaward side, but it has a wonderful location and natural defences on its knoll.

of the wall, effectively dividing it into two, and includes a door-jamb and a guard cell. Gaps in the wall give entry to long galleries, very much a Hebridean broch-type feature seen in galleried-duns. A C-14 date from the rubble wall base of c. 150 B.C. was obtained.

Dun Ardtrek was excavated in 1965, and it was found that both ends of the wall had been built up to the cliff edge and turned along the edge. This section has fallen into the sea, one assumes, but would have been vital for the inhabitants' safety. It seems as though the dun was occupied on an irregular basis, too.

Of more interest to those with a grizzly nature, was the evidence that pointed to the demise of Dun Ardtrek. Vitrified pottery was found on the original floor, and the iron door handle lay in the entrance, probably where the wooden door had fallen after it had been burned and battered in – for that is how this fort met its end.

The inhabitants seem to have had two choices: fight to the death or jump.

Dun Ardtrek was re-used for some considerable time, after the defences had been demolished. A rubble ramp was made to ease the approach to the entrance and a few shards of Roman pottery have been found, pointing to trading along the Atlantic shore. Semi-broch or not, Dun Ardtrek is a most attractive stronghold and one that would not be easy to attack. Unfortunately, as with brochs, once attackers broke through the entrance there was no escape. Dun Ardtrek enjoys a lovely location, though, and, quite rarely for Iron Age strongholds, provides evidence of its demise.

Other Pre-historic Site
Dun Ard an t'Sabhail (Broch) Map 32 ref. 318333

DUN BARAVAT (Dun)

Lewis O/S Landranger map 13 ref. 156356

Directions: Leave Stornoway on the A859. Turn right onto the A858 and turn left at Garynahine along the B8011. Turn right on the B8059 and cross the bridge to the island of Great Bernera. Park 1/4 mile north of Barraglom and walk in a west north-westerly direction across the moor, to the north shore of Loch Baravat.

Dun Baravat enjoys a degree of common ground with that great American hero, Klark Kent. In the latter's case, he is greeted with the introduction, 'Is he a bird? Is he a plane? No, he's Superman.' As for Dun Baravat, it is the question, is it a dun? Is it a broch? No, it's a semi-broch. Or is it?

At one time or another Dun Baravat, or Bharaphat, has been described as all three. All could be right or, equally, wrong and it is considered a dun in this book for simplicity. Semi-brochs combine dun and broch-like features, and are mainly found in the Western Highlands and Hebrides. So, a semi-broch may have a dun layout, yet would include features associated with brochs, such as entrance plan, galleried-wall and possibly an intra-mural cell. In the main, though, a semi-broch would be of inferior design, and often build quality, to a broch. Also, semi-brochs cannot be instantly recognised as such: they vary widely in design and build, adding to the impression that the semi-broch label is something of a catch-all. The search for a semi-broch is almost a red herring, yet Dun Baravat might just be what is being sought.

It stands on an islet in Loch Baravat and is reached by a narrow causeway. From the land it looks overgrown, but once there you can see more than you might expect. The land hereabouts is typical of Lewis – mainly dreary peat bog, but was probably quite different when Dun Baravat was in use.

Rubble fills an interior measuring about 40 ft. x 30 ft., in the 'D' shape of many duns. The wall, possibly combining galleried and solid sections, ranges between 6 to 9 feet thick, so the ratio of wall width:internal diameter is below the 1:1 of many brochs for which measurements are known. Even the quality of the wall, where it is best seen in the north, is more akin to that of a dun. There is an entrance in the north-west and a stairway within the north wall.

So, Dun Baravat could easily be a dun, but a plan drawn in 1861 indicated that the wall rose to at least a fourth level, via several staircases. Another possibility is that Baravat could have been a broch that was altered – possibly after a collapse – to a dun/broch combination, or, indeed, a semi-broch.

Externally, Dun Baravat is now a little over 10 feet high and a scarcement can just be seen above the rubble, along with part of a first floor gallery. Given, say, an average of only 5 feet per level, four levels – at least – would make Dun Baravat a minimum of 20 feet high. This would probably be taller than most duns, and it is certainly one of the highest to be seen today. However, if it is a 'D'-shaped semi-broch, Dun Baravat is probably the only known example in the Outer Hebrides. But, as has been shown by recent excavations here and at nearby Cnip, much else could lie underneath the extensive blanket of peat awaiting discovery.

More recent underwater archaeology has shown that Dun Baravat may have been the final structure of a long period of settlement on the islet. Material giving a range of C-14 dates from 1000-500 B.C. has been obtained, which is much earlier than that for other duns, yet the site was occupied after the partial collapse of the wall. A modern scientific approach, with a greater sample of material can change the received wisdom on Iron Age strongholds, and much else. If only they had Superman's many powers to offer in support, though.

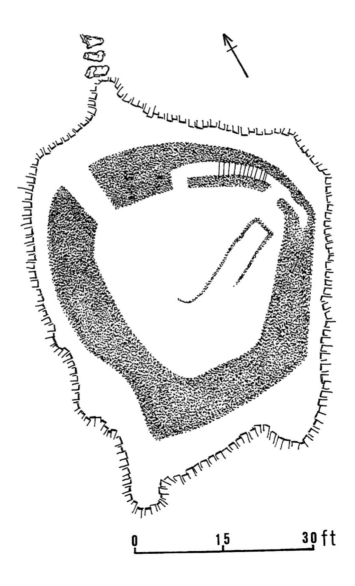

0   15   30 ft

DUN BEAG (Broch)

Skye O/S Landranger map 32 ref. 339387

Directions: Take the A863 north from Sligachan through Bracadale towards Dunvegan. After Struan, there is a car park on the left, and a gate leading to the broch on the opposite side of the road, 200 yards away on the right. A signpost points the way.

Skye has many pre-historic strongholds, but they are not always in the best condition. Quite often, many are a bit of a disappointment, especially as they usually require a fair bit of effort to reach them, and endure the vagaries of the local weather. Dun Beag is by no means in outstanding condition, but is a good example of a somewhat hypothetical, yet typical Hebridean broch.

Pleasingly, Dun Beag is also easy to reach and there is a useful noticeboard with information about artefacts found, some of which are post-Iron Age. Many of its basic features are visible and generally free of tumbled stones. It stands on a rocky knoll some way inland, but still has good views over the coast and Loch Bracadale. The entrance faces the easiest approach, the south-east, and includes the usual door-jambs. There is no guard cell, but, as at a few other brochs, one might open off the courtyard to the right of the entrance passage. On the opposite side is a combined mural cell and stairs leading to the first floor gallery, with fourteen steps.

Almost opposite the entrance, and above the floor level, another gap leads to the fairly wide mural gallery that can be followed in both directions for some distance; it probably

Dun Beag broch from the north-west.

ran almost the circumference of the broch. This, and the well-preserved outer wall-face, with its large rectangular stones, is a feature of several brochs on the island. The wall is about 13 ft. thick and encloses a courtyard 36 ft. across. This suggests that the wall might not have reached the height of, say, Dun Carloway* but would have been pretty tall as there is no sign of any additional out-workings. It still reaches up to 12 feet high in places.

Dun Beag was briefly excavated in during the Great War, but that was hardly the time to indulge in such trivial matters. Although it stands on a knoll, it was discovered that a rubble foundation was used to level the site before building, which gives some indication of the Iron Age builders' understanding and ability to plan. It is also adjacent to land that was probably cultivated or grazed.

Quite a diverse quantity of artefacts in metal, stone, glass and pottery have been unearthed at Dun Beag. These date from the Iron Age initial and secondary use, through intervening centuries to Norse times, and include a gold ring. No doubt, with its strategic potential and wide-ranging views, including to the Cuillins, Dun Beag had its attraction over the centuries, but was probably built because decent farming land was close at hand.

Other Pre-historic Sites

Struanmore (Dun) Map 32 ref. 340390
Dun Beag (Hillfort and broch) Map 32 ref. 462683
Dun Flodigary (Broch) Map 23 ref. 465715
Dun Cruin (Hillfort and possible dun) Map 23 ref. 412516
Dun Gerashader (Hillfort and possible chevaux de frise) Map 23 ref. 489453

DUN BHORARAIG (Broch)

Islay O/S Landranger map 60 ref. 417658

Directions: Head west from Port Askaig on the A846. Turn left at Ballygrant and park at the junction 1/4 mile along the minor road, on the left. Walk along the estate road past Lossit Lodge to Lossit Farm, and follow the track for a further 1/4 mile east. The broch is on top of the hill due north of the track.

As this broch is approached up the steep hill from the south, it looks to be little more than a pile of stones surmounted by a small, modern cairn. That impression is not immediately dispelled on reaching the broch, for a mass of tumbled stones covers the site and is spread somewhat liberally round about. Yes, Dun Bhoraraig may be some way short of being among the best preserved of brochs, but few enjoy such a magnificent, panoramic location.

Arriving from the south and east – the easiest way, a low grass-covered mound round the edge of the broch's platform marks all that is left of an outer wall. It has been heavily robbed, but a dip aligned with the broch's entrance might indicate an entrance in this outer wall. As will soon be apparent, the broch has steep enough natural defences on the north and west sides, so nothing was built there.

The rubble-strewn broch entrance faces south-east, and includes a door-jamb and guard cell to the left of the passage. Neither of these features can be easily seen although, as with much of the broch, they are well preserved under its rubble. The wall is about 15 ft. thick and encloses a courtyard over 40 feet across. Thus, one would not expect this to be one of the great tower brochs – and it probably reached up to no more than 30 feet, that would surely be sufficient considering its spectacular location. Little of the wall facings can be readily seen and virtually nothing of the interior.

There are, what appear to be, three intra-mural cells in the west. The middle one might have an entrance to the interior – and certainly has an end wall in the south, as does the cell to its north. However, when observed in the 19th century, a gallery extended all the way round. This is not visible today, but, as two of the three possible cells have end walls, such a long gallery does not seem likely.

What really makes Dun Bhoraraig so special, apart from being the only broch to survive on the island, is its outstanding location for viewing Islay. Standing at close to 600 ft. above sea level, there are long views to the hills of the south, far across the island's plains, and across to the west coast and Loch Indaal. There are similarly

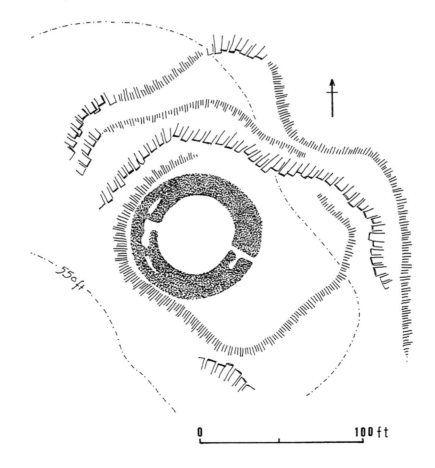

0   100 ft

extensive views over Loch Ballygrant to the north, but the most spectacular views are those to the east. There, across the Sound of Islay, rise the magnificent Paps of Jura, surely some Scotland's most attractive mountains. Go early on a clear morning and you will be rewarded with the eerie sight of the Paps rising above the mist in the sound, like a multiple version of Mount Fuji, in Japan.

The inhabitants of Dun Bhoraraig clearly chose their spot well. An easily defended platform on a hill on which sheep and cattle could be kept, with good arable land to the south, was eminently practical. Above everything – literally, they commanded the area and enjoyed pretty inspiring views most days. Obviously, this so inspired a visitor that he just had to leave his mark. What was a concrete base for a signal station was built on the broch wall in the east last century, on which the cairn now stands. Some pre-historic strongholds have been utterly ruined by such ridiculous additions but, somehow, that is not the case here. The cairn, as with the broch, is fast becoming a tumble of stones itself.

DUN CARLOWAY (Broch)

Lewis O/S Landranger map 8/13 ref. 190412

Directions: Leave Stornoway on the A859 and turn right on the A858. Continue past the Callanish Stone Circles and the broch is visible on the left, about 1 mile south of Carloway. Turn left along the minor road to a car park.

This is a great, pre-historic 'what might've been', for as recently as 1861, when a plan was drawn, Dun Carloway stood 35 feet high with four upper galleries, and part of a fifth being visible. Less than a century before that, it was reputedly even more complete.

Today, Dun Carloway rises to just about 30 feet above the lowest layer of its wall, these points not being aligned, but it remains one of the best brochs to be seen. Stone robbing – that continued into the 20th century – has removed all traces of upper galleries from half of the circumference. In a perverse way, this at least assists inspection of the construction of the galleried-wall – especially the cross-slabs tying it together. That, though, is small compensation for the loss of the second tallest broch, after Mousa*, a century ago.

Dun Carloway sits proudly on a rocky knoll and dominates the nearby loch, the low-lying land to the south and the settlements immediately below. It would have been nigh-impregnable in the Iron Age. The low, north-west entrance faces the easiest approach, and includes a door-jamb and a reasonably large guard cell. The wall is solid at ground level and three low openings lead from the courtyard to the intra-mural cells and the stairs. The wall reaches its greatest height in the south-east, and the cross-slabs that form the floor of a lower gallery and the ceiling of an upper one are readily seen. From outside the entrance, the wall construction, the vertical openings in the south wall and the distinctive taper of the wall's exterior can all be clearly seen to good effect. There is a scarcement about 7 feet above the current floor.

The wall is 11 to 12 feet thick and encloses a courtyard about 24 feet across. This gives the classic 1:1 ratio of wall width:courtyard diameter considered necessary for a broch to reach a good height. Many brochs comfortably exceed this ratio – particularly in north Scotland – and Dun Carloway must surely have reached about 40 feet in height, if it had a minimum of 5 upper levels. There is no questioning the quality of stone and build of Dun Carloway's wall, though. This was intended as a secure stronghold and would have still been standing today had it not been for the stone robbers, unlike a great many other brochs.

Such destructive days are, one hopes, over for Dun Carloway is in the care of Historic Scotland. It was consolidated in 1971, and a mural cell was excavated. Some material was C-14 dated and confirmed use of the cell over an extremely long period of time. Down to c. 1400, in fact, while over 500 pottery shards were also found – dating to 5 to 7th centuries, and few of these seemed to match. This might suggest that

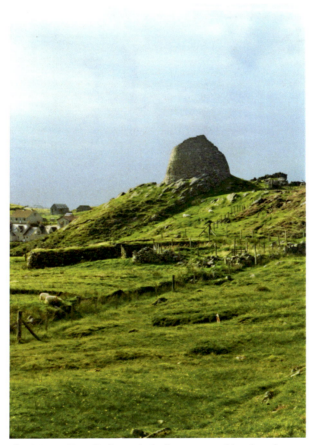

After Mousa, Dun Carloway is the best preserved broch and, as can be clearly seen, dominates its surroundings.

pottery was manufactured there during that time: either that or Dun Carloway had some rather clumsy inhabitants.

Whether Dun Carloway was defensible at that that time is unknown, but it was the scene of a minor spat in the late-medieval period, between the cattle-rustling Morrisons and the MacAulays. The Morrisons took refuge in the broch and a particularly carefree MacAulay supposedly climbed the wall by jamming his dirk in the gaps between the stones. He drove the Morrisons out by throwing burning heather down onto them, a seemingly exhausting, not to say dangerous, task. That seems to suggest that Dun Carloway was still capable of holding an armed band at bay, yet its wall-head might have been missing, otherwise the daring MacAulay would have been easily warded-off.

There is no doubt though, Dun Carloway is one of Scotland's great pre-historic sites. People have been known to travel all the way to Lewis just to see it, and not even call in at the Callanish Stones just along the road. For the non-archaeologist, it gives the clearest insight into how the brochs were built, and also emphasises the essential design and building skills. For those not particularly interested in such minutiae, Dun Carloway is simply a magnificent site to see and visit. With a history of occupation stretching into recent times, it is quite a rare pre-historic stronghold, to boot.

Other Pre-historic Sites
Dun Cromore (Galleried dun) Map 8 ref. 400206
Callanish Stone Circle Map 13 ref. 213330
Cnoc Ceann a'Gharaidh (Stone circle) Map 13 ref. 222326
Cnoc Fillibhir (Stone circle) Map 13 ref. 222325
Ceann Hulavig (Stone circle) Map 13 ref. 230304

DUN CUIER (Broch)

Barra O/S 1:50,000 map 31 ref. 664034

Directions: Head west from Castlebay along the A888 to the north-west of the island, about 1/2 mile west of Cuier. The broch is up the hill due south of the road.

Dun Cuier (on the 'wild and lonely Isle of Barra,' as Pte. Fraser in *Dad's Army* regularly commented) has enjoyed the rare luxury of a relatively recent and quite thorough excavation, in the early 1950s. Although many brochs were, shall we say, dug into during the 19th century – and some were consolidated or cleared out, the chance of finding valuable artefacts was usually high on the list of the excavators' priorities. A great deal of damage was often done, insofar as any future scientific archaeological excavations are concerned, and, since the beginning of the 20th century, brochs have been relatively ignored.

Barra is a small island, but has several archaeological features of interest. Dun Cuier sits on a rocky boss high above the sea and has been described as a galleried-dun, but certainly has most of the trappings of a broch. Its entrance is quite simple, facing east and with a probable door-jamb at the edge of the courtyard. The excavators found the passage was only 4 ft. high originally.

The walls are 14 to 17 ft. thick and enclose a courtyard up to 29 ft. across, so this broch could have risen to a decent height. The walls are interesting – hence the plural, for they comprise two walls that touch and are not joined together at the west, but have long chambers sunk into the outer wall at the north and south ends to form the usual Hebridean galleries. Only on either side of the entrance, is there a solid wall. The walls still rise up to 8 feet above the original floor, with a scarcement about 5 feet above.

Within the courtyard can be seen the footings of what might have been a later retaining wall, or inner buttress. The excavators found a mortared rectangular building within the interior, dating from the 17th century, which used stones from the original broch. This suggested that Dun Cuier was inhabited, on and off, until quite recently – unusual, one might think. That might not quite be so, especially in the Hebridean islands, for Dun Carloway*, Dun Torcuill* and Dun an Sticir* have all been occupied, if only temporarily, within the last five centuries or so. Modern excavations might show this to be even more prevalent.

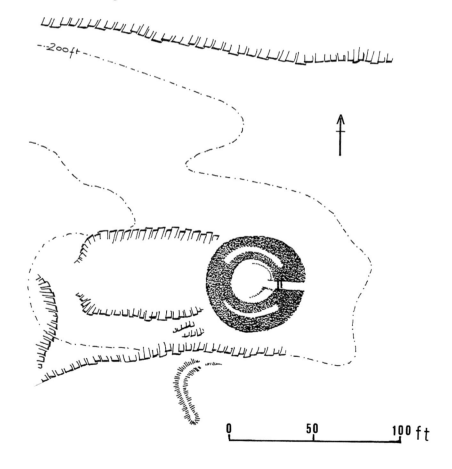

The excavations at Dun Cuier also revealed a central hearth, a bench, rotary quern and paving dating from the middle Iron Age, possibly from a pre-broch settlement on the site. Other artefacts hinted that the broch was occupied in the Dark Ages as gaming counters and a rather impressive high-backed comb, dating from c. 7th century A.D., were also found. Certainly, Dun Cuier enjoyed a lengthy period of use. All this was the result of a relatively modern excavation.

Dun Cuier enjoys good views along the north and west coasts of Barra and has a reasonably commanding position in its locality. This suggests that it might have been the residence of a local chief in the Iron Age, and perhaps even later. One can understand why brochs and duns continued to be used in the Hebridean islands long after they were no longer fortified. As substantial buildings, they were a ready-made residence, the few necessary alterations being far easier than building from scratch. Re-cycling of materials is nothing new.

Other Pre-historic Sites
Dun Bhan (Dun) Map 31 ref. 632003
Dun Scurrival (Dun) Map 31 ref. 695081
Dun Bharpa (Chambered cairn) Map 31 ref. 671019

DUN FIADHAIRT (Broch)

Skye O/S Landranger maps 32/23 ref. 231504

Directions: From Dun Beag, continue along the A863 through Dunvegan. About 1¼ miles north of the castle, the minor road crosses Loch Suardal by a causeway: park at the end of this. Walk in a west-south-westerly direction for about 1,200 yards towards a peninsula with a narrow neck. The broch is just beyond the neck straight ahead.

As you stand on the hill looking over the narrow isthmus to the hill opposite, topped by the unremarkable mound that is Dun Fiadhairt, you might be tempted to turn back. Don't.

In many respects, Dun Fiadhairt is a typical Hebridean broch. Standing on a rocky knoll amid desolate moorland, with walls that are something less in combined thickness than the courtyard is in diameter, and with a long gallery round the east and south, this could be a description of many brochs in the western isles. As you approach, there is nothing that is seemingly special about it.

Naturally, each has its own individual details, such as the number of intra-mural cells – if any. But Dun Fiadhairt has one feature that is unique in these parts, is very rare in brochs in general, and diminishes its defensive capabilities by a considerable margin. It has a second entrance opposite the main one.

The broch was mostly cleared of debris and partially excavated in 1914: this enables the architectural features to be easily seen. The main entrance faces west and has signs of flanking external walls leading from a set of rock-cut steps. These may be original, but could have been cut after a later rock-fall. It is certainly a unique approach to a broch.

The entrance passage features a door-jamb, with guard cells either side: not exactly common-place, but pretty orthodox. This opens onto a courtyard a little more than 30 feet in diameter, with no original features visible on the ground.

The wall is about 12 ft. thick and stands a little over 6 ft. high internally. Within this, there is a double-cell in the north-west, a stair lobby, with six steps, in the north and a gallery running from the north east round to the south. This latter is a feature of Hebridean brochs and is not common in the northern brochs. There are still some lintels over the gallery.

Of most interest, though, is the second entrance, which faces east. This is a much simpler affair than the main entrance – more of a postern-gate. It has no guard cell or door-jambs and is quite narrow. A few lintels remain and it cuts through the long gallery; presumably, a door could have been secured at that point. As far as broch entrances go, this is a pretty mundane affair, yet Dun Fiadhairt appears to have been designed like this, not altered subsequently.

In many respects, the second entrance defeats the whole object of a broch – you might as well insert large windows at first-floor level as well. Surely, such a small stronghold could hardly have needed two entrances. Yet, there it is.

We might well ponder why Dun Fiadhairt has two entrances, and why it was built in such an apparently desolate place. The latter has, of course, changed a fair bit since the Iron Age and one might assume that the broch was adjacent to decent agricultural land.

As for two entrances? Maybe, when this broch was built, times were fairly peaceful. But, if so, why go to all the trouble of building a broch? Perhaps a bit of pre-historic one-upmanship, a stronghold with two entrances belonging a local chief who wanted to impress his peers? Well, it takes all sorts.

Dun Fiadhairt is a splendid broch to visit for its clear internal details, but you will also enjoy some fine coastal views, plus Dunvegan Castle to the south.

DUN GRUGAIG (Dun)

Skye O/S Landranger map 32 ref. 535124

Directions: From Broadford, take the B8083 to Elgol and turn left along the road to the coast, at Glasnakille. Turn right and go to the end of the road, turn round and park by house no. 3 on the left. Follow the fence on the opposite side of the road east and where it ends a path descends quite steeply down to the dun, about 100 yards from the road.

As you walk down the steep hill through the bushes, you are suddenly confronted by this small, magnificent and fascinating promontory dun, in a glorious location. Dun Grugaig has been described as an early, primitive and simple form of semi-broch.

To all intents and purposes, it now looks like an orthodox promontory dun, with a massive stone-wall cutting off the neck of the promontory. Initial impressions of the remains can be deceptive, though, and Dun Grugaig may be deserving of a little flattery in its descriptive title.

The sheer size of the wall is seemingly multiplied further in the way it dominates the promontory. It is currently about 15 feet high and the same in thickness – dimensions not unlike those of many a ruined broch, but gives the impression of something much greater – it might well have been. There is a simple entrance through the middle of the wall, complete with door-jamb, bar hole and lintels. The gaps between the lintels outside the door-jambs might have been for jabbing weapons at uninvited visitors.

Inside and a little to the left, are the remains of stairs through the solid wall to a probable galleried first floor. This is quite ruined, but the gallery is clearly visible, with the back wall being the higher. If this were the wall-head, then it must be close to its original height, but the wall-head may have been a level higher, perhaps reaching to a little over 20 feet. There are traces of a scarcement on the inside of the wall, about 4 feet up.

The interior measures about 50 ft. x 25 ft. with steep cliffs down to the sea, some 50 feet below, on the east, south and west sides. The main wall is carried a little way round the east and west sides at a reduced thickness. Defensive walls were almost certainly

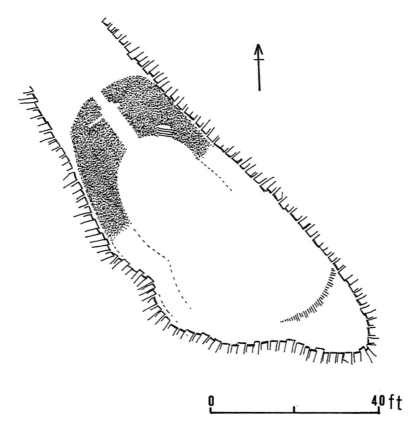

not required at these three sides but, in places, traces of a wall can be seen round the small promontory, making it a much more secure stronghold for the inhabitants.

In most respects, with the whole wall in place, Dun Grugaig would have looked pretty much like a common-place dun, though one perched on a coastal promontory. It might appear to be quite advanced in comparison with some other promontory duns, but is not, overall, built to broch standards. And the title semi-broch? Well, it seems a step in the right direction, but probably dates from the mid-Iron Age.

Never mind the nomenclature that might be attached to Dun Grugaig, it is a lovely example of a defended coastal promontory, which, considering its exposure to nature's more extreme forces, is well preserved. It overlooks the sea lochs Slapin and Eishort, and has good views across to the Sleat peninsula of south-west Skye.

This was not a stronghold where ease of access to water and good agricultural land was given priority over the defensive qualities of the site. The strategic location seems to have taken precedence over any domestic arrangements, giving the distinct impression that Dun Grugaig was far more of a stronghold than a defended homestead. The size of the main wall only adds to that conclusion.

DUN HALLIN (Broch)

Skye O/S Landranger map 23 ref. 257593

Directions: On the Waternish peninsula. Leave Dunvegan heading east on the A850 and turn left along the B886. Continue north through Lusta on the minor road to Hallin. Look out for the drive to houses 16 and 17 on the right. Walk to the end of the drive, go through the gate and up to the dun on a knoll ahead.

From the outside, Dun Hallin bears the stonework typical of Skye's Iron Age strongholds. The use of quite large, rectangular facing-stones can be seen at other Skye brochs and duns – such as Dun Beag* and Dun Ardtrek*, and is quite distinct from the stonework at most Hebridean strongholds, the west and north mainland of Scotland, and the northern isles. Dun Hallin is less typical of Skye duns and brochs, though, as it has an all-enclosing outer defensive wall.

This outer wall encircles a plateau measuring about 150 ft. x 130 ft., from which the sea Lochs Snizort and Dunvegan can be seen either side of the peninsula. The wall appears to be about 6 feet thick, but is difficult to locate in places. Such enclosures are more usually seen at northern brochs, but this was clearly important to Dun Hallin.

The broch's wall is in good condition on the outside and rises up to 12 feet high. It is best seen from north-east and north. It is only about 11 ft. thick and encloses a courtyard 36 feet across. Such a low ratio of wall width:courtyard diameter suggests that the wall was unlikely to have exceeded 30 feet high and, in any case, it is one of the narrowest known broch walls. Perhaps Dun Hallin was a relatively early broch; although it is not known as such, it may even be considered to be a member of the contentious sub-class of semi-brochs.

Dun Hallin has some of the finest external stone facing of any broch. Rising up to about 30 ft. in height, this would have been a most impressive sight.

On the whole, the interior is grass-covered stones – the original floor level is much lower, but the entrance, in the south-east, is badly damaged and its details are impossible to see. Within the wall are two intra-mural cells – possibly guard cells – and a stair-lobby, which are, as one might expect, of no great width. Part of the gallery is also visible, presumably at the first floor level, though it is hard to tell if this goes through to the ground, as is the norm in Hebridean brochs. The broch is better from the outside.

In some respects, Dun Hallin is quite contradictory. It displays the fine stone facing of, one might assume, the middle Iron Age, with the dimensions of what appears to be an early broch. Having such a comprehensive, all-enclosing outer wall is also unique for a broch on the island. Then again, if the gallery does not go most of the way round the wall at ground floor level, in other words Dun Hallin has a solid-based wall, that again would be unique on Skye.

As with most pre-historic strongholds, a thorough excavation would open up a few secrets, and Dun Hallin seems to keep a few close to its chest. It has survived quite well, though, possibly rising to nearly 50 per cent of its original height, and will, no doubt, come under more archaeological scrutiny in the future. In the meantime, it is a splendid place to visit, with long coastal views, and can be appreciated for its fine example of wall-facing so typical of Skye brochs and duns.

Other Pre-historic Sites
Dun Borrafiach (Broch) Map 23 ref. 235637
Dun Gearymore (Broch) Map 23 ref. 236649

DUN KILDONAN (Dun)

Argyll O/S Landranger map 68 ref. 780277

Directions: Take the B842 north from Campbeltown, for 6 1/2 miles, to the Forestry Commission car park at Ballochgair. The dun is across the road, 100 yards to the south-east.

Lying just 40 ft. above the sea, a javelin throw to the east, Dun Kildonan is not only one of Scotland's better preserved duns, but it occupies a panoramic location. It sits on a rocky knoll with a level approach from the west, and a steep descent to the beach. Not only could the inhabitants fish in Kildonan Bay, but there is also a good view across Kilbrannan Sound to the ever-cloud enshrouded Isle of Arran; a spectacular and haunting sight.

Dun Kildonan is often clad in bracken in the summer, but its main features are visible. A D-shaped wall encloses a courtyard measuring about 70 ft. x 40 ft. This wall is stone-faced with a rubble core and varies widely in thickness from 5 to 13 ft., with an additional facing most of the way round. It was probably built in one stage – the inner section not being a later addition, with the median facing stabilising the structure. Perhaps that is one reason why it has survived so well, when many other duns are piles of rubble.

Another reason is that part of the wall was restored during excavations in the late-1930s; stones had been robbed to construct road-side walls, or dykes. The wall is up to 6 ft. high internally, and 8 ft. externally. Despite having some broch-like features, there is no doubt that Kildonan was a dun and the wall was probably only about 15 ft. high.

The west-facing entrance includes a door-jamb and bar-hole, while there is a short length of galleried-wall immediately to the south. This is not very thick and could have been part guard-chamber/part wall strengthening at the entrance. A double intra-mural staircase leads to the wall-head, from which unwanted guests would have been encouraged to go-away. These stairs are in good condition, with tiny steps, while the median wall-face is best viewed from here. There is a small intra-mural cell in the north-east, and a possible bottom step of a ladder to the wall-head in the east.

Dun Kildonan was briefly excavated in 1984. From this, and the earlier excavations, it has been deduced that there were three main periods of occupation. It was built in the 1st century B.C., and occupied for about 300 years. These dates have not been confirmed by C-14 dating so, given recent dating results from other sites, they may need placing a little further back in time. The double-stairs were filled-in soon after, to be cleared out in the 1930s. At least three hearths and up to six small huts were in use at the turn of the pre-historic millennium, suggesting it was possibly occupied by an extended family, rather than a small tribal unit.

Then followed a long period of abandonment, until it was re-occupied in the 7th to 9th centuries A.D. This was a time when the Scotti came over from Ireland and Vikings paid their not always friendly visits. Some huts have been uncovered that might date from this period, along with a brooch and enamelled disc. Finally, after another period of dis-use, Dun Kildonan was re-occupied in the 13th and 14th centuries.

Though many artefacts have been found in or near Dun Kildonan, it was their poor quality that most grabbed the excavators' attention, especially when compared with the high quality build of the dun itself. For the visitor, that is of more importance, and there are few finer duns in Scotland than Kildonan.

With its pleasant views, a fresh-water stream and proximity to the sea, this was a good site for a stronghold and it remains a worthy and easy place to visit. There is a noticeboard and plenty of good walks in the locality.

Other Pre-historic Sites
Ugdale Point (Stack fort) Map 68 ref. 784285
Borgadel Water (Dun) Map 68 ref. 625061
Dun Skeig (Hillfort and Duns) Map 62 ref. 757571

DUN MHUIRICH (Dun)

Argyll O/S Landranger map 55 ref. 722845

Directions: From Lochgilphead, head north-west along the A816. Turn left along the B841 and then turn left on the B8025 through Tayvallich. About 2 1/2 miles south of the village, the dun can be seen between the road and the shore of Linne Mhuirich.

This highly prominent knoll is visible from afar, jutting alongside Linne Mhuirich. It is an obvious location for a stronghold, having considerable natural defences that only needed enhancing. An additional bonus was the ease of reaching the sea.

Quite often, pre-historic strongholds pose the question, 'when is a dun not a dun, but a broch?' Any definition can be difficult to quantify, especially as the height of the tower is crucial. Educated guesswork comes into play, based on the ratio of wall width:interior diameter. As for Dun Mhuirich, the question is a little different and asks, 'when is a dun not a dun, but a hillfort?' True, the inner enclosure on the knoll is small for a hillfort but, if this were in, say, the Borders, it might easily be considered to be one.

As Dun Mhuirich has two stone walls, neither of which seems to contain a core of material dug from a ditch, this could be a deciding factor in it being called a dun. Of course, there are many hillforts with drystone wall defences, and do not forget those with timber-laced ramparts. In any case, Dun Mhuirich has a similar layout to the slightly larger Dun Nosebridge*, which is, without a doubt, a hillfort. Such nomenclatures probably did not concern the Iron Age builders too much ('Look here, if we build the wall with quarried material, we can then say we've got a hillfort and not a dun.'), but it is something to consider when visiting a pre-historic stronghold. Never mind the specialists, what do you think?

Dun Mhuirich is best approached from the north straight to the original entrance. At a lower level, an outer wall encloses the knoll. This is about 9 feet thick at the entrance, reducing to some 6 feet thick in the west – the sheer rock face at the east was more than adequate. The wall varies in height round the circuit, but is still impressive near the entrance.

Higher up, a second wall encloses the knoll at the summit: an area measuring about 55 ft. x 40 ft. This wall is 7 feet thick at the ends, but only 3 feet thick along the sides, and does not appear to have an entrance – not unlike citadels at some hillforts. Thus, it is relatively slight compared with most Iron Age strongholds, but the natural defences must have been quite forbidding. This wall still stands up to 6 feet high in places, resting like a crown on a head.

Nothing is known about the history of this fortified knoll, but the remains of rectangular buildings in the interior – and adjoining the inner wall – possibly date from the Dark Ages, if not later. Quite probably much later, as excavations undertaken in 2012 and 2013 revealed evidence of occupation in the outer enclosure, plus a cruck-framed building and two later ones in the inner enclosure. These suggest re-use during medieval and post-medieval times to the 17th century, although not necessarily fortified.

Dun Mhuirich certainly has a commanding location over Linne Mhuirich and that alone must have made it attractive. Coupled with the natural defences, the knoll was an obvious place to fortify. The later use of the site indicates its strategic value had not diminished with the passing times.

Other Historic Sites
Druim an Duin (Dun) Map 55 ref. 781913
Castle Sween (Medieval castle) Map 55 ref. 713789

DUN MOR (Broch)

Tiree O/S Landranger map 44 ref. 046493

Directions: From the ferry terminal at Scarinish, walk east round Gott Bay and turn left along the road to Vaul. The broch is 1/4 mile beyond the end of the road sitting on a knoll near the shore, and is reached by following the track past a croft.

Lying on the north coast of 'Sunny Tiree', Dun Mor is a typical, ground-galleried, Hebridean broch. It may have led a pretty hum-drum life for such a stronghold – although the knoll was occupied for nearly 1,000 years, but thanks to a comprehensive excavation in the 1960s, Dun Mor leapt into the archaeological limelight. Not only was this the first excavation of a Hebridean broch that was both wide-ranging and comprehensive, but many artefacts were found and a useful series of C-14 dates recorded. Thus, Dun Mor was one of the first brochs to be given a scientifically proved chronology.

The excavator, Dr. Ewan MacKie, also arrived at some conclusions with regards the instigation and chronology of broch-building that went, at the very least, against the grain of orthodox thinking. As if to further confound traditionalists, MacKie also launched his sub-class of semi-brochs on an un-suspecting archaeological world.

His thesis was that immigrants to the Hebrides developed the brochs from the local semi-brochs, and he concluded that the migrants might well be Celts from south-west England. Ultimately, broch-building developed until the final stages were reached, with Mousa*.

Needless to say, the fact that Scotland's unique and most noteworthy pre-historic strongholds might be the product of people from England did not exactly go down too well. MacKie's interpretation of the evidence was perhaps a mite hasty with regards the English connection; the extent of pre-historic trade along Britain's Atlantic coast was far less certain thirty years ago than now. A hornets' nest had been stirred, though.

However, the thesis that brochs were first developed in the Western Highlands and islands, from duns and semi-brochs, and that the ideas were then taken to and improved in the north, has its supporters as well as its critics. In reality, such a scenario might simplify things too much, but MacKie's initial thesis turned the timber-laced wall of the established theories into a vitrifying conflagration. Many recent theories about the all-encompassing term 'Atlantic round-houses' have stemmed from MacKie's initial efforts. The inhabitants of Dun Mor cannot have imagined what their little broch would come to mean 2,000 years later.

As far as visiting is concerned, one major advantage of a modern excavation is that Dun Mor is in a good state of repair. The knoll is surrounded by an out-working up to 7 ft. high, which mostly hides the broch from view; the knoll is quite distinctive, though, set against a back-drop of the sea. The broch's wall is galleried for almost the whole circuit and is about 13 ft. thick. This encloses a courtyard 35 ft. in diameter, so the likelihood is that, as with most brochs in west Scotland, Dun Mor would have been about 20 to 30 feet high, as opposed to the 7 ft. of today. The courtyard is clear of extraneous material and is well built, though lacks the finesse of, say, Mousa*. Perhaps Dun Mor was an early broch, but archaeology has shown that brochs have pre-dated Dun Mor by some considerable time.

The entrance faces east and features a door-jamb, bar hole and, most unusually nowadays, a door pivot. There is a guard cell on the right of the passageway and you need to crawl to get in; even allowing for the current floor level being higher than the original, the entrance must still have been low and narrow.

Three doorways lead from the courtyard to the gallery. Those in the south - where the gallery is wider and where people might have lived - and north-east have been blocked. The door in the north-west also leads to the stairs, and a short section of the first floor gallery can be seen near the guard cell. Apart from a few fallen stones, the gallery is clear, though narrow, for much of its circuit. There is a scarcement about 4 feet up the inner wall-face.

There is, though, rather more to Dun Mor. For a start, it was not the first dwelling on the site. That was a wooden hut with wattle and daub walls, occupied from c. 600 to 300 B.C. There may also have been a second pre-broch phase, possibly of the broch-builders themselves - and it might not have been permanently occupied, but more of a refuge. The broch probably dates to c. 100 B.C. This might not seem an especially early date now, but MacKie was not aware of probable brochs such as Bu and Howe on Orkney, let alone possible build dates of c. 600 B.C.

Doctor MacKie found that the pottery of the broch period was different from pottery of the earlier settlement. That some pieces bore a close resemblance to pottery used in Somerset featured strongly in his migration thesis. Nowadays, and with the benefit of knowledge MacKie never had, trading links might seem more plausible. On the other hand, at a still later date, it was found that native pottery was used again – was this connected with the broch being a communal refuge? Once again, trade or broken trading links, could be the answer.

Then, in a final phase, the broch ceased to be fortified, the tower was removed and an additional inner wall-facing was built. In c. 200 A.D., Dun Mor became a farmstead. A seemingly peaceful century then came to a decidedly violent end, for MacKie found that the farmstead and its inhabitants might have been victims of a hostile raid.

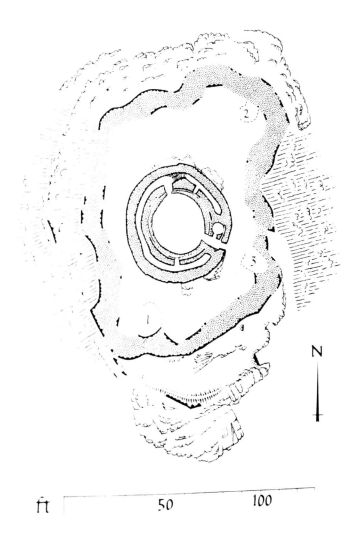

N

ft   50   100

That brought down the curtain on permanent occupation of the site, although more native pottery suggested a later temporary use.

Such a complex chronology is not unique these days, but in the 1960s it was nigh-on revolutionary for the Hebrides, and that was without MacKie's non-standard interpretation. Dun Mor, then, is not only an attractive, well sited broch, but holds a special place in Scottish and archaeological history as well. Much of the current interest and research into brochs and other Atlantic round-houses stems from the work undertaken at Dun Mor, more than 50 years ago. Whether the conclusions drawn are right or wrong - and the latter case is far from being proved, Ewan MacKie led the way; others have only followed. And without him, you and many others might not have had an interest in Scotland's pre-historic strongholds.

Other Pre-historic Site
Dun Beag (Dun) Map 44 ref. 046492

DUN NAN GALL (Broch)

Mull O/S Landranger map 47 ref. 433431

Directions: From Salen, turn south-west along the B8035 and turn right along the B8073. Park at Ballygown and the broch is down by the shore, on the edge of Loch Tuath.

From the road, Dun Nan Gall looks like a mound of tumbled stone just above the water line. As one gets closer, so the broch takes shape, but it is only 10 feet above the sea perched at the end of a low promontory. Thus, even at high tide, there was no additional protection apart from the broch's wall.

Despite the fallen stone, most of the main features are visible, though not easy to reach. The east-facing entrance is blocked for a start, but under the stones are the door-jamb and bar hole, and a socket for a door, with lintels above. Much of the intra-mural gallery is equally full of stones, but can be seen for most of its circuit, as can parts of the inner and outer wall faces. The scarcement is almost complete, though, and there are traces of an upper gallery with openings to the interior.

The wall is up to 13 feet thick and encloses a courtyard 35 feet in diameter. Height would have been this broch's main defence, yet its dimensions suggest that it would not have risen to more than 30 feet. Then again, 2,000 years ago that would have been pretty impressive, especially given the dearth of brochs on Mull. Other features, such as the interior, are similarly encumbered with fallen stones, while only three stairs still appear in place.

Dun Nan Gall certainly has an unusual location. Its name means the fortress of the foreigners (which, if dating from the Iron Age, may support Dr. Ewan MacKie's theory of brochs being the strongholds of people emigrating to the Hebrides), but it seems precariously positioned. It has been partially excavated, but this was before modern scientific techniques came about, so there is nothing to reliably date its building or use.

Dun Nan Gall's location is quite beautiful. With the sea lapping up to it – decidedly useful for fishing and trade, a fresh-water stream nearby and a good deal of land for farming, the broch could hardly be better placed. The island of Ulva lies across the loch, but the broch does not hold any great strategic position, being set so low. This would probably have been a pleasant place to live in the Iron Age, but I dare say it would not be easy trying to sleep on a wild, wind-swept winter's night, as waves pounded against the wall. Not a place for the faint hearted, at any rate.

DUN NOSEBRIDGE (Hillfort)

Islay O/S Landranger map 60 ref. 371601

Directions: Leave Port Askaig on the A846 and turn left at Ballygrant along the minor road. Keep right at the junction after about 5 1/2 miles and park after the bridge across the River Laggan. A track leads east to the hillfort, 1/2 mile away.

There are not many true hillforts in the Hebrides, but Dun Nosebridge is a most fascinating and interesting example. It has all the trappings of an enlarged dun, especially with its central citadel, and sits on a grass-covered hillock over-looking the River Laggan and large tracts of central Islay as well. This was surely a stronghold of considerable importance on the island.

Not surprisingly, Dun Nosebridge can be seen from miles about. The River Laggan is neither wide, nor deep enough to be an effective natural barrier, but the south-east

The defences of Dun Nosebridge hillfort overlook much of central Islay, although it is itself overlooked by the hill from where this picture was taken.

side of the hill has an almost sheer-face and is undefended, except for the citadel. Although Dun Nosebridge's defences are pretty comprehensive, it has not been excavated. It appears that the material for the ramparts was quarried from within the hillfort: they are quite unlike the stone walls of a dun and may have been revetted by wood, rather than stone. At least, there are trees in the Laggan valley.

Two outer ramparts enclose three sides of the hill, each on a different level, while there are four ramparts at the south-west: one of these might have formed a cattle enclosure. The outer rampart is not well defined at the north-east and might never have existed near the steep edge. The enclosure is mostly flat and could also have been used for herding cattle. Both within and without the north-east section, traces of cultivation and building foundations can be seen – these are probably relatively recent.

The middle rampart is much better defined and has an entrance in the centre of the north-east wall. This is built on a terrace and presents a formidable outer defence. The enclosure is quite large and could have been an equivalent of a medieval bailey. As with the other lines of defence, careful use was made of the hill's contours to

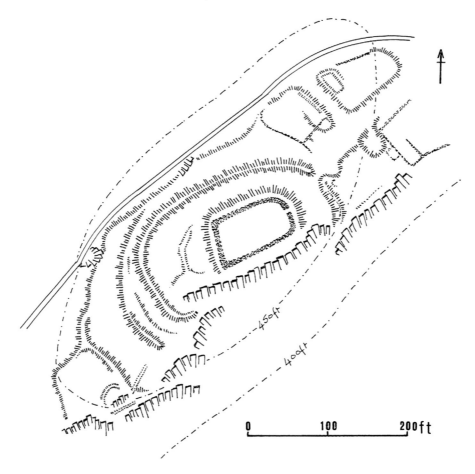

reduce the building work of this highly defended stronghold. Thus, the height of the rampart is far greater from the outside.

On the top of the hill, a citadel measuring about 80 ft. x 50 ft. is enclosed by a substantial rampart. This would have been the main area for the inhabitants and, with three lines of ramparts and the steep hillsides, would have made a secure residence; it is still impressive. There was an entrance in line with that in the middle rampart, but it is not so obviously visible today. From up here, though, the inhabitants would have had a clear view of the surrounding area – a most commanding location.

On the hillock to the north-east there is a second small enclosure overlooking Dun Nosebridge. It is a good way off, though, and could not have been used to bombard the hillfort's habitants. All in all, Dun Nosebridge combines the defensive ideals of height and depth. From every level, the inhabitants would have a height advantage over any raiders while the central citadel, and the houses, would be unlikely to be in range of fire-raising missiles. Dun Nosebridge was, without doubt, a truly formidable stronghold from which to control central Islay and makes an ideal viewing platform today.

Other Pre-historic Sites
Dun Guaire (Hillfort) Map 60 ref. 389648
Dun Bhruichlinn (Dun) Map 60 ref. 370640

DUN RINGILL (Dun)

Skye O/S Landranger map 32 ref. 561170

Directions: Take the B8083 from Broadford towards Elgol and Dun Grugaig. Turn left at Kilmarie and park before a large house on the right. Just before this, a gate on the left leads to a fine bridge across the burn. Cross this, turn right through the woods and follow the field on the left to the end of the fence. Just before crossing the stream, turn left up the hill and go over the stile. Take the path 50 yards further on the right to the dun, about ¼ mile away, above the shore.

Boy, you are in for a treat visiting Dun Ringill, with its fine views over Loch Slapin. Not only was this an Iron Age stronghold, but it was re-fortified and partially re-modelled – with mortared masonry – possibly in medieval times, and has recently been at the centre of another skirmish.

No, not a skirmish with swords and daggers drawn, but one between archaeologists over what exactly is Dun Ringill: a broch; a dun; or a semi-broch – here we go, again… Still, do not let that bother you, 'never mind the quality, feel the width' and what a place to live.

Dun Ringill has been described by Dr. Ewan Mackie (see Dun Mor*) as another semi-broch, due to the building quality and architecture approaching the standards of brochs, yet having an inferior design. Others disagree, but, you must admit, clearly Mackie has a point. Semi-brochs might be a convenient, mid-20th century category, but Dun Ringill – almost certainly a dun and not a broch – is something of a half-way house between the two. Is that enough to legitimise the notion?

Never mind such trivia for now, for sitting on a small promontory with the sea to the south-west, south and east, Dun Ringill had a fully encircling wall not unlike nearby Dun Grugaig*. It can only be approached from the north-west, where a once-massive wall – though in poor condition – confronts the visitor. This is about 15 feet thick, but narrows along the sides facing the sea, while the eastern section has all but vanished – if this were a broch, it surely cannot have been circular. There is a central entrance complete with door-jamb and bar hole, plus a later, mortared extension still

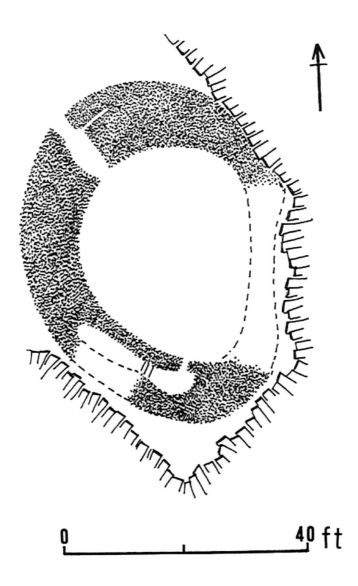

0   40 ft

with lintels in place. This is not unlike a medieval barbican and may, in fact, stem from those times.

The enclosed area measures 50 ft. x 35 ft. and is littered with tumbled stones. Despite this, the inner wall-face is mostly visible and in the south a gap leads to a cell, measuring 18 ft. x 5 ft. This was built within the wall, but is now all a bit confusing, possibly due to later re-use and the passage of time. Traces of an upper gallery on the inner wall can also be seen, so Dun Ringill probably reached about 20 feet high, or more, at least along the entrance section of the wall.

As for the later re-occupation? Dun Ringill was reputedly a stronghold of the local Mackinnon clan in the 9th century, at least for a while. Clearly, as you can see in the extended entrance, beneath the lintels, this may be true as the mortared stonework is not Iron Age.

You can certainly appreciate why the original inhabitants built this dun here and why it was clearly re-fortified centuries later. It is eminently defensible and has a commanding position, abounds useful land, has the sea close by and, if it counted for anything, is a glorious location. Whichever stronghold category Dun Ringill is placed, it clearly fulfilled its purpose twice over and really is a splendidly sited stronghold to visit today.

DUN SKEIG (Hillfort and Duns)

Argyll O/S Landranger map 62 ref. 757571

Directions: Head north along the A83 from Campbeltown. Turn left at Clachan, and park near the house on the right named 'Ardmhur'. Follow the track opposite the house and go through the second gate on the left. The hillfort is on top of the hill before you.

There are many Scottish pre-historic strongholds that have either been expanded or reduced in size: for example, hillforts given extra ramparts or simply being extended. Others, have been transformed from hillfort to broch, and finally become an open settlement: Edinshall* is the prime example here. Sites that have remains of three distinct and different strongholds, though, are rare, especially when they also display the development of design and building techniques.

Dun Skeig is hardly your average, common-or-garden, pre-historic stronghold, though. It crowns an isolated hill 469 feet above the mouth of West Loch Tarbert. In other words, it takes a bit of an effort to get there, but this will be amply rewarded by seeing the three strongholds and the truly majestic coastal views. A heavily robbed, stone wall formed the hillfort, measuring 370 ft. x 120 ft., right at the summit. Most of the stonework is barely visible, but is best seen to the north – with a few short lengths along the east flank, outside the dun, near the dun in the south and to the south of that dun. Presumably, the hillfort's wall was robbed for the later duns, but that was only after it was put to the torch, for traces of vitrified stone have been found.

Chronologically, the next to appear was the large dun that, in part, follows the hillfort rampart at the south. This measures 90 ft. x 55 ft. and has no obvious entrance.

Again, the remains of the wall are some way short of breathtaking, but the whole circuit is visible. The wall is mostly grass-covered, but some signs of vitrification poke through, and confirm that it was of timber-laced construction that came to a grizzly end. This may be an early example of an Argyll dun. As ever, it is unknown whether the dun was burnt down in a raid or by accident, but if one fire was clumsy, a second looks suspiciously like foul play.

Then again, an accident would explain why the second dun was built here: the small dun right at the summit. This is more orthodox in size and build: a circular, single solid stone wall, 10 to 15 feet thick, enclosing an area of 48 ft. x 42 ft. Although the wall is tumbled in places, it still rises to over 6 feet high and good lengths of both facings are visible. There is an entrance in the north-east displaying the door-jamb and a possible bar-hole: these are typical of a later dun. Inspection of the wall shows a that it was not timber-laced, yet falls some way short of the build-quality seen in brochs and many duns. Even so, this is visually the finest of the three strongholds, by some distance.

So, were all three built by people of the same tribe? One may wonder why anyone who had either managed to burn down their own dun, or seen it destroyed, would rebuild in almost the same place, but once at Dun Skeig you will fully understand. The islands of Arran, Gigha, Islay and, in particular, Jura – with its haunting Paps – are all visible. On top of that, Dun Skeig commands the entrance to West Loch Tarbert and has outstanding coastal views. In short, it is magnificently sited and is worth visiting for those reasons alone. Add its unique sequence of strongholds, and you have one of the great pre-historic sites of Scotland.

Other Pre-historic Sites
Dun a'Choin Duibh (Dun) Map 62 ref. 804640
Ballochroy Standing Stones Map 62 ref. 730524
Corriechrevie Cairn Map 62 ref. 738540

DUN TORCUILL (Galleried Dun)

North Uist O/S Landranger map 18 ref. 888737

Directions: Leave Lochmaddy heading north-west on the A865. Park after 3 1/2 miles, about 1/2 mile after the minor road to Lochportain on the right, and walk east across the moors to the north of the small Loch na Creige. Walk for a further 1/4 mile and turn south-east up a spur into Loch an Duin. Dun Torcuill is at the end of the spur.

Here we go again. Once again with a Hebridean stronghold, the problem of its type has to be considered. In essence, when does a dun become a broch, or vice versa? The differences can be very fine, but I doubt there were of much relevance during the Iron Age.

In 1914, an official field visit to Dun Torcuil thought it to be a ruined broch. Then, in 1963, the eminent archaeologist R.W. Feacham called it a galleried dun, but the next year it was referred to as 'the finest example of a broch in North Uist', by the Ordnance Survey (O.S,). That, surely was a defining answer?

Unfortunately, that was a desk-based assumption and, following a field visit in 1965, the O.S. changed its mind and said 'Dun Torcuil is a galleried dun and not a broch'. And now? Still without anything more than field visits, Dun Torcuil has been raised to the status of a broch, to sit (or float?) alongside its near-neighbour, Dun an Sticir*. But for how long this time?

Yes, Dun Torcuill lies on an islet in Loch an Duin, and is reached by a causeway. That, by itself, would have offered a degree of protection and would have been a deciding factor as to the form the rest of the dun took. A galleried wall varying in thickness from 7ft. 6in. to 12ft. 6in. encloses an oval courtyard 38 feet in maximum diameter. The varied width of the wall, and its relative narrowness, marks Dun Torcuill out as being more of a dun than a broch. The build quality of the wall also suggests an earlier date, or at least less skilled work than that often found in the better brochs.

Still, the wall – complete with gallery and a mural-cell – rises to about 10 feet high and, although tumbled in places, has both faces of the walls visible. As such, it looks more stronghold, less a pile of stones than some other similar examples, and is a fine site that has much to show, yet leaves plenty to feed the imagination.

This would have been quite a dominating residence, given the low-lying land, even if Dun Torcuill stood less than 20 feet high. Whether it was a dun, broch or even a semi-broch, one may assume that it was not built for fun.

Other Pre-historic Sites
Dun an t'Siamain (Island dun) Map 18 ref. 885595
Loch Hunder (Dun) Map 18 ref. 905653
Barpa Langass (Chambered cairn) Map 18 ref. 838657

DUNADD (Hillfort and Dark Ages)

Argyll O/S Landranger map 55 ref. 837936

Directions: From Lochgilphead, take the A816 northwards. There is a turning along a farm road on the left to the site, about a mile beyond Bridgend, which is signposted.

Dunadd is one of the most significant sites in early Scottish history. It has an historic past to go with that of pre-history, for it features in the 'Annals of Ulster' when it was besieged, along with Dundurn, in 683 A.D. Dunadd's prominence is further enhanced as the annals relate that, 'Oengus son of Fergus, king of the Picts, laid waste the territory of Dalriada and seized Dunadd,' in 736 A.D. About a hundred years later the Pict and the Dalriadan kingdoms – of which Dunadd was surely an important centre – united under the Dalriadan king Kenneth MacAlpin: Scotland, minus the Norse-ruled western and northern periphery, came into being.

But is that true, or is that all there is to the story of Dunadd? Excavations in 1904 and 1929 enhanced Dunadd's standing, but excavations in the 1980s raised doubts on the written references to Dunadd and yet, at the same time, opened more doors than are visible in a house of mirrors. C-14 dating of artefacts suggested that Dunadd was probably everything that had been claimed for it by the earlier excavations, and then a great deal more – yet possibly much less. Confused?

Occupying a rocky mass that rises above the River Add, Dunadd's defences are located on several levels: such a stronghold is often referred to as a nuclear fort. It is cleverly designed and makes good use of rocky outcrops to reduce the necessary building of defences. The outer enclosure, to the east and south, includes the best preserved defences, while the entrance is through a massive rock: the drystone wall hereabouts is the best at the site. Inside this enclosure are the foundations of two buildings of uncertain date and a well.

A gap in the west through the scant remains of an internal wall passes onto a higher level, from which stairs lead to the summit and the citadel. The defences here are disappointing, grass-covered mounds, but they conceal far more than ever they reveal. After the excavations of 1904 and 1929, Dunadd was assumed to have dated from the Iron Age, but it was the 1980s' excavations that confirmed this beyond question. As for visiting the site, just about everything visible dates from the Dark Ages. In this, Dunadd is not alone.

The recent excavations demonstrated that the citadel dates from two phases of occupation in the Iron Age. The first phase, from c. 400 to 200 B.C., included a dun-like structure that measured about 65 ft. x 40 ft. and was enclosed by a wall 11 to 13 feet thick, with a north-east entrance. This was extended and modified to form the second phase stronghold on the summit, c. 100 B.C. to 100 A.D. With this south-western extension, the enclosure measured 100 ft. x 40 ft. within a wall 13 feet thick. The Iron Age connection might be visually tenuous today, but that is merely a precursor for Dunadd's greatness.

In the 4th/5th centuries A.D., an oval fort was built on the summit to supplant the dun-type stronghold. Additional enclosures were defended by the 7th century, while the summit fort was remodelled to give the distinctive tear-drop shape still visible. Simultaneously, the main outer enclosure wall was built. Further rebuilding and demolition occurred through to the 10th century, as Dunadd became less a stronghold and more a ceremonial centre. Recent C-14 dating suggests Dunadd may have been used as recently as the 13th century, while a series of royal proclamations was certainly made there in 1506. Was this because Dunadd retained some symbolic importance to the people of the West Highlands and islands?

The 20th century excavations revealed that high quality metal-working was undertaken in some scale at Dunadd – it was clearly not your usual domestic residence. There is, though, something of much greater significance that confirms Dunadd's importance. Just outside the summit citadel is a rock with two footprints and basin pecked into the stone. These were probably used to inaugurate the Dalriadan kings, with the new king having to place a foot in a footprint to walk in the footsteps of his ancestors. He may have been anointed with a liquid from the basin. Such rituals have written evidence from late-medieval times, in Ireland and Scotland, and while these mean nothing to Dunadd, the likelihood is that the Dalriadan kings were inaugurated on this very summit.

That is not all. Uniquely, there is a rock-cut outline of a boar or pig, plus faint traces of probable Pictish ogham inscriptions: regrettably, these have defied any translation. Perhaps the boar and the oghams were cut to defile the footprints and basin by the Picts, in 736 A.D.? More recently, the ogham inscription has been considered to be in Irish Gaelic and might have been cut as late as the 10th century. If so, it hints of the continued importance of Dunadd even after the Vikings began to settle in western Scotland. Whatever the real truth about these carvings, they endow Dunadd with a better claim of being the seat of Dalriadan power than anywhere else, the people behind the first united Scotland.

Dunadd is therefore unique. It is most certainly not the only Iron Age site that was re-fortified in the Dark Ages, and those defences are inferior to many hillforts, but Dunadd is a place of such national importance that it must be visited. Dating of moulds and other metal-manufacturing artefacts confirm an Anglo-Saxon influence in Dunadd's metal wares. This mixture of Celtic and Germanic styles marks Dunadd

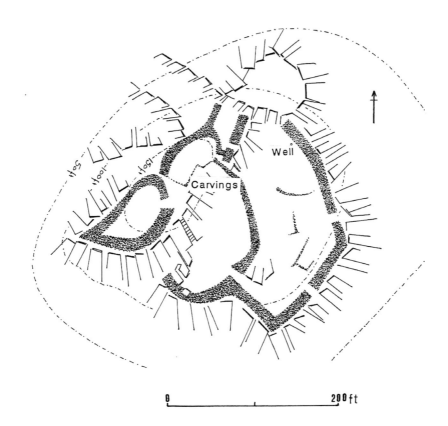

0   200 ft

The Pict fort of Dunadd is one of the most important historical sites in Scotland.
It all began in the Iron Age, though.

out as a place with substantial trading links. It might have even been a welcoming refuge for ousted Northumbrian kings. Did some of these end up in distant Dunadd?

Nobody can confirm absolutely that Dunadd was a ruling or ceremonial centre of Dalriada, but the archaeological evidence suggests this, and much more. It might have been the scene for the founding of the nascent kingdom of Scotland, or not – we shall never really know for sure. Nowhere else has a better claim, though, and as the Stone of Destiny has its symbolic significance for modern Scotland, so the footprints and basin may likewise have been the symbols of a still earlier age of nascent national unity.

There are many Bronze Age stone circles, standing stones and burial cairns only 2 to 3 miles away in the Kilmartin valley.

RUBH 'AN DUNAIN (Dun)

Skye O/S Landranger map 32 ref. 396160

Directions: A compass and map are essential to visit this dun. From Sligachan, head west on the A863, then turn left on the B8009. After a mile or so, turn left along the minor road through Glen Brittle to the west of the Cuillin Hills. Once at Glenbrittle car park, follow the path along the south coast of Loch Brittle. Towards the end, look out for the cairn near the small Loch na h-Airde and the dun is on a small cliff-edge on the coast overlooking Soay Sound in the south-east.

The remote galleried-dun of Rubh' an Dunain that overlooks the island of Soay, has little of the modern world to distract you. As such, it is not difficult to imagine yourself back in the Iron Age. Naturally, there would have been several tracks about, while some of the land nearby would have been either farmed or grazed, but it is the sheer isolation of this dun that gives it a special splendour.

As with several similar strongholds on Skye, a single, curved drystone wall cuts-off a much eroded, though always small, promontory with cliffs on all sides except the north. The area enclosed now measures about 80 ft. x 35 ft. and the wall is 80 feet long, 12 feet thick and stands up to 9 feet high. It is built of large blocks of stone, typical of Skye strongholds and, although ruined, good sections of both wall-faces can be seen.

There is a typical dun/broch-type entrance in the west complete with a set of door-jambs, while most of the wall to the east is galleried. The scarcement may have been used for lean-to houses or as a sentries' platform. Yes, this is typical of many Iron Age Hebridean strongholds – and especially Skye – that possibly belonged to an

Rubh 'an Dunain has been eroded and part has fallen away, but it is a lovely place to visit.
The possible Viking canal, quay and docks are below the waters this side of the dun.

extended family. It probably dates to the last centuries B.C. and must have been remote even for those times.

That very seclusion probably enabled Rubh 'an Dunain to survive quite well and it is one of the better examples of a galleried promontory dun. Great chunks of stone lie at the foot of the cliff where the dun's interior has fallen away, while it must always have been a pretty precarious and exposed place to live. Nobody in pre-historic times would build a defended residence of such strength if it were not to be permanently occupied. So, Rubh 'an Dunain was clearly considered an eminently suitable site on which to live. After all, there were plenty of other choices nearby.

Below Rubh' an Dunain is a canal that links Loch na h-Airde to the sea, plus two boat docks and a quay (now under water). This would have enabled boats to reach the loch or use the quay. These might seem nothing special, but have recently been found to date before 1100 A.D., perhaps even been connected with Vikings, although, I wonder, could they have originated in pre-history and be connected with Rubh' an Dunain? A cairn, ref. 393163, is near a wall at the head of the small sea loch. The O/S map shows other possible routes.

Although a fair old effort is needed to reach this dun, it can be a magnificently uplifting walk, free from man-made sights and sounds and with the ever-present Cuillins for company.

TIREFOUR CASTLE (Broch)

Argyll (Lismore island) O/S Landranger map 49 ref. 867429

Directions: Cross to Lismore by vehicle ferry from Oban. Disembark at Achnacroish Pier and follow the minor road to the B8045. Turn right and after 2 1/2 miles turn right along the minor road towards Balure. After 1/2 mile, just as the road bends to the right, walk south-east towards the coast. The broch is on slightly higher ground near the coast. There is also a boat from Port Appin to Port Ramsay.

Lismore is an attractive island situated at the junctions of the Sound of Mull, the Firth of Lorn and Loch Linnhe. There are fine coastal views all round and the journey to Tirefour Castle is spectacular.

Located on a rocky knoll 150 feet above the Lynn of Lorn, at the north-east coast of Lismore, Tirefour Castle has commanding coastal and internal prospects. Faint traces of outer walls can be seen at the north-east and south-west ends of the knoll, the latter having an entrance in line with that of the broch. It is immediately obvious that this is the ideal place to build a stronghold in this part of the island.

It is not a bad example of a broch either, despite its interior having its fair share of fallen stones. The wall seems to be solid up to first floor level, so is more typical of the northern brochs. It is built of large stones up to about 5 feet in height, with those of more irregular size above, while there is quite a pronounced taper to the outer-face: Tirefour Castle would have had the classic cooling-tower shape, like Mousa*.

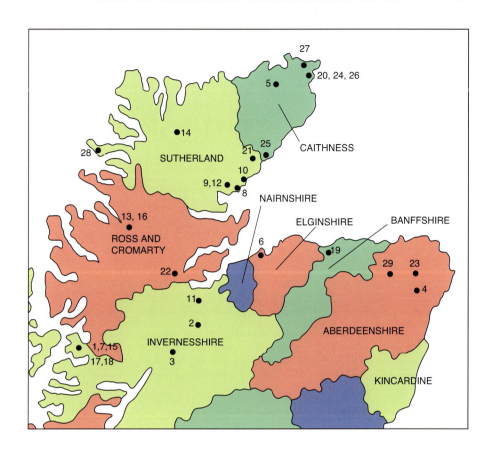

AM BAGHAN BURBLACH (Hillfort)

Inverness-shire O/S Landranger map no. 33 ref. 832199

Directions: Leave Kyle of Lochalsh east and south on the A87. At Shiel Bridge, turn right along the 'Old Military Road' to Glenelg. The hillfort is almost opposite Glenelg Candles, visible from the road part-way up the steep hill.

Am Baghan Burblach hillfort is quite a way off the beaten track and, at barely a third of an acre, is a long way to go for such a small hillfort. However, beyond Shiel Bridge, there are three brochs to see, Duns Telve* and Troddan* and Caisteal Grugaig*, and a dun, Dun Grugaig*, all of which feature in this book.

Generally speaking, hillforts pre-date duns and brochs and so while Am Baghan Burblach has not been dated, it may well be older than any of its renowned pre-historic neighbours. Its tumbled stone wall encloses an area of 170 ft. x 100 ft., and it is not possible to tell whether it was timber-laced; it does not appear to be vitrified. The wall was about 10 ft. thick, but at the south of the entrance, in the east, it was strengthened further.

Within the interior is a hut circle of about 40 ft. diameter. This may be contemporary with the hillfort and, if so, could be about 2,500 years old. Two smaller foundation rings to its west may also date to the Iron Age. That is certainly not the case of the ruined rectangular cottage and its associated gap in the west rampart. If nothing else, this shows that a pre-historic stronghold could be re-used for a considerable period, many centuries after it had originally been abandoned.

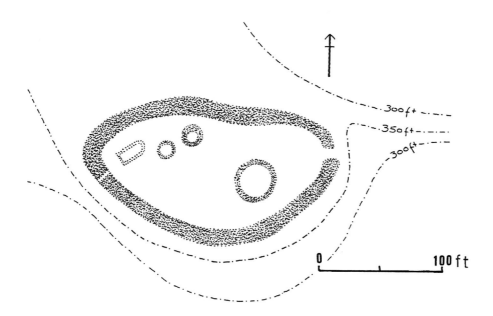

If you travel up Glenmore on a day of unremitting rain, you might just wonder what on earth our Iron Age forebears were doing settling in such a god-forsaken place. When the cloud lifts, though, it becomes obvious just how the hillfort commands Glenmore. Reasonably close to the river, it could have acted as a base for a local chief, hence the large hut circle, or perhaps an outpost for a small tribe based round the coast and Glenelg. Whatever its pre-historic use, from its tumbled rampart one can appreciate its strategic value above the pass, which once was an important route to the Isle of Skye.

Despite the large number of Scottish hillforts, there are very few along the north-west coast. This is a good example of a small hillfort from which the later, more complex, brochs and duns may have developed. The lessons learned in drystone building at hillforts such as this were put to a far more impressive use a little later, as can be seen in nearby Glenelg. That is not to decry Am Baghan Burblach, for a visit here will put the other sites into their proper chronology and perspective.

ASHIE MOOR (Hillfort)

Inverness-shire O/S Landranger map 26 ref. 600316

Directions: Leave Inverness heading south-west on the B862. About 2 miles after the junction with the B852 at Dores, a minor road joins the B862. Park here and the hillfort is on top of the hill 1/2 mile south-east of the junction.

There are several hillforts to the south and west of Inverness many of which, not surprisingly, command extensive views up Loch Ness, the Beauly Firth and Strathconon. The inhabitants of Ashie Moor appear to have had less grand designs, as the hillfort commands the smaller Loch Duntelchaig to the south-east, but still enjoys good views to the north.

Ashie Moor occupies a barren, heather-covered outcrop with a steep approach to the east that did not, apparently, warrant defences. A ruinous stone wall, about 10 feet thick, runs from the north, via the west to the south and encloses an interior measuring about 125 ft. x 75 ft. Though the wall has been robbed – probably to make the nearby roads, some large facing-stones remain in place to give an idea of its former build-quality.

An additional wall, not as wide but equally ruinous, runs from the south-west to form an outer defence on the easiest, southern, approach. It is here that there are simple entrances through both walls, which suggests the hillfort might date from pretty early on in the Iron Age.

Like so many of Scotland's pre-historic strongholds, Ashie Moor has not been excavated and so holds its past close to its chest. It is, though, an impressively sited, small hillfort. Its remote location and apparent lack of any later development, suggests that it might have existed more for strategic purposes, perhaps as an outpost of a small tribe, rather than being a permanently inhabited settlement. Even so, nothing is certain without the benefit of a full excavation.

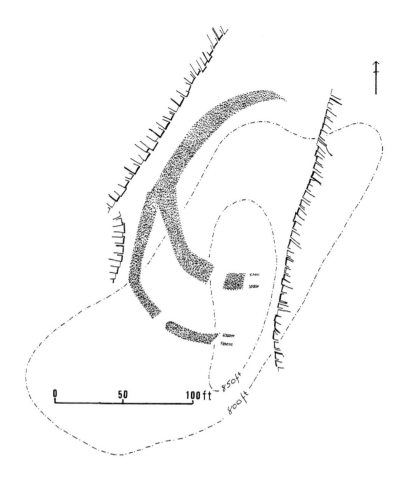

AUCHTERAUR (Vitrified Dun)

Inverness-shire O/S Landranger map 34 ref. 349070

Directions: Assuming you have visited Ashie Moor* hillfort, continue south-west on the B862 to Fort Augustus. Turn right on the A82, cross the Caledonian Canal and turn left up the minor road to Auchteraur. Go beyond the village for about a mile, to where the road curves left alongside a stream. Park and cross the stream, following the track to the left, and go into the woods for about 1/2 mile. The dun is on a rocky promontory above the track.

Vitrified hillforts are found mostly in Scotland. Even then, they are not exactly common-place, but a vitrified dun is genuine rarity. Vitrification, as you may have gathered from the introductory chapters, shows that the wall has been burnt to such an extent that the extreme heat has fused the molten stones together. This suggests that the walls were timber-laced, which usually indicates an early Iron Age phase of building. Auchteraur, then, has an immediate place in any book on pre-historic Scotland.

From over 200 feet above the passage now traversed by the Caledonian Canal, between Loch Oich and Loch Ness, Auchteraur occupies a strong, strategic position. Sited on a rocky promontory, a heavily vitrified inner wall encloses an area measuring 50 ft. x 25 ft., with a south-west entrance. An additional, outer wall offers still further protection on all sides, except the south-east.

This strongly defended dun gives every indication that it was built mainly for strategic purposes. Quite what form of living could have been gained from the nearby land is hardly obvious today, and it is sited a long way from either loch if fish were an important part of the daily diet. Still, such can be said of many Iron Age strongholds. While it is Auchteraur's vitrified wall that gives this dun its historical distinction, it cannot be denied that its spectacular location rewards the energetic and determined visitor.

BARMEKIN OF ECHT (Hillfort)

Aberdeenshire O/S Landranger map 38 ref. 725070

Directions: Leave Aberdeen, heading west, on the A944. Turn left on the B9119 to Echt, and turn north in the village on the B977. After 1/4 mile, turn left along a farm track and ask permission at the farm. Directions will be given and follow the track round the south side until reaching a gateway west of the hill. Then walk up to the hillfort.

With such a wonderful name, a barmkin being a defensive enclosure, one would expect a stronghold of equal standing; you will not be disappointed. At over 1,000 feet high, there are long views towards the coast from the north-east round to the south-east. Ten miles to the north north-west, can be seen the distinctive and prominent hillfort Mither Tap o' Bennachie*, while from there the Tap o' Noth* hillfort is visible. These hillforts might have formed a chain overlooking the fertile coastal lands, and were possibly inhabited by an envious Grampians' tribe who were more than capable of undertaking the occasional raid when the fancy took them.

Without the provision of funds to undertake even a modest excavation, the build sequence of hillforts with multiple ramparts surrounding an inner stone wall, will remain something of a guessing game. This situation is made even more intolerable when one considers the money wasted on layer upon layer of management and administrators in the public sector, churning out poor quality service. The relatively small amount needed to undertake such an excavation would be immensely beneficial to archaeology and enhance knowledge of our pre-historic ancestors: in other words, be of use to society, unlike the bureaucrats.

What greets you on arrival at the top of the hill is a complex hillfort, one that developed over several centuries. It seems that the three tightly spaced, turf-covered ramparts were the first defences to be built. Like those at the Brown Caterthun*, these are now low mounds, but some facing-stones are still visible at the rear of each rampart; it is probable that such stones faced the rampart fronts as well.

Again like the Brown Caterthun*, there are several entrances through the outer ramparts: three close together at the south and one in the north; that at the east is relatively modern. The rampart ends are inturned at each of the pre-historic entrances, to form an elongated passage. Nobody knows why or whether these were in contemporary use, but, as an entrance is the weak-spot of any stronghold – from a hillfort to a modern army base, to have three so close together, and four in total, suggests that defence might not have been this hillfort's priority. These defences enclose a circular area of about 2 1/2 acres, with a diameter of 500 feet.

Within these, and of a more obvious defensive nature, are two circular, tumbled stone walls. The outer one is about 10 feet inside the three earth ramparts, is about 6 feet thick and is now of no great height. The chances are that this post-dates the earth

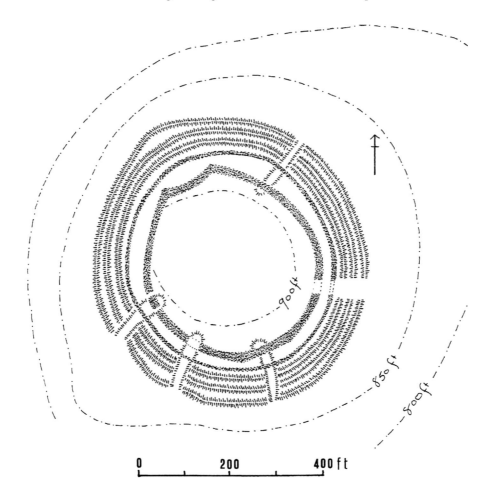

ramparts, and maybe also the inner wall, as, apart from the modern gap, it has no obvious entrance. It is even built over the four pre-historic entrances but, despite this seeming oddity, such a situation is far from unique.

Finally, ranging about 10-40 feet within this, is a second, quite ruinous, stone wall, about 8 feet thick and up to 5 feet high in places, making it the most impressive defence at the hillfort. This encloses an area of about 375 feet diameter and again, curiously, has no obvious entrances; that in the south, although aligning with the passage through the outer banks, may be a more recent addition.

The most obvious question is, how can one have a stronghold without an entrance? A possible answer might be that the original, triple rampart hillfort was little more than a defended enclosure for use in times of danger. Perhaps the chances of an external threat grew, and so the two stone ramparts were built, not necessarily simultaneously. As there is no sign of vitrification, these may not have been timber-laced, as many earlier stone ramparts seem to be, so they could date from well into the Iron Age. Entry to this defended area was probably via step-ladders, or a semi-permanent wooden structure that could be dismantled in times of trouble and strife. The main problem with this theory is that the cattle would have to remain outside the stone citadel.

Another possibility is that the original hillfort was abandoned and, at a later date, the stone stronghold was built for a military use, perhaps one of a chain of hillforts. This could have been an outlying hillfort of the Caledonii, whom the Romans defeated at the Battle of Mons Graupius.

Whatever the true history of this fascinating hillfort, we shall never know with any degree of certainty until such a time that money is found for a decent excavation. You never know, this could have played a key role in one of the most important events to have taken place on Scottish soil, whose location is still elusive: the battle of Mons Graupius. Yet, more men in grey suits, with inflated salaries and handsome pension packages, are meanwhile employed to, seemingly, mis-manage our public services. Historians in 2,000 years' time are going to find it hard to explain our present puerile, prosaic priorities.

BEN FREICEADAIN (Hillfort)

Caithness O/S Landranger map 12 ref. 059557

Directions: From Thurso, take the B870 south. At Scotscalder station, follow the track west for 11/2 miles through Dorrery; keep left at a fork of tracks. After 3/4 mile, turn right towards Torran, a farm. The hillfort is on the hill 3/4 mile due north, not the nearer one to the north-east. You pass some standing stones en route.

The pursuit of Scotland's best pre-historic strongholds will take you to many places far from the usual tourist routes. Ben Freiceadain hillfort is one. Its remote location requires a fair old effort to get there, yet it fully rewards every ounce of energy thus expended.

This is the most northerly, non-promontory, hillfort on mainland Britain and, in this county of countless pre-historic relics, stands out proudly as if making just that point: Ben Freiceadain is no shrinking violet. Ensure that there is good visibility when you visit this hillfort, for there are some magnificent views to enjoy, especially if you like a wind farm. The expanses of north and east Caithness open out before you, and the Orkney Islands sit on the horizon. To the west lie the hills of Sutherland while there are long views to the south over expansive bog-land. In short, whoever commanded Ben Freiceadain probably controlled a considerable area.

Without doubt, this must have been an important focal point in the Iron Age. Compared with the other pre-historic strongholds in this part of Scotland, Ben Freiceadain is massive. The large, mostly flat, summit – measuring about 300 yards by 160 yards at its extremities – is defended on its south and west by a grass-covered rampart of not inconsiderable size. This sits on an apparently natural terrace and was probably faced with stone slabs quarried from the interior. The entrance is in the north-west. This retains an upright stone slab; probably similar to those that once lined the rampart. The steep slopes to the north and east were not deemed to need any additional defences.

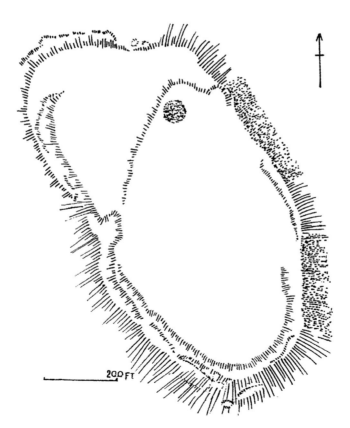

200 FT

If Ben Freiceadain were a major stronghold in the Iron Age, then there is little sign of any permanent habitation. Of course, the huts might have been built in the quarry-ditches behind the rampart, or perhaps lean-to buildings were used instead. As usual with such remote hillforts, though, such a lack of surface evidence is anything but conclusive as to whether it was permanently occupied or not. Only a substantial excavation will shed any decent illumination in that direction.

What can be seen today must not colour your views of the Iron Age. All too often in recent decades, archaeology has discovered that what is often now peat bog was once intensively farmed and settled in pre-historic times. The many, now isolated, brochs that occupy the valleys of east Caithness must have been capable of supporting a steady existence. The same probably applies to Ben Freiceadain, for everything about this once-mighty hillfort suggests that it was a place of considerable local importance.

The hillfort is also known as Buaile Oscar, or Oscar's Town: Oscar being the heroic son of Ossian, the son of the mythical giant Fingal, of Fingal's Cave fame. If that attaches some mystique to the hillfort, something more tangible is the ruined stone burial cairn that occupies the summit itself. This probably pre-dates the hillfort by anything up to 2,000 years and the possibility that the hill was already sacred ground may have influenced the builders. Then again, if one is building a fortified settlement, it is the defensive capabilities of the site that are of utmost importance. On that front, Ben Freiceadain is almost un-rivalled within its locality.

Caithness is a fascinating county to visit for, though much of it now appears rather featureless, there is a substantial number of pre-historic sites, let alone strongholds, to see. Ben Freiceadain is the biggest hillfort north of Inverness and, in this county of innumerable brochs and burial cairns, should not be missed.

BURGHEAD

Morayshire O/S Landranger map 28 ref. 109691

Directions: From Elgin, head west on the A96 and turn left on the B9013, which goes straight to the town of Burghead. What is left of the promontory fort can be seen at the extreme north-west edge of the town, off King Street.

For those familiar with Burghead, you might be wondering what it is doing in a book about pre-historic strongholds. For a start, it is a supposed major Pict stronghold – post-dating the Iron Age, and secondly the site has been virtually destroyed. While both of these claims cannot be denied, for many years Burghead was thought to be an Iron Age promontory hillfort, while some sections are still visible and the location is not un-attractive. Even if you are still not convinced, Burghead serves as a salutary reminder of what could befall our pre-historic strongholds – or anything else – if regulations are ever relaxed.

It is not often that Scotland has cause to thank the mainly English army that put the Young Pretender's supporters to the sword in the 1740s, but that was when General W. Roy had plans of Burghead's massive defences drawn up. Then, early in the 19th century, the local landowner – James Young – decided to improve the village and port and proceeded to destroy the three massive ramparts that cut off the promontory. These were about 270 yards long, measured about 60 yards across and enclosed about 12 acres. This area was divided on an east/west axis by a further wall; the smaller area in the south is several feet higher than the other. In other words, this was a massive fortification on a scale far larger than many other promontory forts in Scotland.

If seeing is believing, then the above may appear as a fantasy. All that is left today is the dividing wall between the ever-encroaching town and the sea. This is fairly impressive but, like many an ageing sportsman, is a mere shadow of its former self. To all intents and purposes, one of the most important historical sites in the country has been wilfully destroyed.

Yet, though all has effectively been lost, Burghead did not go down without a fight, or at least providing some useful archaeological information. The main ramparts were found – by excavation in the 19th century – to have had large beams protruding from the rear. These were joined by iron spikes about 8" long x 1" across, thought to be a unique British application of the building technique introduced by the Gauls in the 1st century B.C., *murus gallicus*. Excavations in the 1960s cast doubt on this thesis as no others were found, and it is now considered that the wood might have been used to get up to the wall-head.

As a further alternative, charcoal from the rampart was Carbon-14 tested and suggested a building date of 3rd to 7th centuries A.D. So, it is possible that the Caledonians occupied the original fort, before it became a major Pict stronghold, possibly known as Torridon. Whatever, there is no doubt that the ramparts were consumed by fire, possibly following the Viking raids of Sigurd the Powerful in the late-9th century, but further details remain elusive.

Other historical events have been connected with Burghead, including a visit by St. Columba to convert the Pictish King Bruide to Christianity, in the 6th century A.D. Such stories and other frivolities from the Celtic revivalists are little more than guesswork and have no basis in fact, insofar as Burghead is concerned. One can assume its former importance from the known scale of its defences, but several carved Pict and Viking stones were also found at the site. These are now in the British and Elgin Museums, and the National Museum of Antiquities. Similar carvings would possibly be found at many Pict settlements, but Burghead was thought to be the only known Pict stronghold of anything like its size. Until, in 2020 Aberdeen University announced that the larger, once considered Iron Age hillfort on Tap o' Noth* dated from the 3rd to 6th centuries A.D., and covered nearly 40 acres – with a possible population of 4,000.

Much about Burghead remains in doubt, including the dating of the large well just off King St. Even this, perhaps the most impressive part of the site, has been considered to be both of Iron Age and later dates. It seems that Burghead cannot win, but we can all benefit from Burghead, even if it is only how not to squander our pre-historic legacy. Once it has gone or been destroyed, there is no going back.

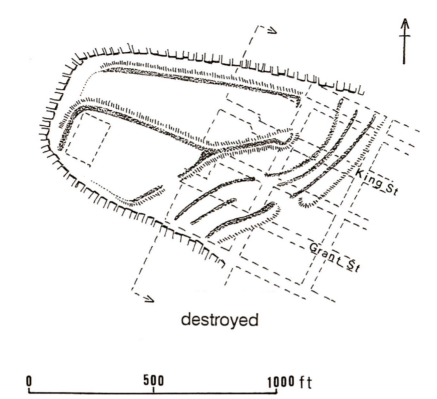

King St

Grant St

destroyed

0   500   1000 ft

Burghead's massive, dividing rampart is all that remains of this once extensive Pict stronghold.

CAISTEAL GRUGAIG (Broch)

Ross and Cromarty O/S Landranger map 33 ref. 866251

Directions: From Kyle of Lochalsh take the A87 east to Shiel Bridge. Turn right on the minor road to Glenelg and turn right on the minor road running along the western shore of Loch Duich. Follow this to Totaig, where the road ends. Continue along the track and footpath that leads directly to the broch, a walk of about 1/2 mile.

Caisteal Grugaig stands within Forestry Commission woods, but the broch is clear of trees and offers good views over the confluence of Lochs Duich, Alsh and Long, while Eilean Donan Castle is just in view. With the trees cleared, as they probably were in the Iron Age, this would have been even more impressive.

Quite why this broch is built part-way up the hill, yet away from the loch, is unclear. The land lower down would surely have been better for farming, while a site near the loch would have been easier for fishing. Perhaps the strategic location was of greater importance, for a considerable stretch of water would have been visible. It may be that the lochs formed a tribal boundary, and that Caisteal Grugaig was a northern outpost of a tribe to the south. This is no more than speculation, but sometimes it helps to consider why a pre-historic stronghold was so sited. In any event, it is harmless fun and can enhance a visit to pre-historic sites.

The most unusual of several features at Caisteal Grugaig is its hillside location, and the consequent slope of about 7 ft. down to the north-east. Now, there are plenty of examples of mortared stone castles built on hill slopes, and even drystone walls at hillforts and duns, but for a drystone tower once probably rising to 30 ft. or so is an adventurous feat. It would certainly be impressive from a distance, though missiles could be thrown into its courtyard from the hill above.

Another feature of interest is the massive triangular lintel over the entrance. Such a stone would spread the load from the wall above and perhaps its visual qualities as well. The entrance is at the lowest level of the broch and is complete with door-jamb, bar hole and a blocked entrance to a large guard cell within the solid wall. The courtyard is some 30 ft. across enclosed by a wall about 12 ft. thick. One would assume that, in order to offer sufficient defence from the hillside above, Caisteal Grugaig would need to be at least 30 ft. high.

The steeply sloping courtyard would be impractical as living space, and there is a wide scarcement visible all round. This is only about 2 ft. above the natural floor in the south-west, but much higher at the entrance, and would have supported a wooden floor which was effectively at first floor level. The courtyard was cleared in 1889, but the present ground floor is still higher than in the Iron Age.

In the south-east there is a small intra-mural cell with a complete corbelled roof. These were found in most solid-wall brochs, but few still have an intact roof. Next door, but separated from it, is the intra-mural stairway to the living quarters. These open onto a gallery and, opposite the entrance, a doorway leads out to the first floor. One can gain a very good impression of the gradient of the slope from this vantage point. The gallery continues farther round, briefly, to a few more steps that led upwards.

In the north-west wall is a, mostly blocked, long intra-mural gallery; entry being gained from the ground floor. Taken together, there are galleries, cells, stairs and an entrance within about half of the solid wall. This is quite a high proportion for such a broch, many of which have little more than an entrance and a single cell. There are also sections of wall visible for most of the circuit above the scarcement, best seen opposite the entrance. This allows a direct comparison to be made of the interior wall-face below the scarcement (solid wall) and above it (galleried wall).

Externally, Caisteal Grugaig's walls stand less than 10 ft. high. As with the interior though, the facing is largely complete and the method of construction can be studied. Remember, these great towers were simply held together by the weight and positioning of their stones. However diminutive the ruins of brochs might appear, one can only marvel at the drystone construction that rose to such heights and lasted several centuries before collapsing through lack of maintenance.

Caisteal Grugaig is spectacularly sited. Its ruins compare unfavourably with the two nearby in Glenelg, the Duns Telve and Troddan, but it demonstrates Iron Age building capabilities, no matter how unpropitious the site. Yes, there is much to appreciate at Caisteal Grugaig, especially its many outstanding detail features.

CARN LIATH (Broch)

Sutherland O/S Landranger 17 ref. 871013

Directions: The North Coast 500 is a useful route to take if you want to visit a few pre-historic strongholds. None is easier than this. Take the A9 north from Golspie, past Dunrobin Castle, for about 1 1/2 miles. The car park is on the left just before crossing the railway. Cross the road to the broch at the south end of the car park.

The coast and valleys of Sutherland and Caithness seem to abound with either known, or suspected brochs. Unfortunately, many have been robbed for building materials, while the remainder are usually mounds of grass-covered rubble. Carn Liath was little different, at one time, but the whole site was tidied up making it a particularly fine and easy broch to visit.

Standing on an enhanced knoll and enjoying spectacular coastal views, particularly to the north-east, Carn Liath commands both the route north and a substantial length of coastline. The knoll is protected by a grass-covered stone wall round its perimeter. Most unusually, a passageway – that was probably covered – leads from the entrance through the outer wall, to that of the broch. This passage entrance has door-jambs, while the broch's main entrance has door-jambs, a bar hole and a, now blocked, guard cell; thus forming one of the most heavily defended broch entrances.

The tower has a solid base and mural stairs lead to the top of the wall. In the courtyard there were two stone-lined pits, one of which was probably a well, while the inner wall-face rises up to 10 ft. above the floor. Much of the wall-face is secondary, built after the tower collapsed and was used as a house, probably in the late-Iron Age. The original courtyard was about 30 ft. across, within an overall diameter of some 70 ft., so the walls are wide and, by implication, possibly reached a height of 40 ft. or so. At the top of the wall, traces of the gallery and a scarcement can be seen. All in all, this broch was designed to appear as the impressively fortified stronghold it most surely was.

The exterior wall-face was restored after a 19th century excavation; rubble was cleared away in the 1970s. Of more interest, though, are the buildings between the broch and the outer wall. These are not to the scale of, say, Gurness Broch*, but were probably more common at brochs than appears to be the case from surface remains today. A few of these may be contemporary with the broch tower, enhancing the theory that brochs did not exist in isolation. Some houses were rebuilt, while others, particularly those built into the outer wall, are likely to be post-broch, but still date from the Iron Age, say c. 300 A.D.

Here, then, is a small settlement, perhaps that of a large, extended family or small village, rather than a single household. The scale of the broch and its outer wall shows that it was intended as a secure stronghold.

Against whom it was built is a mystery, but one can be sure that Iron Age man did not build on this scale for the fun of it. Carn Liath's primary aim was to provide protection, and to show to all and sundry that it was capable of fulfilling that need. If, in the mind's eye, you reconstruct the tower to about 40 ft. high, given the prevailing Iron Age weapons, this would appear as a mighty fortress. It was one of several nearby.

Carn Liath is a fine example of a northern coastal broch; one enhanced by careful restoration. It is a pity that more brochs cannot receive such treatment, without necessarily going to the expense of a full excavation. This would attract a greater interest into these unique pre-historic strongholds that are an important part of Scottish heritage. Perhaps this would help foster the realisation that our pre-historic past was one of great achievement, one deserving of far more attention than it is ever given today.

CARROL BROCH

Sutherland O/S Landranger map 17 ref. 846065

Directions: From Duchary Rock* hillfort, follow a track north-west until it crosses a stream. Follow the stream downhill for 1/2 mile and the broch is on the opposite side. After visiting Carrol Broch, continue downhill to the track at Loch Brora. Head south-east along this, passing another broch on the right after 3/4 mile, and continue through the woods onto the minor road leading back to where you parked.

Also known as Craig Carril, this is a surprisingly well preserved broch, especially as it appears to be a heap of stones from the distance. It is relatively easy to reach from Duchary Rock*, so time ought to be allowed to visit both sites together.

The broch is surrounded by the remains of an outer wall, as at several northern moorland brochs. A gap through this aligns with the east-facing broch entrance.

Although the external wall-facing is barely discernible, thanks to the mass of tumbled rocks, the interior is in particularly good condition: the result of an excavation in the 19th century, which tidied the site up, if nothing else.

The entrance has two sets of door-jambs, rarely seen at brochs, but one that is of obvious additional defensive benefit. Between these, on the right, is a guard cell complete with a high corbelled roof. Most intra-mural cells are now open to the air, so this can be really appreciated in all its finery. The roof construction is always worthy of study, and one might ponder the odd relationship between cells with such a high roof and a low entrance. Sometimes entrances appear low as the present floor is higher than the original one, yet it is surprising to find guard cells – where a quick exit may be required – so encumbered.

Inside the broch, the scarcement is visible and the doorway to the stairs is about 4 feet above ground level, with an intra-mural gallery about 20 feet long leading in an anti-clockwise direction. The internal wall-face is visible up to about 11 feet in height, quite a contrast to the external wall-face. These features make the visit to Carrol Broch all the more rewarding.

Today, the surrounding moorland seems to be a lonely place to live. But with a nearby stream and land that could be farmed, the broch's inhabitants would have regarded this location as eminently suitable for a small stronghold. Carrol Broch was probably one of the latest built, as demonstrated by the two sets of door-jambs, and would have been occupied more recently than Duchary Rock*. Sometimes it can be difficult to reconcile an area of much pre-historic activity with the apparently barren landscape of today.

CINN TROLLA or KINTRADWELL BROCH

Sutherland O/S Landranger map 17 ref. 929081

Directions: Take the A9 north from Carn Liath* broch. About 1 1/2 miles beyond Brora, the railway and road run together. Kintradwell Farm is on the right and park at the next field gate on the right. Walk north-east through the field.

Also known as the Troll's Head, Cinn Trolla is not cared for like Carn Liath*, but it does have secondary, external buildings and is something of a poor man's Gurness Broch*. It was one of many brochs, usually seen as a grass-covered mound, that were cleared in the 19th century. Cinn Trolla was excavated (or cleared) in c. 1870.

This excavation revealed a partially lintelled entrance passage, 18 ft. long and 7 ft. high, with a guard cell 7 ft. across and fully 11 ft. high: sadly, this is now only about 6 ft. and the corbelled roof has gone. Most unusual, though, was the two sets of door-jambs, improving security at a broch's weak-spot. This was a relatively simple method of enhancing the defensive virtues of a broch. It is, perhaps, a little surprising that more brochs did not have two doors.

A large quantity of rotary querns was found inside the broch, along with burials within the intra-mural chambers. The bodies must have been placed there after the broch ceased to be used, and an iron spear-head was found with one body. To date, this appears to be a unique, isolated instance of a later use for a broch.

In all other respects, Cinn Trolla is an orthodox, though well planned, north Scotland broch. With a courtyard some 30 ft. in diameter, and wall about 15 ft. thick, it was most likely of considerable height and, given the apparent lack of any outer walls, that would be its main defence. As usual, there is little of note visible in the interior, but a well was found in the south-east, near the wall with steps leading down 7 ft. There is an intra-mural cell and stair-lobby, and a scarcement can be seen about 8 ft. high, while the wall still stands up to 15 ft. above the original floor level.

The excavations of c. 1870 claimed that the external buildings are post-broch, due to the inferior quality of building. These were mostly built from small stones and human remains were also found in these buildings.

Although the railway now runs close by, Cinn Trolla is only about 1/4 mile from the coast. It would have been ideally situated for farming the coastal plain. As such, it may have been a defended homestead, or possibly a central refuge for the small settlement

This overhead view of Cinn Trolla shows the layout of the broch and the external buildings.

built round it: perhaps that of an extended family. The layout shows that it was well planned, and Cinn Trolla was probably one of the most recent brochs and included the latest innovation, that of double doors.

Other Pre-historic Site
Castle Cole Broch. Map 17 ref. 795133. Also with two door jambs.

CRAIG PHADRIG (Hillfort)

Inverness-shire O/S Landranger map 26 ref. 640453

Directions: Leave Inverness on the A862. After crossing the Caledonian Canal, turn left at the roundabout, along King Brude Rd. Take the fourth turning on the right, cross the roundabout and there is a car park and forest walk to the hillfort.

The hill on which Craig Phadrig stands can be seen from all round Inverness. Unfortunately, being on Forestry Commission land, the views in the opposite direction are not always reciprocated. The hillfort is mostly clear of trees, but as those surrounding it grow ever larger, so the views the Iron Age inhabitants had over the Beuly and Moray Firths, and the Black Isle, are increasingly compromised.

One benefit of Forestry Commission ownership is the provision of car parks, signs and paths that lead to the hillfort. Craig Phadrig is certainly worth visiting as well, for it has much to commend it in fact and fantasy. Happily, it was partially excavated in the 1970s and C-14 dates from both ramparts showed that it was built in about the 4th and 5th centuries B.C. More recently, there have been a geophysical survey, an evaluation and a trench cut, which shed a little more light about the hillfort's past.

An inner grass-covered rampart encloses a rectangular summit of about 1/2 acre, measuring 250 ft. x 75 ft. This rampart is now spread across 30 feet, but was originally about 20 ft. wide; it still stands up to 12 feet high externally and 3 feet above the interior. The 1970s excavations revealed this to be a vitrified, box-shaped, timber-laced stone rampart. The outer rampart runs 50-75 feet beyond the inner defences – round the bottom of the summit – and is a much slighter affair today. It is of similar construction and date and, it is thought, was vitrified at the same time. There are no signs of an obvious entrance through either rampart.

As with other vitrified hillforts and duns, nobody knows whether the fire was started by accident or during a raid. However, as both ramparts seem to have been burned – possibly simultaneously – and are so far apart, it seems that it was either one heck of an unfortunate accident or, more likely, that Craig Phadrig succumbed to an attack. The obvious question is, by whom? That, I am afraid, we are never likely to know but, as C-14 dates were also obtained for the 2nd century B.C., the hillfort enjoyed a decent period of use.

That might have been that for Craig Phadrig, as with so many other vitrified hillforts, except the excavators uncovered some surprises in the interior. A few shards of imported pottery and a clay mould for hanging-basket fittings were unearthed, dating to 5th-8th centuries A.D. The recent trench revealed a palisade ditch cut across the inner rampart, so the site had been re-occupied and the ramparts might have been partially re-constructed as well. If this were the case – and it would be unusual, but not unknown – then Craig Phadrig might have been a place of some importance to the Picts.

That is where the legend enters the story. St. Columba is said to have ventured inland from Iona in the 6th century A.D. and visited the Pictish King Bruide. Reputedly, the gates of the fortress flew open on Columba's approach, and the king and everyone was converted to Christianity – the first to be so in the Highlands. King Bruide was supposed to have had a royal house on the River Ness, so as Craig Phadrig was occupied at that time and, with clay moulds and imported pottery, was probably not your run-of-the-mill settlement, that event might have taken place within this former Iron Age hillfort. Inverness Council seems to favour the site for, as you will have noticed, King Bruide, or Brude, has a road named in his honour. Unfortunately, there are other places that lay claim to be the venue for St. Columba's great conversion, Burghead among them.

Legend or not, Craig Phadrig has its place confirmed both in the early Iron Age, in later Pictish times and, from the most recent results, the inner rampart was probably re-used in the 11th or 12th centuries, for a third time. This seems as though, with three periods of use, Craig Phadrig was a rarity among hillforts, but it may well be, as with duns and brochs, that many smaller pre-historic strongholds were occupied on-and-off on several occasions down the passing centuries.

Today, we can only surmise what Craig Phadrig looked like and who lived there. But you can be certain that it was important enough to warrant a major attack and be razed to the ground. It would certainly have made a spectacular sight as it blazed away.

DUCHARY ROCK (Hillfort)

Sutherland O/S Landranger map 17 ref. 850050

Directions: Take the A9 north from Golspie, past Dunrobin Castle, and turn left along the minor road to Doll. Pass through the village and park just before the ford across the River Brora. Walk along the track opposite the house, 'Tigh na Rosa', and keep right at a fork following the track through the woods to the open moorland. Duchary Rock can be seen along the high ridge on the right.

Considering how close some pre-historic strongholds are to modern transport communications, and they do not come any closer than nearby Carn Liath* broch, it comes as something of a surprise to realise just how remote others can be. Duchary Rock and the nearby Carrol* Broch, which is also included in the book, serve to act as reminders in no uncertain terms.

As with so many things, the greater the effort required, the better the rewards and this is certainly true of the views from Duchary Rock. It is a wonderful example of how to utilise a site's natural defensive qualities to reduce the building required.

One is reminded of how the railways of Britain were, on the whole, built on the backs of the navvies using little more than metal hand tools. River valleys were often followed to ease the tasks of construction and to avoid major earthworks, as is well demonstrated on the line to the north from Inverness. Well, Iron Age people seldom used metal tools nor, so far as is known, wheelbarrows. So, any labour saving in constructing strongholds was most welcome to them.

Duchary Rock encloses about 6 acres, measuring about 800 ft. x 200 ft., yet barely a third of the perimeter defence is man-made, and a decent proportion of that enhances the natural rock. Steep cliffs along the north-east and south-west sides required no further strengthening, and the Iron Age walls are limited to joining these at the south-east and, in particular, the north-west ends. Both walls are of drystone build, often using surprisingly large boulders, and are now quite ruinous. That at the south-east has fared the worst, but a narrow entrance, barely 4 feet wide, can still be made out in the centre.

Much more impressive is the north-west wall, which is three times the length of that in the south-east and has stretches of both inner and outer wall-facings. It was about 12 ft. thick and, although it is quite tumbled, rises to some 4 feet in height. There are two entrances. Both of these are lined with upright slabs typical of several pre-historic strongholds in northern Scotland. There is also a possibility that there were two other entrances, but, given the oft-mentioned matter of an entrance being a stronghold's weak-spot, four entrances rather suggests that either the inhabitants were pushing their luck, or were supremely confident of never being attacked. In which case, why build such a large hillfort? Of course, not all of these supposed entrances need have been in use simultaneously.

The north-west wall is continued round the cliffs at the west side as an additional defensive measure, until they become steep enough not to require buttressing. There is no question that the inhabitants knew the exact amount of work needed to fortify such a site, and were not prepared to compromise its defensive nature. There may have been an additional wall outside the defences at the north-west – this being the easiest approach, but, if so, it is difficult to see.

The interior is covered in peat, except where it has been cut, and is undulating but featureless. The view, though, is tremendous. Loch Brora and the hills beyond open out ahead, while the coastline is visible to the east. Once again, this is another example of a magnificent strategic location chosen for a stronghold by Iron Age people. This is an area of few hillforts, though there are several brochs, so Duchary Rock may have been a mid-Iron Age tribal centre. If so, it was a worthy, if remote site. Carrol Broch* is a little way down the hill to the north-west.

DUN AN RUIGH RUAIDH or RHIROY BROCH

Ross and Cromarty O/S map 20 ref. 149901

Directions: Take the A35 south from Ullapool. Turn right along the minor road that follows the west side of Loch Broom. Stop at the Loggie village sign, go through the metal field gate on the left and the broch is on a rocky bluff about 100 yds. up the hill.

The most obvious thing to notice as you make the short, sharp climb up to this stronghold is that a portion of the wall has fallen down the hill. Thus, Rhiroy is now 'C – shaped, but would have been fully enclosed in the Iron Age.

This stronghold, and nearby Dun Lagaidh*, was excavated in 1968 and was considered to have a flattened circle plan and to be a semi-broch, a sort of half-way house between a dun and a broch. This sub-class of the excavator's, Euan Mackie, has been a source of much, often less than complimentary, academic debate, but if he was once not quite so un-yielding in his view (which he has subsequently modified), there was much validity in his interpretations.

For a start, Rhiroy's galleried wall is up to 14 ft. thick, yet the courtyard's diameter is about 38 ft. Such a low ratio of wall:courtyard suggests that Rhiroy would not have exceeded 30 ft. in height, and falls between a small dun and a broch. Then again, Rhiroy displays several features that can be instantly recognised in many brochs. The, mostly blocked, entrance passage had a door-jamb, while there is a combined entrance to a stair-well and mural cell to the left – a survey in 2015 states that much of this is blocked now. The stairs ran to a landing, which, it was thought, opened onto a wooden floor supported on a scarcement and a circle of post-holes that the excavator uncovered. The stairs then continued up, presumably, to either a second floor, or the wall-head.

There is a mural gallery, nearly 50 ft. long, and it was considered that there were two walls tied together by cross-slabs – quite common in the western isles. The now fallen, assumed narrower, section was not thought to be galleried. However, if part of the cliff has also fallen, there could have been room for the wall to continue in a circle at its usual thickness, thus negating one factor behind the claim of being a semi-broch. This is unlikely to be proved either way, unless the collapsed cliff-face can be shown to have been post-broch.

The wall is almost 10 ft. high above the interior, which slopes about 4 ft. Thus, the scarcement, which is barely 4 ft. above the floor at the uphill end, must have been about 8 ft. up the now collapsed wall. Nothing can be seen of either the post-holes, or the central hearth, while the galleries have been filled-in. The excavator found several rotary querns, and part of one within the core of the wall. He considered that, as a semi-broch, it could date from the 3rd century B.C. Rhiroy undoubtedly enjoyed a considerable post-broch existence and may have been occupied until the 4th century A.D. A sudden collapse of the wall probably hastened its demise.

The views across Loch Bloom are superb and must have made Rhiroy a highly desirable Iron Age stronghold. Despite its nigh-impregnable location, it is close to good farming land and fishing in the loch. As with many strongholds, you should carry a mental image of what it might have looked like, but limit the height to about 25 ft. Once there, all the attractions of the location, and why it may have been occupied over almost seven centuries, become clearly obvious.

DUN DORNADILLA (Broch)

Sutherland O/S Landranger map 9 ref. 460449

Directions: From Tongue, take the A838 west to Hope and turn south along the minor road up Strathmore. The broch is beside the road, about 4 miles south of Loch Hope.

Considering that Dun Dornadilla stands along the route from Strathnaver down Strathmore, a through-route since pre-historic times, it has survived remarkably well. In fact, Dun Dornadilla is the best preserved broch, at least in terms of wall height, in the north of mainland Scotland and is the fifth tallest of all remaining brochs. Mind you, were it not for modern buttressing, that accolade might not have lasted until now.

Standing on the edge of a low terrace just above Strathmore River, it commands views up and down the strath along with access to good agricultural land. The height of the tower would have been its greatest defence and it appears to be a broch of advanced design. The outer wall rises fully 22 ft. above ground, directly over the entrance with its massive triangular lintel. This feature is an impressive embellishment, but also served a useful purpose in spreading the weight of the wall above the entrance passage.

Unfortunately, the entrance is blocked, and the courtyard inaccessible, though the exterior is clear. Thus, the visitor is confined to the outside, which is its best aspect anyway. Here, the distinctive cooling-tower shape is quite obvious and, from a distance, one can add another 20 or more feet to the height and see the broch, in the mind's eye, in all its glory.

The wall is about 14 ft. thick, the courtyard 27 ft. across; comfortably suggesting that Dun Dornadilla was a broch of no mean height. The majority of the wall is about 8 ft. high now, but the exterior facing is in a good state of repair. Indeed, the wall is particularly well put together, as it would need to be, and may possibly have survived had the stone not been robbed at some stage in the past. There is a roofless mural cell opposite the entrance and three levels of galleries were visible in the eighteenth century. If correct, these have now been lost.

Aside from what you can see, Dun Dornadilla's past has not entirely gone unnoticed – a history with a bit of mystery. With references dating from the 17th century, Dun Dornadilla, appropriately, supposedly belonged to King Dornadilla, who reigned from c. 260 B.C. Well, if you believe that… Then again Richard Pocockein, Bishop of Ossory and Meath of the Church of Ireland, and an antiquarian, described the broch in 1760, when the inner wall and outer wall still survived mostly all the way round, although in a 'tottering condition'.

Here, then, not only do we have one of the best surviving brochs, but one can still view it in an environment that might not be too far removed from that of the Iron Age. Certainly, the combination of location and surviving height combine to allow a greater appreciation of how it might have been, than with many brochs. The inhabitants had everything they probably needed: fresh water; fishing; good agricultural land; and a broch that was as secure as they come. Life was never safe and easy in the Iron Age,

It might be remote now, but Dun Dornadilla had all the mod-cons for the Iron Age, with land and water on hand, plus an elaborate and distinctive lintel over the entrance.

as it usually is today, but it was probably little better elsewhere in Scotland than for the inhabitants of Dun Dornadilla.

Other Pre-historic Sites
Dun na Maigh (Broch) Map 10 ref. 552530
Dun Viden (Broch) Map 10 ref. 726518

DUN GRUGAIG (Dun)

Inverness-shire O/S Landranger map 33 ref. 852159

Directions: Continue east along Glen Beag* from Dun Troddan*, until the road ends. Follow the track onwards for about 1/2 mile, crossing a ford. As the track goes uphill and bends right, the dun is down towards the river on a rocky knoll.

Quite spectacularly sited some 100 ft. above the river in its deep ravine, it is perhaps better to visit Dun Grugaig before visiting the two brochs further down the glen. The main reason is that Dun Grugaig pre-dates the brochs, as can be determined by architectural style and build quality, which has led to it being described as a semi-broch. This tag has also been given to the identically named dun on Skye and others that display broch-like features. Such a sub-class is by no means universally accepted among archaeologists and historians, but is a matter that you might consider as you visit more of these pre-historic strongholds.

Dun Grugaig has been described as both a 'C' and 'D'-shaped dun, or semi-broch, but the wall is of the former shape, leaving the cliff side un-defended. There does not appear to have been a fortified wall along the edge, unlike at other similar duns. There would, however, probably have been a fence or wall to safeguard the inhabitants from an injudicious trip and going over the edge.

It is clear that Dun Grugaig's layout shows that some careful planning and skilful building were required. The slope from south to north falls about 10 ft., while there is a gentler slope from east to west. The section of wall at the south is considerably higher than the north, rising to over 7 ft. Much of the outer face is in decent condition and displays a high standard of building. A scarcement is partly visible about 4 ft. high in the interior, and this would have supported the first floor. There may have been a gallery in the wall, certainly at the higher levels, but tumbled rocks make this difficult to see with any real certainty.

The main entrance is in the east, dividing the south and north arcs of the wall and at the end of the higher levels. This is blocked and gives every impression of being difficult to reach, but remember that much has changed in 2,000 years. None of the usual features can be seen, but some lintels are still in place and there may have been a gallery leading to stairs within the south wall.

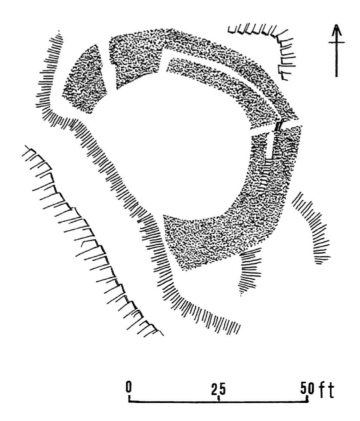

0   25   50 ft

The north wall is nowhere near as impressive and is at a much lower level. Careful observation will show a high quality of build, though, particularly over the falling ground, which includes small clefts and mounds of rock. The builders certainly knew their jobs.

There is another entrance near the cliff edge featuring a door-jamb; as has been mentioned before, the more entrances, the more weak-spots, but several duns and hillforts have two or more. Another gap in the wall, between the two entrances, leads to a mural gallery that appears to run round towards the main entrance. This becomes quite narrow and was probably not a recognised passage for normal use, but such a long gallery connecting with the entrance is unusual.

It is possible that Dun Grugaig might not have had a level wall-head in the Iron Age as did, presumably, most duns and brochs. If the wall were, say, 25 ft. high all round, it would give plenty of protection and saved considerable effort in building just to be level, yet have given a possibly unique, sloping wall-head to the south. This is mere conjecture, but would the builders expend so much effort on defences if not necessary?

The interior is a combination of rubble and the natural rock, and measures about 47 ft. x 38 ft., a decent enough size. Dun Grugaig combines a good defensive location and commanding strategic position, with access to water and reasonably good agricultural land. It seems to hold all the aces.

It is worth considering Dun Grugaig's connection with the later brochs in Glen Beag; were the inhabitants related, or were the brochs and the dun ever occupied simultaneously? We can be sure that, even without excavation, Dun Grugaig is older than the brochs and, whatever label attached to it, such a chronological sequence of pre-historic strongholds can rarely be seen within so short a distance of each other.

DUN LAGAIDH (Hillfort and Dun)

Ross and Cromarty O/S Landranger map 20 ref. 142915

Directions: From Dun an Ruigh Ruaidh, or Rhiroy Broch*, continue along the minor road until it ends at Loggie. A footpath continues north from the road and, after 1/2 mile, the hillfort's knoll rises a little to the north.

Occupying a long ridge in a splendid location above the narrows of Loch Bloom, this site has proved to be an irresistible strategic location for about 2,000 years. There are three separate strongholds on the ridge, each utilising the works or materials of the previous ones. The defences of the earlier strongholds have also been incorporated into the later ones, so that it is not always easy to decipher which is which on the surface.

Dun Lagaidh was excavated in the late-1960s at the same time, and by the same archaeologist, as Rhiroy*. These two might be close together – and even been occupied simultaneously, but the history of the two sites could not be more different. The first fortified settlement at Lagaidh was a hillfort defended by a timber-laced stone wall, about 14 feet thick, which enclosed the summit area measuring about 275 ft. x 100 ft.

There was a very narrow entrance in the east – not even 4 feet wide, and beyond this, protecting the easier approach, an outer timber-framed wall about 8 feet thick, with another narrow entrance in the south.

The hillfort has been C-14 dated from the 8th to 6th centuries B.C., and is typical of those times. Like many such hillforts in Scotland, the inhabitants probably met with a nasty end, for both the main and the outer walls were found to contain much vitrified material dating from the 5th to 4th centuries B.C. Almost certainly, the hillfort was attacked and the ramparts, and perhaps even the inhabitants, burned.

Unfortunately, though, most of the hillfort has vanished. There is a good length of wall in the west, including some exposed vitrified stone, but the rampart near the dun is confusing. The eastern outer wall has also succumbed to later works and is partially covered in trees. As for the walls along the north and south cliff edges, there is no obvious sign of them, but the excavator believes they were used as a quarry for the later dun. This would make sense, as the cliffs are far from precipitous and the stone would be a close-to-hand quarry.

Phase 2 began somewhat closer to the millennium. A circular solid walled-dun was built over the remains of the hillfort's east wall. The dun wall was about 12 feet thick and enclosed a courtyard 36 feet across. There was an entrance in the east, in line with and partially built over that of the hillfort, and this had two sets of door-jambs and a guard cell. A staircase was built opposite the entrance.

Once again, much of this dun has been adulterated by a later building phase. The entrance and guard cell are no longer visible, for example, while the wall was rebuilt in more recent times. In comparison with the hillfort era, the excavator unearthed numerous artefacts in the dun that gave him the opinion that it was the stronghold of, possibly, a local chief. He also drew attention to the marked differences between the stone-work of this dun and at Rhiroy*.

I keep referring to this phase as a 'dun', but when is a dun not a dun, but a broch? In the excavator's opinion, this was a dun – not even a semi-broch, but, along with many similar strongholds, has been considered to be a broch subsequently. Now, though, the tide has turned again, and Dun Lagaidh is considered more likely to be a 'dun'.

One might ask what is the minimum height for a circular, drystone stronghold to be considered a broch, and did the Iron Age people differentiate, or just build to suit a need as they saw fit? Probably the latter, but there is every reason to expect that walls of only about 2/3 the courtyard diameter could have reached, if not Mousa* proportions, 25 feet or more in height. In which case, the stronghold in question, could be far more broch than dun. That is so with Dun Lagaidh, but as there is only a few feet of wall left, it will never be known as to what height it reached, only that it could have been a broch. But, then again…

Phase 3 was much later. Not only had the Iron Age passed, but the Dark Ages had come and gone as well. It is not known whether the site was occupied between the dun/broch falling out of use, whenever that was, but there is no question that the site was not simply re-used, but re-fortified. A hoard of silver pennies dating to the early 13th century A.D. was found, that conveniently places this final fortified phase in its chronological context.

This was no group of squatters holing up for a winter either, as the ruins were transformed into a simple motte and bailey castle. The tower was rebuilt using

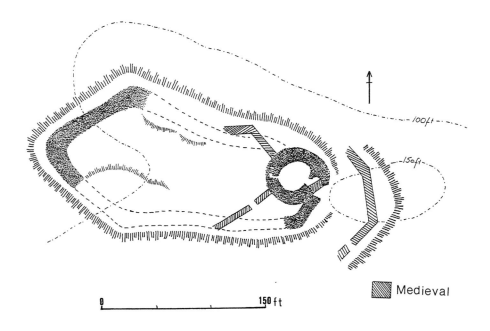

Medieval

0   150 ft

mortared masonry and the old entrance blocked. Entry to the castle was gained at, probably, first floor level down the original intra-mural stairs; a style not unknown in tower-houses. In addition, two mortared walls ran from the castle to join the former north and south walls of the hillfort. These are only half the width of the pre-historic walls and that in the south had an entrance. The whole had become a castle and bailey.

This must have belonged to a local chief of sorts, for it would be far-and-away above the station of a farmer, as was probably the case for a broch in the Iron Age. Unfortunately, this final phase of Dun Lagaidh features neither in any records, nor in local legend, and there are no accounts of derring-do, or even mass slaughter attributed to the castle.

Few pre-historic sites in Scotland can boast three, clearly seen, distinct phases of fortification, let alone such recent defences. Such developments might not make for an easy interpretation, but it is all there. Having seen its wonderful location, one can fully understand why this particular ridge continued to have its strategic attractions. Beauty and the beast in one.

DUN TELVE (Broch)

Inverness-shire O/S Landranger map 33 ref. 829173

Directions: As for Am Baghan Burblach* hillfort, but continue beyond the stream and turn left through Glenelg village. Turn left up the next valley, Glen Beag, and follow this for about 1 1/2 miles. Dun Telve is beside the road on the right.

Glen Beag must have been some place in the Iron Age. With two brochs – plus Dun Grugaig* a bit farther along – this fertile valley, with its crystal-clear burn and good agricultural land, would have been of some local importance in those times. Today, as you travel east from the coast, there is that element of excitement in knowing that you are about to visit two of the finest surviving brochs, which lie within sight of each other.

Dun Telve is in slightly the better condition of the two. Aside from Mousa*, it is the highest broch, still reaching to almost 34 ft. It rises to more than 30 ft. for about one third of its circumference, the rest being curtailed at first floor level, but in 1722 it stood at least 6 ft. higher and the outer galleried-wall completed its circuit, although the inner probably did not.

The wall has a solid base to first floor level 14 ft. thick, enclosing a courtyard 32 ft. across which suggests the ratio of wall:internal diameter used to assess the height of a broch, has its limitations. The ratio for Dun Telve is less than 1:1, yet it certainly once stood at about 40 ft. high. However well built is Dun Telve – and it does not take long to realise that Glen Beag's brochs are very advanced, this cannot hide the reservations required for such arbitrary guidelines. As a rule-of-thumb, it has its merits, but wall build-quality ought to be taken into consideration. After all, Dun Carloway's* wall is only 11 ft. thick, yet it also probably rose to 40 ft. in height.

All this apart, one cannot fail to be impressed by Dun Telve; the wall is wonderfully built. Heavy boulders are used for the solid wall at ground level, but lighter and thinner stone is used at the galleried levels. The classic, tapered cooling-tower shape of the outer wall is apparent and, when shrouded in the drifting mist that can gather in Glen Beag, it would have resembled a miniature power station cooling tower.

The west-facing entrance has the remains of out-works, or possibly even a barbican-type of structure, which leads to additional outer buildings. The entrance is a reasonable height and has a door-jamb, bar hole and an unusually long guard chamber; these features are complete and clearly seen. Only the lintel supporting the outer wall remains.

Both wall faces are in a good state of repair and are impressive. However, it is the height that overshadows everything. A scarcement is visible at first floor level, about 6 ft. 6 in. high. There is no obvious opening to this now; presumably, there was one where the wall is missing. At the north, there is a combined mural cell, complete with corbelled roof and stairs leading to the first floor. The gallery walls are quite smooth at this level and it may have been a passage, but was probably used for storage. At the higher levels, the galleries are much narrower and not so well finished.

There are five complete storeys and part of a sixth above a second scarcement at about 30 ft. high. This may have supported either a fully, or partially enclosed roof, but would still have been a good 10 ft. below the wall-head. It is worth contemplating the living arrangements, the internal layout and how shelter was gained; the useful information board shows only one possibility.

The different levels and method of building, using cross-slabs to tie the walls, can be clearly seen at the demolished ends. Here the true genius of the broch is exposed; however they developed, they are the ultimate in drystone building. A solid wall would soon collapse under its own weight once it reached a height considerably above its thickness. The galleried-wall not only allowed brochs to be developed, but was one of the major breakthroughs in world building.

Above the entrance in the interior, a series of vertical openings run up the wall, as at Mousa*; another set begins higher up. These were most likely a means to lighten the load over the various door-ways, and would also have aided air-flow in the galleries; all part of the accoutrements of the most advanced brochs. The interior is now covered in small stones, but Dun Telve was cleared out in 1914 and a large number of stone lamps,

The interior wall of Dun Telve, showing the upper scarcement and the vertical lines of gaps, possibly for lessening the weight and allowing air, and light, to circulate.

querns and spindle wheels were found. These are quite common artefacts from Iron Age sites, but also suggest that Dun Telve was a later settlement.

Height was Dun Telve's main defence. It has been considered that the foundations of the rectangular building outside the entrance may have formed part of a surrounding wall; this is unlikely. There are a few other remains of outbuildings further round, and lesser traces to the south of the entrance. As can be seen, the stonework of the rectangular building is different from that of the broch, so it could be secondary, though not necessarily post-broch. Such outbuildings are not so common at brochs in the west, but here may have been a development not dissimilar from some brochs in the north.

Dun Telve's location is not as remote as that of many brochs away from the far north. Certainly, such a location would surely not have been defended before brochs. Whether Dun Telve has survived because it was so well built and did not collapse is a matter for debate, but it is significant that the brochs that have survived to over 20 ft. all display advanced building traits and a high quality finish, as seen at Dun Telve and at Dun Troddan*. That they have survived so well may not simply be down to co-incidence.

DUN TRODDAN (Broch)

Inverness-shire O/S Landranger map 33 ref. 834173

Directions: As for Dun Telve*, but a little farther east along Glen Beag on the left.

Much of what has been written about Dun Telve* applies to Dun Troddan, although they are some way short of being identical twins. Nevertheless, they bear a similarity in their present ruined state, even to the extent of how they have deteriorated. In 1720, Dun Troddan stood 33 ft. high, two years later it had been deliberately reduced to its present height of 25 ft. Dun Telve was also similarly reduced at that time, supposedly to provide stone for a spurious public building. The brochs' seem to have had a shared fate.

Like its neighbour, Dun Troddan has a solid wall to first floor level, which is also about 14 ft. thick. Even more co-incidentally, only a third of the wall's circumference exists above this. The solid wall is built of large stones packed with smaller ones and, as with Dun Telve*, smaller stones are used for the galleried levels, and the standard is very high. The classic, tapered shape can be seen to good effect and, considering the entrance design and the gaps up the inner wall – over the stairs and further round – it looks that, to all intents and purposes, the people of both brochs were very close.

Dun Troddan though, stands on a terrace, a little higher than Dun Telve*. Another important difference is that there is no sign of any exterior buildings at Dun Troddan, which might indicate that Dun Telve's* were a later addition.

The courtyard is 28 ft. across, some 4 ft. less than Dun Telve*, and gives the classic 1:1 ratio of combined wall thickness:courtyard diameter. If such a measurement means anything at all, the implication is that Dun Troddan was the higher, despite being on a terrace; Dun Telve*, is known to have reached 40 ft., at least.

Although the two brochs have similar entrances, that at Dun Troddan faces south and does not have a section of galleried wall above. Its long guard cell runs off the left of the passage, as opposed to the right at Dun Telve*, and this is only partially lintelled, but is otherwise very similar.

There is a combined entrance to a roofed mural cell and stairs in the same location in relation to the entrance as that at Dun Telve*. The staircase leads to the first floor, while a little further along is the first step of a flight to the higher levels. It is possible that, between these flights of stairs, there was an opening onto the interior, where a scarcement is seen. Being about 8 ft. lower than Dun Telve*, there is no upper scarcement, but conclusions should not be drawn from this. One interesting theory suggests that, due to the inferior inner wall facing at ground floor level, compared with above, that level may have been used to house animals, with humans living on the mezzanine floor(s) above. Interpreting pre-history can be fun, and you do not have to be a specialist to have a go, either.

Both brochs were cleared of debris before 1920, but Dun Troddan was excavated to a 'good standard'. Several central hearths were found on a layer of rubble, suggesting its continued use, while the original hearth contained part of a rotary quern.

Most significant, though, was a circle of 11 post-holes. This was the first effective evidence that either a complete or mezzanine floor was supported in this way. No sweeping generalisations should be drawn from this, although post-holes have since been found in other brochs. Many brochs have a scarcement, but too many have been badly disturbed to find post-holes. On the other hand, perhaps only those brochs with multiple levels of mezzanine-type floors required additional supports.

More recently, inspections and surveys between 2010 and 2012 suggest that the post-holes discovered in 1920 may not have reached the original floor level. They appeared to be set into deposits above the lowest level and may have been a later addition, or part of a 'home improvement'. As yet, nothing is absolutely certain. So, you are free to decide for yourself without fear of contradiction – yet.

Dun Troddan would have made an even more imposing stronghold in the Iron Age than its neighbour, thanks to its elevated location. The view of its great, gaunt exterior wall, gives a good indication of the sight a broch would present to unwelcome visitors. Let us make no mistake about this, in Iron Age Scotland a broch would look, and be, almost impregnable.

DURN HILL (Hillfort)

Banff-shire O/S Landranger map 29 ref. 571638

Directions: Leave Banff, heading west, on the A98. Turn left on the B9022 just before Portsoy and turn second right just after passing under some power lines. Follow the minor road for about 1/2 mile to Damheads, then turn right and take the track 100 yards on the left. Follow this round the wood to the top of the hill.

The vast majority of strongholds in this book are suited to both readers interested in Scottish history, and those simply wishing to get out and see the country. Durn Hill, though, is really a site for those specifically keen on pre-historic strongholds, and especially hillforts. It is an outstanding example of an un-finished hillfort, and showed how they were planned and built. Or so it was thought…

One beauty of pre-history and history is that a particular thesis or point of view can hold sway for decades – even centuries – and then be swept away, or at least be open to question, by a new discovery. Thanks to some excavations in 2014, through Aberdeen University, it was found that the inner and outer of Durn Hill's three, once-presumed planned, ramparts were not what they seemed and, as a result, its once established past is ripe for revision.

Until recently, then, it was thought that the prominent Durn Hill, at almost 660 feet above sea level and overlooking the north-east coast, was intended to house a bi-vallate hillfort. A marker ditch enclosed the summit area, measuring about 4 1/4 acres, and can be traced for just about the whole circuit. Outside this, and lower down, another shallow ditch marks the site of a second intended rampart, enclosing about 900 ft. x 530 ft.

These two marker ditches have small spoil heaps on their outer lips – an assumed method for placing the intended defences. Then, in 2014, both marker ditches had trenches dug across them and were found to have housed palisade fences. Charred material from the inner trench dated these to the early Iron Age. The conclusion is now that, as a result of the excavations, 'Durn Hill is an exceptionally well preserved fort'.

But – and there is always a 'but', is not a settlement surrounded by a palisade fence merely a palisade enclosure, and hardly a 'fort'? Even in the early Iron Age a palisade enclosure would be a bit old-hat as a defensive measure intended to keep out anything other than wild animals. For example, could the palisade fences have been temporary to be replaced by ramparts, which, for whatever reason, were not built? Perhaps an expected threat did not materialise, so the palisades sufficed and an intended hillfort was simply curtailed? Or were the palisades not up to the job and the inhabitants moved, fled or succumbed to attack before ramparts were begun? There may be many other reasons, too.

Yet, there is more. Between these two former 'marker ditches' is an un-finished rampart. This was marked out with a small bank of stones, enclosing an area measuring about 800 ft. x 450 ft. and some building work was begun at the south. Blocks of quartzite were dug from a ditch and placed up hill, while the spoil was thrown down to form a counterscarp bank. This was only the beginning of construction, but the intention can be clearly seen, if few stones. The 2014 excavators did not cut a trench through this rampart and it is still considered to be an un-finished hillfort – for now. But for whom: the inhabitants of the palisade settlement or a different group of people? Another excavation is awaited.

Durn Hill was once considered to be unique not just in Scotland, but Britain, as a site of two un-finished hillforts. Perhaps, or perhaps not now. Un-finished hillforts are rare and at Durn Hill progress was considerably less than at most. So, if you hope to see a large, multivallate hillfort in a good condition, Durn Hill is not the place for you, the remains are slight.

On the other hand, if you wish to see just how many hundreds of hillforts were probably planned and, at the same time, to enjoy fine coastal and inland views, while pondering changing historical theories, Durn Hill will be very rewarding. Here is another site of major importance in understanding Scottish pre-history that is rarely visited and even less appreciated. At least you will not experience over-crowding.

KEISS BROCHS

Caithness O/S Landranger map 12 ref. 348615 (road broch), ref. 353611 (harbour broch), ref. 353612 (coast broch)

Directions: From Wick, take the A9 north and turn right to Keiss harbour. At the very sharp right-hand bend just before the harbour, a footpath leads through a gate. The harbour broch is on the left. The coast broch is farther north towards the castle, past the pillbox. For the road broch, return to the A9, turn right and park next to the war memorial on the left. Pass through to the broch.

The three brochs at Keiss are all easy to reach and offer an opportunity to enjoy the beautiful coastal scenery of north-east Caithness. The harbour broch is in poor condition. It was dug into in 1864 and was found to have a wall 12 feet thick enclosing a courtyard 38 feet in diameter. There was a scarcement about 6 feet above the floor level and the wall still rises to 8 feet in the west. In 1901, it was 12 feet high.

The entrance faced the sea, but was closed in the Iron Age. Another entrance was opened in the north-east and given a large triangular lintel, but this collapsed and the original entrance was re-opened. In this third phase, the outer wall was rebuilt, incorporating the triangular lintel, and the interior was divided by vertical stone slabs. Following more recent observations, the sequence of some of the above has been questioned, but re-excavating such a damaged site is unlikely to provide any conclusive evidence.

The external buildings are post-broch and almost certainly re-used stones from the broch itself. This broch is now quite ruinous, but is merely a starter for the main courses to follow.

Walk on towards Keiss old castle, perched precariously on the cliff edge, and you soon arrive at the coast broch. Although the castle looks as though it is about to topple over the edge, drawings made more than 150 years ago show that it has deteriorated surprisingly little in the intervening years. A visit is worthwhile.

The coast broch is rather better preserved and appears to be a more recent design, to boot. The tower is only 4 feet high, but both wall-faces are visible – if one does not mind nettles – for most of the circuit. The solid wall is 13 feet thick and encloses a courtyard 26 feet across. Thus, one might surmise that this was taller than the harbour broch, while several other features hint at a more recent date. For example, the east-facing entrance has two sets of door-jambs and at least one bar hole: double-door brochs are not only rare, but are assumed to be some of the last built. To the right of the entrance is an aumbry, or cupboard, sunk into the wall, while the interior was divided by vertical slabs, as at Mid-Howe* and Gurness*, although these cannot be seen today. There is another aumbry opposite the entrance.

The most impressive aspect of the coast broch is the curved passage leading outwards from the entrance between various external buildings: a possible pre-historic version of the medieval barbican. One wonders whether, as at Carn Liath*, this passage ever had a roof. Broch entrance extensions of any kind are very thin on the ground, although, paradoxically, there is another just along the coast at Nybster*. There are also the remains of several rectangular and circular buildings. The largest of these measures 45 ft. x 25 ft., though the walls are low. When excavated, signs of other buildings were found to the north, although these, and any to the west, have now been destroyed.

The relationship between the inhabitants of these brochs must have been interesting, assuming, of course, that the brochs were inhabited simultaneously. While it is easy to conclude that a broch was the stronghold of a local chief, two being so close together does make one wonder. Surely rival chiefs would not have their headquarters quite so close to each other?

Then, there is the road broch! This is the best preserved of the three, although bracken obscures the site in the summer. The complex was enclosed by a massive, encircling wall, some 150 feet in diameter. This is now either missing, or much reduced, but shows that additional defences were sometimes used at brochs in exposed locations, many of which are no longer visible.

The road broch was extensively developed in antiquity, for there is a great circular court outside the original north-east entrance – of inferior build to the broch tower – and many remains of buildings all round. Nature has made these, at best, a confusing jumble in the height of summer, but, I dare say – as with other pre-historic strongholds – a visit in the other seasons will prove more rewarding.

As with the other brochs at Keiss, this was excavated by Sir Francis Tress Barry at the end of the 19th century. The solid wall is 16 feet thick and encloses a courtyard 34 feet across. However, the wall was originally only about 12 feet thick: it was buttressed later, showing that the outer court and buildings are secondary. These may have been built by the original inhabitants or their descendants, or possibly after a period of disuse. The wall is still about 8 feet high.

The original north-east entrance leads from the outer court to the main broch courtyard and features a set of door-jambs, bar hole and a small collapsed guard cell. In the south-east sector of the wall are a set of stairs and a mural gallery, with another set of stairs and an even longer gallery directly opposite. A broch with two sets of stairs is pretty rare, but a second entrance has been knocked through the stair-well in the north-west. This is not as clear as the main entrance and, it was thought, was probably built when the external buildings, and possibly the outer wall, were added. Again, the build-sequence has been questioned, with the suggestion that the main entrance may have been at the north-west and the north-east being secondary.

There are various alcoves in the inner wall-face, while the well had stairs leading down to it and was covered by stone slabs: these are often obscured by grass in the summer. At this secondary phase, this courtyard was divided by vertical stone slabs, which, like those at the other Keiss brochs, have now vanished.

The trio of brochs at Keiss are particularly fine examples to visit for their different architectural features, despite none being of any great height. On the other hand, their relative similarity is only to be expected. So, including Nybster, there are four brochs within 2 miles along this stretch of exposed coastline, each with a developed group of external buildings and sometimes defences. Such a situation, though not unique, is rarely seen and makes for easy, instructive and immensely enjoyable visiting today.

KILPHEDIR BROCH

Sutherland O/S Landranger map 17 ref. 995187

Directions: Take the A897 from Helmsdale to the bridge over Kilphedir Burn, about 3 1/2 miles. Park in the old quarry beyond the bridge. Walk about 50 yds. farther on and look back over the quarry up the hill across the burn; the broch is visible on a ridge. Go back and cross the bridge and walk up the hill.

From afar, Kilpheder Broch gives the impression it is a pile of stones. Do not be put-off or mis-led, it takes on a more meaningful shape from close by. The best view is from the hillside immediately above. Its most impressive aspect is the scale of the outer defences, large enough in their day, no doubt, to grace many a hillfort.

There are numerous brochs in north Scotland, in all sorts of locations, built to a wide variety of styles. Kilphedir stands on a knoll to the east of the burn and commands good views along Strath Kildonan. The area thereabouts has several singleton and groups of hut circles, so the broch may have been the home of the local chief. It would certainly have been prominent and dominant.

The broch's wall is 15 ft. thick, enclosing a courtyard 32 ft. in diameter. The entrance is in the north-west and includes three lintels and a door-jamb still in place, but no guard chamber. Opposite, a door leads into an intra-mural cell, or gallery, but that is that for internal details. The inner wall-face is mostly clear, but the mass of tumbled stones completely obscures the external face.

Remains of similar quality can be seen at several brochs, but Kilphedir's trump card is the well-preserved outer defences. The knoll is encircled by a ditch over 20 ft. wide and still about 10 ft. deep. There is an impressive, heather-covered stone rampart, almost 15 ft. thick and still rising some considerable height from the bottom of the ditch. An apparent counterscarp bank runs round the lip if the ditch, which is further protected by an additional ditch in the vicinity of the entrance where, not surprisingly, the approach is easiest.

The whole site is still impressive. If you re-create the broch tower – in excess of 30 ft. high – and the outer defences, in the mind's eye, one can begin to appreciate Kilphedir's defensive qualities. Not only was it probably the home of the local chief, but one's first sight would confirm that.

*Kilphedir Broch commands Strath Kildonan and, with its outworks,
would have been a formidable stronghold in the Iron Age.*

As far as is known, the broch dates to the so-called classic period of brochs, the first two centuries either side of the B.C./A.D. divide. As mentioned, there are numerous huts hereabouts some of which have been excavated. These date back long into the 1st millennium B.C., while others were rebuilt nearer to the age of the broch. The area was thus occupied by open settlements, possibly from the late-Bronze Age, for well over 500 years. The fair-sized pre-historic population bears quite a contrast to the sparse one today.

The countryside hereabouts is relatively easy for walking and there are several huts marked on the O/S map. Many are in surprisingly good condition, though most are covered in heather. Some are listed below.

Other Pre-historic Sites
Hut Circles Map 17 ref. 989194
Hut Circles and souterrain Map 17 ref. 991190
Learable Stone Rows and Standing Stone Map 17 ref. 892234

KNOCKFARRIL (Hillfort)

Ross & Cromarty O/S Landranger map 26 ref. 507586

Directions: Leave Dingwall on the A862 and head west along the A835 at Mayburgh. After 1/4 mile, turn right along a minor road and a mile later turn right again, and continue just beyond Ussie. Turn right, yet again, keeping right at the T-junction, and continue almost to the farm. Walk past this at the end of the road, and a footpath heads east and then back west to the summit of the hill.

Dominating a ridge between Dingwall and Strathpeffer, Knockfarril commands long views to the south over the Black Isle and Strathconon, and to the northern hills and Cromarty Firth in the north-east. It is a fitting location for a hillfort whose single rampart encloses 425 ft. x 125 ft. Not the grandest of defences perhaps, but one with much vitrified material to be seen.

The rectangular hillfort was almost certainly defended by a timber-laced stone wall and, despite being mostly covered in grass, parts can be seen where the stone has liquefied, run and then cooled. The heat generated in the conflagration must have been great, and probably brought about a pretty nasty end to this pre-historic stronghold and, possibly, its inhabitants.

At each end, and extending from the rampart in an east/west direction, run two lengths of vitrified wall. Though unusual, there are parallels elsewhere and they may have formed entrance passages or sections of wall reached by ladders. The vitrification suggests that Knockfarril dates far back into the first millennium B.C., though three ditches cutting across the site from north to south are later.

Nothing is really known of Knockfarril's history, but it offers many good views. More importantly, the vitrified rock, some of which is in large lumps, give this hillfort its distinction and allow careful study of the results of its destruction, whether by accident or very intentional and effective design.

The steep sides of the hill, on all sides, made just a single rampart necessary for defence.
Knockfarril has a commanding location, too.

MITHER TAP O' BENNACHIE (Hillfort)

Aberdeenshire O/S Landranger map 38 ref. 683224

Directions: Leave Inverurie heading north-west on the A96 and turn left along the minor road at Drummies. Turn left at Chapel of Gairloch and follow this road for 2 miles. Just after the turning on the left, back to Inverurie, turn right into the Bennachie Centre car park. Follow the path through the woods in a north-westerly direction to the summit. One mile walk.

At 1,698 feet above sea level, the journey through the enclosing woods opens out to reveal marvellous views. The hillfort surrounds the eastern tor of the Bennachie hill, the summit of which is to the west and a little higher. Nothing to the east or north rises to anything like the height of the hillfort, so there are extensive views in these directions.

Two walls surround the tor to form the hillfort. The first, at about 100 feet below the summit, is the most obvious and was about 15 feet thick. It is now tumbled and can be difficult to trace, being mixed in with the fragmented rock of the tor itself. Stretches of both wall faces can be seen in places and, so it is claimed, part of a parapet, but this is not entirely convincing. Certainly, this wall was of massive proportions and would have been a formidable defensive feature in the Iron Age.

About half-way between this wall and the summit can be seen a second wall of slighter proportions. As with the outer wall, this is not easy to follow for its whole circuit either, for the same reasons. It is likely that these walls were built at different times, probably quite early in the Iron Age. Some parts of the hillfort were excavated in 2019, but little was unearthed to give a chronology, although a well at the summit has been discovered. A few hut circles that can be seen between the walls, but these might be post-hillfort, while the hill itself was occupied in the 19th and 20th centuries by people evicted elsewhere. Still, that such strongholds in excess of 2,000 years old can casually be seen throughout the countryside is something not to be taken for granted.

The name Mother of the Top, suggests the hill might have had some sort of religious significance at one time, but on a clear day one can see the hillforts on Barmekin of Echt*, to the south south-east, and Tap O' Noth* to the north north-west. Whether these three formed a series of lookouts for the Caledonii, over the coastal area is impossible to tell, but, between them, they certainly command extensive views.

In fact, the Mither Tap has been suggested as a possible site for the battle of Mons Graupius. One of many such admittedly, but Professor J.K. St. Joseph reached this conclusion after much research, including the study of aerial photographs. It does seem rather a strange place for 30,000 Caledonii to fight 20,000 Romans, though, and, presumably, this must have been on the lower slopes of Bennachie hill and not the hillfort. However, there is no real evidence to favour this site over anywhere else, within reason.

The tumbled walls denote a hillfort of some importance, and one with considerable strategic advantages. This value could be reflected in the scale of the outer wall, which must have taken quite a while to build. Certainly, one would expect the hillfort to provide a stronghold for far more people than there are huts visible. This is but one of the mysteries associated with hillforts.

Other Pre-historic Sites
Pittodrie (Hillfort) Map 38 ref. 694244
Easter Aquorthies (Stone Circle) Map 38 ref. 732208

NYBSTER BROCH

Caithness O/S Landranger map 12 ref. 370632

Directions: From Keiss*, follow the A9 north for about 2 miles. A sign-post on the right points to a car park on the coast. A path leads south to the broch.

Nybster is not only an easy broch to visit, but is very attractively located, has clear evidence of a pre-broch stronghold and, if that is not enough, has a rather un-necessary monument to the landowner and excavator. This unfortunate embellishment dominates the site and can be seen clearly from the A9: fortunately, it is easy to ignore once there.

The pre-broch fort is beyond the monument on a small promontory jutting into the North Sea. It is defended by a curved stone wall, about 150 feet long and 10 feet thick and an outer ditch, about 20 ft. wide. The wall is about 4 feet high, but would undoubtedly have been imposing in the Iron Age. These defences were subsequently modified and enhanced. The central entrance has two sets of door-jambs, while stairs lead up to, presumably, the wall-head from the interior on either side of the entrance. This wall rather brings to mind the blockhouses found in the Shetland Isles, and is not unlike the promontory hillfort at St. John's Point.

Leading from the wall, especially to the north, are passages connecting an extensive network of buildings that surround, and in some cases are built against, the broch. Thus, the chronology seems to have been the promontory fort, broch and lastly external buildings. That is not to say that some substantial stone buildings were not pre-broch, except those built against the tower.

The broch, like the rest of the site, was cleared when excavated by Sir Francis Tress Barry, in 1898. This must once have been a particularly impressive stronghold in the Iron Age, standing on the headland. The broch's wall is about 15 feet thick, yet the courtyard is only a little over 20 feet across. One can assume that such a high ratio of wall:courtyard meant that the broch was tall, possibly every bit the equal of Mousa*. However, there is no trace of a galleried wall, which would be essential if it were to be a tall, drystone tower, so doubts remain. There are no intra-mural cells or galleries within the solid wall either, but this is only up to 8 feet high externally, and even less internally, so regarding a galleried wall, absence of evidence is not evidence of absence.

Both wall-faces are visible and display a high standard of building. At least one stone tank can be seen in the broch floor and there was another. The entrance, facing north-east, has the faintest trace of a door-jamb, but this is nowhere near as prominent as in many brochs. A passage leads from the entrance, between the buildings towards the outer end of the promontory, as at the Keiss* coast broch and Gurness*.

Fortunately, Nybster has been excavated a couple of times this century and while there is some doubt as to whether it was a broch or not, an area of flat slabs possibly being a doorway into the wall was discovered. This leaves the possibility that it may have had a galleried wall and, therefore, is a broch. Visually, though, one can easily imagine Nybster being a broch of a more than decent height and, standing where it does, would have been very impressive.

Unfortunately, a large pile of the excavators' spoil, which, rather like the monument, dominates the site, now obscures some of the circular buildings between the broch and the coast. Grateful though we should be for such mapping and consolidation of a broch and fort, it is a matter of debate which of these highly conspicuous monuments is the most appropriate to the rather rustic methods then adopted.

One cannot doubt that Nybster is magnificently located amid the splendid coastal scenery of north-east Caithness. The land is good for farming as well and one can

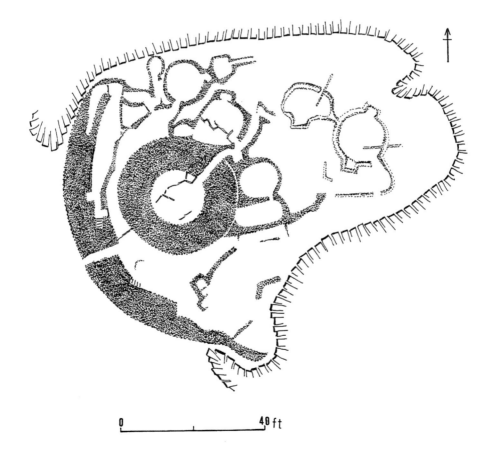

0   40 ft

imagine this coastal strip being a hive of activity in the Iron Age, especially with the number of brochs and duns hereabouts. Nybster was a comprehensively defended settlement. The promontory wall would undoubtedly have been an effective height, making the whole site as safe a place to reside as anywhere in those far-off times. Now, despite its unwanted warts, it makes a particularly attractive place to see Iron Age fortified developments on the ground.

Other Site
The Caithness Broch Centre and John Nicolson Collection Tel. 01955-631377.

The Caithness Broch Project intends to build a replica broch in the near future. See www.thebrochproject.co.uk

OUSDALE BROCH

Caithness O/S Landranger map 17 ref. 072188

Directions: From Helmsdale, take the A9 north for about 4 miles. There is a parking area on the right. The broch is about 600 yds. down towards the sea, above the Ousdale burn and a little beyond a spread of stones that was once a small settlement. Walk down to the high wire fence, follow this to the burn and the latter to the broch.

If you like a bit of adventure, this could be the broch for you. Being about 300 ft. below the road, and still 350 ft. above the sea, Ousdale occupies precarious ground above the burn. The interior was cleared out in 1891 and the broch restored, but it is not easily visible from afar. That would not have been a problem back in the Iron Age, for Ousdale was one of the most modern brochs, and would most likely have been of quite a height.

This was not its only defensive measure, though. The north and west sides are protected by a walled enclosure, the former about 8 ft. thick, so it is a bit more than would be required for keeping a few cattle. The steep descents at the south and east needed no further protection.

The broch is compact, with the courtyard being about 24 ft. across and the solid wall 14 ft. thick. There is thus a high wall:courtyard ratio, with the implication that Ousdale rose to a considerable height. Although the exterior wall-face is not fully visible, the interior wall is in good condition, rising to more than 10 ft.; part, near the entrance, seems to be restored or rebuilt. A fine scarcement is visible about 8 ft. higher than the original floor.

The entrance, in the south-west, has two sets of door-jambs with a large guard cell – complete with corbelled roof – between these. The outer door has a good bar hole as well. Double-door brochs are virtually unknown outside the north and are thought to be about the most recent.

There is a further mural cell in the west while the stairs are in the north-west, showing this had the essential galleried-wall for height. A scarcement is visible in places, and the wall has been buttressed near the entrance, possibly in 1891. Although nothing is known of Ousdale's history, it must have been particularly impressive standing sentinel high above the burn. This is a fine example of the most recent of brochs and is easy to inspect. It is a joy to visit and imagine in all its 40 ft. high days of glory.

This is another broch with which the Caithness Broch Project has been involved. See www.thebrochproject.co.uk

SGARBACH (Dun)

Caithness O/S Landranger map 12 ref. 373637

Directions: From Nybster* broch, walk along the cliff-top to the north for about 1/2 mile.

Although the ruins are not as widespread as the nearby brochs of Nybster* and Keiss*, Sgarbach is more akin to a Hebridean promontory dun, than the more usual pre-historic stronghold to be found in north Scotland. It is, thus, quite a distinct rarity in these parts.

A single wall about 60 feet long, 12 feet thick and nowhere 5 feet high, cuts off an L-shaped promontory on its western side. As with the aforementioned brochs, there are some very pleasant coastal views. Another similarity with Nybster*, is that the latter's broch was a later addition to what was probably a very similar promontory dun to that at Sgarbach.

The central entrance passage had a set of door-jambs, a bar-hole and a guard cell when excavated by Sir Francis Tress Barry – as at Nybster – in the 19th century. Unfortunately, Sgarbach has since deteriorated and these features are now not readily seen, if not downright invisible. The entrance led straight into the interior where there may have been lean-to buildings against the dun wall, a not wholly unusual feature. As at Nybster*, most of this area is now under piles of excavators' spoil and it is difficult to make any sense of its layout. A hearth was the only sign of occupation.

Why was Sgarbach not developed, as were many other promontory duns? Was it occupied while Nybster broch was inhabited? Such questions are not easy to answer, but is there any reason to suppose that a stronghold would have been planned to suit the location and prevailing conditions, rather than a specific pattern or type being imposed slavishly?

Although one cannot doubt that brochs were the ultimate drystone pre-historic stronghold, just as the medieval nobility had castles and fortified manor houses – depending on the owner's ability to fund such a building, so the same may have occurred in the Iron Age. A dun, as at Sgarbach, might have dated from the time of brochs, but the owners might not have been in a position to build, or desire, a broch. So, although Sgarbach is an unusual dun for Caithness, perhaps the builders simply found it most appropriate to their needs: nothing more, nothing less.

Other Pre-historic Site
Skirza Broch Map 12 ref. 394684

St. JOHN'S POINT (Promontory Hillfort)

Caithness O/S Landranger map 12 ref. 310751

Directions: From Thurso, take the A836 east towards John o' Groats and about 2 miles after Mey turn left, north, along the minor road. A footpath leads from this road, where it turns sharp left, to the hillfort.

A single stone rampart, still up to 10 feet high, 200 yards long and with an outer ditch and counterscarp bank, cuts-off St. John's Point to create the most northerly promontory hillfort on mainland Britain. About 10 acres is enclosed making this rather simple, yet massive stronghold one of the largest in northern Scotland.

Situated south-west of the island of Stroma, and south of the Orkney Islands, this hillfort offers magnificent coastal views. Given its size, it must surely have been of considerable importance in the Iron Age. There is a simple straight-through entrance near the western end of the rampart and this, plus the general layout of the defences, suggests it pre-dates both the coastal duns and brochs hereabouts.

Drawing such conclusions can be debatable, for there are plenty of exceptions to be found. Some promontory hillforts, such as St. John's Point, were re-used in post-Iron Age times, and there is little doubt that the number of people who lived here could fill several duns and brochs. So, St. John's Point could have been inhabited both before and during the period when duns and brochs were built. There are other, smaller promontory hillforts in north Scotland.

Size might not be everything, but a large stronghold in an area where small ones predominate suggests a degree of assumed importance. Nothing of its pre-historic interior can be seen. St. John's Point certainly has a spectacular location and is by far the largest, pre-historic coastal stronghold in north Scotland. That alone may give some indication of the role it played in pre-historic times.

The scant foundations of the supposed St. John's Chapel are at 310351.

STOER BROCH (Clachtoll)

Sutherland O/S Landranger map 15 ref. 036278

Directions: Take the A835 north from Ullapool and turn left on the A837. Turn right on the B869 before Lochinver and continue past Clachtoll to the cemetery. The broch is 1/4 mile walk round the coast.

Stoer Broch is a real pre-historical rarity. When I first visited, more than thirty years ago, it was named after the bay on which it looked out. It appeared as a mound of stones, like many brochs except, being exposed to the sea weather, it was not grass-covered. You needed to be nimble and agile to inspect some of the features, such as a door-jamb and mural cells, and it was one of the many brochs of which you might think '…if only it had an excavation…'.

Well, due to some essential conservation work undertaken in 2002 and, especially, an investigation in 2011, the benign Stoer Broch transmogrified, just like the modest Clark Kent became Superman, into 'superbroch', with a suitable change of name to Clachtoll, after the nearest village. It was eventually extensively excavated as well. Stoer had hit the jackpot.

Before all this, it was thought that, as with most brochs, Stoer, enveloped in its tumbled stones, was either dismantled, or abandoned and collapsed. Following the 2011 investigation, and excavations in 2017 and 2018, all was revealed – well, alternative scenarios were offered.

Stoer/Clachtoll had not simply been abandoned and decayed through neglect. No, the wall had drastically and dramatically collapsed inwards, rendering the broch useless. Not only that, but it had been consumed by fire, to boot. How did this happen?

Well, the excavators found that many of the stones among the rubble – all 275 tons of it – showed signs of being in a fire. As the tower's upper floor(s) would have been wood – charcoal deposits were found round the scarcement, with even more lower down, dated c. 150 B.C. to c. 50 A.D. – the assumption is that the broch was burnt, collapsed and abandoned. And it was a big fire.

Was the fire caused by the collapsed wall, or could it have been a domestic accident that got out of control, causing the eventual collapse? Worse still, could the fire be the result of a missile during a raid: a conflict conflagration? A fanciful notion? Maybe, but as brochs may have had a roof or part-roof, possibly of thatch, either at the top or some way down a tower, a lighted spear or other object could have started a fire. Then, if the inhabitants were distracted, by having to defend the broch, the fire could have taken hold and…

Whatever the cause of the abandonment and collapse, one benefit is that this offered archaeologists an opportunity to study a broch literally as it fell out of use; its Iron Age past preserved was beneath the stones. Numerous artefacts were found at the excavations, including stone lamps and cups, querns, combs, pins, beads, bone and iron objects and decorated ceramics, etc., while grain may have been stored in a mural cell. Perhaps most surprising of all was some charred matting. Analysis of these is on-going.

Today, Stoer/Clachtoll Broch no longer appears as an, attractive, rocky mound; the excavations changed that. The landward side is defended by an outer stone wall. Although tumbled, the layout is visible, with the stones cleared from the entrance. Between the wall and the broch, the remains are less distinct, but a route leads from the wall entrance to the broch entrance, which had a secondary structure added. A paved floor and door-jambs were found in 2018.

The broch entrance has a large triangular lintel, no doubt to spread the load above the doorway and to make a distinctive impression. Some conservation work has been undertaken here and the door-jamb, bar-hole and two guard chambers can be seen without having to be a contortionist.

The rubble that filled the courtyard has been removed and many features unseen, or difficult to see, are now clear. The courtyard is 32 ft. in diameter and the wall about 14 ft. thick. It is likely that Stoer/Clachtoll would have been a tall broch – possibly

40 ft. – and, given its low-lying position, would need to be; it now rises to 10 ft. or more in places. The remains of an intra-mural gallery and galleried wall at an upper level, including a scarcement are all clear. Much fine stone-work can be seen, inside and out, and the floor is also at varied heights. After nearly 2,000 years as a pile of stones, this broch has been transformed.

Located just above the shore line, Stoer/Clachtoll broch is susceptible to nature's extremes. Undoubtedly, it would have been impressive in the Iron Age and a special place to live. Its large stones are more typical of brochs on Skye than those on the west coast of the mainland, but this was probably a local affair, despite similarities with northern coastal brochs. Although, it is one of few brochs on the west coast of Sutherland, following the excavations, Stoer/Clachtoll may become one of the most important for revealing details of its past. 'Superbroch' indeed.

See www.clachtoll.aocarchaeology.com

Other Pre-historic Sites
Culkein (Promontory hillfort) Map 15 ref. 041340
Clashnessie (Dun) Map 15 ref. 055315

Stoer is more than just an attractively sited broch. Recent excavations have revealed more about its pre-historic past than most brochs to date.

TAP o' NOTH (Hillforts)

Aberdeenshire O/S Landranger map 37 ref. 485293

Directions: Take the A97 south from Huntly and turn right along the A941. After 1 1/2 miles, at Howtown, a farm track winds up north-west past the west flank of the hillfort, which is at the summit of the hill.

This dominating hill towers over Strathbogie and houses not only Scotland's second highest hillfort, at 1,848 feet, but the largest known pre-historic stronghold as well. Rather surprisingly, Ingleborough hillfort in England is higher than any in Scotland. This business about Tap o' Noth hillfort being bigger than any other in Scotland needs a bit of explaining, too.

You might recall that both Traprain Law* and Eildon Hill* hillforts, each enclosing about 40 acres, are regarded as about the biggest in the country. Both of these great, tribal centres began as small hillforts and, eventually, expanded to become *oppida* – the only really large examples in Scotland. The development at Tap o' Noth was thought to be the reverse, the large hillfort pre-dating that at the summit. But time waits for no man and neither does archaeology. Just when you thought you knew the history of a stronghold, the worm turns.

A low grass- and heather-covered wall almost surrounds the hill a fair distance below the summit. This links a number of boulders on all sides except the south-east. About 50 acres are enclosed, considerably more than at either Traprain Law* or Eildon Hill*, and ten entrances have been noted – health over safety, eh? This, then, seemed to be a major pre-historic stronghold.

It was presumed that this great hillfort dated from early in the Iron Age. Many tracks and hut circles or platforms could be seen within the massive enclosure, especially on the slopes at the northern half. All in all, the larger Tap o' Noth hillfort must have had one of largest concentrations of huts in pre-historic Scotland.

Of much more obvious interest, though, are the massive ruins of the smaller, assumed later, rectangular hillfort at the summit. A collapsed, heavily vitrified, timber-laced stone wall encloses about 350 ft. x 100 ft. Ironically, given the ten possible entrances in the outer hillfort, the inner one is yet another timber-laced hillfort with no obvious entrance. The wall was more than 20 feet thick and must have made a formidable sight, and a pre-historic pyromaniacs' delight as it burned away; large lumps of vitrified stone are still visible. While accidents, and deliberate slighting, can happen, it is preferable to think of this mighty hillfort succumbing in battle – a far more dignified end.

Both hillforts were excavated in 1891 from which came the chronology that the smaller hillfort was the most recent. This one may be contemporary with the hillforts of Mither Tap o' Bennachie* and Barmekin of Echt* and there have been theories as to the connection between these. Did they form a tribal frontier, for example? From such a great height, fully 1,300 feet above Rhynie, one could oversee the land to the sea, 30 miles away, but not on many days in a year. You can, though, see the strategic potential of the three hillforts demarcating a tribal boundary. Still, it was but a theory.

In 1997, Tap o' Noth was surveyed and an enclosure within the larger hillfort, comprising two ramparts, barely 2 ft. high, with a median ditch, was noted. This is easily missed unless you look for it. Other than that, though, Tap o' Noth still housed a couple of Iron Age hillforts about which little was known, despite its likely importance in the region. Until…the pre-historic world at Tap o' Noth was turned upside down.

Recently, Aberdeen University began investigating Pict influence and settlements in the north-east. Excavations were carried out at Tap o' Noth from 2017 to 2019, and included both hillforts and hut platforms in the lower hillfort. One of the entrances at the lower hillfort was confirmed as such, and remnants of a palisade defining the front of a rampart was found, along with holes for timber-lacing within the tumbled wall of the upper hillfort. Some materials, suitable for C-14 dating, were also recovered. And this provided the real shock.

Far from being the first hillfort on the hill, let alone dating from the early Iron Age, C-14 results showed the large enclosure hailed from the 5th to 6th centuries A.D. This was a radical revision, but one backed by evidence. Yet, there was more.

Results from land and aerial surveys indicated about 800 potential houses on Tap o' Noth, perhaps housing up to 4,000 people, mostly in the lower hillfort. But the real surprise was that these dated from the 3rd to 6th centuries, A.D., not B.C. Tap o' Noth may no longer be the largest pre-historic hillfort in Scotland, but it is, easily, the largest known Pict settlement. By comparison, the revelation that the once-assumed, later summit hillfort was dated to 400 to 100 B.C. merely raised eyebrows. Topsy turvy or what? And, undoubtedly, there will be more to come.

More than 30 years ago, I wrote (Tap o' Noth) '…is possibly a site of considerable national importance and surely cannot be overlooked (for an excavation) for much longer…' And just look at the results – so far. They have turned heads and turned previous theories head-over-heels. Could this not happen at excavations at other pre-historic strongholds?

Before you visit, and visit you must, look out for the latest reports from the University of Aberdeen's Department of Archaeology. You never know what will be revealed next.

Other Pre-historic Site
Cairnmore (Hillfort) Map 37 ref. 503248

ORKNEY AND SHETLAND ISLANDS
STRONGHOLDS AND MAP

SITE	ISLAND GROUP	O/S MAP	MAP ref.	OTHER
1 Borwick Broch	Orkney	6	225168	
2 Broch of Burland	Shetland	4	446360	
3 Broch of Gurness	Orkney	6	383268	Broch & Fort
4 Brough of Stoal	Shetland	1	547873	Promontory H/F
5 Burgi Geos	Shetland	1	478034	H/F & Blockhouse
6 Burra Ness Broch	Shetland	1	556957	
7 Burrian Broch	Orkney	5	762513	
8 Clickhimin	Shetland	4	465408	Broch & Blockhouse
9 Culswick Broch	Shetland	4	254448	
10 Hoxa Broch	Orkney	7	425940	
11 Jarlshof	Shetland	4	397096	Multi-phase site
12 Loch of Houlland	Shetland	3	213792	Broch
13 Loch of Huxter	Shetland	2	558620	Fort & Blockhouse
14 Mid-Howe Broch	Orkney	6	371308	& Chambered barrow
15 Mousa Broch	Shetland	4	457237	
16 Ness of Burgi	Shetland	4	388084	Fort & Blockhouse

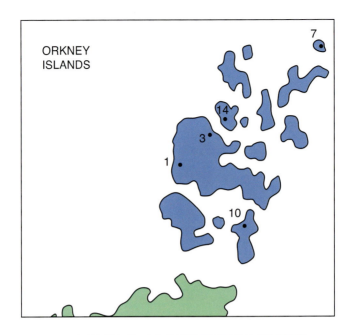

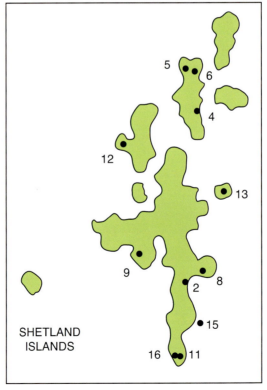

BORWICK BROCH

Orkney (Mainland) O/S Landranger map 6 ref. 225168

Directions: Leave Stromness on the A965 and turn left on the A967. Turn left along the B9056 and first left along the minor road through Yesnaby to the coast. Park in the car park and walk north along the coast, over and down the Hill of Borwick. Cross the stream at the bottom, and the broch is on the second small promontory to the north of the stream. About 1/2 mile walk.

Brochs perched on a tight-fitting promontory are something of a northern isles' speciality. The Broch of Burland is one such on Shetland, but Borwick – sometimes known as Borthwick – was built a mite too close to the edge, for much of its western side has gone over. Borwick has succumbed badly to the combined effects of a precarious site, nature and excavation, but is still attractive and there is more than just a broch to see.

Before it was excavated in 1881, like Mid-Howe*, Gurness* and many brochs today, Borwick was a turf-covered, seemingly natural mound. Those were early days for such work and archaeological investigation was not the sole reason for these undertakings: the hope of finding valuable artefacts often featured high in the diggers' priorities. So, apart from clearing out the broch and giving various dimensions, many of the exterior buildings were covered in excavators' spoil – as at Nybster Broch*.

While it is dramatic to see where the broch has fallen over the cliff edge, Borwick is still attractive due to its gold-coloured stone. About half of the wall's circumference survives and the exterior face shows the classical broch taper, even though it is only about 8 feet high. That is considerably lower than when excavated, for it then stood up to 16 feet, and averaged 11 feet. The broch wall was only about 11 feet thick in the west, but up to 16 feet in the north. Although broch walls seldom have an exact and consistent width round the circumference, such a difference is exceptional.

The entrance faces south-east, and is complete with lintels as far as the door-jambs. Inside this is an entrance to a badly damaged guard cell, but there are no other cells at ground level – though there may be the remains of a small one above the entrance. The courtyard has been described as having a diameter of both 24 and 27 feet, neither of which are relevant today as part of the broch is missing. The internal face is not that of the broch, but a secondary wall built on 3 feet of rubble above the original floor. This brought the diameter of the broch down to about 16 feet, as does the building of wheelhouses within a few brochs.

Most of the promontory, if not all, was further protected by a stone-faced wall about 160 feet long and 6 feet wide, with a ditch beyond: the wall is now covered in turf. A midden near the broch produced a few shards of pottery dating to the middle Iron Age, plus ash and animal bone.

So, Borwick bears similarities with Nybster* and Mid-Howe* brochs. This wall vaguely resembles a blockhouse, without an apparent entrance, although a secondary hut is built over the middle where it may have been. This promontory wall obscures the view of the broch as you walk up the hill from the stream, though the original tower would have been visible.

Between the broch and the outer defences were several dwellings. These may, or may not be secondary and it will need quite a fair effort to find out, as spoil covers much of the area. Useful though many of these 19th century excavations of brochs were, the damage they caused is clearly apparent at Borwick. Much of the broch has vanished over the cliff edge, while it is now only half the height it was when excavated. The chances are that the broch's interior, and especially the external buildings, has been so disturbed that a modern excavation would produce results that were, at best, unreliable. Then again, if it were still a green mound, Borwick Broch would not really be a site worth visiting.

Borwick broch is pleasingly located on the west coast of Mainland, with some spectacular cliff scenery, yet is easy to reach. It was a splendid site in the Iron Age as well, for there is a stream and sheltered landing to the south, good agricultural land all round and, probably of considerable importance, it is strategically commanding. In addition, there is a bit of glamour attached to how Borwick might have met its end. The secondary internal wall was exposed to fierce heat. Was Borwick Broch, in its last phase of occupation, burned in a successful raid?

There is no comparison between the brochs of Mid-Howe* and Gurness*, and Borwick, but the latter is probably a more typical Orcadian broch. There are many similar brochs in these islands, but precious few to see. In the evening sun, Borwick certainly makes up for that.

Other Pre-historic Sites
Skara Brae (Neolithic Settlement) Map 6 ref. 230187
Oxtro Broch Map 6 ref. 253267
Brough of Birsay (Dark Ages/Viking site) Map 6 ref. 239285
Ring of Brodgar (Stone Circle) Map 6 ref. 294133
Standing Stones of Stenness Map 6 ref. 306125
Maes Howe (Chambered Cairn) Map 6 ref. 318127

BROCH OF BURLAND

Shetland Islands (Mainland) Landranger map 4 ref. 446360

Directions: Leave Lerwick, heading south-west, on the A970. After 3 miles, the Loch of Brindister appears on the right, along with the old road. Park just beyond, next to the crash barriers on the left. The broch is visible on the headland to the south-east. Climb over the barrier and walk down round the south of the quarry perimeter fence, keeping the broch in sight. Cross the stream by the bridge leading to the ruined croft nearby. About 1 mile difficult walk.

This is one of the more heavily defended and spectacularly sited brochs. Its location alone, with long coastal views and looking over to Bressay island, makes it worth visiting. Add to this the reasonably well preserved broch and a most impressive set of outer defences, and the Broch of Burland will fully repay all the effort required to get there.

Though the broch is unexcavated, it is thought to date from the main period of brochs, that is the early centuries B.C. and A.D. With sheer cliffs of over 50 feet high on three sides, the broch still stands impressively against the sea, despite being only about 10 feet high. The wall is about 15 feet thick and encloses a rubble-filled courtyard 35 feet across, so it could have risen to 30 feet or more in height. This was probably as much as most brochs had for defensive purposes, but Burland – like some other northern isles' brochs – has much more, to which we will return shortly.

The outer face of the broch wall is best where it faces the sea. Traces of an upper gallery are visible and it appears to be a later broch tower. The entrance is rather close to the cliff-edge in the south-west, and is cluttered with debris. Nevertheless, a guard cell is visible and just one lintel is in position (all were in 1996). All this gives a good impression of the detail design that made brochs so advanced. There is evidence of later occupation, as the broch was altered and, all in all, the Broch of Burland is a pretty well preserved, not to say spectacular, broch of 2,000 years ago.

On the other hand, as clearly seen as you approach, Burland has further defences of considerable strength. The narrow headland is cut off by a massive grass-covered stone wall – with a ditch in front. Behind these are two more walls and ditches. An entrance causeway runs through all these outer defences. They can be viewed in cross-section from the adjacent cliffs to the east. A short excavation in the 1990s, of the outer and central walls at their western ends, subjected to erosion, showed that they both had a rubble and spoil core, but both had stone facings. It was assumed, but not confirmed, that the inner wall was of similar build.

Unlike most brochs, that stand without any apparent external protection, many of those on the Orkney and Shetland Islands have defensive outworks. Few are better than those at the Broch of Burland and, with all its natural advantages, it must have been quite impregnable.

As with so many brochs, that seem to bear the personal touch not applicable to either hillforts or duns, one needs to consider the people who had it built in the first place. This was surely not the dwelling of a simple farmer. Even if Caithness and parts of Orkney are heavily 'brochulated', to the point where they may have been the equivalent of the small hillforts in the Borders, and probably belonged to an extended family, brochs such as Burland suggest that the owner was, at least, of local importance – such as a chief. If so, where did other people live and, like the early medieval castles, was the broch used as a place of communal refuge in times of danger?

These questions, and a great many more, cannot be answered. In fact, the more brochs one visits, the more questions are raised than are answered. Whatever the reasons for building Burland broch, it makes for spectacular and invigorating investigation today. One that is certainly worth the effort required to cross the heather moor and bog.

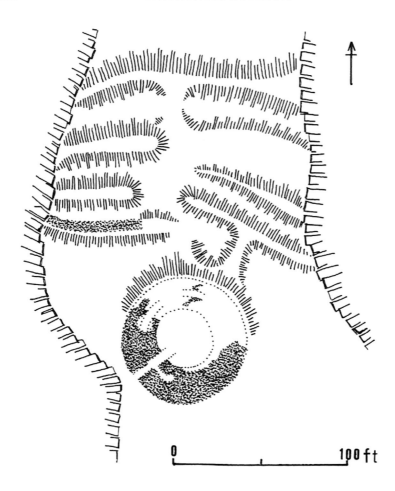

BROCH OF GURNESS

Orkney Islands (Mainland) O/S Landranger map 6 ref. 383268

Directions: From Stromness, take the A967 north and turn right on the B9057 to the north coast. Turn right on the A966 and left along the minor road leading to the coast. The site includes a museum. (Historic Scotland)

While neither displaying the majesty of Mousa* broch, nor the massive build of the White Caterthun* hillfort, Gurness is, nevertheless, one of Scotland's great pre-historic strongholds. Its location, facing the island of Rousay across the magnificence of the Eynhallow Sound, adds to the atmosphere and impression that one is venturing back 2,000 years in time. That there are eight other known brochs along this stretch of water

*The outer defences and some outer buildings at Gurness can be seen,
along with the island of Rousay across the Eynhallow Sound.*

shows just how important it must have been in the Iron Age. Gurness, though, was more than simply a broch, but was a thriving community centred round the broch tower.

Gurness's appearance today is but one brief period in its long history. Until the late-1920s and 1930s, a grass-covered mound covered the broch and settlements. Excavators cleared this to reveal the broch, with the, now re-positioned, most extensive set of surroundings buildings then discovered – and that still applies.

Higher still in the mound, was a Pictish shamrock courtyard house and a probable Viking longhouse. These were re-sited beside the museum, but were originally to the north-east of the broch. Unfortunately, nature had already taken a hand in events and the northern section had suffered from coastal erosion. This, then, is an exposed location, yet one that was inhabited for possibly one thousand years.

The broch is probably the earliest building on the site, though an earlier occupation is possible, despite a lack of visible evidence. The wall is about 15 feet thick – with an intra-mural gallery, and encloses a courtyard 34 feet in diameter. The wall rises to 12 feet above the present floor level; the original floor is several feet below. Thus, the broch could easily have been over 30 feet high – despite the model in the museum depicting it as being little over 20 feet, and would have been a stoutly defended place to live.

The entrance – with its later out-workings appearing almost as a miniature barbican – has door-jambs, a bar hole and, most rarely, a door pivot. The passage is flanked by intra-mural cells with the gallery leading off these. In the courtyard, there is an entrance to an upper level that was reached by ladders, while steps within the galleried-wall led to the higher levels. A scarcement is visible and, most impressively, so are numerous secondary internal features. Prominent among these are the great vertical stone slabs that divide the broch's interior into several chambers, a hearth and two sets of stairs. A hearth, a well and water tank still survive at the original floor level. This was no simple broch, and yet many others might have enjoyed a similar level of sophistication. The plan is useful here, for Gurness is one of the few brochs where the pre-historic internal layout exists to any extent, let alone the level seen here.

There is, though, rather more to Gurness than the broch. Unlike some brochs that stand in splendid isolation, Gurness is further protected on the landward side by a unique rampart with projecting bastions, a drystone-faced ditch about 6 feet deep and two more ramparts. It is not known whether these fully encircled the broch, but the site has eroded since the 1930s, so this is distinctly possible.

Yet, there is more. The broch is surrounded by 14 courtyard houses. The excavators' thought that these were built after the broch was abandoned – and probably used stones from the tower – but, more recently, ideas have changed. There is still little doubt that the broch was built first, but some archaeologists now consider that the courtyard houses – each with their various chambers and shelters, formed part of a

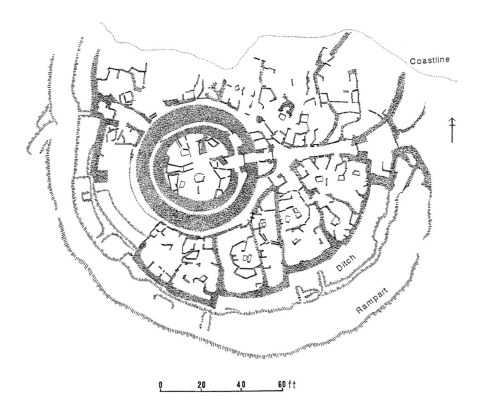

surrounding village. Was the broch either a communal refuge, or the home of a local chief? This theory is given further credence, as the track from the broch to the rampart entrance is not encroached upon by any of these buildings. As such, Gurness has much in common with Norman motte and bailey castles, and must surely have been the fortified base of someone of considerable local stature. Perhaps a king of the Orkney's who, reputedly, submitted to Emperor Claudius before 43 A.D.?

While Gurness broch is unique in the scale of its external buildings and defences, there is evidence of additional buildings at several other brochs, though invariably not so grand. These buildings have usually been considered to belong to a post-broch era, but such ideas might need revising. As with all pre-historic matters, there can be no set model and just because Gurness broch was contemporary with its surrounding buildings does not mean that was the case everywhere. It is likely that the site was abandoned before the Picts re-used it, but who knows what happened between then and the building of the longhouse?

The similarity to Mid-Howe* broch, just across the water on Rousay Island cannot be denied. At the latter, though, some of the external buildings are built over the outer-defences. The scale of the Gurness site, its visible remains from at least three periods of occupation, the museum and its magnificent, if exposed, location make this one of the most important and impressive pre-historic sites in Scotland. Gurness is an essential place to visit for anyone with an inkling of an interest in Scotland's past, and one – given half decent weather – that will be a truly memorable experience.

BROUGH OF STOAL (Promontory Hillfort)

Shetland (Yell) O/S Landranger map 1 ref. 547873

Directions: From Ulsta, take the B9081 round the east of the island. After Otterswick, turn right towards Aywick and take the second road on the right to the north side of the bay. Go through the five-bar gate about 100 yards before the road ends, and follow the track up the hill. Keep right where the tracks fork, immediately after going through the third gate, and follow the track past the ruined croft. The hillfort is on a promontory into the sea.

Most of the Shetland Islands abound with spectacular coastal scenery; Yell is no different, despite the ever-present canopy of peat. This is not quite so apparent in the more sheltered east, where the occasional field just about holds its own, but peat is a remorseless enemy to any agriculture. In contrast, my abiding memory of west Yell is cycling along in a ferocious, gale-blown sleet storm. Nothing necessarily wrong with that, except that it was the middle of August and the locals treated it pretty much as the norm for the time of the year.

Promontory hillforts are ten-a-penny in Cornwall and Pembrokeshire, but they become less common northwards and are decidedly rare in Shetland. Few are as small as the Brough of Stoal, nowadays barely 50 feet wide and only a little longer.

It is heavily eroded but, even so, it is one of the most precipitous pre-historic strongholds anywhere. One wonders why such an exposed place was ever defended and lived on, for it is 150 feet above the sea with no obvious place to launch a boat nearby, and who on earth needed protection from whom at this outpost?

The bare figures do not do the Brough of Stoal any justice, though. The approach enables you to see the three ramparts and two ditches that cut across the neck of the fragile promontory, against the eastern sky. Their zigzag profile has mellowed over the centuries, but there is no mistaking that these most definitely were for defence and not decoration. And that is the best location from which to appreciate the defences, for although the middle rampart still rises to some 8 feet above its ditch, it is the extent of the decay that is most apparent from close-quarters. For example, the remains of the entrance can be seen at the inner rampart, but it has long-since gone over the edge at the others. Were these ramparts all of contemporary build? If not, why not?

But the real magic of the Brough of Stoal can only be appreciated by going right out beyond the defences. There are the remains of a building. Was this a broch, as at similarly located Broch of Burland*? Possibly, or possibly/probably not, for there is masonry amongst all the detritus, but it appears as a promontory hillfort today.

Out here, you can appreciate just what an exposed place it was to live. The clouds swirl above, the sea crackles and pounds the cliffs below, birds swoop and dart overhead and the long, tousled grass rocks frenetically back and forth in the ever-stiff wind. Nature can be compelling, and all the above is on a calm day. There are fine views to the south, while the island of Fetlar rises away to the east. Such sights in the Lowlands could be spoiled by people, cars and other trappings of our modern world. On Yell, you can appreciate this beauty in splendid and absolute isolation.

Be sure of one thing, for all the majesty and natural dynamism of its location, the Brough of Stoal is a splendid small promontory hillfort, on an island often overlooked by visitors to the Shetland Islands. There are bigger and better strongholds elsewhere, some with equally spectacular scenery, but the combination of pre-historic remains and nature make this easily visited stronghold a particularly pleasing experience.

BURGI GEOS (Blockhouse hillfort)

Shetland (Yell) O/S Landranger map 1 ref. 478034

Directions: From Gutcher, follow the B9082 and continuing minor road to Gloup. Walk down the east side of Gloup Voe, cross the burn at the bottom, and walk up the steep west slope. Head due west over the peat-covered terrain, over the northern slopes of the Hill of Vigon, until the coast is reached. Having maintained a due west course, the hillfort is a little to the north on a promontory into the Burgi Geos. About 7 mile walk, round trip.

No pre-historic stronghold featured in this book is as remote, or difficult to reach as Burgi Geos. In this day and age, when advice is showered down – like the heaviest Yell downpour – about not setting foot outside the car without taking every conceivable precaution imaginable, to really enjoy a visit to Burgi Geos one or two little extras would not go amiss. Yes, you can walk over the peat moorland in good trainers, and no, a bivouac-bag is not vital, but wet feet are a racing certainty, at the very least. The relevant O/S map is essential and a compass is not a bad idea either. Allow about four hours for the trip: peat moorland is tiring after a while, it is easy to wander a little off course and, having made the effort to get there, you might as well enjoy the experience to the full.

Do not, though, let any of the above deter you from visiting this remote blockhouse and fort for, if the weather is reasonably dry and not misty (and Yell is usually so on at least one day a year), then it will be a day to remember for years to come. The site is extremely hazardous as well, sitting as it does on cliffs about 200 feet above the Atlantic Ocean, but what magnificence. No other pre-historic monument in Britain can quite prepare you for the journey and experience on which you are about to embark.

In essence, Burgi Geos is a long, narrow promontory jutting into the Burgi Geos inlet, protected by a complex, if not incoherent, group of Iron Age defences. It features an earth bank, rows of stones, a stone-walled enclosure, the blockhouse – for which it is best known, and the only example of a *chevaux de frise* north of Edinburgh. Despite this plethora of defences, which give the impression that the builders had all the necessary pieces for the jigsaw puzzle – but no idea how to assemble them, the promontory itself is not cut off. It could, no doubt with some difficulty, be penetrated a lot easier than at first appears to be the case. That assumes, of course, anyone in their right mind ever came out here to do so in the first place.

As one looks from the east, the southern approach is guarded by an earth mound, while a line of boulders cuts off the north. Behind the latter, a row of stones runs west, seemingly forming a path along the promontory itself. South of these stones, another mound has been built to house the upright stones of the chevaux de frise. Considering that these were intended to prevent an all-out charge, either on foot – or by horse, the area between the *chevaux de frise* and the row of stones is not only convenient for the inhabitants but, seemingly, provides a nicely marked-out passage for any attackers as well.

The narrowness of the promontory neck is a daunting passage from afar, but is easy enough to traverse once there. One is then faced by the remains of the blockhouse on the promontory itself. The blockhouse is within a small, rectangular, walled enclosure: not unlike that at the Loch of Huxter*, though not forming part of the wall. Unlike Shetland's other blockhouses, there appears to be no entrance and the interior was apparently one large cell. This enclosure is slightly offset from the promontory neck, so it would be possible to surround the small fort and blockhouse, if archers or men using slings and javelins could keep the inhabitants pinned down. You can see what is meant by an incoherent layout of the defences.

Few strongholds are as remote as Burgi Geos. It may not look much, but the trek across Yell,
aside from being an adventure, will reveal two rarities: a chevaux-de-frise; *and a blockhouse.*

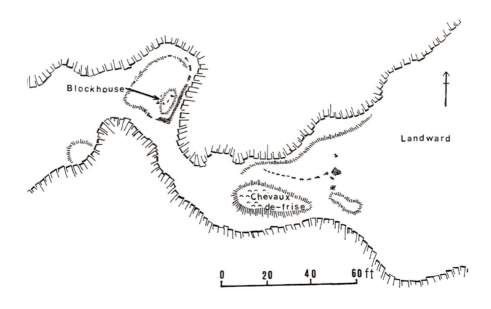

One wonders, today, why anyone ever lived at, and built, Burgi Geos. Despite what has been written elsewhere, the only way you can reach it from the sea is by climbing precarious cliffs, or by flying. The builders seem uncertain of how best to combine all the splendid defensive features – especially the *chevaux de frise* – into an impregnable whole. However, the inhabitants must have been open to influences from either south Scotland or even Ireland (via the Atlantic trading routes?), or the remains have been mis-interpreted.

North-west Yell has successfully resisted all attempts to settle for any length of time, at least since the Neolithic Age. A nearby 19th century settlement was unsuccessful, and the environment traversed in getting to Burgi Geos shows that man is onto a loser almost before he starts. Surely, Burgi Geos was also isolated in the Iron Age? And if it were the stronghold residence of a local chief, where was the rest of the tribe?

Blockhouses may derive from promontory forts, and that at Burgi Geos may have been added to the fort after it was built. There is a hut circle further out along the promontory, which may be of a more recent date than the fort, but why live in such a precarious place? More than any pre-historic stronghold, Burgi Geos is an enigma. Who built it, from where did they come, and from whom was it defended? All these questions can be asked about any pre-historic stronghold with little chance of finding an accurate answer. At many sites, though, one can hypothesise, as there are other strongholds or homesteads nearby, or perhaps other known events, such as a Roman invasion. At Burgi Geos, there seems to be nothing within many miles, and history is a blank page. All of which leaves much to ponder as you make your way back east, enjoying the contents of the friendly hip-flask.

BURRA NESS (Broch)

Shetland, Yell Island O/S Landranger map 1 ref. 556957

Directions: Take the A698 north across Yell. At Gutcher, take the minor road south to North Sandwick and park at the end. Walk down to the beach and follow the coast path south round to the broch, visible on the headland.

As you will undoubtedly have discovered, visiting pre-historic strongholds is not simply a question of driving up, paying your money and going in. Quite often, you have to make a bit of effort to get nearby in the first place, while you usually have to stretch your legs a bit thereafter. Such is the case with Burra Ness broch.

Situated on the east coast of Yell, you most certainly have to put yourself out to visit this broch. Perched on a low, large promontory, Burra Ness has fine views over to Fetlar, Unst and a scattering of other small islands. It is a remote location, which makes it all the more enjoyable to visit, while the rare sea otter can be seen in the vicinity, if you are very lucky.

You might not believe it today but, 200 years ago, corn was grown almost right up to the broch; so it may have been in the Iron Age. The ploughing has damaged what appear to be two encircling ramparts, and there are foundations of various buildings between these and the broch. To all appearances, then, here is another northern isles' broch that might have been a refuge tower for a chief and small settlement, and does not stand in isolation.

The broch wall is 15 feet thick and encloses a courtyard 27 feet in diameter, though little of the interior wall facing is visible. Thus, Burra Ness could have been quite tall, and might have been built in the mid-Iron Age. A small part of the scarcement is visible about 12 feet above the original floor level. An intra-mural gallery can just about be made out among the fallen stones, along with a possible cell, but the interior is anything but impressive.

It is quite another matter with the outer wall-face, especially the eastern side facing Fetlar. This rises to about 15 feet high and is in good condition, despite the continuous battering it has received from the elements. The broch is clearly visible from North Sandwick, but if you double its present height – in the mind's eye, and perhaps add a little more – you can soon see that Burra Ness would have been a most impressively located stronghold 2,000 years ago. The outer wall-face is mostly complete and helps you to visualise how it would have looked; the stonework is, for example, quite different from that of Mousa*.

Pre-historic strongholds are found in all sorts of places, but few are as remote as this. With a sheltered bay to the west offering easy landing, good farming land right outside the ramparts and the broch combining strategic defensive qualities with a command of its immediate vicinity, the builders of Burra Ness found themselves an ideal location. Though remote today, one can easily appreciate the advantages of such a place in less sophisticated times. The remains are more than sufficient to allow you to re-create an overall view of how the site and area might have appeared in the Iron Age.

BURRIAN BROCH

Nth. Ronaldsay (Orkney Islands) O/S Landranger map 5 ref. 762513

Directions: Orkney Ferries runs a weekly service from Kirkwall, while Loganair flies twice daily, Sundays excepted. After leaving the boat at South Bay pier, you can either follow the coast eastwards until you come to the broch on the southern point of the island, a walk of just over a mile, or follow the road inland to Holland. Turn right there for 1/2 mile and turn right again, heading south. This road joins a track to Howar farm, but carry on in a south-easterly direction until you reach the coast. The broch is at the south-east extremity of the Point of Burrian.

Whatever mode of transport you take to North Ronaldsay, you will have an enjoyable and picturesque journey. It is a small island and transport is not needed. Apart from a few burnt mounds, and the unusual Holland House standing stone (ref. 753529) – which can be seen from the road, there is little of pre-historic interest to see. Burrian broch, though, is a fine start for a visit to the island. In addition, the dykes that divide the island might be pre-historic, while the sheep-dyke on the coast is more recent.

The broch nestles right up to the coast and looks out across North Ronaldsay Firth to the island of Sanday. It was one of the earliest brochs to be excavated, in 1870-1, to a very high standard for those times. A large number and variety of bone and stone artefacts were found, such as combs, needles and spindles, as well as iron nails and a glass bead. Unlike many brochs, Burrian has not deteriorated much since then.

The solid wall is 15 feet thick and encloses a courtyard about 30 feet in diameter. So, Burrian might have risen to about 30+ feet in height: it still reaches about 10 feet on the landward side. Much of the exterior facing has gone, but there is some additional buttressing at the north-west. The wall shows that Burrian had the classic cooling tower shape, the distinctive taper being visible. A recessed scarcement can be seen about 3 feet above the present floor and a 'reversed' scarcement about 4 ft. higher, opposite the entrance. This is very rare – so rare, in fact, that it is considered to be a construction of the excavators, whether those of 1870 or not, who knows?

As with other coastal brochs in the northern islands, the entrance faces the sea, in the south-east. The door-jamb is visible and there is an intra-mural cell in the north-west of the wall. The adjoining walls in the north-east and south-west are part of the

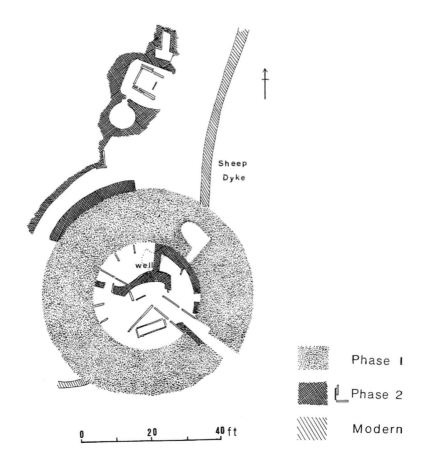

Sheep Dyke

well

Phase I

Phase 2

Modern

0   20   40 ft

island's unique sheep-dyke. This communal system of agriculture could just possibly be similar to that which existed in the Iron Age, at least on North Ronaldsay.

Typical of northern isles' brochs, Burrian also had outer defences: four ramparts provided a particularly effective barrier. Regrettably, these are badly eroded and are almost invisible on the ground. A geophysics survey in 2005 revealed traces of structures outside these defences. Why did so many brochs in the northern islands have such impressive outer defences, while others did without? As many brochs in Caithness have such outer defences, could it be that the occupants of the north were less than harmonious neighbours, or were they occasionally raided by sea-farers? There could also have been a bit of the 'keeping up with the Joneses' as well.

Again, as with so many northern brochs, Burrian underwent a transformation to a semi-wheelhouse. A secondary paved floor and stone partition were built on 2 feet of debris above the original paved floor. It is not known when this took place, but there is no doubt Picts were here at some stage, for the excavators in 1870 found a stone more than 2ft. long with a cross and Ogham inscription. This is now in the National Museum of Scotland, in Edinburgh

There is no obvious sign that the broch was empty for any length of time before rebuilding, but, after finally being abandoned, it was later occupied by squatters. No doubt, some of the broch's stonework found itself used in the sheep-dyke.

North Ronaldsay is a fascinating island to visit. It retains the vestiges of a communal agricultural system that might have had its beginnings in pre-history. This is virtually unique; especially when one includes the enigmatic broch and the various dykes.

CLICKHIMIN (Fort and Broch)

Shetland (Mainland) O/S map 4 ref. 465408

Directions: Turn left out of the Lerwick ferry terminal. Turn right at the roundabout and turn right along North Lochside. Turn right onto the A970, Clickhimin is on the right.

Without a doubt, Clickhimin is one of the most important and visual pre-historic strongholds in the whole of Britain, let alone Shetland or even Scotland. The site was extensively excavated, from 1953 to 1957, with the various artefacts, chronological and building sequences having been revised – and the revisions revised – by several archaeologists since.

Ultimately – and unfortunately – there is no definitive version and much of the original excavator's interpretation and later re-assessments are open to doubt. What, on the surface, appears to be a fairly logical and extensive build-sequence, becomes enshrouded in a confusing mass of theories. To get the most enjoyment from a visit, it is best to simply enjoy the extensive remains and have a bit of fun making an attempt at your own chronological order. There information boards to help.

Sitting in a land-locked freshwater loch, Clickhimin stands on a low islet connected by a long causeway to the shore. From the road, the site reminds one of the castles built by King Henry VIII along the south coast of England; this is further enhanced when Clickhimin is floodlit at night. At one time, although when is a source of considerable debate – with dates being bandied about a thousand or more years apart, the islet was not connected to the shore.

Fortunately, it is today and, before reaching the entrance, the remains of the original causeway with a stone bearing traces of two footprints – beneath a covering stone – can be seen. This may be connected with an inaugural ceremony for a chief (see Dunadd*) and, if nothing else, suggests that Clickhimin was a site of considerable local importance.

That, though, is stating the obvious. One does not need a pretty rustic hammered stone to show that Clickhimin was important; the sheer scale of its defences let you know in no uncertain terms. Although the large outer wall that encloses most of the islet is the first defensive feature you encounter, it was not the first man-made structure. That was a homestead lying to the north-west of the broch, one fairly complete building of which can still be seen. This dates to c. 700 B.C. and may have been undefended.

Clickhimin's outer wall is up to 12 ft. thick, encloses an area of about 140 ft. x 125 ft. and still stands over 8 ft. high. The top courses may have been rebuilt in the 19th century, but it was originally higher still. There is a landing stage at the south of the wall, but there is some debate as to whether this was pre-historic or not: the main wall may date to the 4th century B.C. The entrance is pretty simple, but once inside one is faced with the finest surviving example of a Shetland blockhouse.

Blockhouses are only found on the Shetland Islands, and there are only four other examples (see Ness of Burgi*, Burgi Geos* and Lock of Huxter*). One at Scatness East was discovered fairly recently and cannot really be seen, while that at Huxter forms part of the encircling wall. This is not the case at Clickhimin, but some archaeologists have suggested that it may have formed part of an inner wall that was dismantled when the broch was built. That is but a theory and the surface evidence upon which it was based is hardly persuasive.

Then again, a blockhouse standing within the defensive wall is not exactly its most effective location. It has a central entrance passage, complete with door-jambs and a cell at either side. That on the west is reached by stairs, but entry to the east cell was by ladders. The blockhouse is currently two storeys high, but was probably higher still. There is a scarcement along its inner wall that possibly supported lean-to buildings, but the gap between the rear of the blockhouse and the base on which the broch stands is not great. It could have been a defensive citadel – a pre-historic castle keep, but remains something of an enigma. Yet the blockhouse was clearly of enough use to be retained, even if not to its full height, during Clickhimin's next phase: that of the broch.

Undoubtedly, the broch tower is the most impressive building at Clickhimin. For one thing it is large, measuring about 65 feet across and having a courtyard diameter about half that. Thus, this broch was probably tall, possibly in excess of 40 ft. high, of which about 17 ft. survives. The entrance faces west and has the usual door-jamb and also gaps in the lintels to either view, or jab spears into any unwanted guests.

Initially, the courtyard does not seem as large as the figures suggest, but, as with some other brochs, this was later converted into a wheelhouse. Most unusually, if not uniquely, the broch has two further gaps in the outer wall. One at the north end connects with the intra-mural gallery and stairs to run round to the second-floor level, in the south-west; the other is in the east. These are thought to be original features and show the inhabitants had enough faith in the outer defences to diminish their broch's defensive capabilities.

The plan shows the location of the two cells. The east cell has a magnificent, fully corbelled roof – will your house roof last 2,000 years? The wheelhouse, with its darker stone than the broch, was quite substantial and has its own cell. This dates from c. 200 A.D. and, along with those elsewhere, possibly suggests that the threat that caused brochs, duns and hillforts to be built had receded. Until being cleared out in 1861-2, the wheelhouse still had its distinctive radial piers, not unlike wheel spokes. The floor level seen today is not that of the original broch.

Still there is more to see at this fascinating site. To the west of the broch are several houses. That in the north-west dates from the late-Bronze Age, but the others may have been occupied before, during and after the main broch period. Presumably, the ground beneath the broch would have had huts built on it to fully utilise the space enclosed by the outer wall. The existence of these are somewhat incompatible with the theory of the blockhouse being an entrance to an all-enclosing inner wall. It may be that Clickhimin was home to between 30 and 50 people.

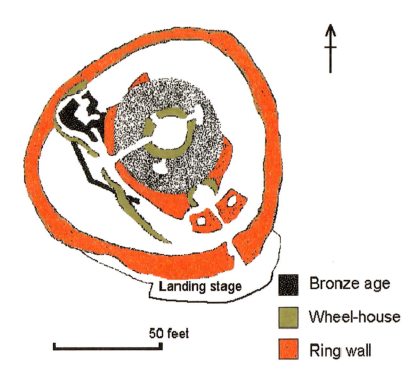

Landing stage   ■ Bronze age

                     ■ Wheel-house

50 feet   ■ Ring wall

Clickhimin, standing on its islet, was possibly occupied for 1,000 years, although not always fortified. The inhabitants were not cut-off from the rest of the world: fragments of Roman glass – possibly made in Alexandria c. 100 A.D. – show that. They developed their island stronghold using the latest defensive ideas: a strong encircling wall, perhaps the mightiest blockhouse ever built, and a broch that, if it really was over 40 ft. tall, would have put Mousa* firmly in its place.

Whatever the status of the pre-historic Shetland Islanders, such development is testament to their building and planning skills. The sheer scale of these defences may make Clickhimin the ultimate, small pre-historic stronghold.

Clickhimin is in the care of Historic Scotland, but is one place where a guide would be very useful. On one of my visits, a coach party arrived, alighted for no more than 10 minutes and was off again. Somehow, one felt, they had missed out. After all, where else can you see a fort, broch, wheelhouse and blockhouse all in one?

CULSWICK BROCH

Shetland (Mainland) O/S Landranger map 4 ref. 254448

Directions: Take the A970, north from Lerwick and turn left along the A971. After 16 miles, take the first road on the left after the B9071, go past Stanydale Temple and turn left at the cross-roads. Continue along this road and turn right onto the B9071. Go up the hill and turn right to Culswick. Park at the Methodist Chapel, signed from beside the telephone box. Follow the track westwards to the north of three small lochs; the broch can be seen towering over the third loch. To return, follow the coast south to Culswick inlet. About a 3 mile round trip.

It is mentioned in the entry for Mousa* Broch that, after seeing the best of its kind, every other broch will seem distinctly second rate, a bit of a let-down. The ideal antidote for a bout of post-Mousa* blues is Culswick Broch. Despite being ruined and standing at less than half the height of Mousa*, the combination of the nature and location of Culswick, probably the most spectacularly sited of all brochs, makes it as attractive to visit as the greatest of them all.

A little over 200 years ago, before the broch was pillaged for stone to build some – now abandoned – crofts, Culswick was, apparently, approaching Mousa's* height. Superficially, as with most brochs, the two had close connections, but in detail, particularly in the stonework, Culswick and Mousa* brochs could not be more different. Large blocks of marvellous red granite give Culswick not only a distinctive hue, but an appearance of solidity that makes the smaller slabs, of which Mousa* is built, look like the left-overs. Even in its present condition, with fallen stones all round, Culswick is anything but a pile of rubble; it is easy to envisage this as a very powerful stronghold.

Culswick Broch's bare physical figures read impressively as well. The solid wall is at least 14 feet thick, enclosing a courtyard about 25 feet in diameter; not quite as high a wall:courtyard ratio as Mousa*, but enough to suggest that Culswick was not a minnow. The interior wall-face is visible up to 8 feet in height in places, but this is above the tumble of stones that fills the interior; the true height is much more. The outer wall-face is even higher, especially in the south and east, and this rises up to nearly 20 feet above the true ground level, buried beneath yet more fallen stones.

Enough of such dry figures, though, for they can be matched by other brochs that could not hold a candle to Culswick. There is an intra-mural cell and gallery in the north-east, with a blocked entrance, and traces of a gallery in the north-west. The entrance, facing south-east, is also blocked, but its door-jambs can be seen and many lintels are in place. Culswick is one of several brochs with a large triangular lintel above the entrance. This served not only to spread the weight of the stones above, but would impress visitors, too. Not only was Culswick Broch an almost impregnable, it looked every inch the part.

That is not all, for Culswick still has an outer defensive wall. This is about 14 feet thick and stands over 6 feet high, although most of it is missing in the north and north-east. Both wall-faces are visible for good sections, but much of the area between the broch and the wall is filled with fallen stones. There may have been some external buildings, but it is currently impossible to tell.

The combination of mighty broch tower, substantial outer wall and location on a large rocky boss overlooking the entrance to Gruting Voe, the lighthouse and the Atlantic Ocean, makes Culswick Broch a formidable stronghold in its commanding magnificence. It is visible for all and sundry to see, especially from the sea. Two thousand years ago, the mighty tower of red granite, glinting in the evening sun, must have made a daunting and dominating sight; one not to be meddled with lightly. From the broch, one can see Foula in the west, and down to Fitful Head in the south, not far from the Ness of Burgi* fort. Oh yes, strategic location featured very high in the planning of this great broch as well.

All this might appear a little over-enthusiastic about Culswick Broch, but, having visited many brochs – including Mousa* the day before, one can become a bit blasé. Culswick certainly refreshed parts that other brochs could not reach. Approaching from the north of the lochs, there it towers in the distance; what an impact it must have made in the Iron Age, or even 250 years ago.

This corner of the Shetland Isles is quiet even by local standards. The various Neolithic settlements to the north show that this was not always the case, but once the blanket of peat began to envelop the land, so man was forced out, or at least onto a narrow coastal strip. Culswick Broch is all that survives from the Iron Age hereabouts. The area must surely have been something less than a hive of activity, yet the broch emphatically contradicts the notion of a barren landscape.

There is access to the sea, farmland and, of course, fresh water lochs nearby. So, although quite isolated, the broch's inhabitants had everything they could need. They certainly built the broch as if they meant to stay.

Other Pre-historic Sites
Gruting School (Neolithic Settlement) Map 3 ref. 281498
Pinhoulland (Neolithic Settlement) Map 3 ref. 259497
Scord of Brouster (Neolithic Settlement) Map 3 ref. 255516
Stanydale (Neolithic Settlement and 'Temple') Map 3 ref. 285502

HOXA BROCH

Orkney (Sth. Ronaldsay) O/S Landranger map 7 ref. 425940

Directions: From Kirkwall, take the A961 south across the Churchill Barriers to South Ronaldsay and turn right on the B9043. Continue through St. Margaret's Hope and park at the Sands of Wight car park. Walk west for 100 yards and turn right along the road up the hill. Where the road turns sharp left, turn right along the track to the house. The broch is in the back garden. Ask permission.

Also known as the Howe of Hoxa, this was one of the first brochs to be excavated, in 1848. Unfortunately, misguided attempts at conservation were then made, while it was turned into a feature of the house's garden: a sort of roofless summer-house. When visiting this site, this appeared to be unused and features of the floor were becoming difficult to see.

Hoxa was first recorded in 1781 and was claimed to have a galleried-wall. By the time it was dug into, the wall was described as having a rubble core, faced with stones on either side. It is extremely unlikely that a broch would ever have a rubble core, as many hillforts do, so the gallery could have filled up with fallen stones. In any case, it was an odd description for the exterior wall-face was revealed down to the ground. The wall was 14 feet thick and enclosed a courtyard 29 feet in diameter. Despite the un-propitious external view, the wall is still about 10 feet high internally.

The entrance faced east, towards the house, and had a set of door-jambs, bar hole and a guard cell entered from the courtyard. Inside the courtyard were a stone-lined tank and some upright dividing slabs, as at Mid-Howe*. In all, this was a decent start at excavating a broch, with many features that soon became recognised in many others.

Things then started to go awry. The landowner decided to fill in the trench exposing much of the exterior wall-face to conserve it, and then mortared the inner wall-face. The wall-head was similarly capped and, while it must be admitted that these measures have preserved the wall in a better condition than many others excavated in the 19th century, the broch was transformed into garden ornamentation. The entrance was opened out to form a gateway, while a set of stone stairs, leading to a platform and flagpole, was built outside this.

As such, Hoxa is an unusual broch to visit, especially after seeing others in a more natural state. Of course, if all brochs had been dressed up and transformed into a garden feature, the loss would be incalculable. This is not the case and Hoxa has a unique and distinctive air about it. The internal slab dividers, on nothing like the scale of those at Mid-Howe*, are still there, as is the tank sunk into the floor. So, although one cannot see the exterior walls, and the entrance has been transformed, there is still plenty to see and the internal height is still impressive.

The location of Hoxa is interesting as well. It overlooks a small bay and beach and there are good views from the wall-head over Scapa Flow. Though marshy in places, the surrounding land could be farmed. Not a bad place to live, really.

Nobody ought to bemoan the loss of Hoxa as a true broch. It was one of the first brochs to be excavated and mistakes were bound to be made. In many ways, it is an example of what might lie beneath the hundreds of similar possible broch mounds, if ever they are excavated. In any case, one cannot just go to a garden centre and order a broch summer-house, so that is one up to the present owners. Thinking about it, I would quite fancy a broch in my back garden.

Other Pre-historic Sites
Broch of Burray (Burray) Map 7 ref. 490998
Castle of Burwick (Promontory Fort) Sth. Ronaldsay Map 7 ref. 434842
St. Mary's Broch (Mainland) Map 7 ref. 470013

JARLSHOF (Broch and multi-phase site)

Shetland (Mainland) O/S Landranger map 4 ref. 397096

Directions: Take the A970 south from Lerwick to beyond Sumburgh Airport. Once south of the airport, turn right to the hotel and Jarlshof is by the coast. Tel. 01950-460112

Jarlshof is one of the great archaeological sites, not only of Britain, but of Europe as well. Here, like Jericho, you can see many phases of development on one site, several of which overlay each other encompassing a period of three and a half millennia. Yet, this site of great archaeological importance was never matched in reality. None of the many residences at Jarlshof seem to have belonged to people of anything but local significance. Jarlshof has not played any great part in history, but it is the combination of the remains themselves that give it such prominence.

During a particularly nasty storm in 1897, the sand was blown from the shore beneath the ruined 17th century laird's house to reveal what was to become the most uniquely settled site in Britain. Today, the site covers about 3 acres, but it is much eroded by the sea. It was excavated in the 1930s and again in 1949 to 1952, each uncovering yet more dwellings. There is a museum while the guidebook is quite invaluable. Although only one of the seven main phases currently visible concerns this book, a brief run-down of the whole history of the site is more than useful.

It dates back to c. 2000 B.C., perhaps before bronze was first manufactured in Shetland. The earliest dwellings are the scant remains of huts to the right of the museum, beneath the medieval farm. As one looks from right to left, so the huts become progressively younger, from Bronze Age to the Iron Age, the latter including souterrains that, unfortunately, cannot be entered. None of these remains, from what may have been a series of larger settlements, are thought to have been fortified.

A little to the north-west, and half eroded by the sea, is the remains of a broch. It has a solid wall, about 18 feet thick and the courtyard is 30 feet across. It is particularly well built, with signs of two mural cells and, given its dimensions, it may have been of considerable height, dating to about the turn of the 1st millennium A.D. Inside the broch, much of the inner wall-face has been obscured by its conversion to a wheelhouse, one of several outstanding examples at the site.

A view over the Iron Age houses at Jarlshof, across to the Scatness peninsula.

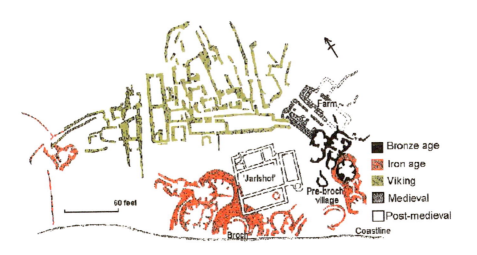

This, and the still better adjacent examples, are the finest wheelhouses to be seen and are extremely well built. If the fact that there is only half a broch at Jarlshof is a little disappointing, the magnificence of the wheelhouses, dating to c. 200 A.D., more than compensates.

At the north-west end of the site there are some late-Iron Age huts and, working back east from these, there is a confusion of Norse buildings from the 9th to 13th centuries. This group of Norse buildings was first discovered in the 1930s. The long-house is the earliest, and the multitude of later buildings have been pushed out in all directions, but especially north. The arrival of the Norsemen in Britain is usually connected with deeds of destruction, so it seems strange to see a considerable Norse settlement of people who were but farmers and fishermen; well, after they had killed off all the locals first...

Still there is more. To the right of the long-house are the remains of a medieval farm, some of these have been removed to uncover the Bronze Age buildings; more of these could lie beneath the farm. Finally, and the only stronghold on the site other than the broch, there is the laird's tower-house that dominates the lot, at least from afar. From the top of this, one gains a panoramic view of most of the site and the surrounding area, helping to un-ravel it all.

Jarlshof, then, is unique in Britain and demands to be visited. People from all over Europe travel to Shetland to see Jarlshof before any other place on the islands. It is that important and stunningly visual.

Other Site
Old Scatness, broch and re-created wheelhouse.

LOCH OF HOULLAND

Shetland (Mainland) O/S Landranger map 3 ref. 213972

Directions: From Hillswick, take the B9078 west and turn right on the road to Esha Ness lighthouse. Park at the top of the hill. Walk north, parallel to the coast, and the loch comes into view after about 1/4 mile. The broch is on a promontory on the west side of the loch.

There are two islets into the loch on its west side and, with a cursory glance, that without the broch seems the better of the two to occupy. Still, it could have been quite another matter in the Iron Age. Though mostly surrounded by water, the remains of an outer bank and a row of boulders cuts-off the landward side of the broch's islet. This may be post-broch, as the stones appear to have come from the fallen broch tower.

This is another broch that gives the impression of being a tumbled mass of stones from afar – and almost until on the islet. The sheer mass of tumbled stone, whether lying about or re-used in later building, gives some indication of the vast quantity required to build a broch: this can be difficult to comprehend, even at Mousa*. It also shows that this was more than a short squat broch. The best aspect of the broch is from the opposite side of the loch.

Many brochs today have been cleared out or tidied up a little – that is certainly not the case here. As such, its features are mostly obscured by stones: the interior, for example, is full of them. Likewise the west-facing entrance, although some lintels are in place and, with a bit of a nimble squeeze, one can reach the guard cell. The wall, of indeterminate thickness, is best seen in the north, where its outer-face is visible for about 6 feet in height: a true height of about 15 feet, but the rubble obscures the lower courses. Also at this point, can be seen part of the upper intra-mural gallery.

Much of the area between the broch and the rampart, and right down to the shore, is filled with secondary buildings. These almost certainly date from the immediate post-broch period for they utilise stones from the broch tower: some are even built into the original rampart. The site would have been particularly attractive in the Iron Age for it had fresh water, land that could be farmed and, of course, outstanding defensive qualities; all one could ever ask for in pre-historic times. Why abandon the broch and build a relatively undefended settlement, though?

Given the quantity of fallen stone, and that it might have been robbed to build later, nearby crofts, the broch gives every impression of being a large tower of advanced design. The location would have been ideal and is similar to many duns and brochs in the Hebridean islands. That ought not goad one into thinking that the builders migrated from the west of Scotland, merely that Iron Age man was capable of adapting a specific stronghold to the local terrain.

The Esha Ness peninsula can be a wild and windy place, yet has much outstanding coastal scenery. The Loch of Houlland broch occupies as sheltered a spot as can be found and would have been particularly attractive to Iron Age man. A walk along the north coast back to the lighthouse is particularly rewarding.

Other Pre-historic Site
Sae Breck Broch Map 3 ref. 210780

LOCH OF HUXTER (Hillfort and Blockhouse)

Shetland (Whalsay) O/S Landranger map 2 ref. 558620

Directions: From Voe, take the B9071 to Laxo for the boat to Whalsay. From Symbister, take the southern road to Isbister. A track leads from the right to the loch and a causeway to the island in the loch.

In the case of the other three blockhouse forts featured in this book, they are all currently free-standing, even if that was not always the case. The blockhouse at the Loch of Huxter still forms the gatehouse of an enclosed fort. As such, one can see similarities between the blockhouse on Whalsay and a barbican entrance to a medieval castle, at least in principle.

The fort stands on a small islet in the loch, connected to the shore by a man-made causeway: unlike the Loch of Houlland* broch, this is a genuine island. As recently as 1881, the blockhouse was recorded as being as tall as that at Clickhimin*; even in 1963 it rose to more than 6 ft. Regrettably, such a source of good quality stone could not be resisted and it was pillaged to build both a school and the planticrues on the shore; these are now becoming quite ruinous. So, here was yet another relatively recent tragedy to blight our pre-historic sites, which makes it all the more remarkable that, say, Mousa* has survived.

Unfortunately, the blockhouse is in a rather poor state and is obscured by tumbled stones. It is about 40 feet long and 10 feet wide and the central, now open, entrance – which is offset from the causeway – has both a set of door-jambs and a bar hole. The cells on either side are entered from the rear, but it stands at nothing like the height of the Clickhimin* blockhouse. Debris is now all around, though there may have been an additional wall between the blockhouse and the causeway.

The main fort wall is connected to the rear of the blockhouse at the south, and to the side at the north. This enclosed an area up to 70 feet in diameter: the wall is a little under 10 feet thick for most of its circuit. As with the blockhouse, this is now quite ruined and a section is missing in the north. The build sequence of the blockhouse and fort wall has not been determined, but it is probable that the two were planned separately, even if built at about the same time. Perhaps a walled fort was being built when the idea of the blockhouse for the entrance was either conceived or copied. The two do not appear to have been built as a whole.

Here, one can appreciate the sole surviving example of an un-modified island blockhouse fort, unique to the Shetland Islands. Its condition could be far better, but it is by no means a disappointment. This is an example of Iron Age man developing and building a stronghold for a specific site. That the Hebrideans would probably have built a dun on the island is merely due to local tradition at any one time. One cannot really say that a blockhouse-type fort was part of a chronological sequence of pre-historic drystone stronghold building, at least in the sense that it was an obvious stage between, say, a dun and a broch.

In the main, the Loch of Huxter fort is a fine site to visit, especially if one is going to Whalsay. Still, it is immensely annoying to think just how much better preserved it was a little over half-a-century ago. Yet another important historic site sacrificed for short-term gain: a lesson that has still not been learned, even today.

Other Pre-historic Site
Pettigarths Field (Neolithic Settlement and tomb) Map 2 refs. 587652, 584653

MID-HOWE (Broch)

Orkney (Rousay) O/S Landranger map 6 ref. 371307

Directions: About 5 miles west of Brinian Pier, down by the coast. Follow the B9064 west until the car park is reached.

Eynhallow Sound, dividing Rousay from Mainland, must surely have been the scene of much pre-historic activity. Apart from the Neolithic burial-chambers hereabouts, there are at least nine broch sites along both shore-lines. Mid-Howe and Gurness* are easily the finest and both have much in common. They are inter-visible across the sound, which, on a clear day, offers some magnificent scenery. Certainly, the broch builders, quite apart from more practical matters, chose a beautiful location in which to live.

The similarities between Mid-Howe and Gurness* brochs are considerable. Both are close to the shore, have outer defences, a ground floor intra-mural gallery, many outer buildings and, until 90 years ago, both were large turf-covered mounds, as many brochs became. In addition, each was excavated and protected from further erosion, and both are now in the care of the state. Mid-Howe was uncovered and excavated by the landowner from 1930 to 1933. Unlike Gurness*, entry is free and, in all honesty, it is the better site: it is seldom busy. There are two other brochs close by, both being turf mounds – one is in the adjacent field. A century ago, that mound is just how Mid-Howe looked.

Mid-Howe sits on a small promontory into Eynhallow Sound, cut-off by a massive rampart with ditches either side. The bank is 20 feet wide, while the truncated, stone-faced inner ditch is 10 feet deep. The east entrance has two sets of rock-cut steps leading to a harbour in Stenchna Geo. The inner ditch is very impressive: too often ditches are silted and bereft of any revetting, and do not convey just what effective defensive obstacles they once were. That is not the case here, for one can fully appreciate just how vulnerable an attacker would be caught at the bottom with javelins and sling-stones raining down.

Further round, the inner ditch has been part filled-in and built over, unlike at Gurness*, where the buildings may be contemporary with the broch. It is possible that Mid-Howe was a promontory fort before the broch was built although, as yet, there is no hard evidence of such a development. A modern excavation might elicit something to back that theory.

The path through the outer defences leads to the broch entrance with its additional structures. The entrance includes the remains of a door-jamb, bar-hole and gaps between the lintels through which spears could be jabbed into attackers trapped in the cramped passage. There is a corbelled guard-cell on the right – almost 8 feet high, and another opposite. Like those at Gurness*, this cell leads into the intra-mural gallery, which was blocked in antiquity when the wall began to collapse. There is a door pivot-hole at the inner-end of the entrance.

The wall is 15 feet thick and the courtyard 30 feet across and, like Gurness*, is full of impressive, secondary structures. If you have visited many brochs before Mid-Howe, or Gurness* for that matter, the interior will be a revelation for you. If this is your first broch, then, I am afraid, it is down hill from here on.

The courtyard is divided, and sub-divided, by large vertical slabs. Each half has a water tank, while the southern half contains a tall stone cupboard, spit holes beside a hearth, an entrance to the galleries and stairs leading to a secondary intra-mural cell that blocked the original first floor gallery. The northern half features a hearth, a cellar, a tall cubicle – not unlike a guard box at royal palaces – and a particularly grand alcove. An opening leads to the first floor gallery and stairs, presumably reached by a ladder. Although all these are secondary features, Gurness* they offer a magnificent insight into Iron Age life. True, the accoutrements are different from today, but the general domestic duties were not dissimilar. It seems probable that while the practicalities were undertaken on the ground floor, the living space was at a higher level.

There is a scarcement 12 feet above the current ground level, for about half the circuit. This possibly supported a mezzanine floor. There is also an intra-mural cell over the entrance passage. The broch's wall, which is up to 14 feet high, has marvellously preserved inner and outer faces and, from the top, one has a good panoramic view of the site and its layout.

Of course, Mid-Howe's original height is unknown, although the galleried-wall to ground level suggests it might be quite an early broch, along with Gurness*. Thus, neither might have quite reached 40 ft. in height, but the museum's projection of Gurness* being 25 feet high, and having a low thatched roof is by no means the only interpretation.

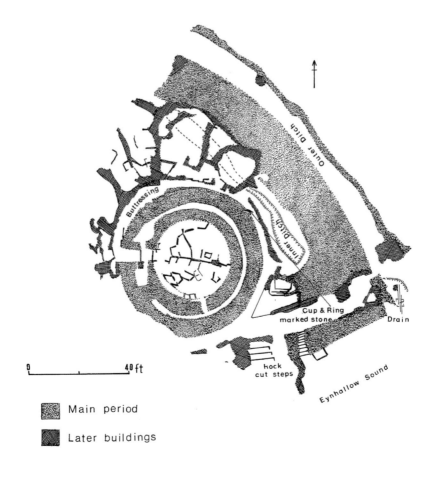

Mid-Howe probably needed to be about 40 feet high and, one has to remember, that a fully thatched roof would not only make the interior very dark, but would be susceptible to fire. This would severely compromise a broch's otherwise impregnable defences.

Mid-Howe's exterior is equally fascinating. Though much-eroded, a considerable number of buildings once occupied what must have been a very cramped site. Vertical slabs buttress the broch wall at the north, where the gallery was blocked in antiquity. This adds further evidence to the contention that Mid-Howe is an older broch, for the builders clearly got their dimensions wrong. Was the tower too tall? There are several particularly good examples of secondary buildings – from two building phases – to the north of the broch. In particular, a smithy's hearth shows that metals were manufactured on the site. Mid-Howe may have been cramped, but it was certainly a comprehensive little village.

As might be expected, Mid-Howe's extensive excavation produced various artefacts, including some Roman pottery. This probably came via trade with intermediaries rather than directly with the Romans, but shows that even the smaller Orkney islands did not exist in isolation. Clearly, Mid-Howe was an important Iron Age settlement. Quite why there were so many brochs either side of Eynhallow Sound, or why the three brochs of Howe were so close together, remains something for future discovery, but shows that this was a route of some importance.

The location of Mid-Howe, opposite Eynhallow Island, makes it a splendid and atmospheric broch to visit, and certainly gives a good reason to visit Rousay. There are four chambered burial cairns between the broch and the Brinian Pier, all worth visiting, easy to reach and sign-posted.

Other Pre-historic Sites
Mid-Howe Stalled cairn Map 6 ref. 371307
Knowe of Yarso (Chambered cairn) Map 6 ref. 403281
Blackhammer Stalled cairn Map 6 ref. 414276
Taversoe Tuick (D/deck cairn) Map 6 ref. 426276

MOUSA (Broch)

Shetland (Mousa) O/S Landranger map 4 ref. 457237

Directions: From Lerwick, take the A970 south for about 12 miles and turn left along the minor road to the pier at Leebotten. It is important to telephone Rodney Smith on 07901-872339 at least a day in advance to book the boat trip to Mousa island.

The approach to Mousa broch, from first seeing the island, to journeying across the sound on the small boat and, finally, the approach from over the island's hills, is one of the most invigorating of any pre-historic stronghold. A quite appropriate way of greeting not only the sole surviving, relatively complete broch, but the finest example of a pre-historic drystone building in Britain. As such, if not one of the Seven Wonders of the Ancient World, Mousa is certainly right at the forefront of any pre-historic works in Britain and is one of the most significant in Europe. Mousa is truly majestic.

Having seen hundreds of pre-historic strongholds before visiting Mousa, one could be forgiven for having muted expectations. Yet, Mousa was everything, and more, that could be expected. To fully appreciate Mousa, it is best to visit several pre-historic sites before venturing out there. Most pre-historic strongholds are ruins and compared with these, Mousa's enormity and majesty is astounding.

The most obvious question is, why is Mousa the only broch to survive almost intact? Its remote location probably helped. More important, though, its wall width is a greater proportion of its size than any other broch, so it was less likely to collapse. Mousa may also have been the ultimate broch, was recognised as such and was left as a monument of a dying age – an unlikely scenario, admittedly. In reality, a combination of circumstances and a dearth of people on the island in the last two or three centuries, probably prevented Mousa being destroyed for building prosaic huts or, worst of all, roads. After all, the brochs of Duns Telve*, Troddan* and Carloway* have all suffered from considerable stone-robbing in recent centuries.

Mousa has an overall diameter of 50 feet, but barely 40 feet at the top, some 44 ft. above ground, hence the distinctive cooling-tower shape and taper of the wall. The wall is solid to the first scarcement – at just over 6 feet high, and is 15 feet thick; the courtyard is only 20 feet across. The wall thus makes up 2/3 of the overall diameter, a higher fraction than any known broch. So, perhaps Mousa was the tallest broch, though written evidence suggests that both Dun Telve* and Dun Carloway*, neither with such a high ratio of wall to diameter, were about 40 feet high within the last 250 years.

What these figures do not show is the sheer magnificence of the structure. Using relatively small stones – even for the lowest courses, one has to remember that this is purely drystone built. No mortar was used, and there was unlikely to be any scaffolding either. One does not have to go to the Egyptian pyramids, the Inca temples or the Greek cities to see some of the finest stone work in history; if not quite on our own doorstep, Mousa is very much a part of Britain.

Fully 9 feet of rubble was removed from the courtyard in 1861, and it was cleared again in 1919. The entrance is much higher than it was originally and, even now, there is a secondary floor that dates from Mousa's conversion into a wheelhouse. One pier still exists, but two others have been removed since 1861. The entrance features a door-jamb and bar-hole, but no guard cells. Instead, there are three intra-mural cells, each with a low entrance, small cupboards – or aumbries, and with corbelled roofs almost 12 feet high. Torches are provided, so one can fully appreciate these otherwise hidden details.

Several larger aumbries are built into the courtyard wall. As with most aspects of Mousa, these are about the finest examples to be found in brochs. At the lower scarcement level, a doorway – now reached by steps, but originally by a wooden ladder – leads to the intra-mural stairs. These wind clockwise within the galleried-wall, through fully six levels and via two landings, to the wall-head. There is a second scarcement at about 12 feet – the lowest known example, which may have been for a roof as there is no obvious entrance to a floor at this level. The galleries are relatively wide, even near the top, and the wall features vertical rows of openings, probably to reduce the weight over the lintels and to give light and air to the galleries.

Once on the wall-head, Mousa really comes into its own. It may once have been about 50 feet high, but many brochs would have stood over 30 feet high in the north of Scotland and the northern islands. In other words, brochs built to within, say, 8 feet of Mousa's present height, if not more, may not have been unknown. That is not to diminish Mousa's magnificence, but indicates the general level of building skills at that time.

From the wall-head, one can see south to Sumburgh Head, across the sound to the ruined Broch of Burraland on Mainland, and command the vicinity of the island. Immediately below are traces of the stone wall that cut-off the promontory, but height was Mousa's main defence and one can see just how invincible a broch would be in an Iron Age raid or a short siege. Arrows, javelins, ladders; none of these would have any real effect on defenders on the wall-head, although lighted arrows or javelins onto an enclosed, thatched roof would be an extremely weak Achilles' heal. This is one reason to doubt that brochs, the ultimate in pre-historic defensive homesteads, ever had an all-enclosing, thatched roof.

A dramatic overhead view of Mousa broch enables you to see the galleried-wall plus the line of the surrounding outwork.

Without a modern excavation, no date can accurately be ascribed to Mousa, but, from its architectural details, it may herald from the 1st century A.D. The wheelhouse era may date anywhere from the 2nd-5th centuries A.D. but, as with Dun Carloway* and some other brochs, Mousa features briefly in later accounts of derring-do. Twice, in the 10th and 12th centuries, lovers were besieged within its walls and, on each occasion, the old stronghold was able to protect the nuptials from their attackers. Legends these may be, but somebody opened out the original entrance, probably to give entry to the rubble-filled interior. Could this have occurred at those times?

Whatever one does in life, there are precious few occasions that remain vivid for the rest of our days. Of the many places one visits, most are usually, if not forgotten, pushed far into one's personal mists of time. If you have an interest in pre-historic sites, history in general or just the world about you, a visit to Mousa is not one that will quickly, if ever, be forgotten.

Other Pre-historic Stronghold
Broch of Burraland O/S map 4 ref. 446231

NESS OF BURGI (Hillfort and Blockhouse)

Shetland (Mainland) O/S Landranger map 4 ref. 388084

Directions: Take the A970 south from Lerwick to Sumburgh Airport. As the road turns east round the south of the airport towards Jarlshof*, turn right past the houses, following this road until it ends. The blockhouse can be seen from the road. Follow a track south to the hillfort.

Many visitors to the Shetland Islands visit the main three pre-historic sites of Mousa*, Clickhimin* and Jarlshof*, but there are many others that should not be overlooked. Ness of Burgi, for example, is only about a mile to the south-west of Jarlshof and yet receives hardly any visitors, by comparison.

True, one has to walk about half-a-mile, but it is mostly across pasture land and a short rocky section, and is quite beautiful. Sumburgh Head, with its lighthouse, broods away to the east, while to the south, with decent weather, the Fair Isle can be seen on the horizon. The ruined laird's hall at Jarlshof denotes the location of that famous site and, as one walks to this once remote and seemingly isolated stronghold, it takes on a quite different complexion.

The Scatness peninsula is most amenable. There are five known blockhouse forts – unique to the Shetland Islands, and two of them are here. Scatness North is on a promontory to the north of the Ness of Burgi and was discovered in 1971. It was excavated in 1983 and only the eastern half remains, at a low height. The Ness of Burgi is in an entirely different league.

You can see the blockhouse most of the way from the road, but that is only the inner-most of the defences. Just after crossing the rocky ground that separates the promontory from the main peninsula, a low rampart, with an entrance in the east, cuts-off a large tract of land. Crossing this, one comes to a rectangular mound of stones built from excavation material. Beyond, two rock-cut ditches with a central wall, still about 7 feet high, cut-off the badly eroded promontory on which the fort stands. The wall was originally built of stones, but appears more like an earthen rampart now.

Immediately inside stands the blockhouse. This was restored in 1971 and is in good condition, although is not in the same class as that at Clickhimin*. On the other hand, it is seen in its original context without later additions. The blockhouse is up to 4 feet high, about 75 feet long and 20 feet wide. There is a central entrance, aligned with that through the outer defences, which has a few lintels, door-jamb and particularly good examples of bar-holes through to the cells on either side of the entrance passage.

The cell on the north-east is entered from the passage; and that on the south-west from inside the fort. Both of these are in good condition and are clear of rubble. There is an additional outer cell at the south-west, most of which has fallen over the edge of the cliff. This gives a good indication of how the promontory has eroded since the Iron Age, for the grassy interior is now very small.

Few artefacts were found when the site was excavated in 1935, and there was no obvious sign of huts. If the blockhouse at Clickhimin* were a guide, this one would probably have been much taller, possibly with lean-to houses against the inner edge. Such an arrangement would make sense of the Ness of Burgi, but many are the pitfalls of extrapolating information from one site and applying them to another. Blockhouses may originate from Shetland's pre-broch era, but that does not necessarily mean that Ness of Burgi pre-dates all the islands' brochs.

Ness of Burgi is well preserved and a joy to visit. Its location is magnificent and, although remote, made sense in the Iron Age with the good land to the north.

The Ness of Burgi is the most complete blockhouse to be seen unencumbered by other additions.

The relationship with the inhabitants of Scatness north blockhouse and fort must have been interesting, but they might not have been contemporary. Here, in every way, is a site that is a complete contrast to nearby Jarlshof*, with all its visitors, and it is no less enjoyable. Do not miss out.

Other site
Scatness north (Tonga) – blockhouse, Map 4 ref. 388087

GLOSSARY

AMPHORA	Large pottery container used by the Romans to carry liquids, etc., for trading purposes, especially wine.
ARD	Simple, early plough without a mould-board to turn the sod. Often with metal-tipped plough-share, and either pulled by man or animals.
AUMBRY	Small storage cupboard or recess in a wall.
BANK-BARROW	Very long, long barrow.
BARROWS	Burial mounds. Usually long (Neolithic), or round (mostly Bronze Age).
BERM	A flat piece of ground separating a rampart from its ditch.
BI-VALLATE	Hillfort with two ramparts.
BLOCKHOUSE	Perhaps citadel or entrance/guard-chamber complex of larger stronghold. Currently unique to the Shetland Islands.
BRITONS	Original Celt-speaking inhabitants of the island.
BROCH	Iron Age circular drystone defensive tower. Had galleried-walls upwards from the first floor, at least.
BRONZE AGE	Preceding the Iron Age, c. 2000-600 B.C.
CARBON-14 DATING	Also Radio-carbon 14 (RC-14) dating. Method of dating organic matter. There is a fixed proportion of Carbon-14 to Carbon-12 in a living organism. Once dead, this proportion is not maintained and falls to about half the former level in c. 5,700 years; a half-life. By measuring the C-14:C-12 ratio in organic matter, an approximate date of death can be calculated. This cannot be determined with absolute accuracy, and is usually expressed scientifically as, e.g. 500 BC ±100, that is 600 to 400 BC. In this book, Carbon-14 dates have been expressed as the middle date.
CELL	Small room within a drystone wall.
CELTIC-FIELDS	Small rectangular fields often with lynchets defining the sides. Date from the Bronze Age, but used in the Iron Age.

CELTS	Iron using peoples from central Europe. Migrated to Scotland probably beginning in the early first millennium B.C.
CHEVAUX DE FRISE	Upright stones, or wooden stakes, in front of a fort or defensive barrier to prevent a mass charge by attackers on foot or horse.
CIRCA or c.	About, approximately. Used with a date, e.g. c. 600 B.C.
COUNTERSCARP BANK	A bank on the outer edge of a ditch. Usually the product of clearing out the ditch.
CRANNOG	Fortified island dwelling in a loch. Usually the island is artificial as well.
CROSS-DYKES	Lengths of bank and ditch used to define territory or create boundaries.
CUP and RING MARKS	Stone carving of circular depression with surrounding rings. Usually made by pecking the stone.
CURSUS	Neolithic avenue bounded by a bank and ditches. Some are several miles long.
DALRIADA	Kingdom of Scotti tribe from Ireland in western Scotland, from c. 5th century A.D.
DARK AGES	Period from the end of Roman rule in England, c. 5th century A.D. to the Middle Ages, c. 11th century A.D.
DITCH	Get off with you!
DUN	Small, Iron Age drystone fort. Usually larger than a broch and lower.
DRUIDS	Celtic priests. Probably late-Iron Age.
GLACIS RAMPART GROUND-GALLERIED	Stone, earth, and spoil covered rampart. (usually broch or dun) Hollow galleried wall from ground level upwards.
HENGE	Circular bank and ditch enclosed earthwork from the Neolithic Age. Probably for ceremonial purposes. Some later adapted by Bronze Age people.
HILLFORTS	Defended settlement usually on hills.
HUT CIRCLE	The wall footings, usually turf-covered, of huts or houses.
HUT PLATFORM	A level platform cut into the side of a hill, on which a hut or house was built.
IRON AGE	The period immediately prior to the Roman invasion of 43 A.D. For this book it approximates to c. 600 B.C. - 500 A.D.
LYNCHET	Bank of soil on the downward side of a Celtic field, created by continuous ploughing.
MIDDEN	Rubbish tip.

MULTI-VALLATE	Two or more lines of ramparts at a hillfort.
NEOLITHIC AGE	New Stone Age. c. 4500-2000 B.C.
OPPIDUM	Large Iron Age settlement, equivalent to a town or a chief's stronghold.
PICTS	Dark Ages' inhabitants of north-east, central and possibly north Scotland.
PILLOW MOUND	Oblong shaped mounds. Date and use uncertain, but possibly rabbit warrens.
PROMONTORY FORT	Hillfort created by ramparts cutting across the level approach, with steep natural defences on all other sides.
QUERN	Either rotary or saddle types. Used for grinding corn. A rotary quern can be tried out at the Broch of Gurness museum.
RAMPART	The banks which, along with the ditch, defend the perimeter of a hillfort.
REVETMENT	The wood or stone facing of the rampart. May or may not have been structurally supporting.
SCARCEMENT	Ledge projecting from a wall, or the wall being set back, on which a floor or roof could be supported.
SCOTS or SCOTTI	Tribe from Ulster that settled in Argyll in c. 5th century A.D. Dalriadans.
SHERD (Potsherds)	Broken fragments of pottery.
SOUTERRAIN	Drystone underground passage or cell, used for storage.
STORAGE PITS	Holes within a hillfort used for the long-term storage of grain or salted meat. Could also be used as rubbish pits.
TIMBER LACING/ *MURUS GALLICUS*	Horizontal cross-timbers through the rampart connecting vertical posts at the front and rear. Essential to prevent collapse of revetment and rampart.
UNI-VALLATE	Single rampart at a hillfort.
VITRIFIED FORT	Usually a hillfort. Drystone wall that had timber-lacing through the wall that had been burnt. The heat fused the stones or rubble together.
WALL RAMPART	Rampart with only one vertical face, to the outside.
WHEELHOUSE	Circular dry-stone house, usually of the later Iron Age with radial stone piers to support the roof.

Other books by
Geoffrey Williams

McLaren: A Racing History

The Iron Age Hillforts of England: A Visitor's Guide

The Elegance of Edwardian Railways

Stronghold Britain

Stars of Steam